The TRASH Phenomenon

The TRASH

The University of Georgia Press

Athens and London

CONTEMPORARY

LITERATURE,

POPULAR CULTURE,

AND THE

MAKING OF THE

AMERICAN CENTURY

Phenomenon

STACEY OLSTER

© 2003 by the University of Georgia Press

Athens, Georgia 30602

All rights reserved

Designed by Jennifer Smith

Set in Minion and Scala Sans by Bookcomp, Inc.

Printed and bound by Maple-Vail

The paper in this book meets the guidelines for

permanence and durability of the Committee on

Production Guidelines for Book Longevity of the

Council on Library Resources.

Printed in the United States of America

07 06 05 04 03 C 5 4 3 2 1

07 06 05 04 03 P 5 4 3 2 1

Library of Congress Cataloging-in-Publication Data

Olster, Stacey Michele.

The trash phenomenon :

contemporary literature, popular culture,

and the making of the American century / Stacey Olster.

p.   cm.

Includes bibliographical references (p.) and index.

ISBN 0-8203-2484-1 (alk. paper)

— ISBN 0-8203-2521-x (pbk. : alk. paper)

1. American literature—20th century—History and criticism.

2. Books and reading—United States—History—20th century.

3. Popular literature—United States—History and criticism.

4. Popular culture—United States—History—20th century.

5. United States—Civilization—20th century.

6. Popular culture in literature. I. Title.

PS228.P67 O45 2003

810.9'005—dc21   2002013116

British Library Cataloging-in-Publication Data available

For my mother,
who reads John Grisham,
and my sister,
who alternates between
gulags and godfathers

CONTENTS

ACKNOWLEDGMENTS

I suppose I can blame it all on my mother. Pregnant with her first child, whom she planned to name after her grandmother Sophie, she went to the movies one day to see *Love Is Better Than Ever* (1952)—a forgettable Elizabeth Taylor vehicle (a "foolish little fable," wrote Bosley Crowther, that "manifests no improvement in either movies or love") distinguished only by the fact that the character Taylor played, Anastacia Macaboy, was called "Stacey" throughout the film. And so, to be disgustingly Dickensian, I am born (or, to be precise, denoted). Such origins no doubt contributed to an early predilection for darkened rooms lit only by projectors and a lifelong aversion to anything connected with the great outdoors. Equally certain, such beginnings also destined me for any number of possible futures: multiple marriages (not yet), multiple diamonds (not on my salary), or the writing of a book like this one (bingo!).

In helping me transform destiny into reality, however, a number of people deserve mention. I am grateful to the staffs of the Museum of Modern Art, the Museum of Television and Radio, the New York Public Library, and, that great unsung resource, the Brooklyn Library at Grand Army Plaza for their assistance in supplying me with the films, videotapes, and microfilms I needed to compose this book. I also am indebted to the staff of the Interlibrary Loan Office at the State University of New York at Stony Brook Melville Library for complying with my numerous requests (often for material unbecoming a professor) with constant patience, astonishing speed, and a remarkable lack of snickering.

My more personal thanks go to those whose intellectual generosity and emotional support both improved this book and made it possible. Some, such as Suzanne Jill Levine and Matthew Strecher, offered help on the basis of e-mails from someone they had never before met. Their expertise in, respectively, Latin American and Asian literature expanded my (North) Americanist's limited sensibility and their generosity reminded me that the academic community need not be restricted to one's home institution. Other individuals, I am happy to say, are people whom I am fortunate to count as friends for many years. Joseph Angier functioned as a virtual media hotline, providing information about films and access to videotapes that I could not have seen without his help. Marlon Ross continued to serve as my unflagging theoretical conscience. My commuting companion, Eric Haralson, a "guy's guy," clarified the intricacies of football to me as effortlessly as he discussed American literature with me. My other commuting companion, Joaquín Martínez Pizarro, not a "guy's guy" (at least in that sense) but a trash *maven's maven*, helped save me from my own rhetorical convolutions; readers who can follow my arguments without difficulty should be grateful to him for his advice. Daniel Harris answered any and all computer questions without ever making me feel like the technology moron I am. Peter Manning and Paul Dolan answered any and all publishing questions without ever making me feel like the nervous *chayellyah* (exact meaning unknown) I also am. And Walter Maddox kept me from derailing just when the proverbial light at the end of the tunnel was starting to become visible.

My final thanks are reserved for those people connected with the University of Georgia Press who made the processes of review and publication nothing short of a dream come true: Alison Waldenberg, who, as acquisitions editor, reviewed the initial proposal and manuscript; Jon Davies, who, as project editor, guided the book through its various stages of production; and, perhaps most of all, Emily Montjoy, who, as editor (or, as I like to think of her, text godmother), oversaw the entire publication process from start to finish with all the care and concern that anyone could desire. Jerome Klinkowitz and John N. Duvall, in their capacity as manuscript readers, provided both extremely expeditious and extremely helpful suggestions for revision. And Jeanée Ledoux contributed copy editing that was as attentive to detail as it was sensitive to nuance.

Chapter 8 originally appeared in *Critical Inquiry* 25.1 (1998): 77–94. Other chapters originally were published in significantly shorter versions. Chapter 2 first appeared in *Modern Fiction Studies* 37.1 (1991): 45–59, copyright © 1991 the Purdue Research Foundation, reprinted by permission of the Johns Hopkins University Press. Chapter 3 first appeared in *Critique* 40.4 (1999): 387–98; reprinted by permission of the Helen Dwight Reid Educational Foundation; published by Heldref Publications, 1319 Eighteenth Street, NW, Washington, D.C. 20036–1802; copyright © 1999. Chapter 7 is reprinted by permission from *Productive Postmodernism: Consuming Histories and Cultural Studies*, edited by John N. Duvall, the State University of New York Press, copyright © 2002 State University of New York, all rights reserved. Permission to reprint in all cases is gratefully acknowledged.

Like a trainer behind runners who forces them to keep moving, my sister, Deborah Olster, kept telling me I was done with chapters before I'd gotten close to finishing them. This is not the trashy novel that will make us a lot of money that she urges me to write, but its completion frees me to embrace commercialism both wholeheartedly and without guilt, inspired, as always, by my beloved Desmond, already cited in the opening to chapter 7, who leaves me endless varieties of trash to pick up.

Brooklyn, New York

2002

The TRASH Phenomenon

We like books that have a lot of *dreck* in them.

—Donald Barthelme, *Snow White* (1967)

Introduction

Dreckologists par excellence, the dwarfs who express this preference in Donald Barthelme's 1967 book also provide the title for the investigation of popular culture and contemporary literature that forms the subject of my book.[1] "It's that we want to be on the leading edge of this trash phenomenon," state these diminutive devotees of movies, music, and Miller High Life (97). Aware that "the per-capita production of trash" in the United States is "up from 2.75 pounds per day in 1920 to 4.5 pounds per day in 1965," is increasing "at the rate of about four percent a year," and will undoubtedly keep increasing until "we may very well soon reach a point where it's 100 percent," the dwarfs conclude with the obvious, and only, response that such a projected saturation demands:

> Now at such a point, you will agree, the question turns from a question of disposing of this 'trash' to a question of appreciating its qualities, because, after all, it's 100 percent,

right? And there can no longer be any question of 'disposing' of it, because it's all there is, and we will simply have to learn how to 'dig' it—that's slang, but peculiarly appropriate here. (97)

And also somewhat disingenuous. For the celebration of cultural trash that liberates Barthelme's novel from the cul-de-sac of exhaustion that John Barth addressed the same year[2]—and whose stylistic high jinks fracture fairy tales and Freud, Dickinson and Disney with equal irreverence—ends with the containment of those subversive energies that the integration of popular culture has previously produced. Obsessed with rules, recipes, and the restoration of "equanimity" that Snow White's withdrawal from them has occasioned, the dwarfs "dig" trash only until they can canonize it into respectability. Once the disobedient heroine is revirginized and sent packing (into the sky!), they can "depart in search of a new principle" (heigh-ho!), safe in the knowledge that they do not, as Pound would have it, "make it new" so much as "old" (181). In this conservative aesthetic impulse they are, as the President who makes war on poetry notes, " 'My Americans' " (81).

By the time of Don DeLillo's *Underworld* (1997), however, simply "digging" cultural trash—in the most literal sense of the term—is no longer a viable option. When one of DeLillo's waste analysts visits the Fresh Kills landfill on Staten Island, he sees that what he earlier has dubbed the " 'King Kong of American garbage mounds' " is already twenty-five times the size of the Great Pyramid at Giza (163), and getting bigger all the time: "And the thing was organic, ever growing and shifting, its shape computer-plotted by the day and the hour. In a few years this would be the highest mountain on the Atlantic Coast between Boston and Miami" (184). Indeed, so consumed by this prospect is DeLillo's featured protagonist Nick Shay that he sees every discarded can and carton in a planetary context and mentally reprocesses items as garbage even while they sit gleaming on supermarket shelves. Unlike Barthelme's dwarfs, though, DeLillo's characters are offered additional ways to deal with an endless proliferation of American trash: not just incorporation and cooptation, but exportation and recycling. Shay engages in all three activities. He works for a company called Waste Containment that designs and manages landfills. He assumes that " 'terrible substances were dumped routinely in LDCs,' " or "less developed countries" (278). He separates household rubbish so that it can be "sorted, compressed and baled, [and] transformed in the end to square-edged units, products again, wire-ground and smartly stacked and ready to be marketed" (809). He is, like Barthelme's dwarfs, a model American citizen.

In Shay's world, of course, the existence of nuclear as well as cultural waste makes disposal of trash very much a matter of life and death. Yet to look at the remarks of those who, over the years, have condemned American popular culture as trash and censored its exportation to other countries as evidence of cultural imperialism, one would think that the stakes were equally momentous. I refer here not just to the usual mid-twentieth-century suspects whose juxtapositions of American mass culture against an unsullied modernism, on the one hand, and indigenous folk cultures, on the other, reflected what Andreas Huyssen has correctly termed an "anxiety of contamination" (vii, ix): Max Horkheimer and Theodor W. Adorno, who mourned "art renounc[ing] its own autonomy and proudly tak[ing] its place among consumption goods" as "use value in the reception of cultural commodities is replaced by exchange value" (157, 158); Clement Greenberg, who imagined kitsch embarked on "a triumphal tour of the world, crowding out and defacing native cultures in one colonial country after another" (103); Dwight Macdonald, who diagnosed mass culture as "a parasitic, a cancerous growth on High Culture" (59); Herbert I. Schiller, who viewed electronic innovations as "widen[ing] the perimeter of American influence, and the indivisibility of military and commercial activity operat[ing] to promote even greater expansion" (124). These claims have since been—in fact, have long been—qualified, if not directly refuted, by the work of sociologists who question the empirical bases upon which they rest, cultural theorists who separate the processes of production from those of reception, historians who supplant fixed aesthetic categories with temporally evolving forms, and literary scholars who portray the integration of high and low as mutually sustaining.[3] Nevertheless, the cultural binarism underlying the midcentury accusations, which harks back to Arnold's "best which has been thought and said in the world" (5), still persists in the remarks of more recent critics, often of decidedly different predilections, as the titles and subtitles of their works make clear. I cite two representative examples. When Arthur Kroker and David Cook juxtapose "Excremental Culture and Hyper-Aesthetics," all they can find are "[s]igns of detritus, wreckage and refuse which, moving at the edge of fascination and despair, signal that this is the age of the death of the social and the triumph of excremental culture" and "a *fin-de-millenium* consciousness which [. . .] uncovers a great arc of disintegration and decay against the background radiation of parody, kitsch, and burnout" (7, 8). When James B. Twitchell contemplates the rapidly approaching "point where there will be no border between Lower Aesthetica and Upper Vulgaria" (23), he sees just "Carnival Culture" ahead, our hesitance even to employ the word "vulgar" any longer hastening "The Trashing of Taste in America," since refusing to categorize vulgarity as such means sacrificing the ability to recognize its opposite as art (2).

Twitchell's *kvetchfest* locates this anarchic undermining of taste in the 1960s, and it is on literature published in the second half of the twentieth century that

I want to focus in my own examination of the integration of popular culture and contemporary writing. As David S. Reynolds's exhaustive study of what lies "Beneath the American Renaissance" attests, American writers of the twentieth century are hardly the first to incorporate popular modes and neglected materials into their works; far from being the products of social *isolatoes,* the canonical texts of the nineteenth century were, according to Reynolds, open texts in which a multiplicity of contemporary idioms and voices democratically mingled through acts of "socioliterary dialogism" in which their authors engaged (564). Conversely, Paula Marantz Cohen has recently traced the "Triumph of the American Myth" in twentieth-century silent films to their elaboration of the values found in nineteenth-century literature (21–42). My focus is somewhat different. What I examine is the way in which writers of the late twentieth century do not just integrate popular culture into their works, but employ those works to investigate a very specific use to which popular culture has been put over the years: the process of nation building.

DeLillo signals a similar exploratory intention in his portrayal of the baseball game that opens *Underworld,* the 3 October 1951 confrontation in which Bobby Thomson's three-run homer clinched the National League pennant for the New York Giants. Suffused by trash as people in the bleachers are shown tossing onto the field crushed cups, waxy napkins, and used tissues—a veritable "contagion of paper" (38) that brings to mind Huyssen's metaphor of contamination—even before Ralph Branca pitches the ball that will become "The Shot Heard 'Round The World," the game explodes into a celebration of "happy garbage" after Thomson's stupendous swing as fans throughout the Polo Grounds express their wish to be "connected to the event" by way of a profusion of personal waste and pocket litter (45). " 'Mark the spot,' " announcer Russ Hodges's producer instructs him. " 'Like where Lee surrendered to Grant or some such thing' " (59). Hodges goes still further. He imagines the moment of "people's history" that they have witnessed as more communally binding than any moment of national consolidation heretofore produced by military conquest: "Isn't it possible that this midcentury moment enters the skin more lastingly than the vast shaping strategies of eminent leaders, generals steely in their sunglasses— the mapped visions that pierce our dreams?" (59–60).

Given the identical space and typeface accorded the home run and that other shot heard 'round the world on 3 October, the Soviet explosion of a second nuclear device, on the next day's *New York Times* front page, one would have to say that Hodges has a point. The loyalty to team and country that distinguishes the response to both adheres to the same inclusion/exclusion principle that defines the modern nation-state within a system of territorially bound nation-states and joins individuals as citizens by relativizing ethnic and class differences vis-à-vis the irreducible differences that characterize foreign others (Breuilly 355–56; Balibar 139). More to the point, such loyalty adheres to the specific binary that has been crucial in determining the concept of American citizenship from the start, whether conceived as Manicheanism, exceptionalism, or what Michael Rogin has termed "American political demonology" (Ronald 272–300). Thomson/Branca, Giants/Dodgers, U.S./U.S.S.R.: all depend on a "connection between Us and Them," as DeLillo's figure of J. Edgar Hoover realizes, to "bring each other to deep completion" (51).[4]

An avid Giants fan all his life, my father taught me this lesson years ago when explaining his rooting for the Yankees, a team I knew he hated, against the Dodgers in the 1963 World Series because, as he put it, "I hate the Dodgers more." What he did not live to see was how the Thomson/Branca binary would be ritualized in years to come in DeLillo's book and the popular cultural event impressed into service as a symbol of national consolidation. In this sense, the scattered pictures of Thomson and Branca that are referred to throughout *Underworld*—in which the two pose with Dwight D. Eisenhower on a golf course (529), flank Richard M. Nixon (465), stand with Jimmy Carter in the Rose Garden (323), and surround Ronald Reagan in the Oval Office, a tasseled flag behind them (190), just "a couple of ballplayers, old-time guys, a winner-loser sort of thing, joined at the hip for life," and a president whose party affiliation is less important than his role as Leader of the Free World (465)—truly are memories, as the song would have it, of the way we were prior to the age of globalization. And not just as a symbol of national consensus. As John N. Duvall has cogently argued, the heroic traits cultivated by the " 'great American pastime' " of baseball were invoked by print media throughout the 1940s and 1950s as both explanation for the defeat of Germany and Japan in World War II and justification for cultural imperialism throughout the Cold War that followed (288–300). DeLillo's book just applies those qualities to American territorial expansion as well: the photograph of Thomson and Branca with Nixon that he includes appears in a quonset hut in Vietnam.

Were the matter left here in DeLillo's book, we would remain with three conclusions about the role that popular culture is shown to play in the process of nation building. First, because it is a photograph of Thomson and Branca that is circulated over the years rather than a newspaper clipping or tape recording, it is the imagistic transformation rather than the originary moment in American history that is impressed into imperialistic duty. So much power do such visual renderings acquire in contemporary literature that citizenship is defined to the degree that one is conversant not with actual American history but with its cinematic transpositions, as the following exchange between an author and television producer in Gore Vidal's *Duluth* (1983) confirms:

"Whatever happened to Kim Stanley?" asks her co-producer.

"I think she's teaching," says Rosemary.

"I liked her in *Planet of the Apes*."

"That's Kim *Hunter*," says Rosemary disgustedly. These young people have no sense of history, she thinks. (56)

Second, such visual representations are obviously never transparent renderings. As Stuart Hall asserts, "representation is a very different notion from that of reflection," for representation "implies the active work of selecting and presenting, of structuring and shaping: not merely the transmitting of an already-existing meaning, but the more active labour of *making things mean*" ("Rediscovery" 64). Third, while interpretation of those popular representations will be amenable to different individual proclivities, it will be guided by those historical/intellectual processes that have left upon every person what Antonio Gramsci has called an "infinity of traces" that favor the collective views that already have been validated in daily life (324). Thus, there always will be preferred meanings that tend to support the dominant culture, as even those critics who see popular culture as inherently polysemous and its texts as sites of conflict between producers and receivers are forced to admit.[5] With some of those meanings the residue of earlier popular artifacts, "You Must Remember This," the subtitle to Robert Coover's *A Night at the Movies* (1987), becomes an injunction, not a choice.

At the same time, in order for those popular artifacts that promote nationhood to remain effective, they must continue to remain relevant. When DeLillo tracks the history of the most important relic of the 3 October 1951 game, he discovers that the ball for which some characters search like a grail is "more or less lost" or taken by an estranged wife or "accidentally dumped with the household trash" and that "Bobby Thomson and Ralph Branca meant nothing" in 1969 to the man who has been given it as an heirloom by his father (611). More than just evidence of filial ingratitude, the neglect also signals a rupture in the concept of patriarchy that underlies the nation since Charlie Wainwright's purchase of the ball for his son in 1951 occurs amidst masses of fathers and sons who cluster to Yankee Stadium for World Series tickets, singing "Yankee Doodle" all the way, a crowd so powerful that even the black man who has come only to sell the ball is inspired by "wanting-to-be-among-them" elation (366). With that "them" implying a "we" that is anything but all embracing, and their referents altering with respect to the positions of individual characters, any nostalgic memories of the way we were that the book invokes must be set against its own interrogation of just who it is that all such plural pronouns denote.

Barthelme's portrayal of popular culture offers no such interrogation, concerned as it is with metafiction more than mimesis. Joined " 'together forever under the red, white and blue' " of the National Parks in which they all have been born (62), the seven men who cohabit with Snow White are so indistinguishable in their voices as to comprise an uncontested white, male, bourgeois (their word) "we." If Barthelme characterizes them as dwarfs, and the President worries about them as " 'My Americans' " (81), it is because they have become so paralyzed by the artistic legacy they have inherited (signaled by those formulaic Chinese baby food recipes bequeathed to them by their father) as to be incapable of any heroic imaginative endeavor (signaled by the current inability to climb Snow White's hair and longstanding impossibility to have ridden with Pershing against Pancho Villa since the year 1900). The only way to ride a horse now is to buy a Buick or Pontiac with the appropriate hood ornament. Hence the weight of patriarchal authority with which Barthelme most contends—and that later will infuse his portrait of a thirty-two-hundred-cubit-long *Dead Father* (1975) being dragged across a landscape by nineteen followers—is aesthetic. DeLillo, however, questions the imagined national community that a patriarchal popular culture supports in his first sentence, "He speaks in your voice, American" (11), because the adolescent Cotter Martin to whom the "he" refers—not just an African American and "flat broke" boy, but the "youngest" and "scrawniest" such boy (12)—is never completely one with the "assembling crowd" he joins at the Polo Grounds on 3 October 1951 (11). The "people's history" of which Russ Hodges finds "this old safe game of ours" such a potent emblem does not include Martin (60). Nor does it include women, as Nick Shay and his colleagues affirm when reminiscing about the baseball game during a business lunch in 1992, at which the one woman present is pointedly excluded. And it only includes Leonard Alfred Schneider, another one of the " 'wastelings of the lost world, the lost country that exists right here in America,' " to the extent that the name Lenny Bruce draws him closer " 'toward the invisible middle' " (628, 592).

Prior to the publication of *Underworld,* it was Thomas Pynchon's *The Crying of Lot 49* (1966) that most famously employed this metaphor of waste to expose how ideologically complicit the entire notion of "the people" is as an emblem of an American nation divided by elect and preterite. But the failed suicides, scarred outcasts, alienated elderly, and " 'whole underworld' " who comprise an alternative "We [Who] Await Silent Tristero's Empire" (W.A.S.T.E.) in his work respond to their exclusion by choosing "a calculated withdrawal, from the life of the Republic, from its machinery" that is "their own, unpublicized, private" and that is decidedly "not an act of treason, nor possibly even of defiance" (85, 92). DeLillo's marginalized misfits, by contrast, engage in guerrilla warfare. Fueled by the belief that in a culture saturated with images, " '[w]hoever controls your eyeballs runs the world' " (530), they appropriate the very forms of popular culture that have been used to manufacture and maintain a "people-nation," to borrow Gramsci's term (418), and redesign them for their own purposes.[6]

The paradigm for this reconstructive process is established when the Eisenstein film *Unterwelt* that DeLillo invents is "shown" at the midpoint of his own *Underworld*. Detailing the attempted escape of "people who existed outside nationality and strict historical context" from a mad government scientist who experiments on them with zapping ray guns, and a search party sent afterward to apprehend them (443), the silent film is premised on the inclusion/exclusion binary that, as we have already seen, underlies the modern nation-state:

> This is a film about Us and Them, isn't it?
>
> They can say who they are, you have to lie. They control the language, you have to improvise and dissemble. They establish the limits of your existence. (444)

Within the context of a novel whose opening links Thomson's popular blast to Russia's atomic blast, the facial deformities that are displayed with the victims' recapture obviously suggest the kind of terror now at the disposal of the state during the nuclear age. For my purposes, however, it is the "politics of montage" that governs both the movie's creation and its exhibition that is more noteworthy (443). Because it is in Radio City Music Hall, "showplace of the nation," that the "legendary lost" Eisenstein film receives its first viewing (424), the film is just one part of a huge elaborate program. And within the context of the Sousa marches, curtains lit by stars and stripes, and chorus-girl parades that open that theatrical extravaganza, the film repressed by both GDR and U.S.S.R. since the 1930s assumes a place in 1974 amid a history of popular forms that for years have reified state control. "[R]emade as interchangeable parts," the thirty-six Rockettes who emerge "high-kicking in machine unison" (428) testify to the Taylorization of leisure-time industries with which Siegfried Kracauer characterized the "mass ornaments" emerging from America's " 'distraction factories' " (67). The "kaleidoscopic bursts" and "methodical geometry" (428) that are projected onto a back screen revive Busby Berkeley configurations that endorsed New Deal cohesion and adherence to a single leader, choreography that, in turn, was borrowed for similar purposes (though a different leader) by the German revue films produced under Joseph Goebbels.[7] And yet the Rockettes of 1974 do not simply repeat the gestures of 1934. Adding bondage collars to West Point gray uniforms, and joining pulsing sexual rhythms to Swiss-clock precision alignments, the Rockettes' stylized movements provide a cross-dressing event that climaxes with their formation of a large red Russian star that they insert right in the middle of America's premiere proscenium ("think of all the

Easter shows and Lassie movies" [429]). Introduced by the most patriotic of fanfare, "the camp elements of the program, the choreography and some of the music, now tended to resemble sneak attacks on the dominant culture" (444).

But hardly the only such attacks, proof that, as a waste theorist once arrested for rifling through J. Edgar Hoover's trash cans claims, garbage "pushed back" (287). For the rumbling that the Radio City hipeoisie hear "shaking under their feet" is the sound of the Sixth Avenue IND train that carries the tag of graffiti master Moonman 157, another artist who is driven by a need to "get inside people's heads and vandalize their eyeballs" (432, 435). And he is joined later in time by Klara Sax, who exhibits a comparable " 'graffiti instinct' " to " 'trespass and declare ourselves' " when painting over abandoned B-52 bombers in the desert and who, even with military cooperation, manufacturers' donations, and grants from foundations, will still " 'scratch and steal' " to get many of the things she needs as a matter of principle (77, 69). And she is inspired by Sabato Rodia, who turns "innocent anarchist visions" into the architectural mélange of Watts Towers, but whose initials carved in archways "like the gang graffiti in the streets outside" attest to the subversive instinct behind their construction (276, 277).

A gay Hispanic, a Jewish woman, an Italian immigrant. Graffiti *writers*, as Moonman's crew is called (437–38), these are DeLillo's surrogates, who fight Eisenstein's ray guns with spray guns, whose strata blues, neon greens, geranium reds, rampant reds, and cherry-bomb reds "fairly exploded in your face" and whose anthropomorphized letters "sweat" and "live and breathe and eat and sleep" and "dance and play the sax" (395, 433).[8] They also are surrogates for the writers that I consider in this book. In their appropriation of castoffs as immaterial as 7-Up bottles or as monumental as nuclear bombers, they fashion an "art that can't stand still"—quite literally in the case of Moonman's trains that climb "across your eyeballs night and day, the flickery jumping art of the slums and dumpsters, flashing those colors in your face—like I'm your movie, motherfucker" (441)—and typify the authors I examine who incorporate all sorts of cultural trash into their work: silent films and war movies, Disney cartoons and Tin Pan Alley tunes, celebrity autobiographies and television miniseries.[9]

Mark Osteen employs the Derridean term " 'iterable' " to describe the resulting intertextual literature that is "simultaneously derivative and original, a tissue of citations that is thereby one of a kind" ("Children" 455). Yet focusing on issues of derivation and originality—even if only to contest them—ends up privileging an interpretive model that, as Thomas Strychacz argues, continues to view literature and mass culture as mutually exclusive in that sources are identified only to have their value denied, and authorial ability derives from a "process of rewriting" that "contributes to a literary end that has been in sight from the beginning" (108, 105). Not only does this reverse the emphasis of literary symbiosis that David Cowart has proposed as a model for texts that attach themselves to antecedent hosts with "bracing candor" (2), it also returns to what might be an erroneous interpretive model. For if DeLillo's waste theorist Jesse Detwiler is correct, and "garbage rose first, inciting people to build a civilization in response," it is the "science, art, music, [and] mathematics" that follows in garbage's wake that is derivative (287)—which might provide an alternative aesthetic paradigm were it not for the fact that the popular culture on which literary texts are based now is produced by technological media for which, as Fredric Jameson reminds us, "there is no 'first time' of repetition, no 'original' of which succeeding repetitions are mere copies" ("Reification" 137).

Like DeLillo, I am content to call the intertextual literature that results the "rambling art that has no category" (*Underworld* 276). But the model for its integration of popular trash that I would propose is that of *recycling*, not repetition.[10] As E. L. Doctorow's portrayal of duplicable events in *Ragtime* (1975) attests, the same processes of repetition—whether as gramophone records, moving pictures, or baseball games—that provide emotional support within a universe depicted as volatile and indeterminate (symbolized by Admiral Peary's inability to locate the North Pole with any precision) also provide ideological support to a nation whose union is revealed to be equally unstable (symbolized by Coalhouse Walker's campaign of terror). Recycling, by contrast, is predicated on the possibility of change. The incorporation of popular culture into literature that it denotes—what Barthelme calls the penetration of one "universe of discourse" by another—destabilizes the alleged autonomy or, to use Barthelme's term, "sufficiency" of both in that "[n]ew things can rush into your plenum displacing old things, things that were formerly there" (*Snow White* 44, 45), without prioritizing, as Eliot did, an "ideal order" of "existing monuments" into which the "new" must "fit in" as a test of its value (101–2). On the contrary, the displacement of which I speak is premised upon aesthetic categorization resulting from an evolving history of audience reception wherein, as Lawrence W. Levine has documented, "exoteric or popular art is transformed into esoteric or high art at precisely that time when it in fact *becomes* esoteric, that is, when it becomes or is rendered inaccessible to the types of people who appreciated it earlier" (234). Thus, even films like *Gidget* (1959) and *Friday the Thirteenth* (1980) may one day require authors to acknowledge their enhanced status by including the years of their release in brackets, as Thomas Pynchon comically suggests in *Vineland* (1990). Moreover, the *contextual* shifts in which such *temporal* shifts result make whatever ideological resonance artifacts, high or low, possess a function of the surroundings within which they are cast. In particular, in filtering the kind of meanings—dominant or subaltern—with which cultural artifacts are encoded, contexts play a crucial role in determining what range of meanings will be available for their decoding. Klara Sax, who views her aesthetic activities in *Underworld* as " 'a work in perpetual progress' " (79), also conceives of her repainted B-52 bombers as " 'a landscape painting' " for which the desert supplies " 'the framing device' " (70), since it is only the awe and terror inspired by the desert that can adequately suggest to viewers the terrible refutation of progress she wants the abandoned nuclear carriers to convey.

My own decision to explore the literary recycling of popular culture in an expansive manner—looking at texts that return to the start of the American Century and texts that spotlight the scopophilic society at its end, supplementing the study of American popular culture's internal dynamics with a consideration of its impact abroad—is governed by an awareness that the particular context within which I write is one that assumes as givens the end of the Cold War and the emergence of a globalized economy in which, to quote DeLillo, "[c]apital burns off the nuance in a culture" (*Underworld* 785). These conditions have led Anthony Giddens to proclaim the entire era of the nation-state as over and dismiss the apparatuses that supported it as " 'shell institutions' " (*Runaway* 26, 37), and David Held to propose a loss of national autonomy, defined as the ability to *achieve* goals, as the factor behind anxieties about a loss of national sovereignty, defined as the initial *determination* of goals (407). Yet, as Stephen Greenblatt has eloquently argued, the celebration of identity politics and local knowledge that the much heralded demise of the nation-state has prompted should not blind us to "the overwhelming evidence of cultural *métissage*, a global circulation, mutual influence, and cross-breeding" that comes from the fact that "[w]ith few exceptions, in matters of culture the local has always been irradiated, as it were, by the global" (59, 58). The nation-state may well be a "fiction" and the United States a particularly "strange anomaly" entering a phase of "hysteresis" defined by inertia, as scholars have claimed, but it is "the fiction of America" that continues to persist. Jean Baudrillard, in fact, goes so far as to venture that it is "on this fictive basis that it dominates the world."[11]

It is appropriate, then, that in exploring this alleged "fiction" I have chosen to focus primarily—though not exclusively—on the novel, for the novel has been the literary form most associated with the rise of modern nation-states since their late-eighteenth- and early-nineteenth-century inception. This is particularly true of the classical historical novel, which, as Georg Lukács has argued, was forced to present nationhood as the product of, on the one hand, turbulent transformations and, on the other, a developmental national history within which those transformations were given meaning (23–26). Struggles between Saxons and Normans in Sir Walter Scott's novels thus yield an English nation neither Saxon nor Norman; bloody Wars of the Roses usher in a magnificent

Tudor dynasty (32). Because Lukács also viewed events like the French Revolution and the rise and fall of Napoleon as turning history for the first time into a *"mass experience"* (23), however, he also recognized that the historical novel's epic qualities were offset by its popular components: the "mediocre hero" of Scott's (and, after him, Fenimore Cooper's) works, whose decency is a function of typicality more than towering stature (36–37); the portrayal of historical crises as crises in popular life, so that what happens locally becomes the material basis for what happens nationally (48–49).

This expanded "zone of contact," which Mikhail Bakhtin used to define the entire genre's internal characteristics (32–33), was complemented externally by conditions of production and distribution that further enhanced the novel's role as popular medium. Dependent as it was on the book, and therefore on the print-language that theorists of nationhood have found so pivotal to the emergence of national consciousness (Gellner 35–38, 137–43; B. Anderson 41–49, 61–65), the novel joined the newspaper in fostering community among the bourgeoisie separated by space but connected by similar reading experiences. Yet removed, at the same time, from the control of patrons and subjected by booksellers to the laws of the marketplace, the novel also developed a brand of social realism that, as Erich Auerbach has made clear, embraced "the whole reality of contemporary civilization, in which to be sure the bourgeoisie played a dominant role, but in which the masses were beginning to press threateningly ahead as they became ever more conscious of their own function and power" (497). Many of these functions, of course, are now performed by visual media. Reflecting this shift, I have included in my discussion television and film as vehicles of national consolidation. My concentration on the novel, in contrast, derives from the subversive role that its "uncrowning" of the epic, to borrow Bakhtin's term (23), has enabled it to assume in those affairs—a point Bakhtin himself fully recognized. More than simply replacing the "distanced image of the absolute past" with an "inconclusive present-day reality" (39), or "a congealed and half-moribund genre" with "the only developing genre" (14, 7), the novel emerged for him as the genre with—most relevant to my purposes—the greatest potential to provide "parody and travesty of all high genres and of all lofty models embodied in national myth" (21).

In selecting the contemporary writers whose appropriation of popular culture most contributes to such parodic ends, I have imposed upon myself a criterion that is as exclusive as it is inclusive. For while a plethora of American writers incorporate popular culture into their works, not all do so with respect to the particular issue of American nation building. This, as it turns out, has been the case with many women writers who, for all their differences in style, would otherwise seem to be obvious candidates for discussion—Ann Beattie, Bobbie

Ann Mason, Joan Didion, Susan Sontag, and Kathy Acker come immediately to mind—but whose very diversity makes any gender-based theory of which writers choose to link popular culture and nation building reductive. Neorealists, at one extreme, tend to subordinate political to psychological consciousness. The listing of who's where in rock 'n' roll heaven (Janis Joplin, Brian Jones, Jim Morrison, even Jim Morrison's widow) that signals " 'the end of the sixties,' " which, in turn, signals " 'the end of the world' " to the characters in Beattie's *Chilly Scenes of Winter* (1976) signals nothing more than their own paralysis (215), paralysis that stems from emotional traumas that predate the sixties by years. Likewise, the sixties' songs and *M*A*S*H* reruns that enable the teenage Samantha Hughes to apprehend the Vietnam War, and her father's death in it, in Mason's *In Country* (1985) offer no commentary on what the American presence in that war signifies. Avant-gardists, at the other extreme, tend either to refuse to consider popular culture's ideological components or impress those components to support their view of nation building as purely—and, to my mind, too indiscriminately—an offshoot of patriarchy, the subject with which they are most concerned. Thus, the celebration of Happenings (1962) and Camp (1964) that marks Sontag's early works is predicated on their remaining "disengaged, depoliticized—or at least apolitical" phenomena, reflecting her antipathy toward "putting art to use—for such purposes as inquiring into the history of ideas, diagnosing contemporary culture, or creating social solidarity" (*Against* 277, 21). By contrast, the demand for "a sharp tool, a powerful destroyer" to cut away the "vision world" that "creates us" (37) in *Blood and Guts in High School* (1978), and the corresponding use of graffiti within her texts that makes Acker such a potentially fine exemplar of the graffiti impulse displayed in DeLillo's *Underworld,* stem from a view of empire as unilaterally Western, harking back to 29 B.C. (*Great Expectations* [1982] 104), unrefined by any sense of historical contingency or national specificity.[12]

In the end, however, my selection of texts has been guided most by what Leslie A. Fiedler has felicitously called " 'ecstatics,' " a term he derives from the Greek *"ekstasis"* to denote the effect "not necessarily achieved by works highly regarded by critics, or necessarily excluded from the most debased popular art" (*What* 139). In so doing, I hope to avoid (the state of my desk notwithstanding) the " 'unreal' " situation in which Tommy Chan, America's "first baseball memorabilist," finds himself in *Underworld* (322, 321): stuck in a basement, surrounded by crumbling paper, suffering " '[t]he revenge of popular culture on those who take it too seriously' " (323). The three sections into which this book is divided do not dispense with aesthetic judgments completely, yet they do try to infuse the "serious" analyses that they provide with a genuine pleasure I take in the objects of their study.

Part one, "Central Casting," examines the role played by popular culture in the creation of the American Century, the casting, in effect, of the United States as the century's preeminent (or central) power. By portraying this imperial construction with respect to the works of three authors—Gore Vidal, John Updike, and Larry Beinhart—that collectively span the years 1898 (and the Spanish-American War) through 1991 (and the Persian Gulf War), this section chronicles the rise as well as, to quote the title of a Vidal essay collection, "the decline and fall of the American empire." On the one hand, the mating of Hollywood and Washington, D.C., that gave birth to this imperial creation is shown to be the product of an extended courtship; as such, the 1980 election of Ronald Reagan as president that would seem to have been its apotheosis turns out to be the result of a union that had produced George Creel's Committee on Public Information as early as 1917. On the other hand, the myth of American exceptionalism underlying that creation is shown to have been propagated by different media operating at different periods of time to support it. In the American Chronicle novels that depict the first decades of the twentieth century, then, Vidal focuses not just on the role played by the yellow press and silent films in fomenting American expansion—and the complicated role played by William Randolph Hearst in defining the shape of those two media—but on the replacement of words by images as the most effective vehicles of achieving that end. Updike's Rabbit tetralogy, which returns to the 1930s while tracing its eponymous character's life between 1959 and 1989, depicts the medium of film, symbolized by Walt Disney's ubiquitous enterprise, as superseded by the medium of television. By the time of the Gulf War, which Beinhart portrays as a miniseries staged by Hollywood professionals armed with video-satellite-computer systems, empire is delineated as a function of which nation can most successfully use the newest communications technology at its disposal.

More than instruments of military expansion, these artifacts of popular culture are also treated as part of a history of economic expansion that, as Brooks Adams outlined at the turn of the century, has long been predicated on the search for foreign markets. Reflecting this fact, as well as the fact that the fiction of America was first promulgated in popular European texts (More's *Utopia*, Shakespeare's *The Tempest*, Tocqueville's *Democracy in America*, to name but a few), part two, "Imports/Exports," focuses on the works of non-American writers—Dennis Potter, Manuel Puig, and Murakami Haruki—in order to investigate the effects produced when the popular artifacts of that imagined nation are exported back to Europe, and elsewhere, for consumption. The products of a mining village near the Wales border, a pampas town fourteen hours from Buenos Aires, and a suburb of the port city of Kobe respectively, these three authors have candidly acknowledged the influence that American popular culture had upon them while growing up in provincial regions, some even citing each other when describing the nature of that similar impact. Even more important, growing up in England, Argentina, and Japan respectively, these authors come from nations whose economic relationships with the United States during the twentieth century mirror the processes of imperial decline and fall that part one covers from the perspective of militarism. England's supersession by the United States as world power was confirmed in 1914 when New York replaced London as the financial capital of the world. Argentina became one nation in which that exchange of roles was illustrated as the country Lenin once called a "semi-colony" of Great Britain[13] (due, in large part, to British railway investments) shifted, beginning in the 1920s and culminating in 1955, to being a subsidiary of Standard Oil. And Japan, whose occupation by the United States between 1945 and 1952 coincided with the period Vidal dubs America's "Golden Age," was the country whose buildup during that period eventuated in U.S. economic devastation during the 1980s. Hence the story of the American Century told in part one is told again in part two, albeit from a different perspective.

Yet contrary to UNESCO's MacBride Commission Report (*Many Voices, One World* [1980]), in which a nation whose mass media are under foreign domination was deemed unable to claim to be a nation (34), the extent to which the writers discussed in this section portray America's exported popular culture as a form of cultural imperialism is shown to depend upon the degree to which each values the indigenous culture that American popular culture threatens to displace. Potter sets television's promotion of a classless "common culture" against its commercialization by American artifacts that contribute to England's becoming a nation of "mimic men." Puig juxtaposes imported American popular culture against the populism of Peronism as competing means of consolidating Argentines of the lower and middle classes into one nation. Murakami, who inherits the history of one of the few nations alleged to have an ethnically homogeneous culture, depicts popular culture—even the popular culture of the one occupying force that ever inhabited Japan—as liberating it from the kind of militarism that *Nihonjinron* consensus actively promoted.[14]

Finally, part three, "W.A.S.T.E.," returns to American literature to explore the degree to which the media spectacle and the representative figure have become sources of national consolidation in the wake of those 5.6 seconds that, in DeLillo's view, "broke the back of the American century" in Dallas ("American" 21). Here, too, the story of the American Century is told, once again from a different perspective. For in serving as potential sources of national consolidation, the three spectacles that are the focus of this section—the assassination of John F. Kennedy, the Scarsdale Diet Doctor murder, and the O. J. Simpson trial—follow a whole series of (in)famous promoters of national unity during the twentieth century, whose fictionalizations may be thought to begin with Theodore Dreiser's treatment of the Chester Gillette case (1906) in *An American Tragedy* (1925) and extend through Meyer Levin's treatment of the Leopold and Loeb case (1924) in *Compulsion* (1956), E. L. Doctorow's treatment of the Harry K. Thaw trial (1906) in *Ragtime* (1975) and the Rosenberg trial (1951) in *The Book of Daniel* (1971), and Robert Coover's treatment of the Rosenberg trial in *The Public Burning* (1977). Indeed, in featuring protagonists—Lee Harvey Oswald, Jean Harris, and O. J. Simpson—who, marginalized by the dominant culture, nevertheless construct their own identities with respect to the formulae proffered by that culture's popular media (formulae that, as these particular cases prove, bypass differences of class, gender, and race), the texts explored in this section portray the central figures of contemporary spectacles as assuming roles first performed by actors in earlier arenas. One thinks, for instance, of Dreiser's delineation of Clyde Griffiths exchanging the "down-and-out laborers, loafers, drunkards, [and] wastrels" of his parents' *American Tragedy* mission for the lead in a trial for which vendors selling peanuts and popcorn compete with salesmen pitching copies of a victim's love letters (17, 630). Or one thinks of Doctorow's depiction of the Thaw proceedings in *Ragtime* as "establish[ing] certain individuals in the public consciousness as larger than life" (71), notably Thaw's wife, Evelyn Nesbit, a woman "ahead of her time" in "provid[ing] the inspiration for the concept of the movie star system and the model for every sex goddess from Theda Bara to Marilyn Monroe" (70, 71). Most of all, one thinks of Coover's portrayal of Julius and Ethel Rosenberg in *The Public Burning* as "hav[ing] become—no less than Valentino and Garbo, Caruso and Bernhardt, the Barrymores and the Bumsteads, Rin Tin Tin and Trigger—true Stars, their performances forever engraved upon the American imagination, their fame assured for generations to come" (264).

As Coover also makes clear, the *"little morality play for our generation"* in which not just the Rosenbergs but "just about everyone in the nation" is "behaving like actors caught up in a play" (147, 145) is the age-old script of American binarism—the very scenario that DeLillo invokes in *Underworld*—delineated here as a battle between "Sons of Light" and "Sons of Darkness" (448) that will be resolved when the executions staged by Cecil B. De Mille in Times Square, "The American Showcase, Playland U.S.A." (206), reaffirm the " *'untransacted destiny of the American people'* " to "go out and take over the world and 'create the first great American Century' " (615, 399). An invented tradition, as Richard Nixon discovers when he goes over the trial in private and its narrative begins to unravel, it proves a communally imperative tradition, as he learns after his public exposure of it as *"a war against the lie of purpose"* leaves people terrorized into a frenzy by "their own sudden and unprecedented impotence" (499, 604). As Uncle Sam, who restores equanimity with the " '*NEW New Enlightenment*' " that he brings (612), confirms in the book's final pages, " 'It ain't easy holdin' a community together, order ain't what comes natural' " (657).

Much the same can be said of the three spectacles that comprise the last section of my book, since just how much the media's representation of them produces "national narrative[s]" that, according to Toni Morrison, restore order and minimize confusion (xv), or celebrities who, as Guy Debord claims, are "guarantor[s] of the system's totalitarian cohesiveness" (42), or merely "event strike[s]" of the kind Baudrillard defines by a "refusal to signify anything whatever" (*Illusion* 21) remain matters of some debate. By entering into that debate with an examination of some of the written texts with which participants inscribed their own images and parasites marketed them, this last section can end with reference to the Barthelme/DeLillo metaphor with which the book begins: troping a 1954 song recorded by The Clovers, but inverting the words of Charles Calhoun's lyrics so as to suggest that, in this day and age at least, "your trash ain't nothin' but cash."

As the individual chapters in these sections suggest, not every popular artifact lends itself equally well to authorial recycling. DeLillo distinguishes between waste and shit in *Underworld* (302), the latter, as is illustrated by the sludge tanker that drifts from port to port for two years without docking (329–30), defined by no reusable potential. Likewise, Dennis Potter's appropriation of the American movie musical examines just what happens when a popular form becomes so exhausted as to turn parody into pastiche—or, put simply, when retro should be let go—since popular forms, much like those literary forms cited by John Barth in 1967, also have histories and historical contingencies.[15] Nor do these chapters suggest that different forms of mass media are recycled or received in the same way. In the fiction of Murakami Haruki, for instance, movies and music promote the possibilities of imaginative resistance, whereas television and video turn people into complacent sheep. And the chapters certainly do not suggest that aesthetic recycling is always, or even necessarily, conducive to ideological reform. The war movie formulae employed by Larry Beinhart may enable him to produce a work that questions militaristic values, but that does not negate the legitimizing of such values that a history of splicing clips from earlier war movies into later ones in fact produced. Nevertheless, what underlies all my chapters is a consideration of under what conditions American popular culture can be recycled so as to change the nationalistic imperative behind its inception, conditions in which the sign, as scholars of media culture have claimed, can be turned into an arena in which different ideological accents intersect and compete.[16]

Underworld draws to a close with the depiction of one such struggle. The crowd that gathers in the South Bronx to witness a billboard on which the face of a murdered child is alleged to appear after nightfall consists of obese women, men in dreadlocks, drifters, squatters, and shopkeepers—all those "people" whose histories are not considered by Russ Hodges when glorifying the crowd that opens the book. At the same time, the advertised product whose image the doomed Esmeralda's face is supposed to displace is orange juice, the acidic base the mayor's office has used locally in its war to erase graffiti and the colored agent the government has used globally in its war to defoliate Southeast Asia. " 'It's just the undersheet,' " says one observing nun to another after the headlights of a train reveal the visage that the crowd has awaited. " 'A technical flaw that causes the image underneath, the image from the papered-over ad to show through the current ad' " (822). And, indeed, there is evidence aplenty that testifies that this is the meaning that should be ascribed to the appearance: the lights that reveal it belong to a train that is "ungraffiti'd" (821), the "great gone era of wildstyle graffiti" having long since succumbed to the correct spelling of a Michelangelo who is last seen puffing on a cigar and planning to sell scrap metal on-line to countries looking to build a military (815). Yet even if DeLillo *continues* his account, much like Barthelme does in *Snow White*, with the immediate commodification of Esmeralda on prayer cards hawked by vendors within days of her first (re)appearance, he does not, like Barthelme, *conclude* his account with an uncontested victory of dominant over subaltern. Two days later the billboard is blank, the sign now just a white sheet announcing room for abject intervention, or, simply, *"Space Available"* (824).

Part I

Central Casting

The industry has always refused to endorse any school pretending to train people to be extras. [. . .] And right here the distinction should be pointed out between an extra and an actor. The extra is not an apprentice or a kind of junior-grade actor who may, simply because he is an extra, aspire to better roles. Unlike Napoleon's recruit, he carries no marshal's baton in his knapsack. It is notable that of the seventy thousand or so people who have been extras at one time or another, not more than a dozen have risen to stardom.

—Will H. Hays, *The Memoirs of Will H. Hays* (1955)

In the end, he who screens the history makes the history.

—Gore Vidal, *Screening History* (1992)

Vidal's *Empire* Strikes Back
Hearst, *Hollywood*, and the Invention of American Hegemony

The 1930 Production Code was not the only innovation spearheaded by Will H. Hays during his term as president of the Motion Picture Producers and Distributors of America. Four years earlier, Hays had been responsible for the formation of both the Central Casting Corporation and the Central Casting Bureau, attempts to eliminate graft in the industry by regulating the employment of performers through what was to be in effect a free placement service. Indeed, Hays admitted in his memoirs that, next to the Production Code, he was prouder of the Central Casting Bureau than of anything else he had accomplished during the quarter of a century he spent as Hollywood "czar." Yet in distinguishing as sharply as he did between "extra" and "actor," and dismissing all educational efforts to turn one into the other as "manifestly rackets" (382), Hays expressed more than sympathetic concern for those thousands of aspirants who flocked to Hollywood each year and more than a realistic appraisal of their chances for success. He revealed an inherent bias at the foundation of the entire idea of central casting: the extra could never be an actor—much less a star!—because the extra did not possess the necessary qualities to become one.

When the United States took its own turn at center stage with its victory in that "splendid little war" that was, for Secretary of State John Hay, the Spanish-American War (1898), the rhetoric surrounding the inauguration of the American Century that followed smacked of similar essentializing sentiments. In place of his brother Henry's historical phobias, for instance, Brooks Adams offered imperial historical prophecies: *The Law of Civilization and Decay* (1895), based upon "accepted scientific principle[s]" of physics (59); *America's Economic Supremacy* (1900), a function of natural selection; and *The New Empire* (1902), determined by mineral lodes and geographical location. Albert J. Beveridge campaigned for the Senate in 1898 by condemning those who resisted America's "resistless march toward the commercial supremacy of the world" as "triflers with nature's laws" (57, 62).

Having surveyed the history of the United States in his seven-part American Chronicle series, Gore Vidal would argue, I suspect, that the transformation of the United States from republic to empire was, if not inevitable, at least probable—not because of some predetermined Manifest Destiny or immutable law of civilization and exchanges, but because of the way in which the country was originally conceived. After all, what could one expect of a country whose first president was a land surveyor? And aware, therefore, of how much the discourse of American global preeminence is an invented tradition, Vidal also is aware of the role played by the popular media in constructing it, from crude block-wood engravings of a twenty-one-year-old Aaron Burr carrying a dead General Montgomery through the Quebec snow in the text that depicts the earliest chronological period of the series (*Burr* 51) to Franklin Delano Roosevelt opening a television studio in one of the two texts that delineate the latest (*Washington, D.C.* 18). Just as it is no coincidence to Vidal that the father of the country was a land surveyor, so it is no coincidence that the president who transformed the United States into a nation-state with the consolidation of the Union after the Civil War also re-created himself as "the nation's true Father Abraham" by growing a beard to soften his features in photographs (*Lincoln* 34).

In the two novels that focus on the first decades of the American Century in particular, *Empire* (1987) and *Hollywood* (1990), Vidal turns his attention to the role played by the mass media, especially film, in the invention of American hegemony. In these two works, which span the years 1898–1908 and 1917–23 respectively, Vidal's examination of the rise of American expansion abroad is complemented by his portrayal of the concurrent rise of the movie industry at home, the increasing role of silent films in the dissemination of American propaganda, and the early matings of Hollywood and Washington, D.C., that resulted in the creation of George Creel's Committee on Public Information (1917) and, later, the Hays Office (1922). As such, it is appropriate that Vidal introduce as his linchpins two characters whose careers personify the shift from manufactured history of yellow journalism to invented history of commercial cinematography: the fictional Caroline Sanford, great-granddaughter of Aaron Burr, who becomes first a newspaper publisher, then a film actress, and finally a movie producer; and her factual counterpart, William Randolph Hearst, who as newspaper-magnate-turned-politician-turned-movie-mogul ably serves as her mentor. Yet focusing on Hearst also enables Vidal to reveal the fault line in the naturalizing discourse with which the century began. For while beginning from many of the same premises as the president most associated with turn-of-the-century imperialism, the Roosevelt Henry James dubbed "Theodore Rex," Hearst's interpretation of the Monroe Doctrine placed limits on the extension of American empire. More to the point, the movies he produced, notably his preparedness serials *Patria* (1917) and, to a lesser extent, *The Romance of Elaine* (1915), inverted those assumptions about separate spheres and masculine virility that Roosevelt continually invoked in the advance of civilization.

For Vidal, who since the start of his career has refused to conflate gender and sexuality, viewing the words "heterosexual" and "homosexual" as adjectives denoting specific practices rather than nouns denoting inherent traits, such an inversion has dramatic consequences. If those qualities that justified American expansion as "natural" no longer apply, then the inevitability of American expansion itself becomes less certain. And if the inevitability of American expansion becomes less certain, then American history itself becomes a chronicle of not just chance events (Roosevelt becoming president by virtue of McKinley being assassinated, Truman by virtue of a predecessor's death in office) but choices consciously made (Jefferson not Burr in 1800, Hays not Tilden in 1876, Bush not Gore in 2000) and roads deliberately not taken.

To Be Continued . . .

The private meeting between Theodore Roosevelt and William Randolph Hearst that concludes *Empire* did in fact occur, although just what was spoken during it remains unknown. Ostensibly arranged by the president to discuss Hearst's acquisition of the Archbold letters, potentially damning documents linking Roosevelt to Standard Oil payoffs, the encounter, as portrayed by Vidal, takes a different direction as the two enemies quickly scuttle the subject of incriminating evidence and move to a more important issue: to whom does the United States belong? The more literal-minded Roosevelt can only think in terms of elections won and property owned. Hearst, in contrast, responds with a lecture about invention, both of the 1898 war with Spain and Roosevelt himself, imaginative endeavors that have made Hearst American history incarnate: " 'It's my story, isn't it? This country. The author's always safe. It's his characters who better watch out' " (472).

Critical theorists who study space accord great weight to the role of the story in preparing the way for conquest. Michel de Certeau, for example, traces that role back to the *fās* ritual performed by Romans prior to any ventures involving other nations, in which the renewal and repetition of originary founding acts legitimized new enterprises whose success it also assured (123–26). We also know just how many different stories Hearst manufactured to justify American intervention in Cuba, such as the 1897 tale of Evangelina Cosio y Cisneros, whose imprisonment for protecting her chastity from a crazed Spanish colonel merely updated earlier American captivity narratives. Yet recent Hearst scholars tend to downplay the impact of the Hearst press in fomenting war with Spain in 1898.[1] And for Vidal, 1898 is merely the date that the American empire "started officially" (*United* 1021). Therefore, acclamations in *Empire* about McKinley's delivering an " 'Augustan age' " without once stirring from the White House telegraph and telephone (14, 199),[2] applause for Hay's "open door" policy in China "buying time until the United States was in a stronger position to exert its will on the Asian mainland" (230), and anticipation at Roosevelt's being positioned to " 'give America the hegemony of the earth, which is our destiny, written in stars!' " (290) must be set against earlier schemes for conquest that punctuate the other novels of Vidal's series, schemes that resonate both backward and forward in time.[3] *Lincoln* (1984) shows William Seward planning to unite warring North and South in a " 'glorious logical *American* solution to all our problems' " by sweeping into Mexico, and then Central and South America, to oust the French, Spanish, and Portuguese from the Western Hemisphere (532). *Burr* (1973) has Andrew Jackson plotting for the republic of Texas to lay claim to the Pacific Coast and then rejoin the United States (328), Thomas Jefferson "setting for the west and the south an imperial course as coldly and resourcefully as any Bonaparte" (160), and assorted statesmen competing with each other to become emperor of Mexico—Alexander Hamilton through connivance with Great Britain, Aaron Burr in alliance with the United States (213, 261).

This is not to suggest that the United States of 1898 (or, for that matter, 1998) is no different from the United States of 1776, for Vidal's essays divide American history into three distinct periods corresponding to three distinct republics: the first, a loose confederation of former British colonies that began with the 1776 Revolution and ended with the 1788 adoption of the Constitution; the second, another fairly loose assemblage that ended in 1861 when Lincoln, "the American Bismarck," took the position that no state could ever leave the Union; the third, a "most imperial republic" ushered in with the 1865 end of the Civil War and peaking in 1945 when it became "the world's master" (*United* 941).[4] At the same time, imperial desire in Vidal's novels always coexists with imperial discomfort. The three-year war in the Pacific between Emilio Aguinaldo's Filipino troops and United States forces cannot be called an "insurrection" because that would imply the country that liberated the islands from Spanish bondage now constitutes a legitimate government, which would turn the conflict into a war of independence with Aguinaldo playing the role of George Washington and McKinley that of George III (*Empire* 106). Secretary of War Elihu Root cannot use the word "possession" when talking about Cuba because, as Secretary of State John Hay amusingly notes, to do so would make Cuba look all too much like what it is—a colonial possession (*Empire* 165).[5]

Hay—the official most burdened with the linguistic acrobatics of coining new words—is not just any statesman, however, but a former secretary to Abraham Lincoln and current member of Henry Adams's Five of Hearts coterie. A bridge between nineteenth- and twentieth-century values, and the man most conscience stricken at the circumambulations required by his position, he traces the difficulties he faces to the tenets of American exceptionalism that still dictate America's uniqueness as residing in a morality untainted by Old World practices:

> Although Hay did not in the least disapprove of the coming American hegemony, as outlined by Brooks [Adams] in his soon-to-be-published polemic *The New Empire*, he felt that the Administration ought never to associate itself with such un-American concepts as empire. Let the empire come in the name of—the pursuit of happiness, of liberty, of freedom. If the United States was not always high-minded, the world might take less seriously the great new-world charter that set off this extension of the British empire not only from the motherland but from all other restless, expanding nations. (*Empire* 321)

Subscribing to the same tenets, Woodrow Wilson later insists on tying the 1919 Paris peace talks to a League of Nations because not to do so is to admit that the United States is " 'just another belligerent out for loot,' " something he refuses to concede, believing as he does that " 'We are not like other people. We must not be like other people' " (*Hollywood* 184).

Nor *is* American belligerence like that of other people because, in Vidal's work, American belligerence is rooted as much in dollars as in actual dominions. " 'I do think that we are the first empire in history to *buy* its territory rather than to conquer it,' " remarks Thomas Jefferson in *Burr*, to which his eponymous vice president admits, " 'There has never been any doubt, anywhere, of our uniqueness' " (319). Jefferson should know, of course, since his purchase of Louisiana—portrayed by Vidal as a fire sale bargain in which Napoleon, "desperate for cash" to pacify a slave revolt in Santo Domingo, cedes territory at rock-bottom prices ($15 million) that doubles the size of the United States—sets the standard (and precedent) for all such acts of acquisition (*Burr* 252). Thus, Ulysses S. Grant defends his negotiations for Santo Domingo in *1876* (1976) as not inconsistent with his condemnation of the Mexican War by presenting it as a good deal of the kind Jefferson himself would have brokered: " 'The president of Mexico did not invite us to invade his country and attach a part of it to the United States. The president of Santo Domingo *offered* me his country for a fair price. By wanting to buy this island I did no more than Mr. Jefferson when he agreed to buy Louisiana, or than Mr. Johnson when he agreed to buy Alaska' " (198).

Such colonialism defined by cash is fully in keeping with the economic theories of history espoused by Brooks Adams, one of the Four Horsemen Vidal cites as responsible for the United States modern empire (the others being Alfred Thayer Mahan, Theodore Roosevelt, and Henry Cabot Lodge),[6] who, likening himself a student of scientific observation, remained undeterred by moral considerations, concerned as he was solely with practical standards of success (*New* xxiv). Defining capital as stored energy and credit the chosen vehicle of energy in centralized societies (*Law* 297, 301), Adams made national expansion the search for markets for surplus domestic goods and nations themselves the products of trade routes; the word "state" applied when territory tributary to a market was considerable and its administrative machinery somewhat ramified, "empire" when such territory was vast (*America's* 20; *New* 197). Because the crossroads at which such markets arose were a function of natural geography, expansion itself was, in large part, "determined by forces which override the volition of man" (*America's* 25). United States expansion into the nearby Caribbean archipelago, therefore, "only obey[ed] the impulsion of nature, like any other substance" (*America's* 81), just as the country's having been "devised by nature to be the converging point of the cheapest routes between Asia and Europe" made it "preëminently fit" to encroach upon eastern Asia and "reduce it to a part of our economic system" (*New* 167; *America's* 221).[7]

Adams applauded the economic centralization that empires fostered since, in his view, administration of the largest mass proved cheapest (*America's* 85)—hence his celebration of the American trust, as evidenced by the consolidation at Pittsburgh that allowed the United States to undersell the world in steel in 1897 (*New* 177). Yet because Adams also recognized that "[n]ature seldom retraces her steps" and "the seat of empire has seldom tarried in one city more than a century" (*America's* 188–89, 189), he also recognized that shifts in trade routes caused displacements in the seats of empire—from Rome after 250 A.D. to Constantinople, from Holland to Great Britain in 1815 (*Law* 81–82; *America's* 1). The instability of these displacements, in turn, prompted the "energetic races" to compete for those remaining markets able to absorb their surplus for fear of dislocations in their own social systems should no new vents be found abroad (*America's* 29, 33). War became redefined as economic competition in its most acute form (*America's* 12; *New* 113).

Although it is not until *Empire* that Adams's views receive a full hearing in Vidal's fiction, they in fact are anticipated as early as *Burr* when Jefferson is quoted as promoting war as " 'helpful to domestic manufacture' " (164). If the assumption of that stance is treated more as proof of the yeoman president's greed than anything else, it is because of the difficulty of viewing as a central-ized power a nineteenth-century country whose own capital doesn't even have a center, "or rather there are several centres" (*Burr* 409), and that continues to locate its seat of government in an "anomalous ten-mile-square parallelo-gram" whose only completed piece of architecture is a red brick barn adjacent to the Executive Mansion (*Lincoln* 16, 22). No such problem afflicts the nation by the twentieth century. Improved architecturally, " 'from first-century Rome to twelfth-century Avignon' " (*Empire* 143), Washington still remains " 'not a city but a dozen villages,' " as Wilson's wife, Edith, notes (*Hollywood* 86). But Washington, D.C., is now supplemented by another imperial center. While it too exists as a geographical anomaly, as "there was no Hollywood in the sense of a movie capital, only villages set in orange groves and onion fields with dusty roads to connect them" (*Hollywood* 135), what there is, however, is a saleable product, one that can transform this West Coast counterpart into the kind of center at the basis of Adams's speculations and the film industry into a textbook case of Adams's theories.

Love and Marriage (or a Shotgun Wedding)

Film historians agree that war, to recall *Burr*'s Jeffersonian remark, certainly was helpful to the domestic manufacture of film, in fact, to the transformation of the American film industry into a functioning cartel for all intents and purposes.[8] Charles Musser cites the Spanish-American War as reviving the industry after a period of commercial difficulty and the malaise resulting from the motion-picture patent battles (240–61). Kristin Thompson notes the opportunity World War I created for the industry to consolidate its oligarchical structure by fill-ing the gap that suspended European filmmaking had produced. By expanding overseas distribution, leadership in three markets (Great Britain, Germany, and Australasia) was extended to world dominance, the key to which was distribution to non-European countries (61–99).

Conversely, at the same time that American wars promoted American films, American films also promoted American wars.[9] This was particularly the case once the government and the film industry formally began acting in concert through the First Liberty Loan Drive, the War Cooperation Committee, the American Cinema Division, and, most important, the Committee on Public Information. From the very start, George Creel saw film as one of the three most effective weapons at his disposal to "drive home the absolute justice of America's cause, the absolute selflessness of America's aims," as the letter to Woodrow Wilson that opens Creel's *Complete Report of the Chairman of the Committee on Public Information* states (1),[10] and he took full advantage of already existing commercial sources and venues.[11] Four Minute Men used reel changes in movie theaters to give talks on committee-designated topics and Four-Minute Singing joined together movie audiences with committee-selected songs. Seven-reel features produced by a Film Division (*Pershing's Crusaders, America's Answer, Under Four Flags*) received massive distribution (between 80 and 90 percent bookings, as compared with the usual 40 to 50 percent cornered by most commercial films) by arrangement with established film distributors (*Creel* 52–53).[12] A Scenario Department contracted production of one-reelers to companies like Paramount, Pathé, and Universal. A Foreign Picture Service added commercial films to packages of war films and industrial pictures; when "Charlie Chaplin and Mary Pickford led Pershing's Crusaders and America's Answer into the enemy's territory and smashed another Hindenburg line" (*Creel* 7), they also prepared the way for funding companies like Ford, U.S. Steel, and International Harvester whose products were on display for audiences as well. As Creel, in a more unguarded moment, was to admit, "it was a plain publicity proposition, a vast enterprise in salesmanship, the world's greatest adventure in advertising," specifically *How We Advertised America*, as the title of his memoir acknowledged, in which the primary product was the nation itself (4).

Caroline Sanford, the Jamesian heroine of *Empire* and *Hollywood,* is no stranger to saleable products even before she is sent to California as Creel's emissary from Washington. Her attempts in *Empire* to gain a contested inheritance from her half-brother in order to purchase a Washington, D.C., newspaper have nothing to do with any allegiance to news in the forum she intends to devote to " 'literature, of a kind that is meant to entertain and divert and excite our readers so that they will buy the things our advertisers will want to sell them' " (150). As such, the shift from newspaper publisher to silent screen actress to movie producer that *Hollywood* traces is just the next logical step for one who is taught early on that " 'it's the way that things are made to look that matters now' " (*Empire* 11). In the real world war of July 1918, the German army may occupy "more of Europe than anyone had ever held before, including Napoleon Bonaparte," but in the reel war of *Huns from Hell* that Caroline, under the stage name Emma Traxler, is fighting in Santa Monica, "American Marines kept on destroying the Huns and a simple American mother, armed only with her virtue and her haunting photogenic face, with the odd crucifix to hand, was able to save herself from the carnal lusts of the bestial Hun" (*Hollywood* 143). Allied victories from the Marne to the Argonne may occur too late to effect changes in actual filming, but new title cards can be inserted upon the movie's release, even different cards in different countries if necessary, so that, as Thomas H. Ince proposes, " 'everybody gets to win the war except the Huns' " (*Hollywood* 163).[13] Caroline is therefore correct in recognizing the greater potency of film as compared with newspapers, since the universal language of silent films enables what was once done to be completely redone. Caroline's director lover recovers from the prolabor fiasco of *The Strike-Breakers* by simply rewriting the title cards to favor management. Ince, in contrast, makes a pacifist film in 1916 only to have *Civilization* condemned as treasonable two years later when, as Caroline realizes with a shudder, "[t]he great democracy had decreed that one could only have a single view of a most complex war" and designates her "to bully the movie business into creating ever more simplistic rationales" to support it (*Hollywood* 105).

Creel himself never saw his efforts on behalf of the Committee on Public Information as coercive in any way. *"In no degree was the Committee an agency of censorship, a machinery of concealment or repression. [. . .] At no point did it seek or exercise authorities under those war laws that limited the freedom of speech and press,"* he declared at the start of his retrospective account (*How* 4). It didn't have to, as Larry Wayne Ward has argued, since the American film industry, upon whose support the committee's film program depended, was run by men, mainly immigrants, obsessed with gaining official recognition and respectability for their medium (8–10, 136–38). But, then again, Creel never saw himself as engaged in any work of propaganda either, "for that word, in German hands, had come to be associated with deceit and corruption," and American exceptionalism, for him, derived from the United States being "alone of the great nations of the world" in having "never conducted a propaganda movement" (*How* 4; *Creel* 109). Yet, as his summary *Report* clearly indicates, denials of propaganda concern merely uninteresting, which is to say ineffective, propaganda. Thus, the Film Division opens a Scenario Department based on the theory that "propaganda films had never been properly made, and that if skill and care were employed in the preparation of the scenarios the resultant pictures could secure [a] place in regular motion-picture programs" (56). Foreign Section commissioners replace "cut-and-dried propaganda" with "carefully selected" articles (203), insert "an array of facts through *American* sources" to appeal "not through a blatant propaganda but through restrained presentation of the truth" (183), and screen movies to "w[i]n converts to our cause," particularly in countries with high rates of illiteracy (such as Mexico and Brazil) in which film serves as "one of our greatest assets" in "conveying impressions and creating sentiment where the printed word is without value" (159).

Perhaps most important, descriptions of Washington and Hollywood as lovestruck honeymooners, cooperating enthusiastically (and noncompetitively) in common cause, dissolve into one illustration after another of a shotgun wedding, with Creel at the altar presiding: "voluntary censorship" of war stills and motion pictures taken by civilians (4, 61); refused export licenses to commercial films, such as gangster thrillers and outlaw westerns, that "giv[e] false or misleading impressions of American life" (4, 103); required inclusion of "American propaganda film," at least 20 percent "educational pictures" to be exact, in all film shipments intended for abroad (7, 104); proscription of entertainment films from exhibitors that fail to show committee-produced war movies. As a result, no doubt exists as to who leverages whom on the food chain portrayed in Creel's *Report*, in which Hollywood exists solely to service the committee.[14] Even less exists in the more candid memoir Creel published the same year that, with great outrage, depicts the committee as existing only by largesse of Congress, a body of bushwhackers, blackguards, and blatherskites (his words) that Creel personally held responsible for his organization's "annihilation" (alternately expressed as "assassination" and "slaughter"), having maliciously "wiped out" its mandate by an act of 30 June 1919 (*How* ix, 51).

Vidal offers a somewhat different set of marital relations.[15] Few politicians depicted in his American Chronicle series resemble Ulysses S. Grant in openly declaring themselves " 'heartily sick of this show business!' " (*Lincoln* 643), a sentiment that proves most life affirming, as it turns out, since it is his hatred of grasping crowds that, in part, is responsible for Grant's decision not to attend Ford's Theatre on the evening of 14 April 1865 in Vidal's novel. Yet a clear change occurs between those nineteenth-century politicians portrayed as using the media to their own advantage and their twentieth-century descendants portrayed as shackled to the media's whims. Lincoln, a "master of guiding public opinion" through "an uncanny sense of how to use the press to his own ends" (*Lincoln* 34), sets his speeches in type before delivering them so as to provide exact copies for wire services, promotes a log cabin birthplace (even though, as one in-law notes, " 'that's all there was to be born in in those days in that part of Kentucky' ") while withholding all pictures of his Springfield mansion (88), and emerges "Honest Abe, the Rail-Splitter," a national icon (232). In contrast, the amateur vaudevillian and "not inexpert tap-dancer" Wilson gets caught by a newspaper publisher while looking at his "collapsed face" in a Marble Room mirror (*Hollywood* 90, 42), and all he can do is readjust his cretinous mouth, double chins, and slack jaw into the "lean, dour, hard-faced Woodrow Wilson" (41). His political adversary Theodore Roosevelt cannot reassemble even that much of a public mask: when caught by photographers and newsreel crew at the north portico of the White House, the fifty-eight-year-old begins to "impersonate" himself for the benefit of the cameras, his thumping arm and pounding fist a mere parody of the Rough Rider and former president now just "imitating himself with less and less plausibility" (67).

This is not just a function of Vidal endowing early-twentieth-century events with the patina of late-twentieth-century media saturation, as his comments regarding the resemblance between Ronald Reagan and Warren G. Harding might suggest (*United* 994). Rather, it is a function of the very real power wielded by the media in the earlier period. No one epitomized that power more than William Randolph Hearst, whose clout in Vidal's works actually increases as his successive bids for political office—president of the United States (1904), mayor of New York City (1905 and 1909), governor of New York (1906 and 1922), and lieutenant governor of New York (1910)—fail.[16] Recognizing "the rogue publisher was a new Caesarian element upon the scene," Hay locates Hearst's influence as originating in a brazen flouting of class hierarchy, to his being "the wealthy maker of public opinion who, having made common cause with the masses, might yet overthrow the few" (*Empire* 387). Such social destabilization is a celebratory prospect for Vidal, who has long maintained that Lincoln's government of, by, and for the people has always been a piece of demagoguery in a country that first limited its franchise to propertied males and is currently owned by 4.4 percent of its citizenry (*United* 650, 933). It is, however, positively predatory to the few, as epitomized by the Five of Hearts, who are shown dying one by one during the period of *Empire* and *Hollywood*, while the masses that constitute the imaginary entity of "the people" increasingly come from outside the United States.[17] Hay and Henry Adams receive ample proof of this phenomenon in *Empire* when the train on which they are traveling to St. Louis stops in Heidegg, Ohio, and the secretary of state goes out to address the crowd that has gathered, only to have his midwestern homilies fall upon deaf ears because none of the farmers that surround him understands English. Convinced that they are in " '*Mitteleuropa*' " and that the " 'true American' " of whom Roosevelt speaks is " 'as rare as one of those buffalos he helped to kill off' " (389, 390), the appalled Adams—who has retreated with Hay to the comforts of private car and delectable morsels—has no illusions about what the future holds in store:

"We shall," said Hay, mouth filled with roe, "transform those Germans and Slavs into . . . buffalos. All in due course."

"No," said Adams, revelling as always in darkness, "they will transform us." (390)

The actual Hearst, of course, was no more of these masses than was Hay or Adams. For all his heading his *New York American* with the logo "A Paper for People Who Think," and instructing his editors to pitch their wares toward "the NICEST KIND OF PEOPLE—for the great middle class" (*Selections* 330), Hearst gave little imaginative leeway to the very class to which his newspapers were meant to appeal. "We are winnowing for our readers the interesting essentials, or rather the facts of essential interest, and discarding the chaff," he wrote to the managing editor of the *New York American*. "We are doing the work" (*Selections* 309). He thus commanded his individual publishers to avoid "pictures which represent the 'artist's conception,'" what Hearst deemed "wholly imaginative pictures," but to be "conspicuously accurate in everything, pictures as well as text" (318). Moreover, as David Nasaw has recently argued, the "hyphenate" masses for whom Hearst intended his newspapers were not the same as the white-collar professionals for whom he intended his movies: "In publishing, he had made his fortune by extending the audience for daily and Sunday papers downward into the working classes. In moving pictures, he would extend the audience up the social ladder by producing pictures so stylish and expensive-looking that even 'society' would flock to them" (283).

Yet the stylish films for which Hearst's ventures into moviemaking are most remembered, those costume dramas that were intended as star vehicles for Marion Davies, comprised only a portion of Hearst's filmmaking efforts. And the pictures that preceded those lavish efforts released by Paramount and Metro-Goldwyn, the Pathé coproduced and distributed serials with which Hearst broke into the business (*The Perils of Pauline* [1914], *The Exploits of Elaine* [1914], *The Mysteries of Myra* [1916]) were efforts to transfer audiences from one medium to another.[18] In point of fact, they originated as strategic responses to the newspaper circulation wars, in which the novelization of episodes printed in Sunday papers prior to Monday theatrical releases served as a potent weapon.[19] Significantly, it is these serials that are the Hearst films cited by Vidal in his novels. When Hearst "plunge[s] into movie-making" in Vidal's work, then, he does so in the same spirit with which "he had invented 'yellow journalism,'" which obliged reality to mirror not itself, but Hearst's version of it" (*Hollywood* 95). Resolutely unlike D. W. Griffith in his refusal to "'think big'" or artistically at this point in time, he approaches film production as a shrewd businessman who sees an opportunity to take advantage of expertise he already has and receive as a bonus "'the best fun there is,'" as he summarizes for fellow publisher Caroline

Sanford: " 'Sort of like a printer's block, the way you can keep rearranging all the pieces. But without a paper's deadline. You can keep at it until you get all the pieces in the right order. They call that part—just like we do—editing' " (*Hollywood* 99).

But not only "fun." For if Hearst's editing of movies deliberately recalls his editing of newspapers, it also coincides with Vidal's portrayal of Woodrow Wilson in Paris, editing the map of central Europe with a "blue pencil that would create new countries like Czechoslovakia while dismembering, if not erasing, ancient empires like that of Austria" (*Hollywood* 201), which turns the practice of Hearst's filmmaking into an inherently ideological act. This was obviously the case when the films in question were those preparedness serials whose plots concerned the self-protective stance the United States needed to assume during times of global turmoil. Yet no less ideologically loaded were other elements of Hearst's early photoplays—cliff-hanger endings whose lack of narrative resolution invited viewer participation, intrepid women daredevils who renounced (or at least delayed) the claims of conventional domesticity—that often challenged the very proselytizing in which the plots themselves were engaged. In other words, at the same time that George Creel's Committee on Public Information was convincing viewers that *America's Answer* had to lie in an American presence abroad, Hearst's serials were overtly limiting that purview to the Western Hemisphere, or "America First," and covertly interrogating the need for expansion at all.

The Perils of *Patria* and Other Divided Women

Released in fifteen weekly installments beginning on 15 January 1917, Hearst's ninety-thousand-dollar production of *Patria* was touted the "serial supreme" that "makes you want to get up and *scream with the eagle*," "the greatest lesson in favor of *preparedness* ever taught."[20] It was not, however, the first preparedness serial to be screened before the public. Audiences the previous year could see Juanita Hansen and Tom Chatterton preserving *The Secret of the Submarine* from agents of Japan and Russia, Marie Walcamp as *Liberty, A Daughter of the U.S.A.* working with Texas Ranger Jack Holt to foil a plot to finance a revolution against Mexico's legal government, and Pearl White saving the Panama Canal from a band of spies headed by the Silent Menace in *Pearl of the Army*.[21] Nor was *Patria* Hearst's first serial to treat the theme of national defense. *The Perils of Pauline,* his first venture, devoted one episode, "The Tragic Plunge," to the efforts of Pearl White (who else?) to preserve U.S. Navy plans from falling into the hands of "cosmopolitan spies" of undisclosed nationality.[22] *The Romance of Elaine* devoted all twelve of its episodes to her role in safeguarding a wireless torpedo, the Sandy Hook defense plans, and, ultimately, the Peekskill center of American munitions manufacturing from the nefarious Anti-American League, another organization of indeterminate origins (although its leader's emergence in New York from the hatch of a submarine and renewed loyalty to his emperor before dying certainly evoke threats of German U-boats and Kaiser). Yet in depicting a specifically Japanese-Mexican conspiracy to invade the southwestern United States as the basis of its plot, *Patria* distinguished itself from Hearst's earlier efforts in targeting what had been the subjects of his personal campaigns for years: Asia, in general, which he saw as engaged in a race war against the Occident (hence his opposition to World War I as a civil war that left a divided white race vulnerable to Asian attack); Japan, in particular, as the Asian nation nearest to the United States geographically/commercially and farthest from it politically/socially; and Mexico, where, after the 1911 overthrow of Díaz, Hearst's properties had been pillaged by successive revolutionary forces.[23]

Being in release at the precise time the United States formally entered the First World War in April 1917 as an ally of Japan, *Patria* also had the dubious distinction of having to be twice reedited, the second time at the request of President Wilson, who initially proposed withdrawing it from circulation entirely.[24] These diplomatic perils of *Patria*—which form the subject of Vidal's reference in *Hollywood*—could be accommodated by removing the inflammatory depictions of Japanese, with the result that the episodes available for viewing today, while still virulently racist in replacing the mastermind Baron Huroki of Louis Joseph Vance's novelization with the smarmy Manuel Morales created for the screen, are fully in keeping with the government's policies at the time.[25] The occupation of Vera Cruz in 1914 and dispatch of Pershing's first expeditionary force already attested to American intervention south of the border. Far less amenable to editing—and, for me, far more problematic to the portrayal of nation building—is the central figure of Patria herself.

Introduced as a ward whose guardian dies shortly after the photoplay begins, and thus a young woman whose inheritance allows her to pursue a life of independent adventure instead of matrimony, Patria conforms fully to the female paradigm established in *The Perils of Pauline*. Earlier serials dealt with this dual undermining of patriarchal authority quite simply. In response to Pauline proclaiming her "desire to live and realize the greatest thrills so that I can describe them in a romance of adventure" rather than marry the son of her guardian right away, as the dying man asks, she suffers a comeuppance of runaway vehicles (car, horse, motor boat, helium balloon), multiple abductions (Indians, pirates, Bohemians), and uncontrollable natural elements (fire, flood, boulders), thrills from which she must be extricated by her intended, Harry, and which (eventually) teach her the lesson of humble renunciation. But the inheritance bequeathed to Patria involves more than the fortune she gains as heiress to a munitions empire. As "The Last of the 'Fighting Channings,'" the title of both the first filmed episode and first novelized chapter, Patria also inherits a sacred trust. This she discovers when she stumbles down a secret passageway to a basement in which she sees a portrait of her Revolutionary ancestor John Channing, Esq. (B. 1757–D. 1816), "Patriot, Statesman, Soldier, and Founder of the Channing Secret Defense Fund," part of which is stacked before her in boxes labeled $250,000 GOLD. Next to this trust, all her skills in negotiating the same perils that menace her serial sisters and rescuing her love interest from danger as often as he saves her—the very elements that would seem to challenge the gender divisions in the serial prototype—pale by comparison. Rather than reinvest authority in a man, *Patria* accords it to a New Woman—only this time, as her name denotes, the house deprived of its father that she usurps is the Fatherland itself.

For a nation repeatedly emblematized in the guise of female Liberty, Columbia, Republic, and America, such iconographic representation is hardly earth-shaking—it certainly should not have been to Hearst, whose authorized biography, *William Randolph Hearst: American* (1936), would partake of the iconic impulse. Martha Banta provides an exhaustive survey of the numerous artifacts produced between 1876 and 1918 that testified to the superseding of Uncle Sam by a female figure: Frédéric Bartholdi's 1886 *Statue of Liberty* in New York's harbor, Frederick MacMonnies's *Columbia* and Daniel Chester French's *Republic* at the 1893 Columbian Exposition, French's 1906 *America* approaching New York's U.S. Custom House, to cite some of the more colossal examples.[26] Yet the representations that Banta considers are all static models: statues, murals, posters, coins. And just how potentially subversive Hearst's serial is to a nation that imaged expansion in terms of white male virility and movement (think Rough Riders storming up San Juan Hill) becomes abundantly clear when the film is set against those coeval works of D. W. Griffith that make national origins— and not just American origins—contingent upon female elision, if not elimination. Indeed, the interwar period in which Banta sees the female form taking command as the primary container for American values (529–38) is the same period in which film critics see Griffith refining his techniques of female subordination: replacing the larger, more mature actresses of the early Biograph shorts with teenage will-o'-the-wisps, fetishizing eroticized body parts (*Judith of Bethulia* [1914]), recycling nineteenth-century stage melodramas of imperiled virtue and chivalric rescue missions, displacing white women's evocation of incestuous desire onto black males who then are punished for it (*The Birth of a Nation* [1915]).[27] By the time of the later epics, the paradigm had become established. "Be careful yourself of the sharp female called 'Guillotine!'" warns the Committee of Public Safety's chief judge in *Orphans of the Storm* (1921) after the French Revolution has degenerated into a maelstrom of "ANARCHY and BOLSHEVISM," led by a "pussy-footing," feminized Robespierre in ruffled shirts, and prefigured by close-ups of lewd women dancing the Carmagnole with wild abandon. With disorder configured as female, Nathan Holden doesn't have to agonize too long when put in the position of having to "sacrifice either his country or his loved one" in the Revolutionary War epic *America* (1924); he takes off to warn upstate New Yorkers of the threat posed by renegade Tories who seek their slaughter and leaves the woman he loves to the manhandling of the renegade leader.

In print, *Patria*'s destabilizing of conventional gender roles *was* addressed to a certain extent. Vance's novelization countered moments of heroic exploits with reminders of feminine submissiveness. Patria displays "adorable sincerity" when accepting the Channing Defense Fund and, with it, the " 'salvation' " of her country; uses a "dainty little revolver" to separate a burning fuse from a cache of dynamite; and accessorizes a coat skirt with holster and automatic pistol "just for the looks of it" when riding by herself along the Mexican border.[28] Advertisements also made much of the fact that the serial's star, Irene Castle, "a great American woman"—always referred to in male-identified terms as "Mrs. Vernon Castle"—was "recognized as the best gowned woman on this continent," while publicity stills emphasized the "Many Alluring Poses" in which she appeared on screen, poses that typically featured a woman in elegant dress looking discreetly at the camera, feet demurely crossed at the ankles.[29] The film, in contrast, adopts the more radical tactic of dealing with Patria's problematizing of woman's role by turning her into a man. If Vance's novelization gave Patria "a face as rapt and exalted with patriotism innocent of thought of self as ever Jeanne d'Arc wore after listening to the voices of the angels in the fields of Britanny," the film makes good on the masculine imagery implicit in that promise.[30]

The pivotal episodes in this transformation (chapters 14–25 of the novelization) involve the conspirators' attempt to dispose of Patria and substitute in her place a look-alike whom Senior de Lima, one of the Mexicans, will then marry in order to gain control of Channing armaments as well as the treasure of the Secret Defense Fund. Anticipating the Hollywood doubles movie that would flourish in the 1940s, in which the same actress played dual roles (one good, the other evil), the episodes address the precise kind of cultural crisis from which Lucy Fischer sees the female doppelgänger narrative emerging, in which the "fissure" represented by the twinning "seems not so much demarcated along the lines of morality (of vice versus virtue) as it does along the lines of gender identification—of 'masculine' versus 'feminine' poles" (184). Fittingly, the double in this case, Elaine the Cabaret Dancer, is discovered by the conspirators in the very milieu that challenged social and sexual boundaries in the 1910s in a variety of ways: its combination floor show, tables, and dance floor dissolving differences between performers and patrons; its elimination of theatrical footlights, curtains, and orchestra pit removing spatial barriers between stage and spectator; its mixture of people of widely varying backgrounds erasing hierarchies of culture, class, and gender; its public display of women evoking the more threatening aspects of looking (Erenberg 122–32).

Society dancers that rechanneled the sensuality of the new dances into a refined spirituality (no wriggling shoulders, no shaking hips, no low dips), the Castles played a great role in assuaging the fears that such social relaxation evoked, Irene in particular, containing as she did the threat of the New Woman (an early advocate of bobbed hair and looser clothing) in the stability of matrimonial partnership.[31] Elaine, the cabaret dancer in Hearst's serial, is of a decidedly different type. She openly consorts with the Latin Edouard, described by intertitles as her "bibulous and jealous manager"; willingly joins the conspirators at their smoky drink-filled table; and seems light-years away from the Patria who, in the novelization's first installment, rejects de Lima's proposal of marriage by telling him she could never marry anyone but an American. Yet the boredom with " 'the deadly respectable places' " that prompts Patria to seek out cabaret nightlife herself suggests that Elaine is less opposite than alter ego.[32] And this view is compounded further by the series of infinite progression that follows the introduction of the doubles subplot as (pay close attention) Elaine's impersonation of Patria is succeeded by Patria's impersonation of Elaine impersonating Patria in order to gain access to the details of the plot being hatched. Only with Elaine's death, the traditional resolution of the doubles tale, and the exorcising of socially unacceptable traits that have been projected from protagonist onto mirror image (in this case woman as emblem of disruption) does clarification emerge. " 'What does this mean?' " asks one of the conspirators when gazing upon the woman's corpse at his feet, to which Patria (in the guise of his cohort Elaine) declares: " 'It means that Patria Channing is accounted for at last. Somebody had to do it—and you men bungled every time you tried it. . . . Now I've done my part.' "[33]

With her disturbing female traits thus expunged, Patria is free to be remade into what the Jeanne d'Arc role of national savior requires. The next time she visually appears as multiples—in triplicate, no less—she wears the uniform of the Royal Flying Corps, breasts firmly bound beneath high-necked tunic and leather belts, relieved of all traces of feminine adornment, in the three identical shots of her saluting that comprise the split screen of episode 10: "War in the Dooryard." (Consider the contrast to Amelia Earhart's attire a decade later that purposely offset leather jacket and breeches with silk shirts, flying wings with strands of pearls, reflecting the indisputably gendered conception of her as an "aviatrix."[34]) No need to mourn the end of the "Fighting Channings" because, as Patria notes in the first novelized installment, " 'a girl can't fight.' "[35] In the final installments that get to the heart of the serial's message about the need for preparedness, she whose failure to reproduce had once doomed the family to certain extinction can safely embody "The Spirit of Her Progenitors," the title of the chapter that immediately follows the conclusion of the doubles subplot. The New Woman has been transformed into a New Man, able to do the kind of things only accorded men in positions of command: organize munitions workers into a citizens' army, review troops beside an unfurled American flag, raise a division of Rough Riders from cowpunchers on her southwestern properties.

Or maybe not so new. For if, as Gail Bederman has argued, assaults on patriarchy between 1890 and 1917 led to a Victorian "manliness" defined by inculcated morality being supplanted by a "masculinity" of inborn virility, the New Man that emerged yoked both in the service of an American imperialism based on a "millennial evolutionary ideology of civilization" behind which always lay "the [white] race's capacity to wield 'the big stick' " (44, 197). Roosevelt, the figure who best incarnated this stance, thus took great offense at Adams's Darwinian allegation in *The Law of Civilization and Decay* that the advance of civilization was characterized by the "martial type" giving way to the "economic man" (*American* 369–72). Yet what Patria emphatically does not do is allow her troops to cross the border and invade Mexico, not even during the final climactic battle scenes, since to do so would turn her repulsion of foreign aggressors, constitutionally defensible as a Lockean protection of private property, into a criminal vigilantism punishable by law.[36]

Such decidedly manly control in a decidedly masculine undertaking is notable for a number of reasons. Whatever bizarre wish fulfillment the transformation of Patria into avenging warrior might have served the Hearst of flabby handshake and high-pitched voice, chastised by his father to " 'stand in like man,' " and forever chastened by McKinley's rejection of an offer to equip a cavalry regiment so that he might serve as " 'a man in the ranks' " in Cuba, the restraint with which she performs her duties corresponds perfectly to his stated policy of expansion without imperialism.[37] To intervene in Mexico, as Hearst often urged, was not to colonize Mexico, but to apply good Pan-American business sense to a situation in which the "capital to develop latent wealth [was] as necessary for prosperity as the latent wealth which capital develops," and the only impediment to Mexican eagerness and American desire was political instability (*Selections* 427). To engage in foreign entanglements elsewhere was to invite "destructive competition," the taint of Old World "racial hatreds" and "greed for power and added territory" compounded by assumed war debts that would "sacrific[e] American industry and American labor for a bond that is without value" (5, 219, 206). At the same time, the metamorphosis of Patria from woman to man to which a change of clothing so greatly contributes, a change anticipated when *The Romance of Elaine*'s heroine assumes the garb of "young tough" and, later, "presentable man" when investigating the plot to penetrate the nation's coastal defenses,[38] implies that the masculinity upon which American imperialism was based, which had been a function of being born male regardless of race or class, was a socially constructed quality and not an attribute of gender. With the premise upon which American imperialism depended thus exploded, and with it all those notions about an innate "national character" that Roosevelt liked to trumpet (*American* 17, 23; *Strenuous* 208, 229), twentieth-century American history turns into one particular path, the product of human agency.

Vidal, of course, long ago dispensed with rigidly sexualized notions of gender, citing as his source the originary tale that Aristophanes relates in Plato's *Symposium* of male, female, and hermaphrodite globes bisected by Zeus, each left desiring its other half in a continual quest for wholeness (*Palimpsest* 30).[39] According to him, the masculinity that Roosevelt elevated to national type reflected no more than the statesman's need to compensate for being "a classic American sissy" (*United* 736), just as Washington's failure to sire anything in the flesh compelled him to conceive the nation as his " 'unnatural progeny' " (*Burr* 23). But when Vidal traces the career of Caroline Sanford in *Empire* and *Hollywood*, the great-granddaughter of the man not made president despite receiving an equal number of electoral votes as Jefferson in 1800, he explores whether the path of Burr not taken would have led to a historical outcome very different from the one available for consideration.

According to Donald E. Pease, who views Burr's brazen desire for empire as simply a more forthright expression of the Founding Fathers' predilections (269), the question is moot. Yet the degree to which Vidal attributes Caroline's similar predilections to a deterministic genealogy is an issue on which he vacillates. On the one hand, Caroline fully adheres to the vow she makes when she first leaves Europe for America, "that she would now become Burr's great-grand*son*, and live out, on the grandest scale possible, that subtle creature's dream of a true civilization with himself as center" (*Empire* 95). She talks about politics and power when her fiancé, Del Hay, wants to talk about theater and marriage (" 'You'll be the woman? I'll be the man?' Caroline smiled" [*Empire* 25]). She becomes a newspaper publisher after she learns from Hearst that "the ultimate power" does not reside in elected office but in "reinvent[ing] the world for everyone by giving them the dreams that you wanted them to dream"

(*Empire* 96). She even outdoes Hearst in choosing to shape those dreams and " 'invent,' " not just news about people, but " 'the people' " themselves in a series of films she produces that will celebrate "the ordinary in American life," the first of which is to be called *Hometown* (*Hollywood* 360–61, 385). On the other hand, as a woman even more divided than Hearst's Patria in that Caroline Sanford the publisher competes with Emma Traxler the Alsace-Lorraine actress, who in turn competes with whatever character Caroline-as-Emma happens to be playing on the screen at any moment, Caroline literally turns identity into a question of performativity. Not surprisingly, when she finally succumbs to the mandatory Hollywood face-lift, the result is complete self-effacement: "Caroline looked like Emma at her best, who was exactly like, though unlike, the original Caroline long since erased by time and Emma's glory and—now— surgery" (*Hollywood* 384).

Ultimately, just how little Caroline's urge for power has to do with gender or genealogy is exposed by Vidal's most divided hero(ine) of all, Myra Breckinridge (1968), who freely admits that she and nature are on a collision course, and whose entire identity as a "New Woman" results from the flick of a surgical knife (*Myra* 4). Indeed, her mission in *Myron* (1974) to restore MGM as a studio by reviving the street in Carverville where Andy Hardy once lived and green-lighting other projects that will nip in the bud "the moral rot at the center of the United States" (such as *The Beat Years of Our Lives,* in which well-groomed actors will preempt Kerouac and company) outdoes even Caroline's plan for megalomaniacal drive (332). Once Myra has reestablished MGM as "principal purveyor of the world's dreams," she, and she alone, will determine just what is dreamed by the entire human race (*Myron* 359).[40]

Myra concedes an important point, though, when she states, "I have no clear idea as to my ultimate identity once every fantasy has been acted out with living flesh" (*Myra* 166). For all her triumphant claims that her "shatter[ing] the false machismo of the American male" in the late sixties put an end to the American conquest of Asia (*Myron* 278–79), her anal penetration of aspiring actor Rusty Godowski confirms that Myra's millennium will be predicated upon the same masculinist basis as every other imperial historical epoch. Much the same can be said of Caroline's less flamboyantly heralded project, however much it may originate as an attempt by "virtuous conspirators" to " 'make the government do—and be—what we want them to do and be' " during a time when talk of a Hollywood "czar" promises even more government regulation (*Hollywood* 387, 360). The sanitized films that will enable Caroline and her director to capture that proposed "bridge between politics and the movies" and reverse the Hollywood-Washington dynamic so that "Mr. Hays, or whoever, would be *their* transmitter from West to East, from the governed to the governors," still place at their center "a family for the whole nation to love," the very foundation of the patriarchal state (387, 388, 387). No need for overt preaching, as Caroline recognizes, because "if they had done their work properly, their ends would be achieved subliminally" (387). And no need for Caroline to give herself up any longer to the invention of makeup artists and film crews, as Caroline ends the book "now entire herself, one person at last" (437). Power has filled the vacuum.

Addressing the issue of alternative models in his "Notes on Our Patriarchal State" (1990), published the same year as *Hollywood*, Vidal proposed Henry Clay, invoking Hearst's rhetoric in depicting him as "a true America Firster" who, "translated to a modern context," would opt for isolation over global domination (204). Addressing this issue in novels that correlate political power and media power, he takes a different tack: he undermines one by depicting the transient nature of the other. In this regard, Caroline seriously miscalculates in overestimating the shelf life of any mass cultural medium: in her mind, four Poussins *do* equal one moribund newspaper, as the financial exchange that gives her entrée into the world of mass communications indicates. Therefore, it is appropriate that in *The Golden Age* (2000), the final volume of the American Chronicle series, which extends Vidal's saga from 1939 to 1954 (and, briefly, from 31 December 1999 into early 2000), Caroline's *Hometown* series survives only to the extent that it is recalled as having been displaced by MGM's Andy Hardy fantasies (17–18), and William Randolph Hearst's legacy exists only to the extent that people are familiar with Orson Welles in *Citizen Kane* ("'Arson who?'" asks a television journalist [448]). It also is appropriate that of all the major fictional creations in *Empire* and *Hollywood*, Caroline is the only one who makes no appearance in *Washington, D.C.* (1967), the earliest of the American Chronicle novels with respect to publication, which covers a historical period (1937–54) comparable to that of the last. When characters in this first installment peruse the countryside around the nation's East Coast capital, all they see are new houses, each mounted with its own television antenna (342). They also see the barbarians that Caroline wished to mold like shapeless clay not just clamoring at the gates, but opening and closing the gates at their will: by the end of the book, the Sanford home is owned by a parvenu whose idea of interior decorating is replacing a portrait of Aaron Burr with a collage of newspaper clippings (360). In other words, while Caroline learns about the power of the media at the foot of her mentor, she never learns the most important lesson about media transiency that Vidal portrays William Randolph Hearst as knowing all along.

When Hearst observes the arch built over Fifth Avenue to honor Admiral Dewey's victory in the Spanish-American War, a "huge version of Rome's arch of Septimius Severus," he knows right away that the arch made of plaster and cheap wood will fall apart when winter comes: " 'That's the American *way*' " (*Empire* 163, 165). In this awareness, the publisher-producer echoes Brooks Adams, who distinguished Roman and American architecture on the basis of materials and longevity: "the Romans were never wholly sordid, nor did they ever niggle. When they built a wall, that wall was solid masonry, not painted iron" (*Law* 348). It is a crucial difference in that art, according to Adams, "perhaps, even more clearly than religion, love, or war, indicates the pathway of [imperial] consolidation," or, in the case of the "cheap core fantastically adorned," imperial disintegration (340, 348). What Hearst defines as "the American way," then, is simply "the way."

In the end, it is this awareness of the transient nature of all kinds of empires that overshadows those dreams of grandeur that permeate Vidal's work, in which moves toward consolidation in the novels are constantly infused by the centrifugal rush from the center cited in the essays, and the official birth of American empire in 1898 is matched by the contention that its hegemonic tenure, its proverbial "Golden Age," lasted just five years (1945–50).[41] In turning to John Updike's Rabbit tetralogy, another American Chronicle series in that its portrayal of the years 1959 to 1989 picks up where Vidal's works leave off, we will see the process of decline mirrored in the supplanting of movies by television as the dominant medium and the economic hollowing of that electronics industry as production shifts from the United States to Japan. If, according to Vidal, the day the Commerce Department declared the United States a debtor nation turned 16 September 1985 into "The Day the American Empire Ran Out of Gas," as the title of his 1986 essay asserts, Updike will explore what happens when the American type is forced to run on empty.

The evidence, however, seems to point to the conclusion that, when a highly centralized society disintegrates, under the pressure of economic competition, it is because the energy of the race has been exhausted.

—Brooks Adams, 1896 preface to *The Law of Civilization and Decay*

In the Forties, American boys created a world empire because they chose to be James Stewart, Clark Gable and William Eythe. By imitating godlike autonomous men, our boys were able to defeat Hitler, Mussolini and Tojo. Could we do it again? Are the private eyes and denatured cowboys potent enough to serve as imperial exemplars? No. [. . .] Glory has fled and only the television commercials exist to remind us of the Republic's early greatness and virile youth.

—Gore Vidal, *Myra Breckinridge* (1968)

Rabbit Rerun
Updike's End of an American Epoch

Fifty-five years old, toting two hundred thirty pounds, and wallowing in semi-retirement, Harry Angstrom has decided to take up books in *Rabbit at Rest* (1990), so fulfilling an intention that a wall-to-wall carpeted den has inspired at the end of *Rabbit Is Rich* (1981). Not just any books does this newly literate Rabbit read, though—no potboilers or murder mysteries or harlequin romances for him. Harry, as befits his paterfamilias status of grandfather, has taken to reading history, "that sinister mulch of facts our little lives grow out of before joining the mulch themselves" (*Rabbit at Rest* 44), and this last volume of John Updike's tetralogy shows Harry studiously progressing through Barbara W. Tuchman's *The First Salute* (1988). Given the fact that the heart attack that Harry suffers early in the novel provides him with an opportunity to see his own proverbial history pass before his eyes, this desire to review the past is all to the good. In Harry's case, however, the past that he reviews on that occasion is one that lends itself, quite literally, to re-viewing. Sunfishing with his granddaughter when the attack occurs, and aware of the need to deliver the child to safety, Harry asks the girl to sing to him in order to keep him awake at the tiller. Judy quickly exhausts her repertoire of nursery rhymes and shifts to television jingles. When pressed for as yet unused material, she comes up with songs from *The Wizard of Oz, Snow White,* and *Pinocchio,* "children's classics Rabbit saw when they were new, the first time in those old movie theatres with Arabian decors and plush curtains that pulled back and giant mirrors in the lobby" (*Rabbit at Rest* 140), and she and Harry glide safely onto shore. Judy's familiarity with the songs of those classic movies stems from the videotaped versions she has watched over and over in her home since, as *Rabbit Is Rich* depicts, the theaters for which Harry nostalgically yearns have been turned into porno palaces well before her birth, and, as *Rabbit at Rest* adds, even their pleas for historical restoration have themselves succumbed to time, mere shingles whining "ELP SAV ME." Unfortunately, the substitutes that have taken their places offer little in compensation due to artifacts they show that provide still less in the way of innovation. We're no longer off to see the Wizard, just cruising on *The Love Boat;* not wishing upon a star, merely "Stayin' Alive." " 'D'you ever get the feeling everything these days is sequels?' " Harry responds when asked if he has seen *Jaws II.* " 'Like people are running out of ideas' " (*Rabbit Is Rich* 377).

And not just ideas. Whether it is gas, as the opening to *Rabbit Is Rich* asserts, or gumption, as the entirety of *Rabbit Redux* (1971) illustrates, the America that Harry Angstrom is meant to mirror is in steady decline, what with communist aggression in the first two novels replaced by leverage that oil grants the Middle East in the third and the edge that technology grants Japan in the fourth.[1] And not just according to Updike. Tuchman's "View of the American Revolution" that Updike has Harry reading in *Rabbit at Rest* is a view of an American empire succeeding a British empire that succeeds a Dutch empire, all of which suggests a view of empire as an inevitably declining state of affairs. Yet Harry, for all his good intentions, cannot warm to such an intellectual view of history or to such a distant period of time: in point of fact, the book puts him to sleep. The only periods of America's past in which he can immerse himself thoroughly are those through which he himself has lived. Likewise, for all his ranting about global events and crises in American foreign policy, for all his pasting a U.S. flag decal on his car window to show his support of the Vietnam War, the concerns that touch him personally are contained more in the popular than the political, specifically, within those same artifacts of popular culture to which his own weakening heart has responded. To him "[t]he movie palaces of his boyhood, packed with sweet odors and dark velvet, murmurs and giggles and held hands, were history. HELP SAVE ME" (*Rabbit at Rest* 184).

Updike, of course, has always taken his measure of American history from the menial more than the monumental, an authorial preference that he attributes, in part, to his apprenticeship at *The New Yorker,* "a loving respect for facticity— for the exactly *what* of matters" comprising the "shared heritage" he finds common to all those who worked at the magazine under Harold Ross (*Hugging* 848). Yet Updike's likening those minutiae of daily life to archaeological remains that contain "more breathing history" than any official documents, so like the value ascribed to the everyday by social theorists such as Lefebvre and de Certeau,[2] is attributable to his own conception of a layered realism wherein what is visible suggests what is invisible, *both* equally constitutive of what should be considered "real" ("Art" 106). This conception of what he deems "distinctive 'American realism'" he traces back to the writings of Walt Whitman. Quoting Whitman's assertion that " 'the true use for the imaginative faculty of modern times is to give ultimate vivification to facts, to science, and to common lives, endowing them with glows and glories and final illustriousness which belong to every real thing, and to real things only,' " Updike delineates the democratizing ramifications that this credo of such an unlikely prophet of realistic writing augurs. Once the world itself can be "sung in its clean reality," real things can be "assigned the sacred status that in former times was granted to mysteries" (*Hugging* 117). And once real things are allowed to function as "masks for God," "[e]verything can be as interesting as every other thing. An old milk carton is worth a rose; a trolley car has as much right to be there, in terms of aesthetics, as a tree" ("Art" 116; *Picked-Up* 518).[3] Most important, religion can be construed broadly, not just as organized faith, "but in the form of any private system [. . .] that submerges in a transcendent concern the grimly finite facts of our individual human case," be it "adoration of Elvis Presley or hatred of nuclear weapons," "a fetishism of politics or popular culture" (*Self-Consciousness* 226).[4]

Therefore, while the Rabbit tetralogy expressly locates those grimly finite facts in items such as VCRs and televisions, emblems of a consumer culture in which, as Updike writes, " '[p]eople don't buy things because they *need* 'em. [. . .] You buy something because it's be*yond* what you need' " (*Rabbit at Rest* 417), the decline of America that these novels chronicle is measured not just by the facts of where the items consumed originate, or what in particular they disseminate, but by how far beyond the obvious the items in question resonate. In tracing this latter shift, Updike has no better spokesperson than Harry Angstrom, for while Updike's imagistic prowess grows over the course of the tetralogy, to the extent that television screens suggest air traffic control screens, which suggest heart monitors whose twitching lines suggest worms, which suggest the origins of life, Rabbit's steadily declines, to the extent that television screens become places on which to see Vanna White turn around letters on *The*

Wheel of Fortune. With even his forbidden dreams just "intensely colored over-populated rearrangements of old situations stored in his brain cells" (*Rabbit at Rest* 472), summer reruns for his autumnal years, Harry turns not so much into a rabbit redux as a rabbit reduced.

The Hinge of History

According to Vidal's *Myra Breckinridge,* who considers the decade between 1935 and 1945 to be the apogee of American power because during those years "*no irrelevant film was made in the United States*" and "the entire range of human (which is to say, American) legend was put on film" (*Myra* 13), there is no doubt as to exactly when America's imperial decline began: 1948. Viewed from the 1973 Watergate perspective of *Myron,* in fact, 1948 forms nothing less than "the hinge of history," when, as signaled by Dore Schary's sponsorship of *The Boy with Green Hair* and accelerated by the encroachment of television, "the studio system is about to go down the drain, taking with it Andy Hardy, Maisie, Pandro S. Berman, Esther Williams—everything, in fact, that made America great" (332, 249). More than just a reflection of personal idiosyncrasy, Myra has a point. The year she cites as "the hinge of history" is also the year the United States began rebuilding the economy of Japan so as to create a stronghold against communism in Asia, a reversal of Occupation policy of reform and democratization that was directly responsible for Japan's later eclipsing the United States as an economic power. Yet international affairs tend to get short shrift when Myra mourns the passing of the earlier hegemonic period. She recalls instead having fallen in love with Joan Leslie while watching *Sergeant York* (1941) and wonders, "But where is Joan now? Where are all those beautiful years of war and sacrifice and Pandro S. Berman films?" (*Myra* 51). She sits in a booth in Schwab's drugstore and regretfully acknowledges "the present Schwab's does not in the least resemble the Schwab's of thirty years ago" (67).

In lamenting a bygone era in terms of bygone popular artifacts, Myra anticipates the kind of observations that will form a litany of loss for Harry Angstrom by the time he hits middle age a decade or two later. He may wonder "what's the point of being an American?" without that Cold War that " 'gave you a reason to get up in the morning' " to count on (*Rabbit at Rest* 442–43, 353), but the absences that pierce his heart most deeply he expresses with respect to less monumental things. Where have all the Chiclets gone? "Have they really gone the way of penny candy, of gumdrops and sourballs, of those little red ration tokens you had to use during the war? . . ." (97). "Whatever happened to the old-fashioned plain hamburger? Gone wherever the Chiclet went" (100). Whatever happened to movie stars? "Where did they go, all the great Hollywood bitches? . . ." (*Rabbit Is Rich* 66).

At best, Harry can recoup his losses by salvaging the particular item lost, as evidenced, for example, by the junk food he tends to favor, peanut bars that recall the fresh hot nuts he bought as a child from vendors in Brewer. More often, his reclamation of the past is wholly imaginative, a sentimental journey evoked by song to those times when "[l]ife was not only bigger but more solemn" (*Rabbit at Rest* 326), when Franklin Delano Roosevelt was president, when Ronald Reagan shot Japanese fighters from airplanes, when Harry himself saved his little sister, Mim, from falling, from a sled, from a bike, from any heights of danger.[5] Because Harry also remains aware of the limitations that his time-bound position in history presents, that being born in 1933 has placed him at the end of an American epoch, "as the world shrank like an apple going bad and America was no longer the wisest hick town within a boat ride of Europe and Broadway forgot the tune," his nostalgia is not for a time of power and perfection, "decades when Americans moved within the American dream, laughing at it, starving on it, but living it, humming it, the national anthem everywhere" (*Rabbit Redux* 114). Rather, his nostalgia is for a period of time when individual heroism was possible so as to aid an America in time of need. " 'You're what made America great,' " Charlie Stavros tells Harry. " 'A real gunslinger' " (49). Harry himself is more precise: he dreams of when he can have his very own silver bullet (263).

As Ariel Dorfman has pointed out, the 1930s witnessed the emergence of many "superbeings"—the Lone Ranger, Superman, Batman, Green Arrow, the Green Hornet, Flash Gordon—who acted as "representatives of the average citizen" during a period of time in which the average American citizen felt less than in complete control (*Empire's* 115, 116).[6] More than in any one popular protagonist, however, Harry locates the greatest of such beings in a purveyor of popular culture: "*That Disney, he really packed a punch*," he thinks after hearing the last of Judy's songs at sea (*Rabbit at Rest* 140). Harry's father goes even further. In his view, " 'it was Disney more than FDR kept the country from going under to the Commies in the Depression' " (*Rabbit Redux* 315). No wonder Harry, at age twenty-six, still approaches Disney products with reverence in *Rabbit, Run* (1960), watching a grown man cavort in Mouseketeer ears on television because "he respects him," moved to silence when that man wearing mouse ears gives advice in God's name (and years before the PTL) (12). And no wonder that a loss that pains him to grief years later is the loss of that very same spokesman. "Where are they now?" he muses when reminded of Annette and all her cohorts. "Middle-aged parents themselves. Jimmie died years ago, he remembers reading. Died young" (*Rabbit at Rest* 110).

An extreme reaction, perhaps, but not an isolated one or one restricted to those of little insight or intelligence. Citing Mickey Mouse as having been his "first artistic love and inspiration" and admitting that his first ambition was to be an animator for the cartoon's creator (*Self-Consciousness* 242; "Art" 88), Updike himself recalls the ubiquity of the synergistic Disney enterprise: "in that pre-television Thirties world, the world of the movies and the world of the popular press were so entwined, and the specific world of Walt Disney so promiscuously generated animated cartoons and cartoon strips and children's books and children's toys, that it all seemed one art" (*Self-Consciousness* 105). Others, too, have testified to the impact that those Disney products wielded. "No one will ever know to what extent it may be held responsible for pulling us out of the depression," conceded Robert D. Feild when assessing *The Three Little Pigs*, but, as he went on to assert, its porcine heroes taunting a Big Bad Wolf in 1933 "contributed not a little to the raising of people's spirits and to their defiance of circumstances" (46).[7] *Fortune* magazine declared Mickey Mouse "an international hero" one year later, "better known than Roosevelt or Hitler, a part of the folklore of the world" (qtd. in Heide and Gilman 57). Winston Churchill, legend has it, even went so far as to make Franklin Delano Roosevelt see *Victory through American Power,* Disney's 1943 film on long-range bombing, as a means of convincing the United States to adopt a similar strategy (Maltin 64).[8]

More noteworthy than Harry's fascination with the world of Disney is the faith he continues to maintain in it despite the falseness it engenders, both with respect to the mass culture it epitomizes and the nation whose impulses it symbolizes. His sister blatantly announces to their family that her Las Vegas speciality is " 'milk[ing] people' " (*Rabbit Redux* 313), but her memories of having worked at Disneyland evoke just eager queries from their father about how close she came to the grand guru himself. Her wobbly rendition of Lincoln's Gettysburg Address inspires " '[w]hat kind of work did Disney have you do, Mim?' "; her saccharine tour guide's spiel of a model Mt. Vernon elicits " 'you ever get to meet Disney personally?' " (315). Harry, to his credit, actually connects Walt Disney and the MagiPeel Peeler Company that he himself represents as linked in fraud together, the "base of our economy" (*Rabbit, Run* 12), but this equation of his early years lasts hardly as long as it takes for him to make it.

More typical of those few connections Harry makes between American commerce and American popular culture is a response he exhibits toward the end of *Rabbit at Rest*. Running, yet again, from the scene of another Pennsylvania domestic disaster—this time, the discovery of his one-night fling with his daughter-in-law, Pru—Harry gets into his car to drive to Florida, a southern flight that echoes the one that initiated his aborted travels three decades earlier. Listening to the songs of his youth on the radio, much like those he has on that first trip, which have now become (like Harry himself, one may speculate) Golden Oldies, and struck by the fact that singers like Roy Orbison are now being joined into the fold, he realizes "that the songs of his life were as moronic as the rock the brainless kids now feed on, or the Sixties and Seventies stuff that Nelson gobbled up" (*Rabbit at Rest* 460). From his resentment comes the subsequent recognition that the motive force behind all such music is greed: "It's all *disposable*, cooked up to turn a quick profit. They lead us down the garden path, the music manufacturers, then turn around and lead the next generation down with a slightly different flavor of glop" (460–61). The sense of betrayal that this recognition evokes he associates, in turn, with the feeling that the closing of Kroll's department store, "where you could buy the best of everything," and its extended consequences have elicited during his adolescence: "If Kroll's could go, the courthouse could go, the banks could go. When the money stopped, they could close down God Himself" (461). But not Disney, as the next lines make clear, for the claims of fakery that Harry's proximity to Disney World causes him to cast upon those second-string amusement parks that "hold out their cups for the tourist overflow" leave the master showman inviolable (462).

Not So Sublime Prime Time

This is not to say that Disney's media remain invincible, of course, for media empires, as we already have seen in chapter 1, have lives of limited duration. The Lone Ranger who filled Harry's young head with dreams of silver bullets no longer rides roughshod over radio airwaves; he just gets ridiculed on Carol Burnett reruns (*Rabbit Redux* 29–30). The hero with the "right stuff" today, Deion Sanders, hits home runs and scores touchdowns and calls himself "Prime Time"—as well he should if his impact is to reach those up-and-coming acolytes who, as Charlie Stavros puts it, " 'all grew up on television commercials' " with the box " 'the only mother they had' " (*Rabbit at Rest* 470; *Rabbit Is Rich* 250). From those first scenes of Harry's wife Janice staring at the television's flickering "blank radiance" of particles in 1959 (*Rabbit, Run* 213), Updike has been attuned to the power that the medium can wield. His later works compound power with presence. Whether as news source in *Rabbit Redux* (for the Vietnam War, SDS riots, the trial of the Chicago Seven, the moon shot) or news promoter in *Rabbit Is Rich* (Iranians outside the Tehran U.S. Embassy, that "cocky little" pope on his way to Yankee Stadium [256], the plucky Dalai Lama doing the talk show circuit), whether as white noise (Ma Springer's Pennsylvania hometown companion) or silent chaperon (for Harry and wife Janice, Harry and girlfriend Jill, Harry and daughter-in-law Pru), television remains ubiquitous. Indeed, so strong does its impact become that interference with its operations is perceived as tantamount to blasphemy: when broadcast of an NFC playoff is obscured by foggy weather, "[t]he announcers [. . .] seem indignant that God could do this, mess with CBS and blot out a TV show the sponsors are paying a million dollars a minute for and millions are watching" (*Rabbit at Rest* 163).[9]

At the same time, for all its preeminence in circulating American cultural capital, to borrow Pierre Bourdieu's term (267–83), television occupies a very different position in Updike's work with respect to American economic capital.[10] Because the black-and-white box first invented by RCA had become, by 1976, a commodity 98 percent of which was imported from Japan, the growth in television's cultural power coincides with the shift from American to Japanese economic power that *Rabbit at Rest* assumes as a given. Clyde V. Prestowitz Jr., in fact, has gone so far as to find no advance as significant or endowed with as many ramifications as Japan's "conquest of the television industry," its illustration of American manufacturers turning themselves into distributors of goods produced abroad making it "the quintessential example" of the process known as "hollowing" (200, 201). Because it also was the United States that licensed the necessary technology to Japan, for monochrome sets in the 1950s and, again, for color in 1962, the nation that first wooed Asia to maintain its own preeminence in global affairs ends up being hoist by its own petard. Dwight D. Eisenhower's 1962 remark that " '[o]nly Americans can hurt America' " takes on significance beyond the demagogic (Updike, *Assorted* 106).

As Dilvo I. Ristoff correctly notes, however, a large portion of the money invested in the United States between 1973 and 1985 did not come from Japan (*John Updike's* 72). Therefore, "THE ERA OF COROLLA" proclaimed by the banner on Harry's car lot heralds an era in which American industries of all sorts have succumbed to the money of *many* foreign investors (*Rabbit Is Rich* 403). To mourn the decline in Firestone Tire quality as a decline in American-produced goods everywhere, as Harry does (111), is to mourn a company finally bought by Japan's Bridgestone, which, in turn, is to mourn the loss of all those other companies acquired by Japanese investors over the previous two decades: Auburn Steel, Inter-Continental Hotels, CBS Records, and Gould, to name but a few.[11] At the same time, to note changes in gasoline station names, from Humble to Getty, from Atlantic to Arco, as Harry does (*Rabbit Redux* 345), is *also* to note both OPEC ascendancy and the scrambling of other nations for the natural resources market as well: Shell, for example, a product of long-term Anglo-Dutch investment; Standard Oil, a more recent purchase of British Petroleum. Within the larger economic context suggested by those items by which Rabbit gauges his life, even the most menial goods that characterize his consumption, those Double Stuf Oreos and Fruit Newtons that he consumes in the most literal sense, resonate with extended significance when so many of those prototypi-cal American foods are produced by nations other than the United States, from the Burger King Whoppers and Ball Park Franks owned by Britain, to the Wild Turkey bourbon distilled by France's Pernod Ricard, to the Carnation evapo-rated milk controlled by Switzerland's Nestlé.

Harry's resentment of such economic realities comes not from the impact they have on him personally, for his own wealth as a seller of Japanese mer-chandise depends upon their continuation, and his investments literally cash in on American misfortunes: his real estate purchase results from " 'the beauty of inflation,' " his silver rises in value with the Russian invasion of Afghanistan, his contemplation of carpets occurs while Iran still holds Americans hostage (*Rabbit Is Rich* 330, 365, 405). Harry's resentment springs instead from the way that economics has replaced politics and standing armies as the adjudicator of power. Believing that "[t]he only difference between the two old superpowers is they sell their trees to Japan in different directions," Harry acknowledges the feeling of loss with which the erosion of bipolar politics has left him (*Rabbit at Rest* 352). With the loss of personalized rivalry that marked bipolar politics compounded by the loss of that same quality that marked American business practices, as " 'good clean dog eat dog' " is replaced by "Japan, and technology, and the profit motive," why not wonder, as Harry does, about the advantages that come with being an American (*Rabbit Is Rich* 24; *Rabbit at Rest* 272)? With selling reduced to " 'just standing at the checkout counter,' " even Willy Loman would turn over in his grave (*Rabbit at Rest* 39).

Having surveyed the succession of one new empire by another over the course of history, Brooks Adams had one remedy for any nation about to go under: flexibility. Ancient Rome fell because it was "uninventive," unwilling to manu-facture any items that could command the Asian market (*New* 40). Eighteenth-century France "found social innovation so difficult" that it continued to fight rather than undersell potential competitors (149). Nineteenth-century Britain succumbed to large-scale property liquidation because it "proved [too] inflex-ible" to maintain its advantages in transportation (174). "[I]ntellectually slug-gish" Russia retained communal occupancy of land for so long that it had to import foreigners to manage its factories (182). Only the United States displayed "intellectual flexibility" when, "through an exertion of energy and adaptability, perhaps without a parallel," it met the debt contracted between 1860 and 1893 by consolidating into trusts that facilitated maximum utilization of its mines (175).

Harry, a true American, likewise adapts to the times. Just as he and Janice have exchanged their Falcon for a Celica and a Camry Deluxe Wagon, they now have his and her sonys, his in that same den in which he reads Tuchman's ac-count of falling empires, hers in the kitchen to watch while cooking dinner. So, too, does Harry change with respect to the degree of appreciation he accords the medium, from early contempt in *Rabbit, Run* to an incorporation of it as a veritable lifeline, "its wires com[ing] out of the wall behind him, just like oxygen," when hospitalized in *Rabbit at Rest* (294). And functioning as a conduit of information between Harry and the outside world, television *does* serve as a data lifeline. " 'I don't have prejudices, just facts,' " he declares (à la Jack Webb) when discoursing on Italian business practices. " 'The Mafia is a fact. [. . .] It was all on *60 Minutes*' " (259). He also knows that "[s]lave ships, cabins, sold down the river, Ku Klux Klan, James Earl Ray" comprise the principal facts of African American history: "Channel 44 keeps having these documentaries all about it" (*Rabbit Redux* 116).

To the extent that all the Angstroms rely on television as a source of information, Harry is not unique. " 'All I know about cocaine is what's on *Miami Vice* and the talk shows,' " Janice cries when confronted with the fact of her own son's addiction (*Rabbit at Rest* 147–48). Nor is Harry unique with respect to the influence the medium has had on his capacity for independent thought. The idea of dropping televisions on Southeast Asia instead of bombs may not originate with Janice in *Rabbit Redux* (Harry suspects her lover, Charlie Stavros), but it does suggest a way in which those hearts and minds desired by American strategists could be won with much less bloodshed (288–89). What distinguishes the effect that television has had on Harry is less the degree to which it has influenced his independence of thought, for Harry has never been much of an intellectual, and more the way it has diminished in scope the very nature of that thought, for this is a man who had pictured a "quilt-colored map of the U.S." emerging from the head of a sleeping God after hearing of the "American dream" for the first time (*Rabbit Redux* 106).

When assessing this capacity for the expansive, it is important to remember that Harry and even Janice take their original codes for conduct from a different visual medium: film. Harry after a heart attack takes his cues for cool from "Bogey at the airport in Casablanca [*Casablanca*, 1942], Flynn at Little Big Horn [*They Died with Their Boots On*, 1941], George Sanders in the collapsing temple to Dagon, Victor Mature having pushed apart the pillars [*Samson and Delilah*, 1949]" (*Rabbit at Rest* 172). Janice acting casual in a convertible he casts as Liz Taylor in *A Place in the Sun* (1951); Janice talking tough he treats like Ida Lupino (*Rabbit Is Rich* 64, 65). Films all made between that 1938 to 1954 period in which Updike describes himself as having gone to the movies "pretty intensely," and upholding the quality of "debonair grace" he considers "a moral ideal," they typify the kind of films he—eerily echoing Vidal's *Myra*—finds "now all gone to scatter and rumpus in the fight with television for the lowest common denominator" (*Hugging* 843).[12]

Television theorist John Fiske provides a sharp retort to such remarks: " 'The lowest common denominator' may be a useful concept in arithmetic, but in the study of popularity its only possible value is to expose the prejudices of those who use it" (309). So it is with Updike. As representing that "lowest common denominator" within the Angstrom household, Harry's son, Nelson, portrays perfectly the shift in sensibilities in which a shift from movies to television has resulted. Looking at him dressed in a purple paisley robe, and reminded of what rich people wore in the movies of her youth, Janice mourns the reduced sense of aspiration that differentiates his generation from hers:

> Robes, smoking jackets, top hats and white ties, flowing white gowns if you were Ginger Rogers, up to your chin in ostrich feathers or was it white fox? Young people now don't have that to live up to, to strive toward, the rock stars just wear dirty blue jeans and even the baseball players, she has noticed looking over Harry's shoulder at the television, don't bother to shave, like the Arab terrorists. When she was a girl nobody had money but people had dreams. (*Rabbit at Rest* 143)

Nelson, in contrast, experiences no sense of diminution because he experiences no change. Having grown up with Mighty Mouse instead of Mickey Mouse, he finds "the screen of reality" too big for him as a teenager and actually "misses television's running commentary" (*Rabbit Redux* 80). Having learned about John F. Kennedy from watching *PT 109* on TV, Nelson has adult ideas of glamour derived from actors so reduced in stature by the box that they need *People* magazine scandals to make them at all interesting (*Rabbit Is Rich* 265). Harry may accuse Nelson and those his age of having had "[e]verything handed to them on a platter" and "think[ing] life's one big TV," but if television is the medium that gives them this message, its platter of leftovers provides very little, filled as it is with nothing but "ghosts" (150). The shows that Nelson watches most often are reruns.

Used to the size of the silver screen instead of SONY's meager inches, Harry fights the diminished sense of expansiveness to which television contributes. Nowhere is his resistance displayed more clearly than in the media with which he measures America's pursuit of new frontiers, media that provide an almost textbook illustration of those forms designated by Raymond Williams as "residual," "dominant," and "emergent" (*Sociology* 204). "Well, nobody was going to the moon much these days," Updike's narrator admits in 1979 (*Rabbit Is Rich* 85).[13] Only Harry, who "was always worrying about how wide the world was, caring about things like how far the stars are" (*Rabbit Redux* 332), still tries to see space as expansive. He may think of *Alien* and *Moonraker* when Nelson's friend Melanie describes " 'a world with endless possibilities' " because he has just seen those films advertised in a nearby movie complex, but he does not think of *Battlestar Gallactica,* which he has just seen the week before on television (*Rabbit Is Rich* 90, 44). He may shoot space invaders in video parlors in Florida, but he still finds the computer screen too small for him to score a single point (*Rabbit at Rest* 107). Yet with the continual thrust for the smaller a trend he cannot reverse, the forms with which he gauges the expansive get progressively smaller in turn. He thinks of film (residual) when the trend is toward television (dominant), he thinks of television when the trend is to video (emergent), with the result a compounding of media formulae that turn his original gaze at the stars into a star-cast glaze, as his overdetermined perception of the *Challenger* disaster illustrates: "And wasn't that the disgrace of the decade, sending that poor New Hampshire schoolteacher and that frizzy-haired Jewish girl, not to mention the men, one of them black and another Oriental, all like some Hollywood cross-section of America, up to be blown into bits on television a minute later?" (*Rabbit at Rest* 458).

Unique among televised disasters in exploding "the modernist myth of technology (and also the Western frontier myth of the necessity of humans for space exploration) as unifying a dispersed audience," as Patricia Mellencamp has argued, the impact of the 28 January 1986 *Challenger* explosion could not be defused via broadcasts of " 'repetitive alteration' " (255). As such, the televised *Challenger* catastrophe has ramifications with respect to America's grandiosity itself. "Even John Wayne" has died, Harry notes at the opening of *Rabbit Is Rich* (7), although the man who, in Joan Didion's words, "determined forever the shape of certain of our dreams" (*Slouching* 30), had already been reduced to parody from *Red River* to *True Grit* a decade earlier. The president with movie magic and his own "dream distance," Ronald Reagan, is replaced in *Rabbit at Rest* by one whose publicists have turned into " 'a beer commercial,' " George Bush, with the prospects of one who, "like God," might know "nothing or everything" shrinking to the reality of another who "knows something, but it seems a small something" (61, 295). With the freedom that comes with being an American now defined as the freedom to watch whatever television shows he wants, it is no wonder that Harry's standards for excellence have shrunk to the level of quiz shows by the time he hits middle age: "That Vanna! Can she strut! Can she clap her hands when the wheel turns! Can she turn those big letters around! She makes you proud to be a two-legged mammal" (430).[14]

Satisfied by so little, we do turn into a "nation of couch potatoes," as Harry realizes, lulled so easily into complacency (*Rabbit at Rest* 485). Janice worries more about Bryant and Willard not getting along on the *Today* show than she does about "that evil pockmarked Noriega" who "just won't leave" Panama (309, 310). Little Judy watches news of the Pan Am 103 explosion with impatience, "believ[ing] that headlines always happen to other people" (79). And Harry, horrified at first by the Lockerbie disaster and "shocked" at his ability to imagine his own son's plane in flames with "just a cold thrill at being a witness" (10), eventually follows suit when he hears of later airline crashes: "The plane in New York skidded off the end of the runway and two people were killed. Just two. One hundred seventy-one died in the Sahara. A caller in London gave all the credit to Allah. Harry doesn't mind that one as much as the Lockerbie Pan Am bomb. Like everything else on the news, you get bored, it gets to seem a gimmick, like all those TV time-outs in football" (501).

More than just a conditioned response to sensory overload, or proof of what Mellencamp has dubbed "our status as safe outsider" (262), this detachment that television cultivates increasingly renders Harry emotional service as the events that it neutralizes have greater personal reverberations.[15] Watching the landing on the moon on television at the same time that he tries to discuss the most recent breakup of his marriage in *Rabbit Redux,* he acknowledges, " 'I know it's happened, but I don't feel anything yet' " (93). Feeling "peripheral, removed, nostalgic, numb" at the sight of his home later going up in flames, he finds the graffiti that memorializes its wreckage "add[ing] up no better than the cluster of commercials TV stations squeeze into the chinks between programs" (278, 342). And fleeing from his last familial fiasco in *Rabbit at Rest,* and realizing that "TV families and your own are hard to tell apart" (the laugh tracks of one and ennui of the other notwithstanding), he comes to a final conclusion about his own degree of Baudrillardian authenticity: "His own life seems [. . .] to have been unreal, or no realer than the lives on TV shows" (468, 469).

By this time of his life, this is a detachment for which Harry desperately yearns, for the show that has left the greatest impact on his consciousness has been the "Rabbit Angstrom Show," on which he has seen his heart surrounded by specks of plaque that look like Rice Krispies (*Rabbit at Rest* 271, 273). Whereas reading about the detouring of his blood that the angioplasty he is to undergo will entail makes Harry think back to film, to "those horrible old Frankenstein movies with Boris Karloff" (269), watching what is happening to him on an actual monitor forces him to shift his thoughts to terms of television—which is all for the best. Aware as he is that his heart is to lie "dead in its soupy puddle" while a machine does the living for him, and angry that such "Godless technology is fucking the pulsing wet tubes we inherited from the squid" (270, 274), Harry *needs* to conceive of the procedure as a television program, needs to hear his doctors talking with "those voices on television that argue about the virtues of Miller Lite," needs to wonder whether the experience will be discussed on Oprah, needs, in short, to combat "a wave of nausea" with "a test pilot's detachment" and so keep the entire experience "as remote from his body as the records of his sins that angels are keeping" (273–75). The proximity of death simply makes it too frightening for Harry to conceive of himself in any other way.

The reruns that his family watches, then, do not bore him with prepackaged dialogue because in Harry's negotiated meaning, to borrow Stuart Hall's term ("Encoding" 137), they provide proof of continual recycling. Anniversary newscasts of Chappaquidick and the Manson murders do not disgust him, for he sees them as "full of resurrected footage" (*Rabbit at Rest* 372). And Toyota ads virtually inspire him, showing "men and women leaping, average men and women, their clothes lifted in cascading show-motion folds like angels' robes, [. . .] leaping and falling, grinning and then in freeze-frame hanging there, defying gravity," because their defiance of gravity contains within itself the prospects of defying those other natural laws that draw us earthbound (*Rabbit Is Rich* 328). If imagining himself a television star once confirmed his own sense of being special (*Rabbit Redux* 325), Harry now takes pleasure at thoughts of being one with the ordinary. He takes hope from those programs in which "a nation of performers, of smoothly talking heads, has sprung up under the lights, everybody rehearsed for their thirty seconds of nationwide attention," because the celluloid immortality that levels all their *Unsolved Mysteries* into one collective fantasy is an illusion to which Harry himself can subscribe (*Rabbit at Rest* 339).

As it turns out, the closest that Harry comes to the immortality that celebrity inscribes combines both the fetishism of politics and the fetishism of popular culture that Updike earlier used to illustrate the kind of broadly construed religion that caters to the need for "Being a Self Forever" (1989), as the essay bearing that title affirms (*Self-Consciousness* 226). His casting Harry as Uncle Sam in a Fourth of July parade has little to do with klieg lights, cables, and monitors of any sort, but it does enlist every other form of American popular culture to conflate age, class, and, most of all, time. The ceremony that results is an ode to the role of repetition in all celebrations of national origins (Hobsbawm, "Inventing" 1–2; Breuilly 344). An impersonator resurrects John Lennon, a tape recorder revives Kate Smith ("dead as she is"), and as "God Bless[es] America" before a "recycled" crowd of all the people whom Lennon imagined "living for today" and Harry had lamented as lost within his high school past, Harry, too, is rerun as Rabbit, "a legend, a walking cloud," who, as national symbol, is lifted further up "to survey all human history" (*Rabbit at Rest* 368–71). Emotionally sustaining, certainly—but intellectually devastating to all notions of American exceptionalism, in which the typical has been conceived as type.[16]

Sort of Like a Big Canada

In point of fact, Harry dressed as Uncle Sam is the second time in the Rabbit tetralogy that Updike explicitly portrays Harry as national symbol, and the difference between the two characterizations is revealing. In *Rabbit Redux,* which reflects his desire to redress America from a Vietnam War perspective, Updike employs Harry to depict the nation as self-proclaimed philanthropist: misguided, perhaps, in ministrations; unmanned, in the end, by others' manipulations. " 'What did I do wrong?' " exclaims Harry, after his ersatz commune of a house has burned to the ground. " 'I was a fucking Good Samaritan. I took in these orphans. Black, white, I said Hop aboard. Irregardless of color or creed, Hop aboard. Free eats. I was the fucking Statue of Liberty' " (311). In *Rabbit at Rest,* by contrast, Updike transforms the profferer of free eats into the biggest eater of all, as Harry himself realizes when he surveys what he looks like without the Uncle Sam costume that he has worn in the Fourth of July parade: "a fearsome bulk with eyes that see and hands that grab and teeth that bite, a body eating enough at one meal to feed three Ethiopians for a day, a shameless consumer of gasoline, electricity, newspapers, hydrocarbons, carbohydrates" (381).[17] But if this is *all* that lies behind the visible, if, as Harry suspects, "[t]he U.S. is still the U.S., held together by credit cards and Indian names" (*Rabbit at Rest* 457), the decline of America may be less a question of dollars and more a question of definition.

In the past, as presented by Updike's corpus, America simply defeated attempts at definition; its symbols, like those of most nations, were effective in creating collectivity in proportion to their imprecision (Guibernau 81–82). In *Rabbit Redux,* for example, Rabbit's rabid talk as Vietnam warmonger is superseded by his awareness that "to describe any of America's actions as a 'power play' is to miss the point. America is beyond power, it acts as in a dream, as a face of God" (49). And Skeeter, the black revolutionary housed by Rabbit in enforced community, subscribes to much the same belief. As he lectures Rabbit, " 'The thing about these Benighted States all around is that it was never no place like other places where this happens because that happens, and some men have more luck than others [. . .] no, sir, this place was never such a place it was a *dream,* it was a state of mind from those poor fool pilgrims on, right? Some white man see a black man he don't see a man he sees a *symbol,* right?' " (213–14).

To the extent that the later Rabbit novels paint a less ambiguous portrait of the country, they depart from this earlier conceit. The diagnosis of Harry's heart as " 'tired and stiff and full of crud' " and the depiction of Washington, D.C., as the "frozen far heart [. . .] of the grand old republic" could not make for clearer delineation (*Rabbit at Rest* 166, 442). Likewise, the designation of *Rabbit at Rest*'s last section by "MI" (myocardial infarction) instead of an abbreviation derived from a state name (FL, PA) "converts the whole of America into the site of one giant heart attack," as Judie Newman shrewdly observes (*"Rabbit"* 192). Yet it is not just a matter of Updike's reducing the symbolically sacred to the visibly profane, as an author like Thomas Pynchon does when he questions whether there are underground alternatives to America or just America at the end of *The Crying of Lot 49* (137). It is a matter of Updike's later works portraying both Harry and the country he mirrors as pedestrian. When Harry suffers his heart attack in *Rabbit at Rest,* he learns that the myocardial scarring that indicates a dying muscle " 'happens to all of us' " as part of an " 'aging process' " that " 'there's no escaping' " (284). For Harry, who originally has taken his identity from "himself [as] the heart of the universe," with "all the world beyond" him just "frills on himself, like the lace around a plump satin valentine," being endowed with a heart that suffers " '[t]he usual thing' " is unbearable (294, 166). For Updike to designate that organ as " 'a typical American heart' " confirms a view of America that, up until this point in his work, has been absolutely unendurable (166).

At the same time, no adjective better reflects an undercurrent that runs throughout the Rabbit novels from the very start, introduced by the question Harry asks himself early in *Rabbit, Run* as he begins the first of his many aborted escapes: "Is it just these people I'm outside, or is it all America?" (31).[18] Nevertheless, while willing to have Harry question whether he is typical or type—not to mention all those other characters who have no problem judging him simply egocentric—Updike has hesitated when it comes to extrapolating from character to country. As late as *Self-Consciousness* (1989), he praises America as a nation of providentially ordained mission, a "great roughly rectangular country severed from Christ by the breadth of the sea," quoting lines from the "Battle-Hymn of the Republic" as corroboration: *"In the beauty of the lilies Christ was born across the sea"* (103).[19]

With the decision to have Harry read Barbara W. Tuchman's *The First Salute* over the last months of his life, however, Updike's reluctance reaches an end, for Tuchman's book both proposes "A View of the American Revolution" from the perspective of past policies and predicts the downfall of American prominence by extending the conclusions of her own findings. Hence no concern for tender liberty provokes the salute granted an American vessel flying Continental Congress colors by a fort on the Dutch island of St. Eustatius in Tuchman's analysis, just a need to maintain a profitable exchange of colonial tobacco, indigo, timber, and horses and Dutch molasses, sugar, implements of war, and slaves. In fact, little concern for the sovereign status of the Thirteen Colonies motivates the alignment of friends and foes during the entire colonial period, the British public opposed to any act that ascribes more value to the colonies than the commercially rich West Indies, the French intervening to prevent any resurgence of British trade that reconciliation between mother country and colonies might effect. Portrayed by Tuchman as a product of the very mercantilist policies Harry so detests, in which "national power depended on the accumulation of hard currency to pay for the era's increasing costs of government and of maintaining armies and navies for constant conflict" (20), the conflict from which the United States gains its name originates more as "a power struggle of the Old World" that just happens to be played out on New World battlefields (143).

Most relevant for Updike's purposes are the attributes of pride and, its offspring, complacency that Tuchman deems the common denominators behind imperial collapse. The most "self-revealing" British remark of the Revolution in her view is Sir Joseph Yorke's demand for military victory " 'to restore the appearance which Britain had such a right to assume,' " indicating as it does a sense of naturalized invincibility that Tuchman deems tantamount to "mental lethargy" (75, 130). For assuming a position as "the world's moon that pulled the tides of international affairs" just prompts others in that imperial solar system to seek changes in the spheres of orbit (149), " '[e]very nation in Europe,' " according to Benjamin Franklin, wishing " 'to see Britain humbled, having all in their time been offended by her insolence' " (87). Tuchman thus ends her discussion of the surrender at Yorktown by judging the six-year war that it concluded "the historic rebuke to complacency" (290).

But not the last rebuke, nor the last illustration. Updike quotes at great length from one of the earlier passages in Tuchman's book in which an eighteenth-century French pseudo-scholar proclaims the New World " 'formed for happiness, but not for empire' " because, as Tuchman paraphrases, its climate made men " 'listless and indolent,' " " 'happy but never stalwart' " (Rabbit at Rest 86; Tuchman 77). Not coincidentally, indolence and happiness are two qualities emphasized by Updike in the portraits that comprise the last two Rabbit novels, Harry portrayed as " 'so fucking happy' " that he offends others, Nelson snorting cocaine because he sees in it " 'instant happiness,' " each outdoing the other in get-rich-quick schemes that betray a fundamental laziness that joins the two more than any chromosomal connection (Rabbit Is Rich 124; Rabbit at Rest 58). When Harry and his family visit Thomas Edison's home in Florida, this trait is shown to belong as much to Americans as to Angstroms. The "five-dollar pilgrimage" to the shrine of "the amazing great American" reveals Edison to have been the owner of the first prefabricated house and the gadget genius of toasters and waffle irons—in short, the father of all those everyday things like the MagiPeel Peeler that Harry has sold that are designed to make American life easier (*Rabbit at Rest* 97). The grounds around his home only complete the picture, containing as they do a rare and mature *Cecropia palmata* tree, otherwise known as the "sloth tree," whose leaves—much like the trait alluded to by the plant's name—never disintegrate over time (94).

With the indolence that marks American character no different from the complacency that caused the decline of other imperial nations in the past, the commonness of the attribute defeats all notions of American exceptionalism. No news here, of course. Brooks Adams had been predicting as much about empires years before Tuchman's book, citing the same traits of lethargy and torpor in his diagnosis: Britain's decline since 1890, for instance, prefigured by the "dilatory" nature of its firms and "slackness" of London tradesmen (*America's* 147), was only confirmed by a Boer War campaign of such "inertia and feebleness" that troops of "inferior stamina" surrendered without putting up much resistance (162, 172). The only addition made during the latter half of the 1980s, of which Tuchman's and Updike's analyses are symptomatic, was the nation targeted for discussion. Predicating *The Rise and Fall of the Great Powers* on "Economic Change and Military Conflict from 1500 to 2000," as the subtitle of his book indicates, Paul Kennedy saw the "more sluggish" growth rate of America at the time as an "ebbing away" from the nation's having once owned a disproportionately large share of the world's wealth to its owning "a more 'natural' share" (xx, 533). Likewise, he saw as moot all debate about the prospects of maintaining the country's position of preeminence, for, as his extended historical analysis argued, "it simply has not been given to any one society to remain *permanently* ahead of all the others, because that would imply a freezing of the differentiated pattern of growth rates, technological advance, and military developments which has existed since time immemorial" (533).

Once Japan's rising sun began surpassing all previous growth rates as the sun over the West began to set, some saw a pattern that reversed earlier international dynamics. As a Tennessee banker who recruited foreign companies noted, "We rebuilt Japan. In effect, they're helping to rebuild us" (Glickman and Woodward 11). Some, in fact, saw it reversing a role that up until then had been paradigmatically American, as did former U.S. Ambassador to the European Community J. William Middendorf when paraphrasing the words inscribed upon the Statue of Liberty: "Send us your tired. Send us your poor. Send us your money" (Glasgall 84). Some even saw the pattern as downright reactionary, plunging the United States into the throes of what one Kentucky Building and Trades Union representative called "economic colonialism" ("Power without Purpose"). Underlying all such assertions, though, was an awareness of one indisputable fact.

As Henry Kissinger put it, "A point will be reached in which the United States will become less relevant to more and more countries, and those countries, whatever may be their preferences, will be drawn more and more to Japan" ("Power without Purpose").

Fittingly, that point in Rabbit's saga comes during his last basketball games, final attempts on his part to recapture his former days of glory. " 'Hey man, [. . .] you're history!' " taunts one of the racially mixed boys whom Harry challenges to a game of hoops (*Rabbit at Rest* 491). And, fittingly, it is when shooting a worn red, white, and blue basketball that the heart attack that makes real this observation occurs. If earlier in his life Harry has refused to believe in America's not being perfect "any more than he believes at heart that he will die" (*Rabbit Redux* 312), the last pages of Updike's saga call the bluff of what has increasingly become a weakly maintained rationalization. The weary "Enough" that serves as an end to Harry's literary life thus signals a final resignation about no longer having to be at center stage. It also may suggest, for Updike, an acceptance of abdication on the part of the nation whose fate has been so linked all along to that of his Rabbit. Admitting that with Bush's election " 'we're kind of on the sidelines, [. . .] sort of like a big Canada, and what we do doesn't much matter to anybody else,' " Harry also intimates that such a position may not be all that bad: " 'Maybe that's the way it ought to be. It's a kind of relief, I guess, not to be the big cheese' " (*Rabbit at Rest* 358).

Nothing, as the next chapter will explore, could have been further removed from this acknowledgment than the applause that greeted America's actions in the Gulf War sixteen months later. " 'I think it's taken the monkey off our back that's been there since Korea and Vietnam and Beirut and a few places in between,' " declared Harry Kane, editor of *Operation Desert Shield* magazine. " 'VCR's may be made in Japan and Mercedes have their stamp of origin, but what's going on in the Middle East is undeniably made in the U.S.A.' " (Applebome 3). With newspapers depicting a "mail-order despot right out of the Sears catalogue" restoring a feeling of "moral clarity" to American foreign policy, with soldiers abroad enabling mothers to recall " '[a]ll this fighting that this country does for other countries' " and to break their hearts over the fact that " 'they don't appreciate it,' " with high noon deadlines for withdrawal challenging any and all disbelief in " 'the willpower of the United States,' " as George Bush so proudly asserted, the tendency to see the conflict in Manichean terms revived those bipolar politics with which Americans felt so right at home (Friedman, "Desert Fog" 1; Friedman and Tyler 18). No wonder Republican pollsters would resurrect slogans from Ronald Reagan's reelection campaign and declare, " 'It's morning again in America' " (Toner 1).

On my block, in fact, it was morning for many days, as yellow ribbons tied around every available tree remained wrapped around trunks for days after the war officially ended. One would do well to remember, however, what happens to fabric that stays out too long in the sun's harsh glare. Like the American flag decal pasted on the back window of Rabbit's station wagon, the colors fade from too long an exposure.

"My opinion is, you have to fight a war now and then to show you're willing, and it doesn't much matter where it is."
—John Updike, *Rabbit Redux* (1971)

Sir, do we get to win this time?
—*Rambo: First Blood Part II* (1985)

Operation Desert Cloud, I mean Storm, is now under way.
—Peter Jennings, ABC *World News Tonight* 16 January 1991

3 Cut and Print!
The Gulf War as Movie Narrative in Larry Beinhart's *American Hero*

When John J. Rambo asks his commanding officer whether we get to win this time, he articulates an age-old concern that transcends the desire of one Vietnam vet returning to Southeast Asia to search for Americans presumed missing in action: namely, can I do it over? Rambo, of course, does do it over, and not just in Vietnam, where he rescues a group of captured Americans single-handedly and still feels enough shame over America's defeat in Vietnam to attempt yet another rescue mission in Afghanistan. Stallone does it over just as much in a series of three movies, each of which pits the renegade Rambo against the official forces of American law and order, thereby juxtaposing the true patriot who would die defending his country against those bogus bureaucrats more concerned with defending themselves from adverse publicity.

Contrasted with this notion of narratives that repeat the past, however, is another age-old scenario that Larry Beinhart invokes early in *American Hero*

(1993) that warns of the dangers of looking back at the past at all. "The 'don't look' story is one of the primal stories," he writes. "God let Lot leave Sodom. God said, 'Don't look back.' Lot's wife looked back and was turned to a pillar of salt. Orpheus went to hell to bring his wife back from the dead. Hades, god of the underworld said, 'Don't look back until you're out.' Orpheus looked and he lost her." Beinhart thus concludes: "When a story is that pervasive and that basic, there is a reason. Every culture, in its collective wisdom, has a knowing that there are things that are not meant to be looked at" (28).[1]

A writer of detective fiction prior to turning his attention to the mass media in *American Hero,* Beinhart is no stranger to the urge for secrecy that those in power share. Within the three earlier works that make up his Tony Cassella trilogy, a search for an SEC informant uncovers the embezzlement of refugee organization funds during World War II by a Wall Street lawyer (*No One Rides for Free* [1986]), an investigation of an illegal sublet yields a presidential campaign financed by an attorney general's real estate scams and arson (*You Get What You Pay For* [1988]), and an inquiry into a young woman's death in an Austrian avalanche results in post–Cold War plans to unite the secret agents of Eastern Europe in a private industrial espionage network (*Foreign Exchange* [1991]). What his fourth novel offers for display are two particular things that those who orchestrate the Persian Gulf War mean not to have looked at too closely—to leave clouded, to recall the Freudian slip with which Peter Jennings announced the war's onset (qtd. in Kellner, *Persian* 115). One is a memo given by a dying Lee Atwater to James Baker sketching the " 'surefire, ultimate' " plan to assure the reelection of George Bush in 1992 (*American* 8): " 'When all seems like it might be lost, and there are no other options, go to war. It is the classical response to insoluble domestic problems' " (126). The other is the cinematic nature of the war in which Beinhart has Atwater's fictionalized memo culminate. For while the dying kingmaker recognizes war as the grand narrative that has governed American political/presidential history since the time of George Washington, he also understands that in a post-Vietnam age in which " 'modern war is a media event' " (to the extent that winning a war on television is more important than winning a war on the battlefield insofar as the votes of the American electorate are concerned), the war to assure the reelection of an incumbent down in the polls " 'must be run by professionals,' " specifically Hollywood professionals (124, 126). Beinhart, in fact, argues that it was.[2]

Remakes, Updates, and Outtakes

Toward the end of portraying the process by which the Gulf War was packaged by Hollywood professionals, Beinhart's narrative traces the mechanisms whereby a Michael Ovitz–like agent named David Hartman is brought in by Bush and Baker to hire the proper director who has " 'the gut instincts, the style, the sheer artistry, to create a war that America can love—on television' " (126), and the Steven Spielberg–like director chosen, John Lincoln Beagle, devises "a remake—not for theaters, for television—of 1942–45: *World War II Two—The Video*" (240). Interspersed with those chapters devoted to the stage managing of the Gulf War are chapters narrated in the first person by Joe Broz, a Vietnam veteran currently working for a high-tech security and surveillance corporation, hired by an actress to investigate the reasons she has been dropped unexplainably from what she thinks is Beagle's next feature. Linking the two narrative strands to each other is the concept of what it means to be an "American Hero," one of the tentative titles Beagle considers for the cinematic opus that will restore the United States to world preeminence (*Pax Americana* being one of the others) and one of the means by which the decorated war hero Broz introduces himself to the reader.

Conceiving of the Gulf War with respect to a familiar historical narrative—World War II or otherwise—is hardly new, of course, and critics who have analyzed the war in retrospect have described the variety of familiar stories that the media invoked in order to frame the conflict: rape scenarios to depict Iraq's penetration and subsequent refusal to pull out of Kuwait, early American captivity narratives to portray hostage dramas, Manichean dualistic scripts to show Western Christianity pitted against Eastern Islam, Great War tales of Belgian babes hoisted on German bayonets for rumors of infants taken from incubators and left to die on hospital floors, western "Showdown in the Gulf" logos for nightly news broadcasts detailing the latest ultimatums and deadlines, and football game plans for successful bombing missions, these last particularly timely for a forty-three-day war that was punctuated by Super Bowl weekend.[3] Likewise, conceiving of the war as a cinematic spectacle is quite consistent with the way in which journalists at the time articulated the experience of watching "Iraq, the Movie" on television, complete with "glamorous stars, non-stop virtual action and thus far not a single dead body on screen."[4]

Underlying Beinhart's treatment of the Gulf War as recycling familiar cinematic narratives in particular, however, is the contention that images have now replaced words as repositories of history. When Atwater questions what war is to most Americans, he comes up with a list of movies and television shows—

Rambo, Star Wars, Combat, The Rat Patrol—that eventually replaces even the memories of people who have actually been to war (125), as the experiences of Joe Broz illustrate. The war in Vietnam that returns to him while running consists of "just pictures. No sound. No smells" (41). The corollary of such replacement of reality by image, moreover, is the ease with which changes of history can be effected by changes in imagery. When Beagle screens the first wave of Vietnam War movies for himself, in which the story is virtually the same—a series of "Lies and mendacity. Burning children. [. . .] Drug addicts, crazed veterans with guns. [. . .] Rapes. Double veterans. Ambushes, booby traps, balls shot off. Burning huts"—he realizes that the traditional roles of heroes and villains have been unaccountably switched, in which "Americans become the Nazis. Occupying a foreign country. Taking reprisals on civilians. Lidice become My Lai" (178, 179). No cause for concern, though, for when Beagle screens for himself the second wave of Vietnam War films that succeed the masochistic nightmares of Oliver Stone, Michael Cimino, and Francis Ford Coppola, he finds that the exploits of Sylvester Stallone and Chuck Norris have "not just created, but established, a revised memory of what had happened": "Gone was the moral confusion. Gone was the defeatism" (191).[5]

In fact, Beagle's private screening of war movies as research for his own intended epic—perhaps the most vivid section of Beinhart's novel in that its portrait of monitors mounted flush to the wall duplicates so well what John H. Cushman Jr. dubbed the Gulf War's "electronic battlefield" (1)—shows that the entire military history of the twentieth century exists in celluloid form. The director's cutting from Nazi glories in *Victory in the West* and *Triumph of the Will* to Japanese atrocities in *Wake Island,* then shifting to hard-won American triumph in *The Battle of San Pietro* and magnificent precision bombing in *Bombardier,* and climaxing with *The Longest Day*'s invasion of Normandy essentially replays the history of World War II within a ten-screen video room, with German and American films engaging each other as combatants. More to the point, Beagle's screening of war movies shows that the entire military history of the twentieth century exists (and persists) in a relatively small number of cinematic images that get recycled from one film to another. "Hollywood was, contrary to popular opinion, a frugal place," writes Jeanine Basinger in a passage Beinhart quotes in a footnote. "Plots and characters and events were saved like old pieces of string, and taken out of the drawer and re-used," with the result that the generic World War II combat movie was born, which "would then recur and recur and recur" (50; qtd. in Beinhart 236–37). Rumors about Beagle working on the reincarnation of John Wayne through new medical technology—" 'They're going to take the remains of the best of the old stars and, using genetics and microsciences, re-create them' " (87)—thus have a certain degree of validity since one of the titles he tentatively toys with is indeed *"The Reincarnation of John Wayne"* (246).[6] Acknowledging himself that the first principle of all fine art is plagiarism and the first of all commercial art is theft (128), Beagle reassures his Washington, D.C., producers, " 'We're talking about nothing new,' " when pitching Saddam Hussein as a modern-day Hitler invading the Poland stand-in of Kuwait while salivating over a France updated to Saudi Arabia: " 'the issue is only one of framing' " (289).[7]

The issue is also one of representation. "RepCo," the powerhouse agency that packages the Gulf War in Beinhart's book, is both owned and founded by a man who subscribes to Sun Tzu's *Art of War* philosophy, wherein the best strategy is one that *"evades Reality and Confronts through Illusion"* (79). And reviewing the actions of those who actually promulgated the Gulf War offensive shows that illusion was key to promoting the conflict before the first shot was ever fired. For example, the invasion of Kuwait was represented as the defense of Saudi Arabia, even though no evidence existed that Saudi Arabia was threatened by Iraq, because, as a *Washington Post*–ABC News survey revealed on 10 August 1990, 74 percent of Americans polled supported sending troops for purposes of defense, while 68 percent opposed the use of troops to force Iraq to withdraw from Kuwait (Taylor and Morin 26).

Beinhart, in contrast, opens his novel with a statement of intention that aims to set his own record straight. "This is a work of fiction," he states in the book's opening headnote. He then continues to distinguish between what he has devised and what can be documented through a steady series of footnotes that includes everything from attributions of source material to translations of material in languages other than English (notably the various editions of *The Art of War* quoted), clarifications of historical references (such as World War II references to Lidice and Rotterdam), definitions of terms (pertaining to subjects as varied as Hollywood filmmaking, Vietnam War weaponry, and the designation of Jewish male offspring), and, perhaps most important, differentiations of fact from fiction (particularly when the introduction of characters who may approximate living persons requires their being distinguished from real people). "Not a real name," reads the twelfth footnote that intimates the source for Carter Hamilton Bunker, head of Joe Broz's security firm. "But the reader can assume, in this case, that the character is modeled on a very real person with a résumé that includes Yale, the oss, and the CIA prior to starting an investigation and security company" (55). "A pseudonym," reports the fourteenth footnote with reference to pop star Vanessa Swallow's reputed fondness for strap-on dildos (66). "Fictitious name. Real rumor," clarifies the fifteenth footnote with respect to the gerbilectomy undergone by movie star Nick Jackson that is noted in the text proper (67).

Such self-reflexive representation, in theory at least, purports to distinguish Beinhart's work from those works that make no attempt to separate what is devised from what is documented in their re-creations of historical events, as epitomized for Beinhart by the ABC television film he cites after his opening disclaimer, which introduced its *Heroes of Desert Storm* program with the statement: " 'Tonight's film is based on true stories and interweaves news footage and dramatizations with actors and actual participants. To achieve realism no distinction is made among these elements.' " Yet Beinhart's repetition of his own disclaimer about his book being a work of fiction in his second footnote, and the heightened rhetoric that qualifies the speech and actions of his public figures as not just "figments of the author's imagination except where supported by the public record," as his headnote first asserts, but "absolutely figments of the author's imagination" that "should in no way be construed as 'true' or even a 'fictionalization of a truth that can be told no other way' " (4–5), followed by yet a third reminder that "this is a work of fiction" suggests that more is at work here than mere authorial ingenuousness (5). The laborer, quite simply, protests too much.

As it turns out, the most critical fact that establishes Beinhart's work as a work of fiction is the one he significantly—and, given the careful documentation throughout the entire work, intentionally—omits from his conformance to scholarly practice: the fact that the actual Lee Atwater died on 29 March 1991, well after Desert Storm had ended, and therefore cannot be identical to the Lee Atwater whose death is commemorated by Bush and Baker in chapter 6 of Beinhart's book (47), well before any of the planning for the Gulf War is even initiated. Only a short, dated excerpt from Atwater's *New York Times* obituary, camouflaged by three other references devoted to Atwater's character (pun intended) traits in Beinhart's fourth footnote (5), indicates that the entire event upon which Beinhart's scenario is premised is complete fabrication.[8] "[S]cience doesn't really say which theory is true," he writes when discussing what happens when the scientific method that has become the criterion for most contemporary thought is confronted with multiple explanations for an event, "it determines which one to use, as if it were true, because in the context in which you are using it, it will work" (421). Expedience, in other words, proves the final deciding factor—in shaping a scenario for a fictional novel no less than for an actual war.

Beinhart's fictional director of that war, John Lincoln Beagle, exhibits a degree of self-reflexivity as well. Unwilling to remove himself from the noncelluloid world completely, he feels compelled to check into "that parallel universe" called "reality" every now and then (248), even if "somewhere off in reality," to a mind mired in Hollywood, generally translates into the equivalent of "Erie,

Pennsylvania, or Fort Smith, Arkansas, or Eau Claire, Wisconsin" (193). Unfortunately, when Beagle "get[s] into a dialogue with reality," it is mainly because "that was the raw material that he would have to manipulate" (207). Yet here, too, his motives prove less than original, as the documentary films that open his ten-screen "American *Iliad*" indicate (167). The replacement of Spanish flag with Old Glory that constitutes the entirety of *Tearing Down the Spanish Flag* (1898), the first commercial war movie, took place on a downtown Manhattan rooftop, not Manila or Havana (168–69). The victory of America's navy in the producers' *Battle of Santiago Bay* sequel occurred in a bathtub, special effects smoke for naval guns provided gratis by a cigarette puffed by one of the producers' wives (170). The sneak attack recorded in *December 7th* transpired in Hollywood, California, "a place that has never been bombed, torpedoed, or strafed" (171). As Beinhart concludes, "There wasn't enough reality around, so they made some up" (171).

These selections that Beinhart has Beagle make are not just a function of portraying one megalomaniacal director intent on becoming " 'the greatest whatever I am that I am' " (305), for, as film historians have shown, making up some reality was standard practice among both filmmakers and distributors interested in documenting war—*any* war—since the turn-of-the-century Spanish-American War.[9] Pancho Villa, who delayed his 1914 attack on Ojinaga to allow filmmakers time to cross the rebel lines and who pushed back executions to seven or eight in the morning so as to provide cameramen with better light, also agreed as part of his exclusive twenty-five-thousand-dollar contract with the Mutual Film Corporation (which accorded him a 50 percent profit share) to stage a battle in the event that none of the battles fought provided satisfactory film footage; when none proved spectacular enough for *The Life of General Francisco Villa* later planned as a feature film, other battles were simply fabricated (Brownlow 91–92, 102). What makes the films that Beinhart cites cases of "very special fraud," to employ his own term (169), is, most obviously, a similar discrepancy between the facts they purported to document and the fictions they both manufactured and, in so doing, promoted—a manufacturing facilitated by the fact that the men in charge of shooting those films were feature film directors like John Ford, William Wyler, John Huston, and Frank Capra. But compounding the fraud is the way the recycling of formulaic plots and imagery enabled mythologized early films to legitimize the messages of later ones. As Beinhart reminds his readers in a footnote, the Spanish-American War marked the beginning of the American Century (168), a point Atwater acknowledges in his memo when quoting John Hay in proposing the " 'splendid little war' " that Margaret Thatcher mounted in the Falklands as the model Bush should emulate (124). And, as we have already seen in chapter 1, not for nothing did the rise of the movie industry coincide with the rise of American expansion and military intervention abroad.

Clearly, the legitimizing that recycling facilitated occurred when earlier documentary footage from one film was inserted into a later film for purposes of verisimilitude, as happened with Ford's *December 7th* (1943), which won an Oscar for best short documentary the year of its release, and whose images, as Beinhart notes, "became the reference for future films" (170). Yet no less were fictional films invoked if the mythology they rendered proved useful at a later time. When the hero of *Guadalcanal Diary* (1943) is asked whether he thinks he is Sergeant York or Gary Cooper and he repeats Cooper's diversionary gesture of gobbling like a turkey in order to kill an enemy soldier, it is the repentant pacifist of a World War I movie that is cited to validate the actions of marines in World War II rather than the actual Richard Tregaskis journalism upon which the *Diary* is based (Basinger 71–72). Likewise, when Beagle talks to Bush and Baker about the " 'one thing that's absolutely central, imagistically speaking, to the whole production' " that he has been engaged to direct, he cites " 'a shot of one of these smart bombs going right down Saddam's chimney' " in order to convey the message to America that " 'this is surgery, not slaughter' " (295). This image he directly appropriates from the 1943 film *Bombardier*, in which a previously hesitant bombardier " 'put[s] one in the smokestack' " of a Japanese munitions factory, clear of conscience because his chaplain has explained to him the difference between the enemy's mode of indiscriminate saturation bombing and the Americans' mode of precision bombing that avoids noncombatants of any kind (249).

Reel People

The most egregiously fraudulent movie that Beagle screens for himself, according to Beinhart, is Leni Riefenstahl's *Triumph of the Will* (1935), and not only because its staging of the 1934 National Socialist Party Congress for the express purpose of filming it supplanted the manipulation of reality through re-created events by a complete manufacturing of reality (170). Prefiguring the kind of movie Beagle plans to make in the Persian Gulf—and thus suggesting the kind of imperialist position the American presence there assumes by comparison—the German film's use of actual Congress participants as characters also turned real people, by default, into actors. Beagle experiences the casting difficulties such scenarios create when dealing with his secretary's pressure to put her daughter in a film of his in some capacity. " 'I'm not using actresses or actors,' " he informs the desperate mother. " 'Only real people,' " to which she replies, without missing a beat, " 'well, then use her as a real person' " (197).

The problem, as Beinhart understands, is that in a media-congested society, there are no real people left. Nowhere is this absence more clearly displayed than in the story of Joe Broz, whom everyone considers a "real person" due to the fact that his limited connections with the Hollywood industry leave him able to differentiate between role-playing and reality. " 'You're a guy. A man's man. For real,' " says Magdalena Lazlo, the actress who hires him to investigate Beagle's film ventures. " 'Not some actor playing a tough guy' " (21). " 'She's got a real guy's guy,' " report the tabloids of the romance between the two that later becomes public. " 'This one's for real' " (161). Joe, however, is no more real than a plugged nickel, for while his experience behind movie cameras may end with surveillance, his experience in front of movie screens continually determines the way in which he gauges his actions. "You've seen this scene in the movies. Mostly Westerns," he says of his walking into a Watts bar unescorted. "I'm Alan Ladd, but folks just call me Shane" (183). "It's like *Pretty Woman*," he quips when describing the shopping spree that Maggie takes him on to change his wardrobe. "Except I'm playing Julia Roberts and Maggie's playing Richard Gere" (142). He may keep a bourbon bottle filled with tea in his desk drawer, "[a]s a joke, you know" (11), so he can assume the role of TV gumshoe, but his abilities to remain on the discerning end of the humorous divide decrease as the allure of stardom, in the form of Maggie Lazlo, draws him more and more into the Hollywood orbit. "Do movies make us or do we make the movies?" (14), he asks early in the book. When the romance that he and Maggie have been faking to deceive people who start investigating her for Hartman appears to be turning into an actual love affair, and their front to produce movie vehicles for her turns out to attract definite prospects, it becomes impossible for Joe to provide an answer. In the dream factory of Hollywood, his own dreams appear to have come true.

The setting for such star-search anointment, significantly, need not be Hollywood. The closest Joe comes to true celebrity is in Vietnam, where he goes to seek the exotic Orient "[l]ike in the movies I saw when I was a kid" (258), where he approaches combat like "a John Wayne movie" while fighting in the jungles (49), and where his abilities to protect his men from harm make him " 'like a star,' " as his war buddy attests, much like the character played by Christopher Walken in *The Dogs of War* (377). But facilitating greatly the rise to celebrity are those connections between Hollywood and Washington, D.C., that Beinhart, much like Vidal, sees as making each handmaiden to the other. "It's tough being president," Beinhart's Bush admits to James Baker. "Frankly, it's a lot tougher than being an actor" (45). Not so, of course, for the actor that both industries combined to elect president, Ronald Reagan, who had both incarnations of his career overseen by the legendary agent Lew Wasserman.

As Michael Rogin has persuasively documented, the sixteenth-century conflation of political leader's body and body politic that Reagan often invoked while president was attributable to a series of 1940s films (*Santa Fe Trail* [1940], *Knute Rockne, All American* [1940], *King's Row* [1942]) in which Reagan the actor was sacrificed and then reborn on screen (Ronald 1–43); it was this false objectification of Reagan as a vulnerable self that ultimately enabled him to acquire presidential stature (13). Yet, as Leo Braudy has also shown, the professional dovetailing that Reagan embodied extended an even older tradition that went back to ancient Rome, where politicians went to actors to learn oratorical techniques (568). Thus, when David Hartman, Beinhart's Wasserman-of-the-nineties (126), actually journeys to Rome in search of financing for Bush's production, its evidence of wealth and empire and opportunity, "layered in ruin and glory, spoke to him that Hollywood was nothing new" (362). So, too, did Reagan's conflation of performer and politician reflect a centuries-old American tradition in particular: George Washington, according to John Adams, may not have been our finest president, but "he was the best actor of presidency we have ever had" (qtd. in Brownstein 12). In fact, when Beinhart surveys the embarrassing spectacles that amateur performers like Nixon, Ford, Carter, and Bush have made of themselves before the cameras, he concludes that Reagan may "turn out to be the harbinger of things to come and the practice of having someone 'act' as president will be institutionalized" (72), a prediction that, in cinematic circles at least, has already been realized courtesy of a 1993 movie called *Dave* (the wisdom of which, more recently, would seem to have been reinforced by vice presidential candidate Joseph Lieberman's rendition of "My Way" on Conan O'Brien's *Late Night*).

In *Foreign Exchange*, Beinhart traces Reagan's skills as a performer to his ability to tell a good story, a skill whose value Reagan discovered when the teletype from which he would announce Chicago baseball games as a young Des Moines sportscaster went down in the middle of a game. Rather than admit to listeners that he was not broadcasting live from the stadium, Reagan made up plays to cover the time lost, knowing in advance that the game he invented never would match the one that actually was occurring, and thereby learning that "a good story was a good story and *reality did not matter*" (54). In *American Hero*, however, Beinhart's main concern lies less with the performing skills that enable politicians to enact the role of president and more with that mating of Hollywood and Washington, D.C., forces that enable politicians to obtain power as president in the first place. Much as in Vidal's work, Beinhart's investigation reveals the long tradition of mutual back scratching in which the marriage between the two has resulted. If, as early as 1915, *The Battle Cry of Peace,* a film that invoked the threat of German espionage during the years that American sentiment veered toward isolationism, was given twenty-five hundred marines by the military to be used as extras, by the time of World War II, this kind of exchange had evolved into informal contract.[10] As Beinhart writes, "The military gave Hollywood footage, advisors, equipment, soldiers, transport, cooperation. In return, the filmmakers gladly told the story that Washington and its soldiers wanted told, the way they wanted it told" (174).

Yet altering the terms of that prenuptial contract in recent years, as Ronald Brownstein has discussed (206–7), are two changes that have affected the way that candidates get elected to political office: one, 1974 amendments to the federal election laws that limited donations by single individuals to one thousand dollars apiece for primary or general election campaigns and twenty-five thousand dollars annually to all federal candidates; and, two, costs of television advertising that concurrently increased dramatically the amount of money necessary to mount a successful bid for political office (twenty million dollars in 1995 for each prospective 1996 presidential candidate, which translates into seventy-seven thousand dollars per business day or ten thousand dollars per hour, according to analysts [DeParle 30]).[11] With the targets of fund-raising shifting from single individuals who could underwrite campaigns with large checks to individuals who could influence others to write checks, and with fund-raising itself becoming increasingly concerned with uncovering new sources of income that could be drawn upon constantly, Hollywood became more and more important as a source of potential revenue, particularly since Hollywood money, in contrast to contributions from Wall Street and the oil industries, for example, did not arouse much suspicion with respect to disclosure. As Brownstein states, "It was lucre without odor" (208). And once candidates began associating themselves with celebrities in order to grab the quick public relations fix that comes from feeding off the images of cultural icons, it also was legitimacy without onus—especially when the celebrities in question did not even have to countenance their appropriation, as occurred in 1984 when both Republican and Democratic presidential candidates invoked Bruce Springsteen in order to show how much each was "Born in the U.S.A." (Brownstein 370–71). As a result, a practice that signaled "moral chaos" to Vidal, writing of Hollywood in 1923 from the perspective of 1990 (*Hollywood* 414), had become by 2000 a topic appropriate for late-night comedy. Hence David Letterman's 14 September comment about his program's doubling as " 'a special Al Gore fund-raiser' " and his warning that the Democratic nominee's appearance on it would include collecting one thousand dollars apiece from audience members—the same day that a Radio City Music Hall benefit produced by Miramax cochair Harvey Weinstein,

Rolling Stone publisher Jann Wenner, and vh1 president John Sykes garnered the Gore-Lieberman team $6.5 million (Sella 75; Sack A30).

Unlike George Creel, then, who subordinated West Coast to East Coast capital in 1920, Beinhart has few doubts as to where the larger share of the (im)balance of power resides by the time George Bush's reelection campaign starts gearing up in 1991. When he compares the reactions of Washington, D.C., and Hollywood to the mass media, he concludes that whereas Washington sees the media as carnivorous, the Hollywood industry treats the media as totally "pussy-whipped": "Nobody was afraid of television or the press. If a reporter didn't mind his manners, he was cut out of the loop. If he truly offended, he was fired," a point Beinhart illustrates in a footnote that discusses the blackballing of movie reviewer Joseph McBride by Paramount after McBride wrote an unfavorable review of the studio's *Patriot Games* (118). Even more revealing, Beinhart contrasts the vaguely threatening responses of industry insiders who thought he was writing a book containing "a thinly disguised Ovitz" character with the complete lack of any such comments provoked by his use of politicians who were in office during the time his book was being written, "the (then) president or the (then) secretary of state who are not 'characters like,' but named George Bush and James Baker" (100).

Central to the maintenance of power in Beinhart's book is the ability to use the new communications media effectively. Constantly aware of the way words are transmitted over airwaves, to the extent that he " 'controls the conversation with perfect sentences, perfect paragraphs, perfect pages' " even in ordinary dialogues (29), Secretary of State Baker, "the best spin doctor in Spin City" (280), is the perfect person to receive Lee Atwater's memo. Indeed, Atwater's memo to Baker is premised upon America's military victory in Vietnam having been compromised by its defeat on living room television screens, such as occurred with the televised storming of the American embassy in Saigon during the 1968 Tet offensive (124–25). Therefore, when negotiations with Saddam Hussein bog down over his desire for prime time scheduling in order to deliver his message to the world, Hartman advises Bush to accede to the media-unschooled Iraqi leader's demands since " 'Saddam's understanding of television is worse than Michael Dukakis's' " (372). In contrast to Vietnam, then, which Hartman describes as " 'a lousy movie' " that " 'went on too long' " and caused people to walk out, the war Beagle is to direct will be modeled on the " 'well played, well paced' " Second World War through which everyone sat until the end (293), which, in television terms, translates into " 'a miniseries to end all miniseries' " (339).

Such docudrama television, in one sense, can be perceived as defeating its own purposes. As opposed to those World War II movies "shot in the glory days of wide-screen formats like Todd-AO, Ultra-Panavision 70, and Cinemascope" that promoted a nation's sense of epic destiny and grandeur (167), the celluloid meant to immortalize George Bush's place in history testifies only to " 'this sadly diminished day of ours' " (339), as Beagle's research assistant realizes. (" 'It's one thing to be killed for a movie,' " quips Maggie Lazlo after hearing of the assistant's being killed. " 'But for a miniseries?' " [340].) And one is reminded of the difference drawn by Updike's Rabbit Angstrom between the power conveyed by the movie-star president, Reagan, godlike in that "you never knew how much he knew, nothing or everything," and his small-screen successor, Bush, who definitely "knows something, but it seems a small something" (*Rabbit at Rest* 295).

At the same time, the celluloid meant to immortalize George Bush's place in history also testifies to "the leading-edge technoglories of the United States' two foremost exports: arms and entertainment," as Tom Engelhardt points out (87), and, as such, refutes the very challenges to American economic supremacy that Updike's protagonist so decried. That being the case, public-opinion polls revealed that Bush's popularity ratings rose throughout the Gulf crisis, from 55 percent before Iraq's 2 August invasion of Kuwait to 76 percent by midmonth (Smith 162). After Desert Storm finally began in January 1991, polls also revealed that, in contrast to the Vietnam War's poor pacing, the pacing of the Gulf War proved highly engaging: 50 percent of those polled claimed to be addicted to the television coverage, and 58 percent of adults under thirty called themselves "war news addicts" (Kellner, *Persian* 236–37). Part of their addiction, no doubt, resulted from the fact that, in contrast to even hourly delays in receiving film footage from Vietnam, video-satellite-computer systems coverage of the Gulf War enabled them to participate in what George Gerbner has termed "instant history" (244). Part, no doubt, resulted from the thrilling Star Wars technowar they were able to witness without paying the price of theater admission. And part, no doubt, resulted from the sanitized nature of what they were allowed to see due to the fact that, in contrast to Vietnam, where journalists, often working independently, developed the habit of following small units into the field and "shooting bloody" (Combs 272), journalists in the Persian Gulf, much like those in Grenada and Panama in 1983 and 1989 respectively, were limited in what they saw of actual fighting. They only arrived at combat zones as part of media pools supervised by armed forces escorts, and any film they were able to shoot was later subjected to the censorship of "security review."

Despite all these contrasts, Beinhart finally sees the Gulf War as more similar to than different from the war in Vietnam. "A man had been killed to keep *his*—David Hartman's—secrets," Hartman muses after Beagle's research assistant is assassinated for unknowingly trying to pass information on Beagle's doings to Joe Broz. "This was power" (332). Perhaps the primary secret that those in charge tried to keep throughout the Gulf War concerned the impression of little carnage due to the technological superiority of the American offensive. It was this impression that led Jean Baudrillard to characterize the conflict as a "soft war" prior to its onset, marked by "a hyperrealist logic of the deterrence of the real by the virtual" (*Gulf* 27); an "[e]mpty war" once it began, with images of blindings (journalists wearing gas masks in Jerusalem, sea birds blinded by oil spills) replacing images of battles (33, 40); and, finally, a "consensual war" after it concluded, in which "the two adversaries did not even confront each other face to face" (83, 62).

We know now the boomerang effect that such impressions can, and did, produce. "'Hyperreality' cuts both ways," as Margot Norris makes clear (294). Because the Pentagon censorship that concealed dead bodies also deprived the war of the very signifiers that certify any military triumph as real, "[t]he war passed through the public imagination and memory like a video phantom, unable—in the absence of any national pain or suffering—to imprint a lasting inscription on either the national conscience or the national self-image" (295). [12] According to Michael Rogin, such "motivated forgetting" was precisely the point of the series of American spectacles staged in Grenada, Libya, and Honduras, as well as the Persian Gulf, since the "political amnesia" to which it leads "permits repetition of pleasures that, if consciously sustained in memory over time, would have to be called into question" ("Make" 507). Yet we also should be aware, as Christopher Norris takes pains to remind us, that whatever value Baudrillard's terms have as indices of epistemological confusion bears no obvious relation to their ability to delineate ontological concerns (177). In other words, we know now that only 10 percent of the bombs dropped on Iraq were so-called smart bombs, that 70 percent of U.S. bombs missed their targets completely, that Iraqi casualties numbered over one hundred thousand, with civilian deaths estimated at between one and two times that amount. [13] We know now, in short, that the high-tech war was also high-casualty, not unlike Vietnam.

Beinhart prepares us for the resemblance the two wars will share at the end of his book with a raid that Joe Broz stages on the offices of David Hartman. [14] Armed with a battery of assault weapons and the stolen memo that contains Lee Atwater's proposal, the raid duplicates the ambushes in which Broz has participated as a marine in Vietnam. Aimed at freeing the woman he loves from the minions of Hartman who have taken her hostage, the raid also prefigures one of the primary narratives by which the Gulf War later would be framed by the media. "'I will keep your secrets. Forever,'" Broz tells the vanquished Hartman in a reprise of the latter's earlier pronouncement about power (420). In so doing, the character whose degree of realness Beinhart has undermined for four hundred pages of the novel turns into the "authentic American hero" he has introduced himself as being at its start (9)—not because he is successful in rescuing a damsel in distress à la Dudley Do-Right, but because of what this Audie Murphy clone threatens to do to her kidnapper if he welshes on their bargain to exchange memo for Maggie's megastardom. " 'If you break our deal, I will survive and I will come and I will kill you. Because that's what I do,' " states this hero who has now found the formula that defines his American authenticity. " 'I kill' " (420).

Part II

Imports/Exports

If our people are content to witness perpetual rubbish, let it, at any rate, be English rubbish in preference to American rubbish, because in producing English rubbish the money will at least be spent in this country.

—Lord Newton, debate on the British film industry,

House of Lords, 14 May 1925

From chewing-gum and neon, broken noses and juke-boxes, canned imports and noisy drama, delinquent mothers and sobbing saxophones, Good Lord, Deliver Us.

—Dennis Potter, "Why Import This Trash?"

Daily Herald 6 August 1964

4 Dennis Potter, *Pennies from Heaven*, and the Dream of a Common Culture

Cold Lazarus (1996), the final television drama completed by Dennis Potter before his death, is premised upon an arresting image: a cryogenically frozen head.[1] In contrast to his earlier rants against the importation of American television shows, however, Potter's portrayal of the fight to transmit that head's memories around the globe via TV, cable, VRS, and videos offers an exportation opportunity that would warm the cockles of the British Tourist Board's heart. "A goldmine, Harry. We're talking of a goose which'll lay a golden egg whenever we want!" boasts David Siltz, president of Uniplanet Total Entertainment, so convinced is he that the chance to view how people lived four hundred years ago will provide a ratings sweep in the year 2368. "We'll plug that brain into everybody else's! What's his is ours!" (359). And odious as the prospect of consorting with a "Muck Merchant" like Siltz is (331), the scientists who have been attempting to stimulate the head's memories in their laboratory choose to "prostitute" themselves and accede to the impresario's scheme (306). As the biotechnologist who heads (pun intended) the laboratory is advised by one of her colleagues, "You should take the tainted silver, scrape out our poor creature's memories, and show *billions* of people out there that, yes, there were other ways to live. The past can stand in front of us for once, challengingly, and not be safely anaesthetized in the long, long ago. Let the past speak! Let it *accuse!*" (308).

I open my discussion of Potter's work with reference to this frozen head because it encapsulates, in microcosm, Potter's feelings about what the medium of television can do at its best and at its worst, for—make no mistake about it—plugged into neurotransmitters, wired to antennae, and emitting a fluorescent gray light, the head, for all intents and purposes, *is* a television set. As such, it has the potential of creating that common culture that prompted Potter's initial attraction to the medium and made him find *"connect"* (alluding to E. M. Forster) a far better verb than the "merely technical *transmit"* for what the defining activity of television should be (*Seeing* 51). Equally certain is it that the frozen head's memories will show "other ways to live," for its broadcast images of an England of football games and royal family interviews provide marked alternatives to the derelict Whitehall and desolate Albert Hall warehouse that characterize the drama's present setting, relics of a country that has not existed as a political entity for two hundred years. At the same time, the process by which those memories are to interact with the minds of audience members is hardly conducive to the notion of personal sovereignty that Potter saw television's subversive alternatives as promoting (*Seeing* 69). On the contrary, as suggested by Siltz's rhetoric of possession, the process smacks far more of colonization: "Haven't we always tried to get *inside* people's heads? Isn't that what the game is all about, showbiz and that part of it we call politics? *Owning* people. But—and this has been the drag—but we've never been able to get right inside, to *own* the tiniest little fragment of the inside of a person's head. Now we have the chance!" (359).

Potter's most famous use of this metaphor of colonization came in the James MacTaggart Memorial Lecture that he delivered at the Edinburgh Film Festival in 1993. Titling his talk "Occupying Powers," a condition he defined as occurring when "[o]ur own land was in the hands of others, and these others were not interested in our growth, or emancipation," Potter described what it felt like to sell his services to "the strange new generations of broadcasting managements and their proprietors," the extreme of which he found so typified by Rupert Murdoch (for whom he reserved his worst invective) that he later came to call the pancreatic cancer that was killing him by that name (*Seeing* 44, 34, 14). But in making the *Cold Lazarus* character he envisioned as a "Murdoch successor" an

American (*Seeing* 26)—a self-proclaimed "Barnum and Bailey," no less (290)—Potter expanded his metaphor of occupying powers to denote a form of cultural as well as managerial imperialism. Indeed, one of the most revealing memories screened for the scientists is occasioned by Daniel Feeld, the writer whose head has been frozen, lip-synching in a karaoke bar to Bing Crosby crooning "Pennies from Heaven" (309).

Attributing to Daniel Feeld this 1936 song has resonance for anyone remotely familiar with Potter's career, for *Pennies from Heaven* (1978) was the first of three television serials he wrote that employed American popular music in order to explore the phenomenon of popular culture—*The Singing Detective* (1986) and *Lipstick on Your Collar* (1993) being the others—and the device of characters lip-synching to recordings of the past rather than singing themselves in order to show that "these were genuine artefacts from the past that had been cannibalized and transformed into the workings of the head" (*Potter* 85), to recall the governing image of *Cold Lazarus*. What makes *Pennies from Heaven* an especially fruitful subject for examining Potter's ambivalent feelings about popular culture *in general* stems from the way its music satisfies both religious yearnings for a world that is other than it is, shared by all those characters who break out into song, and the commercialist creed that its protagonist's selling of sheet music necessarily raises. In so doing, the serial directly juxtaposes the beatific against the business. What makes *Pennies from Heaven* an especially fruitful subject for examining Potter's view of the parasitic relationship of English and American popular culture *in particular* stems from the fact that Potter wrote two filmed versions of the drama: one, a six-part television serial first broadcast by the BBC in 1978; the other, a feature film released by MGM in 1981.[2] In having the fantasy sequences that accompany the miming of the BBC characters parody the conventions of movie musicals, the serial deals as much with the impact of the American movie industry in England as it does with the American music industry—an impact depicted as longstanding, since Potter's portrait of the 1930s is continually infused with his perceptions of the 1970s. But in having the fantasies of the MGM characters derive completely from specific American movie musicals of the 1930s, the American adaptation moves into pastiche, a practice, as defined by Fredric Jameson, of considerably less vitality, "amputated of the satiric impulse, devoid of laughter and of any conviction that alongside the abnormal tongue you have momentarily borrowed, some healthy linguistic normality still exists" (*Postmodernism* 17). To put it another way, the British Arthur Parker can imagine escaping to Chicago to avoid England in the 1930s. The American Arthur Parker, however, already is in Chicago in 1934 when the movie begins, and the city in which he lives is at the height of the Great Depression.

Common Culture, Popular Culture, and Television Culture

Dennis Potter was not alone in calling for a common culture among those who first began writing in the decade following the Second World War, particularly those whose personal histories as scholarship boys had left them straddling different social classes and, therefore, classless for belonging neither to the class from which they came nor the class for which they had been schooled. Defining culture as "not only a body of intellectual and imaginative work" but "a whole way of life" in *Culture and Society* (325), Raymond Williams decried the lack of any such unifying principle in postwar Britain: "We need a common culture, not for the sake of an abstraction, but because we shall not survive without it" (317). He then went on to found that ideal of culture on the idea of solidarity (332), citing working-class culture, with its "basic collective idea, and the institutions, manners, habits of thought and intentions which proceed from this," as providing the closest approximation of its realization (327). For the Cambridge educated Williams, such institutions were exemplified, for instance, by the local newspaper, "[p]roduced for a known community on a basis of common interest and common knowledge" (312). For Richard Hoggart, descended from northern steelworkers, it was the phenomenon of club singing, in which individual performers remained participants in a group activity, both for following in the wake of folk musicians before them and making the emotions they evoked accepted as common to all those in front of them (129, 188).[3]

Yet calls for a common culture did not mean a leveling of aesthetic cultural distinctions. "We are faced with the fact that there is now a great deal of bad art, bad entertainment, bad journalism, bad advertisement, bad argument," reported Williams (305), who traced the mass culture that these deficient artifacts reflected back to 1870, when the Education Act created a literate but aesthetically undiscriminating public, and even further back to 1730–40, when the emergence of a new middle-class readership led to the emergence of a new literary genre, the novel, to meet its demands (306–7). Admitting that "[n]obody can raise anybody else's cultural standard," he nonetheless advanced "open access to all that has been made and done" and education in the skills necessary for traditional artistic appreciation as an antidote (318–19). References to "bad songs" and "banal verses" (186), "puff-pastry literature" (192), and milk-bars that exhibit an "aesthetic breakdown" so complete as to produce "a sort of spiritual dry-rot amid the odour of boiled milk" likewise punctuate Hoggart's writing (203, 204). Aware of the pretensions and proclivity for the secondhand that often accompany culture vultures of limited means, he, too, endorsed traditional aesthetic criteria in praising an " 'earnest minority' " for choosing "an idealistic love for 'things of the mind' " instead of "arrogant low-browism" (260, 255).

Such differentiating assessments, of course, were fully in keeping with the sense of cultural hierarchy that Britain's postwar welfare state, for all its extension of social services, retained, as Alan Sinfield has pointed out. The Labour Party manifesto of 1945 concerned itself with making culture available, not redefining culture: " 'By the provision of concert halls, modern libraries, theatres and suitable civic centres, we desire to assure to our people full access to the great heritage of culture in this nation' " (50). The BBC's intentionally highbrow Third Programme completed a model conceived by its director general as " 'a broadly based cultural pyramid, slowly aspiring upwards,' " and a process intended " 'to lead listeners from the Light Programme to the Home and from the Home to the Third until eventually the Home and Light should wither away leaving the Third over all' " (51), a cultural Marxism in reverse. The 1946 Fine Arts Council charter dedicated itself to " 'increase the accessibility of the fine arts to the public throughout Our Realm' " (52). And Leavisism in the universities made an appreciation of canonical literature attainable by anyone of any class. As Sinfield concludes, "the traditional conception of 'high' culture persisted, but now with state validation, within the story that it was for all the people" (53).

Williams remained aware of the difficulties attendant upon modeling a common culture on the solidarity of the working class, notably the divisions that an increased specialization of labor invariably produced, and, more dangerous, the provincialism that enforced insularity too often bred ("while the clenched fist is a necessary symbol, the clenching ought never to be such that the hand cannot open, and the fingers extend" [335]). Nevertheless, he ended his pivotal 1958 book by comparing the cultivation of culture to the tending of a garden, in which, with proper care, natural growth can prosper instead of "the selected energies which the dominative mode finds it convenient to enlist" (337). Hoggart, whose confidence in the decency of working-class culture was less unqualified, remained more skeptical. Because he saw the destruction of the urban culture he valued as directly attributable to the rise of mass culture, which already had substituted "centralised palliness" for community (278), and because he viewed "chains of cultural subordination" as "both easier to wear and harder to strike away than those of economic subordination" (201), he questioned "how long this stock of moral capital will last, and whether it is being sufficiently renewed" (266).

Potter's *Singing Detective* provides a most poignant dramatization of the process depicted as inevitable by Hoggart's *The Uses of Literacy* (1957) in a fever dream that its protagonist Philip Marlow has of his father performing birdcalls at the local club in their forest community. Beginning with the child Philip, watching his father with undisguised love, the camera slowly pans the silently appreciative 1940s audience, only to return to Marlow, now an adult, unable even to clap his hands due to the psoriatic arthropathy that has crippled him, sitting alone in the cobweb-strewn room, pictures askew, piano draped.[4] Potter's personal experience of communal decline, however, reveals itself much earlier, as talk of cozy club intimacy to which the collier's son succumbs during a 1961 visit home ends with a litany of social splintering that his Oxford University status forces him to acknowledge: "For I knew, as well, that the pits are closing, the club is losing members, the chapel is falling away, the rugby team cannot always get a full fifteen, and the Foresters are closing up in front of each other as never before. And that many young people want to leave, as I have left. 'There's nothing to kip 'um here, o'butty' " (*Changing* 113).[5] And the atomization that, for Potter, constitutes the Changing Forest of Dean typifies the kind of anomie he finds destroying the changing nation at large.

> "The telly," I was told by a middle-aged miner, "is the best thing 'as ever come to our whum, butty", and he may have been right. After all, the tin baths do not hang outside the back-kitchen walls, and no one can say that we have not gone forward, and forward in the right direction.
>
> But if this surge of achievement alienates us from the basic spirit of community, then it is obvious that all the chrome and comfort is not going to lead us very far towards Socialism. It is going to preclude so many forms of vitality, and help create a dead land, grey in its values, ambitions and pleasures, its people buried in a huge coffin, a glittering coffin. (*Glittering* 45)[6]

Unlike Williams and Hoggart, Potter has no impulse to eject this proverbial machine from the working-class garden. For one thing, the garden depicted in Potter's works is anything but paradisiacal. In his *Blue Remembered Hills* (1979), as opposed to Houseman's, a child is burned to death because his friends shut him inside a barn, not knowing that he has been playing with matches—notably "England's Glory" matches—inside it.[7] For another thing, the alien machine has the potential of being liberating, as Potter's account of the changes mandated by the physical placement of the set suggests. Unsuited to the kitchen chaos of the wireless, television turned the front room from a museum housing nothing but the "lifeless clutter" of its owner's best possessions into a "genuine living space" in which people could eat and drink in full view of the flickering tube (*Changing* 17). Even more important, this kind of domestic liberation promised a much more extensive form of freedom. "I first saw television when I was in my late teens. It made my heart *pound*," recalled Potter in the James MacTaggart lecture he gave at Edinburgh. "Here was a medium of great power, of potentially wondrous delights, that could slice through all the tedious hierarchies of the printed word and help to emancipate us from many of the stifling tyrannies of class and status and gutter-press ignorance. [. . .] Switch on, tune in and *grow*" (*Seeing* 55).

Indeed, far from seeing television in particular, and popular culture in general, as antithetical to common culture, in the manner of Hoggart, Potter saw them as productive of it: "if 'pop' culture is moulded primarily by the economic motive of profit maximization, then it is also shaped in some degree by certain *genuine* desires and needs. [. . .] Somehow we are able to discern that a great deal of that which is true and valuable in traditional working class culture is *still* reflected in the slicker, cheapened 'pop' culture, however obliquely, however much like a ray of light sliding through a filthy window" (*Glittering* 121). And not just working-class culture. As the portrayal of westerns in an early work like *Where the Buffalo Roam* (1966) shows, popular culture cuts across all social classes, joining an unemployed youth from Swansea who wants to be called Shane with the probation officer who tries to help him and the instructor who constantly humiliates him, all of whom find the western so "potent and evocative" a myth as to "knock Robin Hood into a cocked hat." For nineteen-year-old Willy Turner in particular, so illiterate that he can process the word "it" only pictorially, as a man in a hat outside a church, westerns provide the only possibility of escaping an environment defined by the physical abuse of a dead father and the verbal abuse of a living grandfather ("real cowboys out there on the range, free as wild horses"). Willy's probation officer thus realizes that while the printed word does not prompt Willy's imagination, other cultural artifacts do: "There are adults who can look at a neon sign and find it beautiful." If such a claim is compromised somewhat by the fact that it is his mother's purchase of a dime-store paperback called *Dead Man's Gulch* that comes closest to getting Willy to read—suggesting that popular culture functions much as the BBC's Light Programme did to the Third—it is far more undermined by the ending of the drama in which Willy shoots his family in a desperate attempt to make his gunslinger fantasy real ("Four outlaws, four corpses"). It is not, then, simply the fact of popular culture that can promote both personal and communal growth in Potter's world; it is the use that is made of it. As Potter qualified in the introduction to his first published dramas, "Television, in short, is exciting—just so long as we use it boldly and imaginatively" (*Nigel* 21).

Used unimaginatively, in fact, television promotes stagnation. The *New Statesman* newspaper columns that Potter wrote over the years attest to the large number of dismissible television byproducts that stem from the variety of preconceptions held about the medium: schlock from those who just disdain "a box that can be plugged into the same socket as a hairdryer or a coffee percolator" ("Poisonous" 725); misrepresentation, which is to say lies, from documentarians who assume an equivalence between the window onto the world and the world ("Stay Out" 744); historical myopia from those who make period pieces with nothing but fancy costumes and elaborate sets ("Embalmed" 268) and invitations to "[c]ome in, yesterday. The past is the past is the past" ("Flay" 428).[8] These last Potter excoriated most soundly, for in presenting a fossilized past, uninformed by the concerns of the present, they cooperate with those features unique to the medium that already are conducive to passivity and apathy: a "tapwater" quality, on the one hand, what Williams termed "flow" (*Television* 86), in which "[p]rogrammes slide into each other, colour each other, drain each other and contradict each other" (*Nigel* 11; "Take" 940); distancing, on the other, in which viewers can "look down and see the world boiling, and then we can go and put the cat out" ("Violence" 796). As Potter recognized at the start of his career, "most television ends up offering its viewers a means of orienting themselves towards the generally received notions of 'reality'" (*Waiting* 30). As he also recognized, "one of the troubles of supposedly showing things-as-they-really-are (the window problem) is how difficult it then becomes in the same grammar not to make people feel deep in their souls that this is also more or less the way things have to be" (*Seeing* 53).

Combating the naturalistic techniques that contribute to such social stagnation, Potter's dramas force viewers to see the frame in the picture in order to remind them of the constructed nature of all programming.[9] Hence his attempts at reclamation by disorientation, using an arsenal of what would become trademark devices: direct address to break the barrier between actor and audience (*Vote, Vote, Vote for Nigel Barton* [1965]); rapid-fire cuts between past and present to deny each the status of "norm" from which the other deviates (*Stand Up, Nigel Barton* [1965]); adult actors cast as schoolchildren to highlight the continuity between maturity and youth (*Blue Remembered Hills*); and, most famously, lip-synching to popular music (*Pennies from Heaven, The Singing Detective, Lipstick on Your Collar*) so that the music "takes on the reverberations of all that is around it, and then those little lyrics start having added ironies" (*Potter* 91). When, for instance, Private Hopper allows his fantasies to break out in 1950s rock songs in *Lipstick on Your Collar*, "[t]he sort where moon don't rhyme with June and you're not up to your backside in bloody buttercups" (198), he engages in an act subversive of an entire military hierarchical establishment, emblematized throughout the serial by the duty to make the officers' Nescafé, the "barely bloody drinkable" (6).[10]

Less successful was Potter in subverting the impact of commercial television, introduced on 22 September 1955, and personifying in the extreme the phenomenon that J. B. Priestley had termed "Admass" one year earlier after a visit to Texas. For someone like Williams, in fact, the commercialization of television, a medium once distinguished by its limited capitalist component of distribution (the sets viewers had to buy in order to partake of its offerings), became inseparable from the Americanization of television, since the programming of American television had been devoted to advertising from the start (*Television* 25, 68). Such an incursion, of course, only reflected the increasingly dominant role played by the United States in British affairs since the end of the Second World War, as evidenced by the 1945 termination of Lend-Lease, the 1947 forced conversion of sterling to other currencies, the 50 percent rise in British defense expenditures to help finance the Korean War, and, perhaps most clearly, the 1956 Suez fiasco.[11] At the same time, that Americanization of British television became inseparable from what Williams saw as a military-industrial Americanization of the world, what with U.S. Department of Defense and USIA transmitters dumping American programs on unwitting viewers all over the globe and the three American broadcasting giants having subsidiaries in over ninety foreign nations, proof to Williams of a "planned operation" spearheaded by "a distant and invisible authority—the American corporations" (*Television* 40–41, 133).

Potter, no less than Williams, found the commercialization of British television a deplorable phenomenon. *Follow the Yellow Brick Road* (1972), the work he later judged his "low point" (*Waiting* 19), shows what happens when commercialism turns people from citizens to consumers— or dwarfs, as is the case with its actor-protagonist who prefers sanitized commercials to the surrounding dramas that "stink" (372), despite the fact that he gets upstaged by even the Great Dane in his own advertisements. And Potter, much like Williams, found that shift the result of changes in Anglo-American relations impossible to ignore, as *The Bonegrinder* (1968), one of his earliest works, illustrates. Depicting the steady intrusion of Sam Adams, an American merchant marine, into the life (and, later, home) of George King, a middle-aged English banker soon to be retired, the drama has no doubts about the relative strengths of the economic positions that each man represents: while the Yank, in a parody of Marshall Plan munificence, flashes wads of "shiny kings and queens" in front of old pensioners and dispenses coins with the reminder of "[w]hat a mess the world would be in without the dollar," King's sister-in-law is choking to death elsewhere over the words "cup of tea." Fully cognizant in his newspaper columns that American inroads into British television had left viewers with reduced choices, between "a monogamous American dog or a bad-tempered American duck on BBC-1, and a 16-year-old Hollywood musical following hard upon a 21-year-old Hollywood musical on BBC-2," as he wrote after the 1975 Spring Bank Holiday ("Bunk" 736), Potter remained equally aware in those columns of the implications of such diminished choices: the transformation of viewers from dwarfs—possessed of at least some free will—into mere "mimic men," since, "[l]ike the mimic men of our old Empire who carried furled umbrellas in the middle of a dry season we, too, have slowly taken on the mental inflexions or infections of a provincial and colonialised people" ("Mimic" 357).

Potter's dramas, however, present a much more ambivalent view. While the scientists in *Cold Lazarus* may claim, "There'll *always* be an England" (273), almost all the other characters in his works who ponder the issue of national identity come up empty handed. Adrian Harris, the fictionalized Kim Philby of *Traitor* (1971), hangs a picture of a Constable landscape on the wall of his Moscow apartment to recall the images of his homeland that still haunt him, "[t]he England of the watermills and the cricket fields and the gentle faces, lemonade, and haystacks," but, as one of the journalists who visits him notes, the painting has no relationship to England in the 1970s. Like the remnants of Camelot for which Harris's archaeologist father has once searched, that nation remains literally and figuratively buried underground, abandoned just like the "green fields and happy groves" of Blake that Harris has had to recite in school. Far more accurate is Jason Cavandish in *Blade on the Feather* (1980), alleged recruiter of Philby, Burgess, and Maclean, who finds that the only things of England left to inherit are rice pudding and baked jam rolls with extra custard. Remnants of an English background, they also are souvenirs of that upper-class background in which "[s]ilver spoons tarnish easily," as the former Cambridge don comments, in which case the demise of all that once accompanied them may not be worth mourning. The culture of America offered by way of contrast may be crass and commercial, on the one hand, but it is also egalitarian in spirit and possessed of vitality, on the other.

Pennies from Heaven (BBC) and the American Movie Musical

In *Pennies from Heaven*, that vitality specifically comes from the activity of mimicking—the mimicking of American music, to be precise. Yet more than just a narrative of the 1930s punctuated by songs of the 1930s, the BBC *Pennies from Heaven* functions as a dramatization of the 1930s American musical. How else to interpret scenes of homeless men accompanying one of their own singing "Serenade in the Night" while standing on shelter beds and playing accordions (177–78) or a prosecutor metamorphosing midtrial into a music hall magician who pulls flowers from his sleeves while crooning "Whistling in the Dark" to the oohs and aahs of the jury (238–39)? Even if much of the credit for the extravagance of such scenes is attributable to the collaborative nature of television production, notably the embellishments of Potter's script by choreographer Tudor

Davies and director Piers Haggard,[12] enough stage directions appear in the published text of the drama to indicate that the musical is the genre with which Potter is deliberately working: from the first strains of Elsie Carlisle's vocal of "The Clouds Will Soon Roll By" that Arthur Parker mimes *"in the conventions of a musical—totally in earnest"* (4), which signal the distinctive way in which singer and song will be joined, to the children who perform "Love Is Good for Anything That Ails You" *"in hideous parody of all children in musicals"* (99), to the pimp who urges a woman about to embark upon a life of vice to "Better Think Twice" while *"swivelling on [a] stool as in a Hollywood musical"* to the piano playing of Carroll Gibbons (138).

Given Potter's nonnaturalist concerns, it's a perfect genre for him to employ since, as Martin Rubin succinctly notes, "[t]he phrase 'realistic musical' can only be a relative term" (26). And taken in broad overview, the story of *Pennies from Heaven*, in fact, *is* a variation on the classic boy meets girl–boy loses girl–boy gets girl plots that underlie so many movies of this kind, with, albeit, the added complications of adultery, unwanted pregnancy, prostitution, and murder. BOY MEETS GIRL: Arthur Parker, a commercial traveler who wholeheartedly shares the sentiments of the sheet music he sells, picks up two people who corroborate his faith while on a business trip from London to Gloucester—a hitchhiking singer of hymns, who functions as his alter ego, and a village schoolteacher, Eileen Everson, who incarnates all the lyrical joys he finds missing from his sexless marriage to a shopkeeper's daughter. BOY LOSES GIRL: Pregnant, forced out of her job, and abandoned by Arthur, who has reconciled with the wife who has agreed to front him money for a record shop, Eileen comes to London; unable to find any kind of work after her funds are depleted, she finds herself forced into prostitution in order to support herself. BOY GETS GIRL: Reunited after a chance meeting at a pub one rainy night, Arthur and Eileen decide to run off together, only to be separated when Arthur is falsely arrested and then hanged for the murder of a blind girl, only to be reunited once again by virtue of a miraculous resurrection that provides the requisite "bleed'n 'appy endin'" dictated by the musical genre (247).

Because Arthur's misfortunes can be seen, in large part, as the result of his unswerving belief in the words of the goods that he purveys ("They tell the truth, songs do" [60]), it is tempting to interpret the drama as offering a wholesale condemnation of popular music for cramming people's heads with visions that cannot be fulfilled in real life (assuming that any agreement exists on what constitutes "real life," of course). Arthur, who explicitly describes himself as "empty" and "blank" (5)—a perfect postmodern subject—is very much constructed by music that fills his head with heart strings that go zing and moons to be wished on (blue or otherwise). But since almost every character in the drama breaks out into song at one point or another, the drama offers the more insidious suggestion that popular music provides, as proponents of the Frankfurt School argue, the means by which not only Arthur is doomed, but all those whose lives are meant for subjection.[13] After all, what else do the lyrics of the title tune propose but acceptance of hard times (storms, rain, clouds, thunder, showers) as necessary prelude to rewards (sunshine, flowers, fortune, and, finally, pennies from heaven), a "planned" arrangement (by whom left unspecified) in which people must punitively "pay" in advance for what they want because years ago no one appreciated the fact that "the best things in life were absolutely free"? The headmaster of Eileen's school thus rebukes her for encouraging students to use their imaginative powers to see invisible desks in forests and draw trees shaped like diamonds in classrooms, since all these children of miners need is enough education to keep a job in the pits, and for that "[c]heap music will do" (116).

Cheap perhaps, but not vulgar. "A pop song is ordinary language put to extraordinary use," writes Simon Frith (168), an extraordinary use that is as much socially interactive as socially isolationist. As Frith later goes on to explain, "what makes music special in this familiar cultural process [of identity formation] is that musical identity is both fantastic—idealizing not just oneself but also the social world one inhabits—and real: it is enacted in activity. [. . .] In this respect, musical pleasure is not derived from fantasy—it is not mediated by daydreams—but is experienced directly: music gives us a real experience of what the ideal could be" (274). Specifically, music in *Pennies from Heaven* provides an experience of what Potter's ideal common culture that defies hierarchies of class and education could be. MPs and bankers break out into song as frequently as miners and buskers in Potter's drama, sometimes even the same song, as occurs when Arthur's frigid wife, Joan, reprises the opening Elsie Carlisle vocal (78). Therefore, popular music is presented as dissolving all those divisions that are embodied in the incessant reminders of etiquette that pervade the drama like a daisy chain of grammatical correctness and proper table manners: the Methodist shopkeeper's daughter, Joan, corrects the Cockney bricklayer's son, Arthur; the sheet music salesman who travels by car, Arthur, corrects the hiker who thumbs rides from place to place singing hymns for spare change.

It is as much to this kind of social commonality that the inarticulate Arthur refers when talking to his fellow salesmen about songs containing "things that is too big and too important and too bleed'n simple to put in all that lah-di-dah, toffee-nosed poetry and stuff, books and that—but everybody feels 'em" (68), as to the more transcendent rewards of "[t]he patch of blue sky. The gold of the, of the bleed'n dawn, or—the light in somebody's eyes—Pennies from Heaven" for which he yearns (69). As such, the "[f]aith in the goods" he sells that Arthur professes is not mere hyperbole (68). Popular songs do not simply inherit the role of the psalms, as Potter has stated in interviews (*Potter* 86; *Seeing* 19) and as *Pennies from Heaven* portrays in making Arthur and the hiker alter egos. Rather, popular songs democratize the psalms in a way that religion no longer does by the time in which the drama is set. The paean to "All Things Bright and Beautiful" that Eileen's schoolchildren sing is a testament to a God whose "order'd estate" keeps the rich man in his castle and the poor man at his gate (41). The hiker who sings hymns for a living falls prey to epileptic fits—the words of the songs he sings are unable in any way to support him.

The salesmen to whom Arthur expresses his credo puncture his rhapsodic sentiments about songs with a quick retort: "Half of 'em were dreamed up in a back office by a couple of Jew-boys with green eyeshades" (70). More than just a remark that distinguishes Arthur's beatitudes from his companions' boorishness, the reply echoes many of the governing assumptions made about the manufacture of those Tin Pan Alley songs about which Arthur tries to wax so eloquently. Writing in 1933, Constant Lambert, for instance, found "the fact that at least ninety per cent of jazz tunes are written by Jews undoubtedly goes far to account for the curiously sagging quality—so typical of Jewish art—the almost masochistic melancholy of the average foxtrot" (qtd. in Pearsall 92). Its underlying anti-Semitism notwithstanding, moreover, the salesmen's reply is not without a certain justification, given the dominating presence of Jewish composers, many with Anglicized names (Berlin for Baline, Rose for Rosenberg), and Jewish publishing houses (M. Witmark and Sons, Joseph W. Stern and Company, Charles K. Harris, Shapiro and Bernstein) in the music industry during the years between the two world wars. "It's just a business, Arthur," his fellow salesmen say (70). What they don't say (at least not explicitly) is how much an *American* business it is, centered first in Manhattan's Union Square and later moving to Twenty-eighth Street between Fifth Avenue and Broadway, or how centralized a business it is, with the 1907 formation of American Music Stores, Inc., setting sheet music prices, and the 1914 establishment of the American Society of Composers, Authors and Publishers protecting against copyright infringement. Nor do they say anything about how formulaic a business it is, complete with "how to" books,[14] or how big a business it is, as a comparison of statistics for sheet music sales illustrates: the hit song of 1853, "My Old Kentucky Home," sold fifty thousand copies (Ewen 5); "After the Ball," published in 1892, sold over five million (Kantor 16).[15]

Arthur, unfortunately, lives in a country in which the national broadcasting company (incorporated on 31 December 1926) was policing what music it would transmit over the radio since its inception, restricting audience access to the most sanitized dance bands while allowing propagandists like Percy Scholes and Sir Walford Davies to lecture listeners on the virtues of classical music. This was in conformance to the dictates of a director general, John Reith, who felt it his mission to "give the public what we think they need—and not what they want," since "few know what they want and very few what they need" (qtd. in Briggs 55).[16] To Arthur, then, the Americanization of British music, exemplified by those songs composed by Americans but performed by British dance bands that punctuate the drama, is liberating.[17] Thrilled by the success that "Roll Along Prairie Moon"—a 1935 Fiorito, MacPherson, and Von Tilzer cowboy song he plugs—has in a land with nary a prairie or cowboy, he even goes so far as to proclaim, "I'd rather be a Yank. They got the best songs" (163). And living as Arthur does in a country in which the national broadcasting service had never wrestled free from what Tom Burns has called the "political swaddling clothes" with which the government had draped it (20), as evidenced by the government's legal authority to commandeer the BBC during the May 1926 General Strike if necessary and its initiation of Empire broadcasting across the world in December 1932, such cultural liberation has definite political ramifications.[18] To the youth who comes into the record shop that Arthur later opens looking for needles with which to play his military band music, however, such liberation signals only a steady and threatening encroachment. "We shall need 'em one day," he tells Arthur, when explaining his musical preferences as preparation for the next war he is certain will come, since the Yanks are "taking over," a point he finds confirmed yet again by the fact that the new records in which Arthur tries to interest him are sung by Bing Crosby (148, 149).

Neither an abstract nor paranoid fear, the youth's comment reflects quite accurately the very real concern that the importation of American popular culture produced in England during the 1930s. Most of that concern centered around the importation of American movies, an industry whose connection to the American music business was already well established, from the vaudevillian background of many of its moguls, to the manufacture of movie theme songs as part of accompanying movie scores and—with the coming of sound—theme songs bearing the same names as the movies in which they appeared, to the final absorption of Tin Pan Alley by Hollywood film companies that had purchased music publishing houses.[19] With exportation of its goods having the advantages that the main item in question, film, was made to a universal world standard (the same width, the same space between sprocket holes) and was supported by an unrivaled vertical structure of production and distribution, the American film industry had little difficulty penetrating foreign markets. By 1918, over 80 percent of all films shown in Great Britain were Hollywood produced (Murphy

51). That initial penetration, in turn, was only exacerbated by the 1927 advent of talkies due to the country's high density of movie houses (3,300 in 1929, 4,967 in 1938) and populace that could understand the language of the films in their original form (Branson and Heinemann 252).

Yet, as Ian Jarvie has meticulously documented, the issue for those MPs who passed regulatory quotas designed to offset the number of American films imported with increasing percentages of homemade products (notably the 1927 and 1938 Cinematograph Films Acts) was not simply one of trade imbalance, in which, as slogans like "trade follows the film" and, later, "bacon before Bogart" and "grub before Grable" suggested, control of films shown in Britain would lead to control of other British industries.[20] Rather, the issue was equally one of culture—not just protecting British culture from "becoming Americanised in manners and customs, habits and methods, speech and idiom through constant familiarity with American films," but promoting culture as a form of imperial nation building, as indicated by parliamentary debates that voiced fears about "the evil of showing to coloured races and to, shall we say, less educated people than the average inhabitant of this country, representations of the lives of white people which are completely contrary to the life the bulk of us live" (qtd. in Jarvie 145, 118).

Exhortations of empire regularly punctuate the entire script of the BBC *Pennies from Heaven*, set in 1935, the Jubilee year of George V. "You live in the greatest country in the world, bar none," intones the headmaster of Eileen's school. "In the greatest Empire the world has yet seen. Bar none" (43). "The Jubilee of His Majesty King George the Fifth is quite properly the occasion for national joy and gratitude," proclaims Major Archibald Paxville, a Conservative MP, to his political cohorts. "The people have shown, the length and breadth of the land, that they are fundamentally at one! They have shown their contempt for the sour and alien creeds which would set one class at the throat of another, which would trample the country's Flag under foot, which would turn its back on our great and united Empire, and level us all down to the same drab, uninspiring and impoverished condition" (184). Much like the commemorative Jubilee jigsaw puzzle that Arthur literally has to put together, however, the united empire to which such jingoistic sentiments refer is very much a matter of rhetorical construction, offered by those in positions of authority to those whose lives (and livelihoods) provide direct contradiction. Jubilee crockery proves an unwanted commodity—the salesman who panders it talks about importing someone like Mussolini to take over in England (64–65). Jubilee Records rarely sells more than a few needles—its owner, Arthur, finally smashes all its contents in frenzied disgust (166). Indeed, far from people of different classes "pull[ing] together" and keeping their hands off each other's throats, as the MP asserts (184), people are depicted as remaining rather far apart—and resenting the fact. Arthur does *not* kill the blind girl for whose strangulation he is arrested (the epileptic hiker does), but he *is* guilty of a crime at the time that he meets her, namely, trespassing upon her family's property. And it is the litter that he deposits upon that land, evidence of a crime against her class, that later gets Arthur convicted for the crime against her person for which he is hanged.

Part of this debunking of empire is attributable to the specific conditions of Depression England, of course. When Eileen informs Arthur that the only legitimate work she has been able to find upon arriving in London is as a dishwasher, and that only sporadically, Arthur's remark, "And this is supposed to be the greatest country in the world!" (163), reveals the falsity of all those exhortations of British Empire in 1935. But, as commentators on Potter's drama have noted, the presentation of the Depression in the BBC *Pennies from Heaven* occurs more by way of amorphous cultural memories of the 1930s—scattered references about people being out of work, allusions to more tramps on the road than ever before (113, 130, 140)—than actual events of the 1930s, such as hunger marches and instances of open class conflict.[21] *Anti*nostalgic in its refusal to keep the past tucked safely in the past, which, in Potter's view, is exactly what the nostalgiac does (*Seeing* 67), the drama continually breaks its time frame in order to show how conterminous the past is with the present. Thus, many of its cultural allusions actually postdate its 1935 time period. Arthur's referring to musicals in which characters "can't get anybody to put on their show in a proper theatre. And they put it on in this barn" (226) is an allusion to *Babes in Arms* and *Babes on Broadway*, Mickey Rooney–Judy Garland vehicles that were not released until 1939 and 1941 respectively. Characters who mime songs such as "Pennies from Heaven" (1936), "Pick Yourself Up" (1936), "Love Is Good for Anything That Ails You" (1937), "Serenade in the Night" (1937), and "Says My Heart" (1938) mime songs that were not composed until after the time in which the drama ends. *"Britons make it—It makes Britons,"* as the box of shredded wheat on Arthur and Joan's breakfast table proclaims ([4], changed to more direct "Force" in the television production), may be a belief it is possible to convey from the perspective of the year in which the drama is set, 1935, and then only with a certain suspension of disbelief. From the perspective of the year in which the drama was written—1977, another Jubilee year—Britons are not making it any longer. Americans are. Fears of losing preeminence in 1935 are not just expressed by characters in the drama, they are exposed as having been validated in the intervening years by the author of the drama.[22]

Pennies from Heaven (MGM)
and the Exhaustion of the American Movie Musical

Stripped of such rhetoric of empire completely, and transferred to a Chicago setting, the *Pennies from Heaven* that Potter later adapted for MGM cannot lay claim to making any statements about British imperial decline. Nor does it make much of a statement about overcoming class divisions. Eileen's working-class father has a car just like the middle-class Arthur; the blind girl, who looks about as shabby as everyone else, is killed underneath a highway overpass, not on her family's property.[23] And eviscerated of these two primary raisons d'être, remembered mainly (if at all) for big Hollywood production numbers that, in Potter's view, acted in contradiction to his use of lip-synched music in having little connection to what the characters themselves would be capable of imaginatively projecting (*Potter* 109–11), one may wonder what reason the MGM *Pennies from Heaven* has for being at all.

And the answer: the production numbers themselves. For if the BBC *Pennies from Heaven* sacrifices historical accuracy to make a statement about the transition of Great Britain from the 1930s to the 1970s, the MGM *Pennies from Heaven* separates itself even more completely from any attempt at 1930s historical verisimilitude. In fact, troping as it does so many actual texts of the period (some postdating the film's 1934 time setting), specifically visual texts, the MGM *Pennies from Heaven* provides a compendium of representations divorced from their referents. Arthur and Eileen at a diner counter are deliberately framed to suggest Edward Hopper's *Nighthawks* (1942), not the Greenwich Avenue restaurant that was the setting for Hopper's painting. Arthur and Eileen sitting in a movie theater, an usherette posed to their side, recalls Hopper's *New York Movie* (1939), not Hopper's wife, Jo, who was the model for the theater's employee. Arthur driving past a billboard of Carole Lombard in *Love before Breakfast* (1936)—the billboard itself a representation of a cinematic representation—invokes Walker Evans's 1936 photograph of Atlanta, Georgia, and the reel—as opposed to the real—Carole Lombard.[24] A movie about visual texts more than an actual historical period, the American *Pennies from Heaven* contemplates the history of American popular cultural aesthetics.

Seen in this light, the dance numbers (choreographed by Danny Daniels) provide a pivotal function, establishing as they do that any set can become a stage. A diner wall slides away and a hiker performs "Pennies from Heaven" in front of a collage of stock Depression photo images: bums asleep on sidewalks, men queuing up on breadlines. A pimp jumps on top of a pool table and turns a bar into a burlesque house for his gyrating striptease. Such blatant stylization is particularly apparent in those elaborate Busby Berkeley–inspired numbers, so different from the elementary choreography that characterizes the BBC numbers (the splendor of Bob Hoskins's star-turn cartwheels aside) that are signaled mainly by changes in lighting. Signaled instead by quick cuts, dramatic set and costume changes, and separating spectacle space from surrounding narrative space, these very literal "showstoppers" follow their 1930s prototypes in enabling viewers to lose all sense of proscenium frame of reference.[25] The scene in which Steve Martin's Arthur, in tails, tap dances to "Yes, Yes (My Baby Said Yes, Yes)," while giant coins roll onto a bank lobby and chorines, photographed from overhead to form kaleidoscopic patterns, acclaim a giant hundred dollar bill with Martin's face on it, not only recycles the opening song of *Gold Diggers of 1933* (commonly known as "We're in the Money"), in which chorines, strategically covered with coins, emerge from a dollar sign doorway to dance in front of huge coins on which "In God We Trust" is prominently displayed; it also expands the bank lobby in which Arthur has been refused money into a Radio City Music Hall clone of a set. Bernadette Peters's Eileen, resplendent in Bob Mackie lamé, shimmying to "Love Is Good for Anything That Ails You," while children dance on the tops of desks turned into grand pianos, not only jazzes up the fifty-six-piano–"The Words Are in My Heart" number from *Gold Diggers of 1935*, exchanging a bevy of ethereal women for a homeroom of Shirley Temples hooked on speed; it also turns the rustic schoolhouse in which Peters previously has been reading fairy tales into the Big White Set celebrated in so many 1930s musicals.

This is not to suggest that these 1930s cinematic antecedents bear absolutely no relationship to the historical milieu in which they were made, for the backstage shows that form the climax to those Berkeley musicals are always set against, and often gain their raisons from, the gritty conditions of Depression America. "Remember My Forgotten Man," the magnificent finale of both *Gold Diggers of 1933* and the show performed in it, casts Joan Blondell's hooker as the "Spirit of the Depression," beseeched by down-and-out war veterans meant to recall the disastrous 1932 Bonus Army March on Washington. "Shanghai Lil," which concludes the show-within-a-show of *Footlight Parade* (also 1933), heralds the American flag, Franklin Delano Roosevelt, and the National Recovery Administration eagle in quick succession through formations of placards and chorus caps. Warner Brothers, the studio that produced these films, was unique among Hollywood studios in being committed to supporting Roosevelt, as was evidenced by its incorporation of the NRA blue eagle into the title cards of its films (Babington and Evans 46–47). And, as Mark Roth has persuasively argued, the very choreography of their production numbers, which subordinates individual star turns to coordinated group (or, in the case of "Forgotten

Man" and "Shanghai Lil," troop) movements, reinforces the New Deal values of social cohesion and harmony just as the instrumental role of the director (both of the show within the movie and the dances performed within it) reaffirms the achievements it is possible to obtain under the hand of a strong leader (44–45, 47–48).

Void of all such political context, the MGM *Pennies from Heaven* functions instead as an American movie about American movie musicals. Thus, three of the numbers included in it that do not appear in the BBC production, for instance, derive from earlier American musicals: "Yes, Yes (My Baby Said Yes, Yes)" (from *Palmy Days* [1931]), "Did You Ever See a Dream Walking?" (from *Sitting Pretty* [1933]), and "I Want to Be Bad" (from *Follow Thru* [1930]).[26] This altered focus becomes even more evident when the movie shifts from the Berkeley-inspired dances to the Fred Astaire–Ginger Rogers "Let's Face the Music and Dance" number (also not included in the BBC production) that serves as its choreographic climax, for, unlike the Warner Brothers–Berkeley films of the 1930s, the RKO-Astaire-Rogers films of the 1930s had virtually nothing to do with the conditions outside their elegant—and fine, as Jerome Kern and Dorothy Fields would say—romances.[27] Only with the insertion of the dance performed to this Irving Berlin song, the MGM film also becomes a movie about the exhaustion of the American movie musical.

It's a remarkable scene, which begins with Arthur and Eileen, on the run from the law, sitting in a movie theater watching *Follow the Fleet*, a 1936 Astaire-Rogers vehicle; then shifts to Arthur and Eileen getting up onto the stage to mimic, with their miniature shapes, the steps that Astaire and Rogers are performing in twenty-foot-high proportions behind them; and ends with Arthur and Eileen magically and seamlessly transported into the movie themselves, in glorious black and white, taking over the Astaire and Rogers roles and costumes. And yet, for all the dexterity of the Martin and Peters performance—the fact, quite simply, that they pull it off so astonishingly well—the entire scene is steeped in aesthetic overload. Heavily bracketed, in terms of the theater stage onto which Arthur and Eileen step prior to their metamorphosis, the screen into which they later are spliced, and the *Follow the Fleet* scene that is itself part of a show within a show, the dance is more detached from the surrounding narrative than any other in the MGM movie.[28] It's also more a testament to artistic cannibalization than any other. As Arlene Croce has pointed out, the problem for those who made the Astaire-Rogers films, which were produced at the rate of two a year, was always originality of plot; the filmmakers solved this problem by falling back on the last script but one, cannibalizing their own earlier products, and later cannibalizing other contemporary Hollywood films as well (83, 104). What Croce doesn't say is how much the Astaire-Rogers films began self-reflexively cannibalizing themselves—as occurs, for instance, in *Top Hat* (1935) when Astaire dances before a chorus of men dressed, like himself, in top hats, white ties, and tails (whom he then "shoots" down with his cane) and in *Shall We Dance* (1937) when Astaire dances with dozens of women masked as Rogers, based on the reasoning that, as it is explained to her, "if he couldn't dance with you, he'd dance with images of you." The corpse has been cannibalized, and there remains nothing left on it for further picking.

It is, paradoxically, as a paean to this very sense of exhaustion that the *Pennies from Heaven* "Let's Face the Music and Dance" number works most effectively—an elegy for all its energy. It is also appropriate that its final image should depict a chorus of men, much like those in *Top Hat*, wearing top hats and tails, holding up their canes here in such a way as to bar Arthur and Eileen from escaping. For, in the end, it is this inability to escape—not just from the authorities insofar as the plot of the movie is concerned, but from the conventions of the genre insofar as the American musical is concerned—that differentiates the BBC and MGM productions most profoundly. When the British Arthur, who wants to live in a world "[w]here the songs come true" (163), is on the run from the police, he thinks of two specific places to which he can go: New York and Chicago. Two cities that meet his and Eileen's minimal requirements in providing a safe haven from extradition (or so he thinks) as well as having both a cinema and a wireless, they also signify two very different possibilities vis-à-vis the 1930s movie lexicon. New York is the home of Broadway musicals, "[t]he place we've dreamed and talked about," as one Mahoney sister says to another in *The Broadway Melody* (1929). "Ain't it swell?" Chicago is the place of gangster underworlds, a town "rollin' in jack" in *Scarface* (1932), in which Tony Camonte seeks to "write [his] name all over [. . .] in big letters" with a machine gun. When Arthur opts for Chicago ("I like the sound of it. You can roll it in your mouth, can't you? Chi-ca-go" [222]), he chooses, whether he realizes it or not, to engage in perhaps the greatest act of transgression of his life, for he seeks to go to a place where the songs do not come true: Ruby Keeler always succeeds in New York; Cagney, Robinson, and Muni all die in Chicago. The American Arthur, however, is never given the opportunity for any such choice. When he pines "to live in a world where the songs come true," asserting, in desperation, that "[t]here must be some place where them songs are for real," Eileen can only respond with a song title from *Chasing Rainbows* (1930), another movie musical: "Happy days are here again, is that it, Arthur?"

That "again," as anyone familiar with Potter's career knows, is a word with much descriptive validity, for Potter didn't just "play it again," to recall another overused cultural idiom, he played it again and again—recycling *Schmoedipus* (1974) as *Track 29* (1988), *Sufficient Carbohydrate* (1983) as *Visitors* (1987), and

Lay Down Your Arms (1970) as *Lipstick on Your Collar* (1993).[29] Whether one judges what is implied by that "again" as cause for despair, as Fredric Jameson does in mourning the political neutering it signifies, or delight, as John Barth does in commending the prospects of reinvesting older forms with contemporary concerns, depends, finally, on one's own theoretical predilections.[30] The last line of the BBC script provides a clue as to which Potter himself might choose, however. "The song is ended, but the melody lingers on" (247). It should, and it does, for it echoes the introductory lyrics of George and Ira Gershwin's "They Can't Take That Away from Me" that Astaire sings to Rogers in *Shall We Dance*. More to the point, it echoes the mantra spoken by those geriatrics who form the Al Bowlly Appreciation Society in Potter's *Moonlight on the Highway* (1969), the first drama he wrote in which he experimented with the use of lip-synched music. These celebrants who gather to commemorate the crooner's 1941 death during the Blitz dedicate themselves to "the sweetness of nostalgia" and have as their magazine editor a younger man who, as his psychiatrist notes, cleaves to "schmaltzy songs from an era he can have known nothing about at first hand." Redefined later as the governing metaphor in *Karaoke* (1996), one of the two final works written by Potter as he was dying of cancer, the impulse would be described as a condition of aesthetic deadlock: "The music's written and performed by someone else, and there's this piddling little space left for you to sing yourself, but only to *their* lyrics, *their* timing. It's that feeling that [. . .] The way we hear—see—*think* that what is so—say *out there.* [. . .] In front of us—the way we feel it's somehow or other been *arranged* in advance by—by [. . .]" (27–28). And so when Arthur and Eileen *do* sing for themselves, as occurs for the very first time at the end of the MGM *Pennies from Heaven,* the sounds they emit are devoid of any resonance. Tinny. Hollow. Both drowned out and upstaged by the "Glory of Love" production number that surrounds them. The song is over, and the melody does linger on. Unfortunately, no one can hear the singers' voices any longer.

We got married because we loved one another, and we loved one another because we both loved the same thing. In different ways we had both wanted to do the same thing: he with intelligence, I with the heart; he, prepared for the fray; I, ready for everything without knowing anything; he cultured and I simple; he great and I small; he master and I pupil.

He is the figure and I the shadow.

—Eva Perón, *My Mission in Life* (1951)

I said a lot of things against him especially at the trial, but I will always admire his masculinity. Wow!

—Hedy Lamarr, on the dissolution of her sixth marriage, *Ecstasy and Me: My Life as a Woman* (1966)

5 Flotsam and Peronism in the Novels of Manuel Puig

Gladys Hebe D'Onofrio, the sculptress in Manuel Puig's *The Buenos Aires Affair* (1973), suffers from a tendency to conform to traditional models while a student in art school, to the extent of unconsciously copying the work of established artists. Having withdrawn to the seashore years later to convalesce from a breakdown to which a decade of artistic inactivity has contributed, she finds salvation—not to mention true vocation—in the debris the surf washes up on the sand: "Flotsam [. . .]. That was my work of art, to bring together scorned objects to share with them a moment of life, or life itself" (103). Gladys Hebe D'Onofrio, as it turns out, also is a sexual masochist, who, in likening a forced ravishment to the torture undergone by the martyred Argentine patriots of 1810 (113), finds pleasure to the degree that female submission advances the cause of the nation-state. Drugged, gagged, and bound during the book's climactic mise-en-scène in which she is penetrated at gunpoint, her ecstasy heightened in proportion to the violation suffered, she thrills with patriotic fervor: "Glory to thee, farmer! You forge with your toughness our beloved country's greatness!" (189).

Gladys is not unique among Puig's characters in her recycling of discarded artifacts: the autobiographical Toto of *Betrayed by Rita Hayworth* (*La traición de Rita Hayworth*, 1968), who draws MGM movies on picture cards, and the incarcerated Molina in *Kiss of the Spider Woman* (*El beso de la mujer araña*, 1976), who narrates cheap American "B" movies, engage in similar practices. Yet as Puig's only protagonist to find her professional calling as an artist, and the one whose approach he explicitly cited as sharing ("Brief" 168), Gladys reflects quite accurately the preoccupations with popular culture and political power that so absorbed Puig himself. For, in contrast to the citizens who comprise Dennis Potter's England of the 1930s and 1940s, the immigrants and children of immigrants who make up Puig's Argentina during that same period have no cultural heritage, common or otherwise. Much like Gladys, who scavenges the beach for cultural castoffs, descendants of Italian or Spanish parents who live in small pampas towns are forced to create a language of their own using the only models available—popular songs, women's magazines, American films—however sentimental or clichéd. Refuting the claims of critics who see such castoffs as artifacts of Camp, and contributing to that process of "cultural disburdenment" that Susan Sontag, for one, deemed the most pervasive modern option (*Styles* 167), Puig portrays them as culturally constructive, as evidenced by the popular genres copied in his own work—the *novela policial* (detective novel) in *The Buenos Aires Affair*, the *folletín* (serialized novel) in *Heartbreak Tango* (*Boquitas pintadas*, 1969)—parody being a word he shunned throughout his life.[1]

With the introduction of Perón and Peronism as backdrop to *The Buenos Aires Affair*, and the explicit consideration of political oppression in *Kiss of the Spider Woman* and *Pubis Angelical* (1979), however, popular culture imported from abroad becomes juxtaposed against an indigenous populism as vehicles for promoting a shared cultural heritage among Argentines of the lower and middle classes. Gladys thus celebrates the overthrow of Perón in 1955 because it prevents further suspension of American films and French fashion magazines. To both phenomena Puig ascribes gendered characteristics: politics depicted as a masculine enterprise, as evidenced by the patriarchal state founded upon the heterosexual family unit; moviegoing as a feminine pursuit, as exemplified by the homosexual Molina, who embellishes movie narratives as sumptuously as he once did window displays. Yet to the extent that the machismo underlying political domination also emanates from Hollywood's "*Fábrica de Sueños*" or "Dream Factory" (*Pubis* 109),[2] American movies typify the kind of "industrially produced fiction" condemned by Ariel Dorfman for teaching people "how not to rebel" (*Empire's* ix)—or, in Puig's terms, how to submit.

In exploring this conflation of what before had been portrayed as competing discourses, I want to focus especially on *Pubis Angelical.* Set in 1975 during the brief reign of Perón's third wife, Isabel, and detailing the story of the Argentine exile Ana, who, while being treated in a Mexican hospital for a cancerous tumor, projects her experiences as a romance novel of the 1930s–40s and a science fiction narrative of the not-too-distant future, the book is modeled on two imported artifacts of American popular culture: Hedy Lamarr's (ghostwritten) autobiography, *Ecstasy and Me: My Life as a Woman* (1966), and George Lucas's *THX 1138* (1970). Escapist in that these projections of imaginative flotsam arise in response to pressure from a former lover to involve herself in Peronist intrigue, they nonetheless reflect accurately Ana's obsession with finding an idealized *"hombre superior."* Yet overshadowing this tale of a woman who searches for a "superior man" throughout her life is the saga of another *"semidiosa de Hollywood,"*[3] Eva Perón, whose (ghostwritten) autobiography, *My Mission in Life* (*La razón de mi vida,* 1951), attests to that same search—indeed, whose place in the Peronist movement was based on an acknowledgment of inherent gender differences and the necessity for feminine submission. With the suggestion that this self-styled "Bridge of Love" became a congressionally anointed "Spiritual Leader of the Nation" by virtue of joining cloying movie melodrama, on the one hand, and patriotic renunciation, on the other, the forces that had originated in Puig's work as opposed vehicles for joining individuals into a collective whole emerge as variations on a single theme.

MGM Machismo

Deemed "the poor man's entertainment," as one United Artists representative put it (qtd. in de Usabel 12), in a country that, excluding Brazil, had more movie houses than all of Latin America combined, film occupied a pivotal position in Juan Perón's nationalization of industry. Beginning while Perón was still secretary of labor and social welfare, and extending into the years of his first presidency (1946–52), increasingly stringent decrees were passed that, among other things, required theaters to show a minimum number of Argentine films (even when the number in question exceeded the number of native films actually made), granted tax rebates to operators in proportion to the percentage of Argentine films exhibited, and placed exhibition of Argentine films on the same percentage basis as American films. By 1948, revenues accrued by foreign films distributed in Argentina were frozen and import permits were reduced to one-quarter of the films distributed the previous year (de Usabel 178–82, 229–38). Yet in legislating content as well as quotas, these measures differed from those Cinematograph Films Acts introduced in Great Britain during the 1920s and 1930s. Starting in 1947, for instance, 10 percent of all films made were to devote themselves to Argentine themes or adaptations of Argentine authors, using completely Argentine staffs and casts. Films classified as "A" for special artistic merit or national concerns were to receive obligatory exhibition, and production of cheaper films designated "B" became available for state funding (Barnard 48, 41).[4]

In a country long divided between the gaucho culture of the interior and the Europeanized culture of the port bourgeoisie, between oligarchic landed interests and an urban working class comprised by immigrants, such measures addressed a population whose links to the nation had never been particularly stable. By 1914, immigrants and the descendants of immigrants since 1850 constituted 80 percent of the population, less than 5 percent of whom took citizenship between 1850 and 1930 (Rock, *Argentina* 166, 143). Directed specifically at an American film industry that had been targeting non-European markets as key to its expansion ever since 1916, and Argentina in particular as one of the two main points of entry to South America, the measures reflected an equally long history of bilateral trade inequities, as evidenced by the closure of American markets to Argentine wool after the Civil War and their longstanding refusal to accept Argentine grain and beef. The incorporation of United Artists as Los Artistas Unidos de Sur América in 1931, then, just continued an invasion of Argentine soil by American companies already initiated by the Chicago meat-packing plants in the 1910s and Standard Oil in the 1920s.[5]

Perón's was not the first era in which film had occasioned nationalist outrage, however. Condemned as "weapon[s] of social corruption" by right-wing Nationalists in the 1930s, American films evoked all the xenophobia that an industry allegedly run by "nation-less Jews" could for those desperate to establish a uniquely Argentine sense of *hispanidad* or essence (qtd. in Rock, *Authoritarian* 24). This was despite the fact that the industry's success during that decade was limited by problems that the conversion to sound had created in Spanish-speaking countries: superimposed titles perceived as interrupting action sequences (when read at all in a country of widespread illiteracy), dubbing rejected because of inauthentic accents (Argentina's *rioplatense* dialect being especially difficult to duplicate properly), efforts at Pan-American awareness (such as the 1939 *Juárez*) dismissed as historically naive, reshot American films with Spanish-speaking casts proving too expensive to continue. What distinguished the industry nationalization introduced by Perón in the 1940s was the way its regulation of film confirmed the replacement of Great Britain by the United States as chief economic bogeyman to the Argentine nation-state.[6] Not that much confirmation was needed by the time the first legislation was passed in 1944. With the embargo of raw film stock from the United States, on which the Argentine industry had become completely dependent during World War II, imposed in response to Argentina's refusal to cut diplomatic relations with the Axis powers, and the deliberate buildup of the Mexican industry by the newly formed Office of the Coordinator for Inter-American Affairs, the country considered the leader in Latin American film production in 1939 was well on its way to the twenty-two-movie annual low it would reach in 1945.[7]

The movie-mad characters who swap film reviews as avidly as recipes in Puig's first novels remain blissfully unconcerned with Argentine politics, nationalist or otherwise. The one exception, as critics have noted (Bacarisse, "Projection" 188; Mac Adam 58–59), is Esther Castagno, the scholarship student in *Betrayed by Rita Hayworth* who, not unlike the Oxford educated Potter, attends "an illustrious high school for rich people" (164) during the period in which Perón's first presidency was being compared to Britain's postwar welfare state. What critics tend to neglect, though, is the way Esther's treacly diary entries of 1947 present her zeal for Perón as being in inverse proportion to her Hollywood-infused fantasies about Toto's cousin Héctor. Indeed, for all the reverence the name Perón evokes as the "word [in which] the heart of a nation is contained" (167), it is the matinée heartthrob Héctor whose name sends the fourteen-year-old into sheer rapture: "Hector, I want to change your name . . . Jasper, or Joseph, or James, don't you see why? Because that way your name will begin with J, like joy. . . ." (169). More to the point, the Sundays that her activist brother-in-law wants "young people to lock themselves up with a committee" are the same days that Esther yearns to join her private school classmates in "the majestic lobby of the most splendid movie theater in Buenos Aires" (174, 172), after which she will retire with her beloved to a milk bar, à la *Date with Judy,* for coffee and "two American-style pancakes" (173). It is only after Toto preempts her "first date with life" by cruelly recalling her class status as " 'riff-raff' " that Esther immerses herself completely in the Peronist movement (172, 178), her final glorification of those dental procedures and peritonitis operations at the heart of the new worker state the direct result of an enforced realization that, as far as her celluloid-induced fantasies are concerned, "[m]y neighbors and I can't touch the stars" (179).

This is not to suggest that Peronism has no place in the fantasies of those other characters whose individual narratives make up Puig's first novel. Toto's reworking of *The Great Waltz* (1938), a Johann Strauss biopic, as "The Movie I Liked Best" in the chapter that follows Esther's diary borrows from Perón in fabricating a "Duke of Hagenbruhl" army officer who, at the beginning of the movie, is "the hope of the Austrian Empire" when Vienna is in political disarray and people are clamoring for bread, and who, by the end, has become "a model emperor who has brought prosperity to his people" (185, 195).[8] Rather, it is to suggest that the alternative that movies provide for Toto is less to the Peronist politics he is too young to appreciate fully and more to the barren landscape of Coronel Vallejos and the machismo ethos of his father, Berto, that constitute his more immediate surroundings. Thus, as Emir Rodríguez Monegal recognized in an important early article, "it is not movie-going in itself that alienates, but rather that movie-going is symptomatic of alienation," an alienation "which has other, deeper causes" ("Literary" 64). When Berto threatens to " 'break [Toto] in two' " for interrupting the siesta during which he and his wife make love, Toto opts for thinking about *Romeo and Juliet* and his infatuation with its star Norma Shearer (28).

Yet the film that best reflects Toto's wish to escape such oppressive conditions also illustrates the problems with assuming that American popular culture offers any alternative to them. Suggested by "romances and incidents in the life of America's greatest showman," as its stylized Broadway credits assert, *The Great Ziegfeld* (1936) is viewed by Toto as a testament to all the glamour that is missing from pampas "dry as rock" and a village without a single green leaf (142–43, 220)—it is, in fact, the film he cites in 1943 as the one movie he'd like to see again (107–8). Reconceived by Toto to include a friend's uncle who, with the help of a solicitous bellboy, saves Luise Rainer from dying in her elegant hotel, it also serves as a modified escapist projection: escapist in that imagining the couple taking the bellboy (who is Toto) away with them to a snowy forest cabin will remove him from a stepfather who (like Berto) is presented as abusive; modified in that the fantasy is curtailed by Toto's consciousness that the uncle's marriage in real life to his friend's aunt prohibits him from running off with Luise Rainer.

What he remains unconscious of, however, is the degree to which the film meant to celebrate a "love of beauty [that] could never be cheap or common," as incarnated in those Follies devoted to "glorifying the American girl," does quite the opposite. It is not so much a question of the spectacular Follies numbers appearing today as monumental examples of kitsch—that the set for "A Pretty Girl Is Like a Melody" looks like a giant meringue rather than an expression of Ziegfeld's untrammeled aestheticism ("I've got to have more steps. I need more steps. I've got to get higher, higher!"), or that the costumes on parade in "You Never Looked So Beautiful Before" resemble an endless cavalcade of tin foil. It is more a question of the glorification of women on display depending on a complete erasure of any individualizing traits by an impresario whose "sublime superiority" (his wife's words) allows him to be father, philanderer, and financier all at once. In this sense, Ziegfeld more than makes good on the promise he makes at the beginning of the film, when he tells a young child, "I'm going to take all the beautiful little girls like you and I'm going to put them together and make pictures with them." In the shift from the petulant solos of Rainer's Anna Held to the Busby Berkeley–inspired "You Gotta Pull Strings" to the final tableau that opens "A Circus Must Be Different in a Ziegfeld Show," the American woman steadily devolves from clotheshorse (Anna Held demanding gowns like Lillian Russell's) to clothes hanger (expressionless clones immobilized in close-ups). As a result, for all its expensive trappings, the circus finale presented as the apotheosis of Ziegfeld's vision expresses much the same stance as the first exhibition he stages at the 1893 Chicago World's Fair, in which the dumbbell hoist by a strongman is revealed to contain two "other dumbbells," in the form of two women, which prompts their barker to acclaim, "Aren't they beautiful? Aren't they glorious?"

This connection between the machismo that underlies Argentine nationalism and the machismo that underlies American popular culture is made even more apparent in *Kiss of the Spider Woman* when Molina, echoing Toto, presents his own version of the one film he would choose "to see all over again" to his Marxist cellmate, Valentín (56).[9] A Nazi movie that details the story of Leni Lamaison, a cabaret singer, who, with the help of a handsome German officer, learns to love the invader of France as its savior, *Her Real Glory* (*Destino* in the original Spanish) makes it abundantly clear that the place of women in the German Fatherland really *is* in *la maison*. As the studio "press-book" created by Puig for the invented film indicates:

> "Our idea of beauty must forever be one of healthy fitness," so our Leader has stated, and more specifically as applied to women, "Her single mission is to be beautiful and bear the sons of the world. [. . .] Because there is no place for women in politics within the ideological context of National Socialism, inasmuch as to drag women into the parliamentary sphere, where they pale, is to rob them of their dignity. The German renaissance is a masculine undertaking [. . .]." (84–85)

Such an invocation of separate spheres was hardly exclusive to Nazism, of course. The virility-obsessed Theodore Roosevelt adhered to much the same principles when assigning to women the role of multiple babymaker in his essay on "National Duties," banishing "the wilfully barren woman" from any place in the social community (*Strenuous* 230). And, in fact, the studies of Otto Rank and Dennis Altman that Puig footnotes posit *all* "powerful system[s] of state run by men" as "prolongation[s] of the same primary repression [paternal domination], whose purpose is the increasingly pronounced exclusion of women," who must, "for economic ends and for purposes of defense," produce a large quantity of children (152).[10] Yet, in Puig's work, the German Leader whose power is depicted as residing in " 'authoritarian government rooted solidly in the people itself' " (94) is also meant to recall the specific Argentine Líder whose authority derived from the same power base and whose praise of women was predicated on the family remaining the foundational unit of the nation-state: "To dignify woman morally and materially is to infuse vigour into family life. To infuse vigour into family life is to strengthen the Nation, of which it is the living cell" (J. Perón 40).

At the same time, as Suzanne Jill Levine astutely points out (262), in loosely modeling his Nazi movie on a 1942 Zarah Leander revue film, *Die grosse Lieb (The Great Love)*, Puig's work also recalls the star-studded extravaganzas of Hollywood's studio system. It was these films that, in managing audience desire through the choreographing of what Siegfried Kracauer earlier termed "mass ornaments" (66–70), served as one prototype for those entertainment vehicles that comprised nearly half the Third Reich's feature filmmaking efforts.[11] Joseph Goebbels's 17 March 1936 diary entry thus commended *Broadway Melody of 1936:* "Fluid, made with great tempo. The Americans are good at this. The content may be utter nonsense, but the way they do things is really something" (qtd. in Rentschler 109). Because "the way" in question, as Karsten Witte has argued (251), generally involved taming unacceptable erotic desires through the desublimation of marriage (in the case of the American films) and "desexualiz[ation] to the point of complete self-sacrifice" (in the case of the German films), Molina's infatuation with *Her Real Glory* is perfectly consistent with his attraction to all those American movies he narrates, even the cheesy ones. The conquering hero "whose love of country makes him invincible, like a god," in the lavish German film acts no differently from the patriarch who colonizes the tropical island of the Val Lewton–inspired zombie film (55, 185). The Alsatian chanteuse whose "destino" is to take a bullet in the chest for the Fatherland acts no differently from the American wife whose role requires her to take a poisoned dagger in the heart from her husband—the commemoration of one as a statue and transformation of the other into a zombie just literalizes the abnegation of will that has characterized their relations with men all along.

As Rainer's portrayal of Strauss's wife illustrates, submission could also be a powerful tool of manipulation. In *The Great Waltz*, it is her enumeration of the myriad ways the composer will need tending that creates doubts in the mind of the manipulative diva to whom she has just (selflessly) ceded him. And Puig's titling his first novel after the *femme fatale* played by Rita Hayworth in *Blood and Sand* (1941) indicates his awareness that renunciation in midcentury American movies could be challenged by the subversive sexuality of some stars and the oppositional ideological positions embodied by others.[12] As far as his characters are concerned, however, the description of zombies who "never complain, because zombies can't talk, they haven't any will left and the only thing they get to do is obey and suffer" (167) does encapsulate the traits shared by those venerated MGM actresses whose excessive glamour was part and parcel of their protagonists' excessive pain: Rainer's abandoned waifs in the Strauss and Ziegfeld biopics ("I have lived all these weeks with a knife in my heart. I am content to leave it there. For his sake," "Maybe you'll have to work a little and to suffer a little. But what is that?"), Garbo's suicidal dancer in *Grand Hotel* ("That's what it comes to at last. You die. I'm not going to wait" [1932]) and stricken courtesan in *Camille* ("It's my heart. It's not used to being happy" [1936]), even Hayworth's abused siren in *Gilda* ("You wouldn't think one woman could marry two insane men in one lifetime, now would you?" [1946]). For the ever analytical Valentín to ask Molina, near the end of the book, "Whoever put that idea in your head?" in response to the latter's confession of finding pleasure, or "kick," in the fear generated by a man's embrace (244) is to miss the point of all those movies he has had narrated to him. For Molina to accept that conjugal dynamic as "the natural thing, because that makes him [the husband] the . . . the man of the house" (244) is to fall prey to the ideology to which Puig admitted subscribing in his youth, a belief in "Clark Gable as a force of Nature," rather than Clark Gable as a "historical-cultural product" ("Interview" [1977] 61).

Viewing the movies meant to extricate Molina emotionally from the cell in which he and Valentín are imprisoned as only reinforcing the terms of that same incarceration means reading *Kiss of the Spider Woman* in a way antithetical to those critics who see in the men's physical union a relinquishing of identity based on sexual practices and a transcendence of all oppression based on gender.[13] Valentín explicitly alludes to such a possibility when he compares the men's habitat to a desert island on which they can "make any damn thing" out of their relationship because "outside of this cell we may have our oppressors," but "[h]ere no one oppresses the other" (202). Yet with Valentín's continued physical relations with Molina compromised by his desire to get the soon-to-be-paroled window dresser to take a message to his revolutionary comrades, and Molina's maternal care of Valentín compromised by the authority that the possession of foodstuffs affords him, there is no way that the cell they inhabit ever can be the isolated *Enchanted Cottage* (1944) of Robert Young and Dorothy McGuire. All there is, and continues to be, is an oppressor and an oppressed, constantly reversing, in a prison cell that Puig, speaking in the guise of invented doctor Anneli Taube, defines as the basic division of roles in "every social cell" (209–10). And all there is, in the end, is a deeper internalization of those gender-inflected roles, as evidenced by the morphine-induced ravings of Valentín that conclude the book, in which the various figures of Molina's films coalesce in the form of Valentín's girlfriend, whose murmured " '*I live deep inside your thoughts and so I'll always remain with you, you'll never be alone*' " is as chilling as any torture he has undergone at the hands of Isabelita's government (281).

Don't Die on Me, Argentina

Imprisoned in a Mexico City hospital, awaiting the results of cancer surgery, the bourgeois Ana of *Pubis Angelical* internalizes those gender-inflected roles in much the same way as Molina and Valentín. Indeed, for all the affected British idioms ("take tea" instead of "drink milk," "have a meal" instead of "have dinner"[39–42]), devotion to haute couture ("Saint-Laurent is a danger for the world" [84]), and allusions to high culture (notably the Teatro Colón) that permeate her conversations with others, Ana's diary entries reveal her familial home to have been "just like all the others from the middle class" and her pleasure in "watching love films" to be like that of "almost everyone else" (60, 166). Accordingly, despite an acrimonious divorce, an adulterous affair gone sour, and a dangerous liaison that has forced her into exile, she continues in her obsession with finding—or, more to the point, waiting for—a "man who'll be worth my time" (13), a "superior man" (77, 194), a "superexceptional person" (84), a "Prince Charming" (165), all the while wondering, in an echo of the question Valentín poses to Molina, "Why am I so foolish? who has put that in my head?" (166).

Given the fact that the majority of *Pubis Angelical* takes place in Ana's head, Puig provides readers with the opportunity to answer that very question, albeit not very easily, since the novel is composed of three interwoven narratives: the story of Ana's hospitalization that takes place in 1975, a 1930s–40s romance that depicts the saga of a Hollywood movie queen, and a post-atomic-age tale of a young sexual conscript who may well be the movie queen's lost descendant. Yet for all the complexity of this narrative juggling act, very little actually happens in *Pubis Angelical*. The story of Ana that anchors the novel alternates between confessional diary entries and dialogues with visitors, in which she considers topics as diverse as Argentine politics, psychoanalysis, women's rights, and the state of the arts while awaiting news of her prognosis. The heavily plotted romance and science fiction narratives that interrupt these entries and dialogues—which include all the twists and turns that tales of espionage and entanglement demand—emanate as imaginative projections in which Ana can escape or address the issues that are raised consciously. Therefore, with the exception of those dialogues that Ana has with a feminist friend and a former lover, *all* of the novel may be considered the product of Ana's proverbial head.

Because of this self-reflective component, Ana, unlike Molina, is able to connect her passivity with men to the kind of spectatorial stance that moviegoing has inculcated, "[b]ecause to shut your eyes and imagine things while a man is embracing you, it's as if you were watching a show" (166). Likewise, she can connect the personal and the political in the abstract in that she knows "a man, even if he doesn't threaten to, can still beat you, and he's much stronger" (74), and that, projected from patriarchal aggression to state-sanctioned totalitarianism, there is no difference between "Hitler and a hysterical husband who comes home drunk and abuses his family" (198). She just refuses to see these abstract postulations as being in any way applicable to her own circumstances. "Don't say we," she reprimands Pozzi, the Peronist ex-lover who has come to Mexico City to ask her help in the kidnapping of a high-ranking right-wing official, Alejandro, who is besotted with her (27). Insisting that her decision to leave Argentina has been the result of "a personal matter," that she has no sympathy with Pozzi's leftist Peronistas, and that she "never got involved in politics and never will," she adamantly concludes, "I'm not a political exile" (28).

She couldn't be more wrong, of course. For the seemingly apolitical musings on masculine and feminine roles that comprise the majority of Ana's speculations, which posit the difference between men and women as springing from women being "all impulse, all sentiment," and presume "it's bad for women to get it into their heads that they're just like men" (76, 77), virtually duplicate the remarks of another devotee of male superiority whose subscription to separate spheres reinforced the pyramidal model of *verticalidad,* originally adopted by Perón to control the trade unions, that came to underlie the entire Peronist nation-state. Already apparent in the lectures Evita delivered at the Peronista Higher School (later published as *Historia del Peronismo* [1951]), which distinguish women, whose "lives are guided more by the heart than by the mind," from men, who "live according to the way they reason," both the product of Nature's "wisdom" (*History* 18), such rhetoric would become full blown in the autobiography that emphasizes a subject so "driven and guided by my feelings," so constitutionally "disorderly in my way of doing things" (*My Mission* 5, 167), that she is unable even to order properly "these untidy notes of mine" into a narrative that is anything more than "muddled up" (171, 139). Viewed in this context, the modesty with which Evita repeatedly cloaked herself (Van Cleef and Arpels jewels and Dior gowns notwithstanding[14])—"a humble woman of the Argentine people," "a humble woman of this country," "a simple woman of the people" (*History* 9, 24, 28)—is not only a function of her lowly origins, a ploy to enlist those *descamisados* (shirtless ones) who were her political bread and butter. It is equally a function of her gender, placing her in the role of "sparrow" to her husband's "gigantic condor," "shadow" to his "superior presence," finally " 'slave,' " albeit one who has never "felt as free as I do now" (*My Mission* iii, 81, 169), and no less a political ploy in that it became part and parcel of the Peronist Women's Party founded on the qualities of "fanaticism" and "total surrender" (*My Mission* 42–43; "My Message" 57–58).

In drawing this connection between Puig's protagonist and Eva Perón's public persona, it is important to acknowledge that Eva Perón's name never figures into Puig's text directly—a curious omission in this most overtly political of Puig's works, in which the conversations of Ana and Pozzi trace the vagaries of Peronism from the trade unionism that characterized its first phase to the combined right-wing nationalism and left-wing liberationism of the third presidency to the guerrilla activism undertaken in its name during the period in which the novel takes place (94–104).[15] And, admittedly, the construction of Evita's public persona was in large part the product of male ghost- and speechwriters, notably Manuel Penella de Silva, who ascribed Nazism's excesses to a failure to integrate into its regime female sensibilities and believed that humanity's salvation depended on bringing those same sensibilities to bear on policy formation.[16] But in infusing political rhetoric with the hyperbolic language of romance, styling herself "a bridge of love between Perón and my people" (*History* n.pag.), her work "a drop of love falling on that immense muddy ocean which is the world of hatred and strife" (*My Mission* 166), and her fanaticism "a permanent and heroic process of dying" ("My Message" 57), Evita drew upon a discourse peculiar to her own history. An avid reader of *Sintonía* ("the magazine of the heavenly stars and of movie stars") and adolescent admirer of Norma Shearer cinema ("I cannot wear my crown upon my heart" [*Marie Antoinette*, 1938]), this was a woman who went on to broadcast "Heroines of History" radio dramas (1943–45) devoted to, among others, *The Amazon of Destiny* (the Life of the Dauphine), *My Kingdom for a Love Affair* (Elizabeth of England), *A Woman on the Barricades* (Madame Chiang Kai-shek), and *Hallucination* (Rosario López Zelada, Martyr of the Yellow Fever Epidemic).[17] A one-time actress whom Europeans likened to Lana Turner ("Eva Perón," *Time* 14 July 1947: 36), this was a woman whose wake would be filmed by a Twentieth Century–Fox cameraman and released as *And Argentina's heart stopped.*[18]

The 1930s–40s romance that opens Puig's novel partakes of an identical discourse, derived as it is from the Hedy Lamarr autobiography that chronicles "the tragic side of love" as experienced by the actress christened "one of the most beautiful women of the century" (*Ecstasy* 20, 86–87): the suicide of a German aristocrat upon her refusal to marry him; marriage at seventeen to a munitions manufacturer "known and feared in every capital of the world" who holds her captive in a "velvet prison" of Austrian luxury (20, 33); five more marriages, stoically accounted "the price an emotional woman has to pay," finally embraced as the "trials and tribulations" that make people "more understanding of each other" (117, 246). Ana, Puig's protagonist, has no evident access to the ghostwritten memoir. What she does have, however, is a belief that the period between the wars "must have been a good time to be a woman" in that women during that time were "mysterious, languorous, stylized" (17). Reflecting this belief, the projection that opens Puig's novel is filled with the props of American cinema that have contributed to Ana's assumption: mink rugs, ermine stools, porcelain telephones, platinum jewelry boxes. What she also has are reminders of her own physical resemblance to Lamarr and enough information about the actress's first marriage to Fritz Mandl to see its correspondences to her own early union to a well-connected engineer, Fito, who has aspired "to be on good terms with the entire country" (24, 23). And to the extent that the resulting scenario addresses—or, more specifically, redresses—these and other elements of Ana's disappointing romantic history, the projected romance functions as a woman's revenge fantasy, very much in the way that theorists of the genre have postulated (Radway 147–52; Modleski 45–48). Within it the heroine escapes from an industrialist husband (like Fito) who imprisons her on an island off the coast of Vienna (!), tosses overboard the faithless Soviet (the former Trotskyist Pozzi) whose talk of renouncing politics for love masks a plan to lure her into the clutches of his "coreligionists" (66), gets to keep a coat so loaded with jewels that its pockets are fit to bursting (Alejandro's gifts), and, as an extra reward, is endowed with the ability to mind read (a variant of separate spheres' intuition) that, in granting her access to unlimited knowledge, will make her capable of "routing the secret plans of any world power" upon her thirtieth birthday (50).

Yet to the extent that the 1930s–40s narrative appropriates so completely the cinematic conventions of the 1930s–40s love story in which the woman who dares to desire must end badly to pay for her presumption (Doane 96–122), it suggests that the American artifacts that Ana has envisioned as subverting the patriarchal forces that have defined her own history, and, by extension, that of Argentina, do quite the opposite. If, as feminist film theorists have argued, classical Hollywood cinema solves the threat of castration that the figure of woman on the screen evokes by depriving her of a gaze, transforming her into an object of male scopophilic desire, and then fetishizing her into a figure of reassurance,[19] the introduction of the heroine identified as "el Ama" (the Mistress) and, later, "la actriz" (the actress) combines all these devices into yet another overdetermined mise-en-scène. "[T]he most beautiful woman in the world" awakens from a dream, in which her body has already been nullified by the male doctor who has cut it open (3), to find a note from her husband, the Master, informing her that he has had to narcotize her the previous evening because " 'if your eyes had been watching me, I wouldn't have dared do to you what I have done,' " so unable is he to " 'accept at the same time the challenge of your intellect, as supernatural as your body' " (4, 5).[20] Subsequent details only reinforce this initial denial of female subjectivity. A constant object of male surveillance—by servants her husband hires, by the Soviet agent Theo, ultimately by the Hollywood cameras that turn her into "Miss Star" (89)—she remains forever subservient to masculine viewing. Her narcissism continually magnified by the reflecting surfaces that punctuate her story—the large Venetian mirror of her island captivity (57), the mirrors in Hollywood by which "she lived surrounded" (88), the waters in her Mexican retreat that serve as a "silver mirror" (110, 113), the mural whose audiovisual mechanism enables viewers to see their own faces reflected (106)—the only thing she is shown to look at is herself. Only the image returned is not the ideal self that the Lacanian psychoanalytic theory cited in other portions of Puig's novel presupposes for a unified ego (145–48).[21] The Venetian mirror falls out of its frame and smashes to smithereens, the mural reveals the skulls of dead people, and the waters return such "an usual image of herself" that the Ama/actriz rips off part of her skirt to make a turban in order to disguise the unattractive image that stares back at her (113). Not surprisingly, her refusal to submit to additional psychological fragmentation at the hands of a lover's analyst leads to the final punishment of all: death in a suspicious hit-and-run accident while in the process of making one last escape.

The heroine of the science fiction narrative that constitutes the second imaginative projection cross-cut with Ana's tale fares little better. A sexual conscript who ministers to elderly men at the beginning as part of a compulsory two-year civil service, w218 ends up arrested for the attempted murder of a lover and sentenced to life imprisonment in the desolation of Ices Everlasting, servicing men so contagiously ill as to make any physical contact inevitably fatal. In the case of this projection, however, such a fate is not so much the result of the particular American artifact upon which Puig loosely models it.[22] On the contrary, at the end of George Lucas's *THX 1138,* the eponymous protagonist escapes the prison defined by uniform whiteness to which he has been condemned for the crimes of "drug evasion" and "sexual perversion" by climbing up a ventilation shaft toward a "superstructure" defined by the colors of a giant sun. In so doing, he also escapes, by extension, an Orwellian society whose omniscient god, omm, sanctifies citizens' actions to the degree that they advance the nation-state ("You are a true believer. Blessings of the State. Blessings of the masses. Thou art a subject of the divine, created in the image of man by the masses for the masses. Let us be thankful we have commerce. Buy more. Buy more now. Buy and be happy"). Rather, the fate of Puig's w218 is a function of the very genre in which the projection is cast, which, in the case of American science fiction, first popularized in the 1930s and 1940s as entertainment for adolescent boys and seemingly unchanged in its values until the 1970s, is a genre that has long been accused of never having outgrown its pulp fiction origins. Hence the charges: American science fiction has totally ignored the social structures governing real women's estate (Russ, "Image" 79–94), predicated its futuristic empires on past ones (notably the Roman Empire) that had subordinated women (Sargent 433–41), and assumed as natural a hierarchy of superiors and inferiors, what Ursula K. Le Guin has termed "a perfect baboon patriarchy, with the Alpha Male on top" ("American" 99). Consistent with this bias, THX 1138's female partner, LUH 3417, disappears from the screen after being arrested for an illegal pregnancy, her last known whereabouts given (by a computer) as the reproduction center, where her code is listed as "consumed" and her registration number as reassigned to a parthenogenetic embryo.[23]

Compounding this deterministic edge in Ana's second projection is the fact that the patriarchal predilections of science fiction are melded with those of romance. Like Ana, W218 yearns for a "man of great worth," a "real man" (134), an "ideal man" (154), a "man of her dreams" (155, 163), whose "superior[ity] to herself" would derive from the fact that "[h]e could be the brains of the pair, while she would bring her pleasant personality, and yes, of course, her much-celebrated beauty" (134). Indeed, to the extent that many details of Ana's 1930s–40s romance reappear in the science fiction narrative of the twenty-first century—a heroine with the ability to read minds (more a convention from science fiction that bleeds into the earlier romance) who physically resembles the actress of *Algiers;* a duplicitous spy, LKJS (another Pozzi stand-in), who woos her with fashion and finery from the forbidden 1930s; a love affair conducted by way of reflected gazes—the second projection may be seen as a recasting of the first. But in setting these details of the 1930s–40s love story within the context of a futuristic tale of the Glacial Year 15, the second projection explicitly connects the subjugation of woman in the former to the subjugation of the masses in the latter. Aware, as are all the men in the love story, that "[a] woman who will read the thought of every man who craves her sexually, and allows her to look into his eyes" is "[a] danger to this planet of men," and thus must be "eliminated, or at least kept under control, the control of men," LKJS appreciates in a way the others do not the role she can play in the extension of empire: "It's even possible that we could use her in our own plans for territorial and economic expansion" (205).

Such extension of the patriarchal nation-state, significantly, is a prospect that the second projection depicts as more than just speculative. John Huntington has commented on the imaginative conservatism of science fiction (not to be confused with the political conservatism of some of its practitioners), in which the envisioned future is an extrapolated version of the past: "by relying on traditional literary conventions and forms, and by repeating historical and psychological patterns from the past, it [science fiction] manages to domesticate the future, to render it habitable and, in spite of a somewhat strange surface, basically familiar" (166). This is especially the case with the dystopian form of science fiction that Ana's projection most closely resembles. As Michael Holquist asserts, utopian fiction is a "literature of the subjunctive mood" in that its putative future settings "reverse, however, the artificial time of the grammatical subjunctive which, in most European languages, is some form of the past" and whose value systems typically contrast idealized with nonidealized options (137, 140). True to these conventions, Ana's dystopian narrative portrays two societies: the valley of Urbis (identified by the reader as Mexico City) in which w218 currently resides, and the City of Aquarius (Buenos Aires, "Queen of the River Plate" [165]) in the neighboring Republic of the Waters in which she has been born. Yet with the former portrayed in terms of a repressive Supreme Government that punishes all talk of life before the "polar inundation of years gone by" (135), prohibits all figurative artistic expression (172), and even bans the eating of spaghetti as "inflaming gluttony" (162), and the latter in terms of a " 'Cenacle of Power' " devoted to making women " 'tremble in fear' " before men and into which boys are ceremoniously inducted by the placing of their fathers' hands upon their penises (205–7), the alternative societies depicted are in fact nonalternatives, just two delineations of patriarchy.

The extended ramifications this has for political life in any Latin American country could not be more disheartening. For all her talk about Argentine control versus Mexican spontaneity (122–24), and Argentine aggression versus Mexican compassion (168–69), the country in which Ana has sought shelter from a regime that has raided half the homes of its citizens may be no haven at all. Pozzi, after all, tracks her down there and finds her in what would seem to be the most protected place of all, a hospital bed. And for all his talk about the "national national" Peronism he practices versus the "national [with a 'z'] socialism" of Argentina's current regime (99), the two are but flip sides of the same coin, the kidnappings of the Montonero guerrillas with whom he claims to deal but not be among (102)—a hair-splitting distinction of dubious merit—and the death squads of the Triple A (Argentine Anti-Communist Alliance) equally reprehensible forms of violence masquerading as public service.[24] Calling him a "dupe" and a "dreamer," Ana ascribes Pozzi's Peronist involvement to his being a "romantic" who "imagined Peronism as you pleased, and you got married to it without knowing it first" (126, 125), equating his own naïveté in politics to her own in love: "Just as I got involved in that business of marrying a man whom I didn't really know" (126). Unfortunately, her own exile in Mexico may be equally a matter of delusion. "I'm embarrassed to be a spectator, I want something more," she claims of herself (166). But what? "I would like Argentina to develop," she continues (167). Yet in what way?

Any answers depend on how one reads the separatist call to arms that informs the novel's conclusion, in which an imprisoned, and later mortally infected, w218 of Ices Everlasting becomes the recipient of three orations: a dying man's impassioned prayer that she recognize "that the ideal man whom she longs for . . . she carries within herself" (225), a fellow patient's account of the reincarnation achieved by a woman whose spirit has been embraced by a loving daughter, and an escapee's tale of miraculous transformation, a bodily transformation no less miraculous for causing the soldiers who witness it to cast down their arms in the middle of a bloody civil war.

> Suddenly a strange gust of wind arose and the nightdress was lifted, showing me to be naked, and the men trembled, and it's that they saw I was a divine creature, my pubis was like that of the angels, without down and without sex, smooth. The soldiers were paralyzed with amazement. An angel had descended to the earth. And the shooting stopped, and the enemies embraced one another and cried, giving thanks to the heavens for having sent a message of peace. (231)

Such prophetic utterances, of course, virtually duplicate those liberationist views that Puig expressed in interviews and essays: his belief, following Theodore Roszak, that "the woman most desperately in need of liberation is the woman every man has locked up in the dungeons of his own psyche" ("Interview" [1979] 26); his denial, much like Vidal, of sexual identities based on specific sexual practices ("Losing" 57). Such utterances also turn what had previously been a dystopian projection into the kind of textbook feminist utopia lauded by recent critics of science fiction. If, as Naomi Jacobs claims, the sexuality that limits women's lot in science fiction to that of breeder is imaged in terms of fertile landscapes, and the seemingly sterile fields of ice—as are found in Ursula K. Le Guin's *The Left Hand of Darkness* (1969) and Joan D. Vinge's *The Snow Queen* (1980)—provide "fertile ground for the female imagination and a place where radical confrontations and reconceptualizations become possible" (190), Puig trumps Le Guin in replacing Gethenian androgyny with a total erasure of sexuality. If, as Marleen S. Barr affirms, patriarchy sometimes convinces mothers to destroy their unborn daughters, and the cloning of women—as occurs in Suzy McKee Charnas's *Motherlines* (1978) and Sydney J. Van Scyoc's *Star Mother* (1976)—enables daughters to replicate, if not literally reproduce, their mothers (*Alien* 7, 143), Puig goes further in enabling daughters to reconnect with mothers who have never given birth to them in the first place. The actress whose history w218 looks up in the library, the actress from the 1930s–40s romance, dies more than twenty years before w218's birth.[25] Moreover, in so extensively focusing on female reunion and reconnection, Puig completely inverts the values that had informed Ana's earlier projection. Apropos the cinematic 1930s–40s love story, the romance that opens Puig's novel forgoes motherhood as displacing female desire away from men: the mother of the Ama/actriz tries to kill her, the Ama/actriz puts her daughter up for adoption, the film character played by the Ama/actriz loses her daughter in a roadside accident. The science fiction narrative that ends it inaugurates a matriarchal millennium. A mother who has imagined her daughter a casualty of war discovers that her daughter is alive and well—more than well in that physically transformed into a "pure angel," like herself, she cannot ever "be a slave to the first scoundrel who sensed that weak point between her legs" (232). Ana, who has thought so infrequently about her daughter in Argentina that she cannot remember her and equated talking to women with talking to a flower vase, asks on the last page that her mother and daughter come visit her in Mexico City so that in "talk[ing] to them," they "would understand each other" (236).

A radical feminist revolution. A sexless Second Coming. Not one of which, I would argue, should be seen as a viable blueprint for nationhood.[26] "It is important to know how to *play* utopia," Holquist warns when comparing the representational strategies governing both chess and utopian writing. "[I]n the game of utopia, men may be reduced to pawns for the sake of a better representation; to attempt the same reduction in life leads to the police state" (145). Puig, who viewed his novels as aiming for "a direct reconstruction of reality" ("Cinema" 288), was well aware of the consequences of putting into practice the particular utopian reduction that informs the conclusion to *Pubis Angelical:* he already knew what a maternal "incarnation of Good" chosen "to demonstrate the path to salvation" was like (232). That was the role in which Evita had cast herself—long before official titles anointed her "Lady of Hope," "Mother of the Innocents," "Spiritual Mother of All Argentine Children," and "Spiritual Leader of the Nation"—having once transformed her twenty-four-year-old self into an aging society woman whose good works earn her the name "mother of the poor" in *La Pródiga (The Prodigal),* her final film (Fraser and Navarro 47). Recasting the Argentine nation as a family, her husband as a common father, and herself as "the mother of all the urchins, and of all the weak and the humble of my land," eventually just "the mother of my people" (*My Mission* 64, 213), dispensing her foundation largess to the expectant poor amid the constant flash of photographers and floodlights, simply meant playing the same role on a larger stage. And not even a very original role, recycling as it did the Marie Antoinette of Norma Shearer, running off to a charity benefit under her patronage despite warnings of possible rioting, having discovered true love in the love of her people (or so the movie would have one believe), as the Count Fersen of Tyrone Power predicted she would.

All that changed over the years was the increasing spiritualization of the performance as the debilitating symptoms of the uterine cancer that would kill her left Evita in fact the asexual figure—a veritable pubis angelical—her publicists had tried to manufacture in myth, kissing lepers and syphilitics with the same renunciatory fervor that infuses w218's request to be assigned to the Hospital for the Contagious at the end of Puig's novel. [27] "When the world is justicialist, love will reign . . . and so will peace," declares the autobiographical persona who discovers that she, like "the women of all the earth," has an "instinctive" and "sublime calling" (*My Mission* 173, 196–97). A limitless calling, too, according to the messianic martyr of the dictated deathbed pages who, by that time, had expanded her purview from "the panorama of my own country" to "the panorama of the world," insisting as part of her "Supreme Will" that the "partisan[s]" and "fanatics" of what had since become the "doctrine" of her husband "impose this Peronist truth on the entire world" ("My Message" 67, 91). With this historical backdrop as his legacy, Puig didn't have to look far to answer the question, "what would the world be like made in the image and likeness of woman?" that he has his *Pubis Angelical* protagonist pose. "It *would* be well decorated, at least," as Ana concludes (199; my emphasis)—just like the roof of Evita's foundation, adorned by statues of herself atop each Doric column; just like the unfinished Monument to the *Descamisado*, whose planned 180-foot muscular worker was to be replaced by a towering figure of the first lady. In short, the world created in the image of woman would be no different from the world created in the image of man.

"I'm an Argentine, he said to himself. I am a space with nothing in it, a timeless place, that has no idea where it's going" (337), says the colonel entrusted with disposing of Evita's corpse in Tomás Eloy Martínez's novelistic account of *Santa Evita* (1995). Much the same could be said of all those exiles who populate Puig's works beginning with *Pubis Angelical:* the labor lawyer seeking political asylum in *Eternal Curse on the Reader of These Pages* (*Maldición eterna a quien lea estas páginas,* 1980), the elderly sisters of *Tropical Night Falling* (*Cae la noche tropical,* 1988), his final novel, who emigrate to Brazil to get away from "stinking old Argentina" (34). That Puig portrays this enforced condition as perpetual reflects, no doubt, the circumstances of his own life: censored by the Right and Left in Argentina, banned in Cuba, condemned by feminist groups in Spain, lambasted by militant gays in Brazil; emigration to Mexico City in 1973, New York in 1976, Rio in 1980, finally Cuernavaca in 1989. This is not to suggest that in moving from home to home Puig found no place like home. In that his initial move to Mexico City was occasioned by personal infatuation as well as the necessities of political flight, the man who referred to himself as "a one-man woman, like Helen Morgan," and never renounced his belief in the couple as the preferred social unit, carried with him the same "invisible net[s] of repression" that he intellectually recognized as forming the "cobwebs" of Argentina's collective unconscious. [28]

As his final novel suggests, those cobwebs do not result only when Argentine machismo is crossed with the mores of American popular culture. "COLONIAL ARCHITECTURE MAY LOSE ONE OF ITS MOST BEAUTIFUL MONUMENTS," declares the headline of one of the newspaper articles quoted in *Tropical Night Falling* (52). Detailing the progressive deterioration of "one of the few remnants of colonial architecture," most recently hastened by a fire, the article nevertheless ends with the qualification that, due to the strength of the material used in its construction, "[t]he façade, however, seems to remain solid, [. . .] fueling the hopes of those who support its preservation" (53). Yet this evidence of the continuing Portuguese presence in Brazil pales beside the much more extensive presence alluded to in a later piece on bikini swimwear. " 'Nobody copies anybody, but everybody copies everybody,' " a Brazilian manufacturer is quoted as stating in the article that surveys the new bathing suit collections (59). Only the statement that follows his remark makes it clear that somebody is being copied more than anybody else. As the article goes on to say, the common element in almost all the new collections is the fabric Lycra, "an international product of Du Pont."

"She said you're doing very well. But Westerners don't understand Japanese students' psychology. [. . .] You're good at memorizing, but when I ask you to translate, you haven't understood the content at all. That's no better than a parrot can do. At this rate, your English will never be of any practical use."
—Tanizaki Jun'ichirō, *Naomi* (1924)

"Last week you—I mean we—wrote the copy for that margarine ad. [. . .] But tell me, have you eaten margarine even once in the past couple years?" [. . .]

"It doesn't matter," I said. "It's the same whether we eat margarine or don't. Dull translation jobs or fraudulent copy, it's basically the same. Sure we're tossing out fluff, but tell me, where does anyone deal in words with substance?"
—Murakami Haruki, *A Wild Sheep Chase* (1982)

6 Murakami Haruki's Garbage-Collecting/Snow-Shoveling Consortium

It is no coincidence that the product that prompts two advertising agency owners to discuss translations and copies in Murakami Haruki's *A Wild Sheep Chase* (*Hitsuji o meguru bōken,* 1982) is margarine, since margarine itself can be considered an imitation or copy of butter.[1] Yet butter also forms the root of the Japanese word *batā-kusai,* literally "stinking of butter," which is used to denote those Japanese who attempt to emulate Western styles too closely. Populated as they are with characters who breakfast at Dunkin' Donuts, lunch at McDonald's, and—to pursue the lactose metaphor a bit further—snack at Dairy Queen, Murakami's novels would seem to reek of butter, as critics of his fiction have observed.[2] The narrators whose work often involves promoting such perishable goods in one way or another describe their activities accordingly: "[C]ollecting garbage and shoveling snow," the narrator of *Dance, Dance, Dance*

(*Dansu dansu dansu,* 1988) asserts of the restaurant reviews he writes for women's magazines. "You know, cultural snow" (7).

The quite literal consumption of foods that Boku's[3] efforts are meant to stimulate/simulate is emblematic, of course, of the kind of consumption that dominates any "advanced capitalist society" (*Dance* 11) in which commodified images have replaced actual goods as objects of desire and that has transformed Japan into an "Empire of Signs," to recall Roland Barthes's characterization, or *shōjo* culture, to employ a more recent term.[4] Boku's tale, however, is given a very specific context, 1983–84, the year that witnessed the opening of Tokyo Disneyland on 15 April 1984, and so that consumption of imported foods to which he contributes also is emblematic of a longstanding relationship between two very particular societies. For as the producer of many of those unsatiated appetites, the imported artifacts of American popular culture that pervade Murakami's work—movies and music no less than food—invoke a relationship with the West and modernization that goes back to the 1868 Meiji Restoration, a purchase of cultural artifacts pivotal to the U.S. conceit of the Pacific as an "American Lake" first enunciated by Whitelaw Reid in 1898.[5]

It would be easy to appropriate Dennis Potter's notion of "Occupying Powers" to describe those artifacts of American popular culture since the United States was, after all, the only nation ever to occupy Japan, for however brief a period (1945–52). It would be equally easy to apply Potter's phrase "mimic men" to those elements of the Japanese response that could be construed as slavish imitations or, to recall the words of the Tanizaki headnote, parrotings: "If you keep eating hamburgers, you will become blond!" proclaimed the slogan of the first McDonald's to open in Japan in 1971 (qtd. in Creighton 46). To do so, however, is to presume that exported artifacts retain their original cultural symbolism, which, as critics have argued, is not necessarily the case.[6] More to the point, to do so is to presume that popular culture imported from abroad displaces an indigenous—and preferable for being more authentic—folk culture, even though much that now is viewed as comprising that folk culture originally came to Japan by way of China.

Neither presumption has much validity as far as Murakami or the nation about which he writes is concerned. An author who compares his adolescent immersion in cheap American paperbacks to Manuel Puig's immersion in cheap Hollywood movies, and who modeled one novel, *A Wild Sheep Chase,* on Raymond Chandler's *The Long Goodbye,* and titled another, *Hear the Wind Sing* (*Kaze no uta o kike,* 1979), after a line in a Truman Capote short story, Murakami has always distanced himself from Japanese *junbungaku,* or "pure" literature, as thoroughly as he has shunned the *shōsetsu,* or "I-novel," that is its most typical expression.[7] A nation in which over 90 percent of its inhabitants categorize themselves (rightly or wrongly) as belonging to the middle class, Japan, unlike Potter's England, has no need for a mass medium to minimize class differences. Indeed, as one of the few nations alleged to be ethnically homogeneous, or " 'mono-racial,' " as Murakami puts it (Buruma, "Becoming" 70), Japan already has what Potter would consider a common culture.[8] And that, for Murakami, is precisely the problem. For unlike the notion of *hispanidad*, which never galvanized the Nationalist movement in Argentina beyond a small fraction of the population, the cultural exceptionalism, *Nihonjinron*, that underlies the common culture of Japan and that posits an essentialized ahistorical Japanese identity has yielded a very real history of Japanese imperialism: notably the Pan-Asian colonialism that initiated, as portrayed by *The Wind-Up Bird Chronicle* (*Nejimaki-dori kuronikuru*, 1994–95), a fifteen-year period of war in the 1930s and 1940s. By joining viewers into one big *uchi* (in-group), Japanese television—on which, in Murakami's work, American programs do not appear, contrary to actual practice—actively promotes that ahistorical consensus. American movies, by contrast, promote historical consciousness—admittedly, a consciousness defined by tremendous slippage, as different movies in Murakami's work can morph into each other by virtue of having the same actress as star—but a sensibility that nevertheless serves as a form of resistance by giving play to individual subjectivity and imagination.

A Delicate Balance

When Commodore Matthew Perry announced his 1853 arrival at Edo Bay with the words, "we didn't come here to fight but to trade" (qtd. in Brannen 628), he could not have realized how much the two activities he juxtaposed against each other would become synonymous a century later or that identities would be exchanged as well as items. Such exchanges have involved more than mere fashions, as occurred, for instance, when ballroom dancing swept Japan in the 1870s and jazz was introduced in the 1920s. For scholars who find the identity of Japan as a nation-state to have originated as an entirely modern response to the threat of Western domination, and even go so far as to contend that the discursive unities of Japanese culture, language, and ethnicity did not exist until the eighteenth century (Sakai 121), they concern the construction of Japan and the United States as "national-cultural imaginaries" (Ivy, *Discourses* 3). As such, the dialectical relationship between the two—whether expressed in terms of self and Other, *wa* and *yō*, or *uchi* and *soto*—is one of continual fluctuation. And their interactions—whether denoted as "transaction," "domestication," or

"internationalization" *(kokusaika)*—are debated to the degree that they produce a "vulgarization" of the East or a "Japanization" of the West.[9]

I write on the day that the *New York Times* front page disclosed the suicide
rate in Japan to be reaching record numbers as people are increasingly throw-
ing themselves in front of trains, jumping off cliffs, or hanging themselves in
response to the cumulative impact produced by the 1990 burst of Japan's economic bubble.[10] But I want to begin my discussion of Murakami with a return
to the years just preceding that pivotal one since his perspective, which entails
destabilizing the Japanese-American dialectic, appears all the more distinctive
when set against texts that depended on maintaining it in order to cope with
the worst years of the trade imbalance.

Nothing in 1989 seemed to symbolize that trade imbalance more than the
purchase of Columbia Pictures Entertainment by Sony Corporation for $3.4
billion.[11] An acquisition particularly threatening to American sensibilities, its
linkage of hardware and software manufacturing in conformance with economics synergy theory was perceived as completely upsetting what Marilyn
Ivy has called the "division of mass cultural labor" ("Formations" 257) upon
which American self-esteem in the years of $50 billion trade deficits had rested:
the consoling belief that "economic prowess does not necessarily entail cultural
dominance" (Ching 200). It did not matter that the primary motive behind the
acquisition still centered around high-tech hardware, specifically HDTV (high-
definition television), for which Sony planned to produce movies so as to avoid
a repeat of its mid-1980s financial nose dive after Betamax lost out to VHS in
consumer videocassette recorder preferences. Nor did it matter that the studio in question, whose moviemaking unit had been floundering for years, remained managed by Americans, that the purchaser was considered the most
Westernized company in Japan ("'almost an American company'" according
to one *U.S. News and World Report* source [Egan 35]), or that the history of
the Japanese in Hollywood had been dismal in the past.[12] Coming two years
after Sony bought CBS records for $2 billion and just two weeks after Australia's
Qintex Group agreed to purchase MGM/UA Communications for $1.45 billion
(Fabrikant A1), Japan's acquiring part of the second largest U.S. export industry of entertainment (from quintessentially American Coca-Cola, no less) after
key technology of the first, aerospace, had already been surrendered as part of
the controversial FSX deal was reported as transgressing the boundaries of mere
economics and undermining the very tenets of American identity: "this time
the Japanese hadn't just snapped up another building; they had bought a piece
of America's soul" (J. Schwartz 62). Not only that, they even had bought land
on which to bury it—in Oxnard, California, beneath a planned theme park to
be called Sonyland.[13]

As holiday headliners became Thanksgiving turkeys (*Hudson Hawk* losing thirty-five million dollars, *Last Action Hero* over three times that amount[14]), and as fiscal redeemers awaited one year were consigned to fiscal purgatory the next (*Mary Shelley's Frankenstein* a "potential commercial and critical success" in 1994, another "expensive dud" in 1995[15]), it became apparent that xenophobic fears for America's soul were premature. Declarations of "From Walkman to Showman" (*Time* [Oct. 1989]) were replaced by doubts of "They Can Make a Walkman, But Can They Make a Batman?" (*Fortune* [June 1995]); the courtship of "*When Columbia Met Sony . . . A Love Story*" (*Business Week* [Oct. 1989]) by laments over "Sony's Heartaches in Hollywood" (*Business Week* [Dec. 1994]); and, most dramatically, the nightmare of "Japan Invades Hollywood" (*Newsweek* [Oct. 1989]) by odes to "Sony's Bad Dream" (*New Yorker* [Feb. 1994]).[16] Unable to eulogize in 1989, however, the media were forced to neutralize the very problem they reported. Some offered reminders of Japan's premodern status, as occurred when the *Atlantic Monthly* illustrated James Fallows's piece on "Containing Japan" (May 1989) with cartoons of *sumo* wrestlers. Others reasserted Western cultural dominance, as occurred when *Newsweek*'s story of the Columbia acquisition invoked that gendered binary long used to delineate dominance of all sorts and displayed a geisha holding the Statue of Liberty's torch on its 9 October cover ("Japan Invades Hollywood").

Significantly, this was a binary employed by Japanese as well as Western writers, as was confirmed by another 1989 media event, the release of a bootlegged translation of *The Japan That Can Say No*, coauthored by Sony chair Morita Akio and Liberal Democratic Party conservative Ishihara Shintaro.[17] Within this work, Japanese who refused to take advantage of the "technology card" (43) that semiconductor sales had given them in the manufacture of nuclear weapons were alternately depicted as unmanned ("like a stud poker player with an ace in the hole who habitually folds his hand" [43]) or simply feminine ("a kept woman, afraid the man will kick her out" [76]).[18] Therefore, if Theodore H. White alerted readers to the economic "Danger from Japan" in 1985 by portraying Japan as a serial rapist—its Ministry of International Trade and Industry "target[ing] the countries and markets to be penetrated" (38), its capital "moving from penetration to control" (38)—and the United States as an unsuspecting "assembly of consumers" that cannot "resist Japanese penetration" (40), *Newsweek*'s replacing Columbia's logo with a geisha in 1989 inverted White's earlier depiction. A figure who not only is unable to penetrate, the geisha is a courtesan specifically intended for penetration. A figure in old-fashioned garb, she also reminded readers of where in the modernity hierarchy Japan deserved to be placed.

Published in 1985, the year the Commerce Department declared the United States a debtor nation, Murakami's "The Elephant Vanishes" ("Zō no shō-metsu"), in contrast, avoids binaries in favor of blendings. At first, the opposite would seem to be the case, as an opening paragraph that cites newspaper accounts of "the trade friction with America" is offset by the narrator's own account of working for a major electronics manufacturer that insists that the room in which its coordinated appliances are meant to go be denoted in English as " '*kit-chin*' " (*Elephant* 308, 320). Undermining this portrait of Japanese economic supremacy countered by continued American cultural supremacy, however, is the event to which the title of the short story refers: the disappearance of an elephant from a zoo in a Tokyo suburb. An image that appears in Murakami's work frequently, the elephant—here an "awfully old elephant" and "feeble old thing" (309, 310)—is associated, as in the West, with the past, which Murakami defines broadly as any period that precedes the postmodern present. Yet in "The Elephant Vanishes," the elephant's identity also is defined with respect to that of the keeper to whom it has been attached—quite literally, by virtue of adjoining domiciles—for ten years. What enables both to disappear, according to the narrator, who is the last person to have seen them before they vanish, is a shift in the size of their respective bodies: " 'The balance seemed to have changed somewhat. I had the feeling that to some extent the difference between them had shrunk' " (325). A function of the narrator's perception, the imagined relationship between elephant and keeper mirrors that between the two nations alluded to in the story's first paragraphs; its collapse makes him think that "things around me have lost their proper balance" (327). That loss, in turn, signals an end to an era for the narrator. He concludes his tale of elephant and keeper who have "vanished completely" by asserting "[t]hey will never be coming back" (327) and announcing the onset of a "new order," one defined, like the coordinated appliances he sells, by the quality of "unity": "Unity of design. Unity of color. Unity of function" (326, 327).

This refusal of Murakami to delineate the Japanese-American dynamic as one of binarism can be explained in several ways. Reflecting the underlying assumptions of Pacific Rim discourse, in which interpenetrating global connections make meaningless all notions of centers and peripheries (Connery 32), for example, it can be seen as emerging from specific contemporary conditions, and the shift in "The Elephant Vanishes" from old to "new order" interpreted as a shift from artifacts in which vestiges of national-cultural pasts are identifiable to artifacts in which all such distinguishing elements are erased. The home of the right-wing Boss that Boku visits in *A Wild Sheep Chase* encapsulates a history of Japan's encounters with the West: a "Meiji-era Western-style manor" adjacent to a "traditional one-story Japanese-style villa" on one side and attached on the other to a wing whose design incarnates a " 'mutual opposition of ideologies,' " a "triple-feature-plus-coming-attractions mélange of a house" that "had evolved blindly, toward who knows what end" (69). The renovated Dolphin Hotel to which Boku journeys in the sequel, *Dance, Dance, Dance,* displays attractions that have already arrived: "a gleaming twenty-six-story Bauhaus Modern–Art Deco symphony of glass and steel, with flags of various nations waving along the driveway, smartly uniformed doormen hailing taxis, a glass elevator shooting up to a penthouse apartment" (21), the Bonaventure Hotel of Los Angeles beamed down onto remote Hokkaido.[19]

Yet the more important reason for Murakami's repudiation of binarism as a means of delineating Japan's connection to the West stems from his recognition that binary oppositions tell only half the story for a nation whose identity derives as much from its relationship—also fluctuating—to China as it does from its relationship to the United States. Therefore, in "A Slow Boat to China" ("Chūgoku-yuki no surō bōto," 1980), the narrator's attempts to determine with certainty what distinguishes Chinese from Japanese fail dismally. He observes the behavioral traits of Chinese classmates but decides "[t]hey were as different from each other as could be, and in that way they were the same as us" (*Elephant* 225). He considers the background of a coworker but discovers that her experiences do not match her ethnicity: "Although Chinese, she herself was Japanese-born and had never once been to China or Hong Kong or Taiwan. Plus, she'd gone to Japanese schools, not Chinese. Hardly spoke a word of Chinese, but was strong in English" (227). Forced to realize that not even empirical research and reading can define what is, in effect, an imaginary community, he learns to satisfy himself with "only my China," "the China that sends messages just to me," not "the big yellow expanse on the globe" but "a part of myself that's been cut off by the word *China*" (238–39).

Poised, then, between the East, represented by China, and the West, represented by the United States, Japan comes into existence by way of a triangular set of interactions. Nowhere does Murakami present this triangular relationship more clearly than in the scene in *Hard-Boiled Wonderland and the End of the World* (*Sekai no owari to hādo-boirudo wandārando,* 1985) in which the narrator reads about the history of the unicorn. An "evolutionary orphan" that, like Japan, has been able to survive by virtue of its isolation (98), the unicorn portrayed in literature conforms to two different types: one Western, originating in Greece, distinguished by a two-cubit-long horn and, consistent with such a defining trait, a masculine penchant for young virgins; the other Chinese, a herbivore of shorter horn, alleged to have caused Genghis Khan to desist in his planned invasion of India. "In the East, peace and tranquility; in the West, aggression and lust," Murakami summarizes, only to end with the caveat: "Nonetheless, the unicorn remains an imaginary animal, an invention that can embody any value one wishes to project" (97).

A critical passage in Murakami's fiction, this projection of Japan as both subject and object of aggression has important ramifications with respect to how Japan's unique heritage as colonized and colonizer is judged. In *A Wild Sheep Chase*, for instance, the titular animal that forms the object of the narrator's pursuit is introduced as an emblem of Japan's enforced modernization. Creatures with " 'no historical connection with the daily life of the Japanese' " prior to the end of the late feudal period, sheep first are imported from America during the Ansei period (1854–60), bred, and then ignored after the Second World War: " 'A tragic animal,' " " 'the very image of modern Japan' " (111). As Murakami later reveals, though, one reason why sheep continue to have no connection to Japanese daily life is because they are bred in response to the military's need for thermal wool to clothe those soldiers being trained for upcoming continental military campaigns—specifically, the Russo-Japanese War of 1904–5 (205) and, after that, the North China campaign of the 1930s (180). Thus, the Sheep Professor who is asked by the army to draw up a plan for " 'ovine productivity in Japan, Manchuria, and Mongolia' " and bred in his turn to be " 'the standard-bearer of agricultural administration for tomorrow's East Asia' " (180, 182)—an ovine analogue of Japan's Greater East Asia Co-Prosperity Sphere—is asked to colonize China in much the same way that America has colonized Japan. Or so it would seem.

Scholars who study the history of Japanese imperialism place great emphasis on this analogical point in explaining Japanese aggression as, simultaneously, a response to—even imitation of—Western aggression and a precursor—even emblem—of liberation in Eastern Asia. His qualifications notwithstanding—the admission that Japanese aggression was the earliest non-Western case of modern imperialism, the acknowledgment of the "brute militarism" that rapidly came to overwhelm it—Masao Miyoshi, for example, still argues that "this aggression also contained a nativist program of fighting back against the Western conquest" (41, 40). Contending that "it is not impossible to discern in the struggle signs of reactive, counter-contestational will and energy," he goes on to assert that through that struggle Japan became "a model for other independence-movement leaders" (41).[20] And Murakami does in fact incorporate this very argument into his work when relating the rationale behind the 1932 creation in Manchuria of Manchukuo, "the great guinea pig of Asia," as John Gunther disparagingly put it (143).

Ishiwara was of the opinion that Japan should not turn Manchukuo into another undisguised Japanese colony, such as Korea or Taiwan, and should instead make Manchukuo a new model Asian nation. In his recognition that Manchukuo would ultimately serve as a logistical base for war against the Soviet Union—and even against the United States and England—Ishiwara was, however, admirably realistic. He believed that Japan was now the only Asian nation with the capability of fighting the coming war against the West (or, as he called it, the "Final War") and that the other countries had the duty to *cooperate* with Japan for their own liberation from the West. (*Wind-Up* 500)

Only Murakami rejects this argument, and with reference to the sheep metaphor with which he first introduces the subject of Japanese aggression in his work. Sheep, as Boku learns from the caretaker in *A Wild Sheep Chase,* do have a pecking order, and so an injury to one animal prompts the others to jockey for position. In the end, however, it does not matter which one reigns supreme and which ones are cowed into submission, for when they get to the butcher block, all suffer the same fate: " 'Just one happy barbecue' " (229).

The question then becomes how to act in such a way as to avoid herd behavior, which, in the elusive yet all-encompassing Japanese state that Murakami portrays, is an increasingly difficult endeavor. The Class-A war-criminal Boss behind Boku's *Wild Sheep Chase* " 'sits squarely on top of a trilateral power base of politicians, information services, and the stock market' " (58–59). The "quasi-governmental" System that "monopolizes everything" in *Hard-Boiled Wonderland* monopolizes even the Factory that allegedly exists to subvert it (33, 137). So convinced is Boku in *Dance, Dance, Dance* of the fact that " '[t]here's no such thing as establishment and antiestablishment anymore. [. . .] The system's got everything sewed up' " that he adopts the boomerang theory of social resistance: "You throw a rock and it'll come right back at you" (169, 55).

Central to such monopolistic control is control of the mass media. The Boss who preselects and packages 95 percent of the information that reaches people is described as having " 'nearly the entire publishing and broadcasting industries under [his] thumb' " (*Wild* 58). And, in point of fact, the Boss's rise to power in the 1930s is predicated on his ability " 'to steer society by using the weaknesses of the masses for leverage' " (117). Yet not all forms of mass media steer the masses to the same degree. According to Kurihara Akira, who divides mass culture into different strata depending upon levels of dissemination and consumption, the mass culture of television, video, and commercials "embodies the technical rationality of industry, while it acts in a rule-governed, standard, and integrated way." Movies and popular music, which provide "ample room for the projection of desires and needs and for the exercise of the imagination," promote the possibility of resistance.[21] What Murakami adds to Kurihara's argument are different ports of origin. The television that turns individuals into a herd of complacent sheep is an entirely homegrown product. The movies and songs that cause them to kick up their heels—if not in protest, at least to dance, dance, dance—come completely from the United States.

(It's) a Small World (after All) and the Cinematic Attempt to Enlarge It

These linked depictions of medium and nation reflect, no doubt, the generic biases of an author who aspired to be a screenwriter while at Waseda University and wrote his thesis on "The Ideology of Journeys in American Films" (Iwamoto 296). They also conspicuously omit certain salient details about the history of the mass media in Japan: the number of American television series broadcast in Japan in the late 1950s and early 1960s (as many as fifty-four in the peak year of 1963–64) and the percentage of American programs (77 percent) that still constitute the vast majority of television imports even among today's greatly diminished numbers (Stronach 138, 128); the long history of Japanese moviemaking dating back to the introduction of film into Japan in 1896 and the establishment of an indigenous film industry around 1907 (Kasza 54; Silverberg 70). The depictions are nonetheless historically accurate in portraying television and film as antagonistic media—the big-screen attendance that peaked at 1.1 billion in 1958 had declined to 373 million in 1965 due to the impact of the little box (Schilling 11; Stronach 136)—and as media whose battle for viewers was clearly decided within a few decades of the 1953 inception of television broadcasting. As early as 1975, surveys were revealing television as having outdistanced not just movies but every other medium in Japan to become the preeminent conveyor of information (Ito 49).

Consistent with Murakami's view that this vehicle of preeminence also acts as a vehicle of consensus, the three mysterious TV People who invade the narrator's home unannounced one Sunday evening in the first sentence of the story "TV People" ("TV pīpuru no gyakushū," 1989) are defined by the quality of complete uniformity, a "singular lack of distinguishing features [that] makes it next to impossible to tell them apart" (*Elephant* 206), a surrendering of individual identity that is reflected in their reduced size, "slightly smaller than you or me. [. . .] About, say, 20 or 30%," and simulated appearance, "as if they were reduced by photocopy, everything mechanically calibrated" (197). Such indistinguishability, moreover, is part and parcel of the very appliance they carry around with them. When they later intrude into the narrator's workplace, interrupting an

afternoon meeting with television in tow, they provoke no reaction from anyone, even though the televison's Sony logo emblazoned for all to see indicates
that the item in question is manufactured by a rival electrical appliance firm.

The independence of the narrator, by contrast, is portrayed as a function of
his not owning a television or vcr—deprivations that cause his colleagues to
refer to him as a "modern-day Luddite" (206)—and from the fact that he structures his day with respect to the nonelectronic medium of print: "I always read
after dinner. I might set the book down after thirty minutes, or I might read for
two hours, but the thing is to read every day" (204). Indeed, as a copywriter,
whose job entails imagining differences between otherwise identical products,
the narrator occupies a potentially radical position, embodying what some critics consider the "creative, playful, and somehow subversive artist" in his ability
to undermine "bureaucratic capitalism from the inside."[22] Once the TV People
imperiously install a Sony in his living room, though, he succumbs more and
more to passive collectivity. Unable to read because his thoughts keep returning
to the television set on the sideboard, unable to sleep because the TV People have
"stayed on in my head" (205), unable to speak now that his "customary world
is no longer absolute" (201), he lapses more and more into silent observation.
He even begins to believe as real the images the television set proffers, despite
the fact that—as occurs with a machine that looks more like a juicer than the
airplane it is represented as being (213)—the forms of those projected images
bear no resemblance to the actualities they are meant to duplicate. With the
shrinkage of his hands noted in its last paragraphs establishing beyond a doubt
that the narrator has become a TV person himself, the story ends by suggesting
that the narrator's loss of personal sovereignty comes hand in hand with a loss
of spatial sensibility, as he asks, *"Which way is front, which way is back?"* (216).

As Andrew A. Painter has argued with respect to Japanese daytime television,
such a collapse of spatial, as well as temporal, boundaries is essential to Japanese
television's promulgation of what he calls " 'televisual quasi-intimacy' " (295),
a quality that derives from television's being experienced "as both public (produced and circulated in society) and private (viewed inside the home) at the
same time" (322). In Murakami's short story, in fact, one of the TV People who
appears on the television screen climbs out from inside the television and steps
into the narrator's living room. Such intimacy, in turn, is fundamental to the
talk or "wide" shows' *(waidoshō)* facilitation of "electronically created *uchi*—
all-purpose 'in-groups' that anyone can join simply by tuning to the right channel" (Painter 296), the ultimate "in-group" being, of course, the nation itself.[23]
Paul A. S. Harvey makes a similar point when discussing morning serialized
television novels, or *asadora,* in which the heroines' seemingly contradictory

quests for independent selfhood through work and for parental surrogates to authorize their acts are resolved by having the heroines' development exemplify that of the modern nation of which they are a part (146–47). As such, these historical dramas enable television to present "an ethic of progress and self-improvement whereby the past is literally left behind" (139).

Given how much "disappears" or "vanishes" in Murakami's work, this consensual erasure of history to which television contributes is not to be taken lightly. "Some things are forgotten, some things disappear, some things die," notes Boku ruefully of the wife who abandons him near the beginning of *A Wild Sheep Chase* (21–22), leaving behind her "[t]hree albums rendered into a revised past" because she has confiscated every photograph of herself that previously appeared in them (20). But these demises are hardly synonymous since things that disappear lack the commemorative rites that are accorded things that die and that establish their having existed in the first place. Three call girls who "disappear" in *Dance, Dance, Dance* (295; "'Practically vanished into a blank wall'" [155]) do not even have proper names with which to identify them, just a maximum of four letters, "'[s]igns tacked up in empty air'" (156), that serve as their *noms d'amour*. The television actor who "disappears" from a Shakey's pizza parlor prior to plowing his Maserati into Tokyo Bay does not even have a scent to mark his presence, just an image: "'A push of the button and—*brrp!*—I'm gone'" (*Dance* 359, 144). And given current statistics that ascribe television ownership to 99.7 percent of Japanese households, each of which has a set turned on for over eight hours each day (Inoue 35),[24] the prospect of historical erasure by an entire collectivity becomes more than a mere possibility, as Murakami knows full well. The desolate northern township of Junitaki to which Boku journeys on his *Wild Sheep Chase* may have had to close one-third of its shops for lack of business, but it still boasts "unimaginably tall television antennae" on every rooftop and inhabitants who watch an average of four hours of television between the time they return from work and the time they go to sleep (214–15, 208).

Movies, in contrast, promote an altogether different historical sensibility with respect to the past. This, significantly, is not simply because the movie titles that Murakami's narrators cite so often refer to older movies, as occurs, for instance, at those times that the narrator of *Hard-Boiled Wonderland and the End of the World* accesses a cinematic data bank that includes *Casablanca* (1942), *The Big Sleep* (1946), *Key Largo* (1948), *The Third Man* (1949), *Rio Grande* (1950), *Fort Defiance* (1951), *The Quiet Man* (1952), *The Enemy Below* (1957), *Ben Hur* (1959), *Spartacus* (1960), and *El Cid* (1961), to name but a few. Nor is it a function of that nostalgic search for lost origins, which, as references to later films like *Easy Rider* (1969) and songs like "Born to Be Wild" (1968) suggest (*Hard-Boiled* 341, 219), constitute Murakami's position vis-à-vis the 1960s.[25] The fact that Boku acclaims Jimmy Gilmer's "Sugar Shack" (1963), a song recorded on a label (Dot) founded by a record mail-order proprietor, as authentic in a way that the " 'mass-produced garbage' " to which his *shōjo* sidekick listens is not (*Dance* 112) confirms John Whittier Treat's theorization of nostalgia (*natsukashisa*) in Japan as "a desire that is produced simply for desire's sake" and the " 'nostalgic subject' " as one whose "longing for another sort of life, one that never actually 'was' because no such life ever 'is' " is doomed to disappointment (383, 384). Rather, movies are distinguished by virtue of the fact that the temporal differences that they acknowledge result from their giving free play to individual subjectivity in the very construction of history.

Typical of this phenomenon is the narrator of another Murakami short story whose Sunday is also interrupted by an unexpected event. Like the narrator of "TV People," who structures his time with respect to print literature before the invasion of his home by little people, the narrator of "The Fall of the Roman Empire, the 1881 Indian Uprising, Hitler's Invasion of Poland, and the Realm of Raging Winds" ("Rōma teikoku no hōkai, 1881-nen no Indeian hōki, Hittorā no pōrando shinnyū, soshite kyōfū no sekai," 1986) structures his time with respect to the keeping of a diary for twenty-two years prior to the onset of those winds cited in the story's title. Unlike most diarists, who transcribe their entries on the days that the events in question occur, Murakami's narrator composes his entries on each Sunday from notes that he jots down throughout the week. He is proud of possessing a memory "as airtight as the lid on a blast furnace" (*Elephant* 113), for his *narration* of the events that he experiences on the Sunday on which the story takes place rivals the precision of Greenwich Mean Time: he hangs laundry at 10:18 A.M. "to be exact" (113), notices the winds beginning to blow at 2:07 P.M. "more precisely" (112), hears the telephone ring at 2:36 and then again at 3:48 (114, 116), and, finally, notes the winds abating at 4:05 "on the dot" (117). Yet his *interpretation* of those events employs cinematic similes that at times bear so little correlation to the events as to border on metaphysical conceits: from his description of the Sunday prior to the onset of heavy winds as "[a] peaceful Sunday afternoon like the heyday of the Roman Empire" (113) that obliquely evokes a 1964 Sophia Loren movie to the pointed comparison of the disturbances in telecommunications the winds cause "like the Indians all rising on the warpath in 1881, [. . .] burning pioneer cabins, cutting telegraph lines, raping Candice Bergen" (114) that conflates two movies released within a year of each other (*Soldier Blue* [1970] and *The Hunting Party* [1971]). Even more outrageously, his account of the prior day's events depends on three movies even more separated in time that bleed into each other:

Saturday, Hitler's armored divisions invaded Poland. Dive bombers over Warsaw—
No, that's not right. That's not what happened. Hitler's invasion of Poland was on
September 1, 1939. Not yesterday. After dinner yesterday, I went to the movies and
saw Meryl Streep in *Sophie's Choice*. Hitler's invasion of Poland only figured in the
film.

In the film, Meryl Streep divorces Dustin Hoffman, but then in a commuter train
she meets this civil engineer played by Robert De Niro, and remarries. A pretty all-
right movie. (115)

To the narrator, who prizes his diarist's "meticulous system" as attributing
"[t]o every meaningful act, its own system" (118), the slippage from a 1982 film
(Sophie's Choice) to a 1979 film *(Kramer vs. Kramer)* to a 1984 film *(Falling in
Love)* is evidence of what he earlier has deemed "the overwhelming tumult of
history" that the unexpected gales have had on a composition policy previously
determined by "[e]ighty percent facts, 20% short comments" (114, 113).[26] To
the reader, it provides evidence of the narrator's replacing—whether he realizes
it or not—the recorder's role of annalist with the more imaginatively incisive
one of historian, which involves not just the recounting of facts but the ordering of facts. As the neurophysiologist who installs software into the brain of
Murakami's *Hard-Boiled Wonderland* narrator recognizes, the aggregate memories that constitute each individual's cognitive system are constantly changing
due to the workings of the subconscious. Stabilizing those memories requires
"'[r]earrangin' everything into a story,'" which, in turn, requires "'[c]uttin'
and pastin', tossin' out some parts, resequencin','" in short, engaging in a process that is "'exactly like film editin','" which, as it turns out, is exactly what the
professor has done before the Second World War (262).

The Wind-Up Bird Chronicle: NHK, Nomonhan, and the Nature of the Body Politic

As it also turns out, "'cuttin','" "'pastin','" and "'resequencin''" perfectly describes the encyclopedic structure of *The Wind-Up Bird Chronicle,* for its story
of Tōru Okada's quest to find the wife who suddenly leaves him is repeatedly interrupted by the interpolated stories—themselves often interrupted and
resumed—told to him by characters who wander in and out of his experiential
orbit. Thus, as the chapter titles indicate, Okada hears the psychic "Creta Kanō's
Long Story" of being unnaturally defiled by his politician brother-in-law (87,
294), his teenage neighbor "May Kasahara's Inquiry into the Nature of Hair-
pieces" (101), the mapmaker "Lieutenant Mamiya's Long Story" in two parts of

being captured in Outer Mongolia by enemy troops in 1938 (135, 151), "The Zoo Attack (or, A Clumsy Massacre)" of 1945 witnessed by a Japanese veterinarian in the capital city of Hsin-ching (400), ultimately "The Wind-Up Bird Chronicle" itself that consists of accessed documents of a computer program (511). Not the least important of the novel's stories are those that Okada himself narrates of what he undergoes at the bottom of a dried-up neighborhood well to which he begins retreating in an attempt "to think about reality" (233), stories often impossible to distinguish as recollections, dreams, or hallucinations. With his return from the well leaving him with visible bodily marks of his descent into it, however, the very contemporary and suburban Okada is forced to acknowledge both the interconnectedness of all the various tales, persons, and periods that the book presents and the common historical source from which they all radiate. Specifically, "[a]ll of these were linked as in a circle, at the center of which stood prewar Manchuria, continental East Asia, and the short war of 1939 in Nomonhan" (502).

Such historical centeredness and specificity mark a tremendous advance in Murakami's work. No longer is the history in danger of being forgotten a generalized past. The history being consciously expunged is the history of Japanese militarism, beginning with the 1931 Manchurian Incident in which, under the pretext of railroad track sabotage actually staged by the Kwantung Army, full-scale military hostilities erupted between Japanese and Chinese troops; extending to the "phantom empire of Manchukuo," which, in later "disappearing into history," removes all traces of its existence as a Japanese puppet state (418); and culminating in the election to the Diet of purged war criminals whose descendants solidify their nepotistic careers by way of television exposure during the present time (1984–85) in which the novel takes place.[27] Consistent with this authorial advance, the novel also attributes to its portrait of the media very precise ideological ramifications. No longer do characters watch television in the abstract. They now watch a very specific station, "the government-supported NHK network," on huge color sets accorded the reverence demanded by any shrine that occupies a room's ceremonial alcove (51).

Strictly speaking, NHK (Nihon Hōsō Kyōkai) is not a "government-supported" network, if by "support" one means direct financial allocations. A noncommercial public corporation (much like the BBC in England), NHK is funded almost entirely by receivers' fees paid by viewers, administered by an autonomous Board of Governors, and, in accordance with the 1950 Broadcast Law, remains financially accountable to the National Diet. As a corporation whose Board of Governors also is appointed by the prime minister, however, NHK justifies Murakami's characterization in that its subjection to government control has been, as Ellis S. Krauss conservatively puts it, "not completely lacking" (90).

Certainly, such control characterized the years prior to World War II, when NHK radio acted as a national monopoly and Japanese officials, impressed by the British government's use of broadcasting during the General Strike of 1926, instituted state controls over daily operations (prebroadcast censorship, circuit breakers to stop programs in progress) and engaged in wholesale commandeering during times of extreme crisis, as occurred after the Manchurian Incident and during the abortive army coup of 26 February 1936 (Kasza 83–97, 153–57).[28] Yet, as Krauss has documented, with NHK television newscasts depicting the state as an omnipresent guardian of the public's interests and transmitting visuals that emphasize the nonconflictive nature of Japanese society (in contrast to images that limit violence to societies outside of Japan), NHK still acts as a source of state legitimation (117–20, 103–6). To put it another way, television's postwar role as a conveyor of imperial spectacles, as evidenced by the increase in television ownership that coincided with the 1959 wedding of Crown Prince Akihito and the 1964 Tokyo Olympics, just extends the state-sanctioning role that radio had played in prewar years, as evidenced by the completion date for NHK's national network being pushed forward so as to enable it to transmit the official coronation of Emperor Hirohito in 1928.[29] As such, the role of television just emblematizes the longstanding role that Japanese mass culture itself has played in the construction of what Miriam Silverberg aptly terms "consumer-subjects" (61–83).[30]

Read schematically, *The Wind-Up Bird Chronicle* can be viewed as a battle between two men, Okada and his despised brother-in-law, Noboru Wataya, over the soul of one such consumer-citizen, the wife that leaves Okada at the beginning of the novel and goes over " 'to the world of Noboru Wataya' " (582). As one of the psychics that Okada consults in an effort to discover his wife Kumiko's whereabouts correctly states, " 'Noboru Wataya is a person who belongs to a world that is the exact opposite of yours [. . .]. In a world where you are losing everything, Mr. Okada, Noboru Wataya is gaining everything. In a world where you are rejected, he is accepted' " (314). These opposed worlds, significantly, correlate with each man's relationship to the medium of television: the unemployed Okada does not own a set; the Tokyo University grad economist-cum–popular author–cum–activist intellectual Wataya predicates his entire career on broadcast appearances.

We watched his sudden transformation in amazement. [. . .] On the television screen, he looked far more intelligent and reliable than the real Noboru Wataya. I'm not sure how he accomplished this. He certainly wasn't handsome. But he was tall and slim and had an air of good breeding. In the medium of television, Noboru Wataya had found the place where he belonged. (75)

In fact, the very amount of time that Okada has lived without a television, the six years of his marriage, is the same amount of time that it takes for the anointed Wataya to become elected to the House of Representatives, and, with that election, gain " 'a very real kind of power that he can exercise in this world, a power that grows stronger every day' " (437).

One measure of that power is the extent to which Wataya wields it in Okada's own dream world. No longer just a man who "talked the way people on television talked" and "moved the way people on television moved" even while off camera (199), he intrudes into the world of magic realism that Okada experiences while sitting in the bottom of a dried-up well. There, as in the world of waking life, Wataya produces the same stunningly preemptive effect on his audience: "The face of Noboru Wataya was being projected on the screen of a large television in the center of a broad lobby. [. . .] There must have been over a hundred people in the lobby, and each and every one of them stopped what they were doing to listen to him, with serious expressions on their faces. Noboru Wataya was about to announce something that would determine people's fate" (243). So preemptive is that impact that it survives, in a later vision, even after NHK reporters announce Wataya's bludgeoning at the hands of an unknown assailant whose description matches that of Okada. Try as he might to dissuade the hotel viewers that he has not beaten Wataya with a baseball bat, Okada recognizes his endeavors to be futile: "But they would never believe me, I was sure. They believed only what they saw on television" (573).

More than mere acquiescence, such belief results from what Murakami explicitly terms acts of defilement that Wataya perpetrates (41–42, 213–14, 606). The psychic Creta Kanō experiences that defilement individually as a penetration of her body from behind by Wataya and the removal of one bodily organ after another, resulting in a voiding of " 'all my memories, all my consciousness' " (304). As Kumiko, who finally does kill Wataya in the novel's real world in revenge for her own violation, clarifies: "The freedom to do anything at all was taken from me" (606). From the collective unconscious of his television audience, however, Wataya tries to extract something far more sinister:

"Through television and the other media, he gained the ability to train his magnified power on society at large. Now he is trying to bring out something that the great mass of people keep hidden in the darkness of their unconscious. He wants to use it for his own political advantage. It's a tremendously dangerous thing, this thing he is trying to draw out: it's fatally smeared with violence and blood, and it's directly connected to the darkest depths of history, because its final effect is to destroy and obliterate people on a massive scale." (583)

Coming near the conclusion of a novel that—atypically for Murakami—has been drenched in violence and blood, this passage, perhaps the most crucial in the work, recalls a series of earlier incidents in which the massive obliteration of life, and not just human life, by Japanese troops has been depicted, often in horrifying detail: the execution of five hundred prisoners of war in North China (117), the disposal of people in wells into which hand grenades are then tossed in Nanking (143), the liquidation of animals in a Hsin-ching zoo that turns into a clumsy massacre when the animals refuse to surrender their lives immediately (404–8, 411–13). At the same time, coming from an author who admits to a belief in blood transmission,[31] such a passage also veers uncomfortably close to postulating another form of essentializing *Nihonjinron,* this time with violence as the defining quality of Japanese uniqueness. Okada even surmises " 'there was some kind of inherited tendency in the Wataya family bloodline' " (582), and attributes Kumiko's decision to abort their child to her unwillingness to propagate that quality any further.

This is hardly the first time that a rhetoric of autochthonous Japanese identity has been invoked to explain social behavior during wartime, as H. D. Harootunian has illustrated. The intellectuals who met to discuss " 'overcoming the modern' " *(kindai no chōkoku)* in a 1942 symposium held six months after the start of the Pacific War acclaimed pre–Meiji era tradition as distinguishing " 'the blood of the Japanese' " from that superimposed " 'Western knowledge' " they found incarnated in the materialism of imported American mass culture (Harootunian 67, 68). And, in a very literal sense, there *is* a blood connection in Murakami's book between Noboru Wataya and the history of Japanese militarism. The uncle whose Liberal Democratic Party constituency Noboru inherits with his election to the Diet has been a collaborator in Manchukuo with Kanji Ishiwara, one of the ringleaders behind the Manchurian Incident that "later would prove to have been the first act in fifteen years of war" (499). More to the point, there is a historical connection between Yoshitaka Wataya's technocratic activities in the 1930s and his nephew's bureaucratic activities in the 1980s. For if what distinguished Japanese colonialism in the 1930s was the exploitation of Manchukuo's natural resources for Japan's own war machine, as Perry Anderson has argued (14–15), what constitutes Japanese colonialism in the 1980s, according to Murakami, is the very same quality of industrialization. The wig company for which Okada's teenage neighbor, May, works gets its hair from women in Southeast Asia. And since wigs, as May astutely notes, are " 'the ultimate consumer product' "—" 'Once they get their hooks into a guy, he's a customer for life' " (110)—the history of Japanese imperialism continues to repeat itself in insidious, for being less noticeable, form. No wonder Okada envisions in his dream state a "large map of the world hung on the wall" as the back-drop for Noboru Wataya's announcing "something that would determine peo-ple's fate" (243). With Japan's already having "overcome the modern"—indeed, "conque[red] the modern" according to Prime Minister Ōhira Masayoshi (qtd. in Harootunian 78)—to *be* the modern after the era of high-speed growth, the fate in question is nothing less than the future of Japan itself.[32]

But having set his book a decade earlier than the one in which he writes it, Murakami—much like Potter in *Pennies from Heaven*—has access to that envi-sioned future: the 1989 end of LDP hegemony and death of Emperor Hirohito, the 1992 stock market collapse and fall in the economic growth rate, the appre-ciation of the yen and reduced sales of Japanese exports, the depression in real estate and increase of bad loans. To the extent that he deems anything unique to the Japanese character, then, it is not a propensity for violence per se. Too many references in the book to the massive obliteration of life committed by people of other nations—Mongols who crush hundreds of Russian aristocrats beneath thick planks in Kiev (157), Soviets who slaughter thousands of Lamaist priests and landowners in concentration camps (543), Americans who wipe out one hundred thousand people with a " 'special new bomb' " in Hiroshima (522)—preclude that possibility. It is, instead, a propensity for unreasonable overexten-sion that often manifests itself in acts of violence so irrational because so des-tined to defeat from the beginning. Hence the 1939 battle of Nomonhan (52–54), in which outnumbered Japanese foot soldiers, armed with bolt-rifles, satchel charges, and Molotov cocktails, fought motorized Soviet troops, armed with tanks, flamethrowers, and long-range artillery, over a barren patch of land on the Manchurian-Mongolian border based on the belief that superior spiritual training, *seishin kyōiku,* would triumph over vastly superior matériel power.

As Alvin D. Cook has exhaustively documented, such faith in the compen-satory force of *bushidō* continued to prevail even after that slaughter of eigh-teen thousand men, as evidenced by Japan's embarking on a second campaign against the United States, Great Britain, and the Netherlands barely two years later and while still at war with China, again supported by the belief that "lack of equipment gave us Japanese a chance to demonstrate our superior fighting spirit and valor," as a reservist arriving at Truk Island in 1943 was informed (qtd. in A. Cook 2: 1082). In Murakami's view, such belief still continues to prevail over forty years later. After all, even the skeptic Okada deems Nomonhan "a mag-nificent battle" (53). The ear model in *A Wild Sheep Chase* who concludes, after being told Japan's history of twentieth-century militarism, that " 'we Japanese seem to live from war to war,' " thus misses half the point in her assessment (210). Much more accurate is the Sheep Professor who ascribes that history to a refusal to learn from past experiences, a form of blindness that may or may not be willful: " 'In other words, we don't have our feet on solid ground' " (188). In other words, the stroke that leaves Noboru Wataya vulnerable to his sister's fatal attack in *The Wind-Up Bird Chronicle* results from a weakened blood vessel in his brain that doctors diagnose as " 'probably' " congenital (602).

Earlier Murakami protagonists respond to this quasi-determinist scenario by opting out of it into solitary bachelorhood, as critics have noted (Strecher, "Murakami" 67), cultivating a world-weary Raymond Chandler pose, much like the "lone-wolf Calcutec" of *Hard-Boiled Wonderland* (80), a self-described "leftover wrapped in black plastic" (21), or the snow-shoveling writer of *Dance, Dance, Dance*, whose most intimate relationship is with a used Subaru (31). They then spend the remainder of the novels coaxing themselves out of social semiretirement. Okada, in contrast, begins *The Wind-Up Bird Chronicle* in a socially subversive position since his decision to quit his job and become a househusband inverts the tenets of the traditional gender-based household upon which patriarchal Japanese society rests. He cannot solidify that subversion by way of American movies, for *The Wind-Up Bird Chronicle* is almost devoid of all such references, and the American music he does hear around him comes mainly in the form of processed Muzak. He instead appropriates another Western import, the idea of individual identity, a concept for which Miyoshi finds the word *shutaisei* increasingly invoked after 1945 (97–98), and a concept for which Murakami finds no Japanese linguistic equivalent at all.[33]

Such individual identity is not to be confused with selfhood, since Murakami shows the self to be both literally and figuratively skin deep. "The human fruit is always ripe for peeling," notes his *Hard-Boiled Wonderland* narrator (157). And when humans in *The Wind-Up Bird Chronicle* are deprived of that epidermal covering that allegedly serves as boundary between body and mind, they find not only that this border is easily permeable but that the interior exposed immediately beneath it is nothing but raw meat. Okada, for instance, dreams of a Hokkaido guitar player "peel[ing] his own skin as if it were the skin of an apple" until he uncovers a "bright-red lump of flesh," only to have the skin crawl up Okada's own body and, so generic is it, plaster itself upon him as a new overlay (339). Lieutenant Mamiya, whose tale of being forced to witness a man being skinned alive in Outer Mongolia until a "bloody red lump of meat" is the real-life source of Okada's nightmare (160), experiences that staged dismemberment as so disruptive of his sense of human embodiment that he loses all sense of himself as a unified entity in response. Never particularly stable to begin with, as he recalls the way that he "as an individual human being" became slowly "unraveled" in the vast spaces of the borderless steppe even before being captured by Mongol soldiers, his "mind swell[ing] out to fill the entire landscape, becoming so diffuse in the process that one loses the ability to keep it fastened to the physical self" (139), Mamiya deteriorates completely when forced into the bottom of a well. Deprived of all sense of agency, "unable to do—or even to think—anything at all," he emerges "a dried-up carcass, the cast-off shell of an insect" (167).

Cast-off shells. Vacant houses. Empty containers.[34] Murakami's litany of bodily imagery proliferates, all in keeping with poststructuralist dictates that refute all semblance of a totalizing ego and, with it, what Homi K. Bhabha terms "that *perspective of depth* through which the authenticity of identity comes to be reflected in the glassy metaphorics of the mirror and its mimetic or realist narratives" ("Interrogating" 191). Yet in postulating a "core of consciousness" as the source of individual identity (210), Murakami deviates sharply from contemporary theoretical practices in endorsing depth as an operative model for both mimesis and human subjectivity. " 'Two-thirds of the earth's surface is ocean,' " Creta Kanō reminds Okada, " 'and all we can see of it with the naked eye is the surface: the skin. We hardly know anything about what's underneath the skin' " (228). Certainly, with the naked eye we don't: one red lump looks much like another. But by joining Western notions of identity with Eastern conceptions of an underground that can be reached through the underground of the mind we do. The teenage May, by concentrating on manual labor and *"not thinking about myself,"* assumes she *"can get closer to the core of my self,"* the " 'real me' " (451). Okada, who discovers he earlier has known only "the most superficial layer of the person Kumiko herself," recovers "[t]he real Kumiko" by accessing a computer program whose password is "Sub" (280, 490).[35]

Of what does the "real Kumiko" consist, however? In *The Wind-Up Bird Chronicle*, it consists of Kumiko responding to her husband's computer query by recollecting a trip they made to the aquarium long before they ever were married. Reflecting an even more fundamentally Western sense of identity, Kumiko's means of identification conforms to the one Bhabha deems "the most decisive and influential formulation on personal identity in the English empiricist tradition" ("Interrogating" 191–92), which John Locke founded upon a consciousness of the past: "so far as this consciousness can be extended *backwards* to any past action or thought, so far reaches the identity of that person" (qtd. in Bhabha, "Interrogating" 192). The difference is that in Murakami's novel that past is extended backward beyond the span of any one person's lifetime. What distinguishes Okada's personally reconstructive experience at the bottom of a well from the personally disintegrative one of Lieutenant Mamiya is the mark on his cheek that Okada takes away from his ordeal. In contrast to those imposed bodily markers that, as Robyn Wiegman has discussed (24–25), historically served as emblems of social hierarchy and, in particular, enslavement, the "blue-black stain" on Okada's cheek is portrayed as inherently organic: "It seemed to have penetrated deep into the skin" (287). In the world of Murakami, in which, as Matthew C. Strecher claims, "the paranormal is free to operate, in order to ground a more concrete, mimetic subtext" ("Hidden" 142), and in which individuals remain "[c]aught in the cross hair of the real and the imaginary" (*Dance* 161), the mark, on the one hand, establishes the real and the imaginary as in no way synonymous: "*That was no dream*, they were telling me through the mark," Okada realizes. "*It really happened*" (289). On the other hand, as a mark that also appears on the cheek of the Manchukuo veterinarian who witnesses the massacre of zoo animals in 1945 (404), which connects Okada to the generation past, and as a mark "about the size of an infant's palm" (288), which connects Okada to an unspecified generation of the future, the mark on his face also transforms Okada's body into an emblem of the body politic.

Critics who investigate the body are quick to comment upon the portrayal of the body as nation-state (E. Martin 126) and consider the ideological ramifications of situating the body as a locus for the enactment of state power. Michel Foucault, for instance, imagines a "political 'anatomy'" that would study the body politic as a "set of material elements and techniques that serve as weapons, relays, communication routes and supports for the power and knowledge relations that invest human bodies and subjugate them by turning them into objects of knowledge" (28). By having the body of his *Hard-Boiled Wonderland* narrator surgically reconstructed so as to process, or "launder," information for the System more efficiently, and by depicting his *Dance, Dance, Dance* protagonist as a telephone switchboard that connects the other characters to each other, Murakami turns the human body in his earlier novels into just such a locus. But by defining human identity in terms of historical relationships in *The Wind-Up Bird Chronicle*, Murakami accords it a degree of agency that he denies his earlier characters. Okada, in the end, *does* rescue his Eurydice of a wife, and not in spite of, but precisely *because of* the fact that this Orpheus of a husband has finally decided to look back.

A similar kind of agency was suggested in a brief article printed by the *New York Times* on the same day that it ran its front-page story about people committing suicide in record numbers in Japan in response to the nation's economic recession. The piece in question, which ran right beside the continuation of the article on suicide, concerned the controversy surrounding the attempts to provide Japan with an official national anthem (Kristof A8). As the newspaper reported, the title of the song in question, "Kimigayo," literally means "Your Majesty's Era," which, the piece went on to state, government authorities were scrambling to redefine so as not to signify "The Reign of Our Emperor," as the Foreign Ministry did in a leaflet that was promptly recalled, but as something more like "The Reign of Our Emperor—But Only as a Symbol of the People." As the newspaper also indicated, however, "Nobody has seemed very convinced by that." Like Murakami's *Wind-Up Bird Chronicle[r]*, they, too, looked back and, this time, decided they did not like what they saw.

Part III
W.A.S.T.E.

If you research the life of Jesus, you see that Mary mother of Jesus disappears from the record once he is crucified and risen. Where is the mother who raised the boy?
—Marguerite Oswald in *Libra* (1988)

And we have stories galore, believe me—with documents and everything.
—Marguerite Oswald, *Hearings before the President's Commission on the Assassination of President Kennedy, Vol. I* (1964)

A Mother (and a son, and a brother, and a wife, et al.) in History
Stories Galore in *Libra* and the
Warren Commission *Report*

One more story for the record:

Uncertain about how to begin my discussion of Don DeLillo's *Libra* (1988) and the Warren Commission *Report* (1964), the first of my chapters to examine those marginalized individuals that Thomas Pynchon had characterized as human W.A.S.T.E., I decided to prolong my state of procrastination by having a cup of tea. No sooner had I sat down to drink it than I heard the sound of teeth gnashing material unintended for internal consumption, and, upon immediate investigation, saw my seventy-five-pound canine deconstructing DeLillo's book in a way neither de Man nor Derrida could have anticipated. Two things saved him from the reprimand he deserved: one, my recognition that pasting together—quite literally—the papers that comprise Don DeLillo's postmodern historical novel made me, Scotch tape in hand, just another of the people DeLillo portrays trying to construct a unified narrative out of disparate pieces;

two, the fact that the narration of this incident has enabled me to open my examination with a story about myself, for if anything distinguishes DeLillo's account of the Kennedy assassination and its aftermath, it is the need of everyone involved to fashion it as a story, or fashion from it a story, with the self as star. Not just any kind of story, moreover, but a story that would dramatize the role each played in those spectacular 5.6 seconds that, in DeLillo's view, "broke the back of the American century."[1]

Such a nationally deconstructive diagnosis, which invokes only to discredit the triumphant term chronicled in the first section of my book, is one that continues to haunt DeLillo. *Underworld* portrays the assassination as "an event that took place at the beginning of the sixties, [. . .] that now marked the conceptual end, carrying all the delirium that floated through the age," a slow-motion replay of it in the Zapruder film testifying to an entropic "running down, a sense of greatness really, the car's regal gleam and the murder of some figure out of dimmest lore—a greatness, a kingliness, the terrible mist of tissue and skull, [. . .] on Elm Street" (496). Yet, as Ernest Renan argued over a century ago, shared suffering may be more valuable than shared joy in constituting the legacy of memories required by a nation, for common griefs promote "the feeling of the sacrifices that one has made in the past and of those that one is prepared to make in the future" (19). Hence the obsessive recollection of those alive in 1963 as to where they were on 22 November. But if, as other theorists of nationhood have emphasized, it is print-language that is fundamental to the maintenance of that imagined community in an industrial age (Gellner 50–51), particularly in the Americas, in which historically an almost perfect isomorphism existed between the stretches of empire and their vernaculars (B. Anderson 75), the question then becomes what written forms the narration of the Kennedy assassination must take in order to be communally binding.

As the cover to my paperback copy of *Libra* now so clearly attests, mine is hardly the kind of seamless (re)construction favored by dominant cultures. But then neither is DeLillo's, composed as it is by two juxtaposed story lines, one defined by time, which traces a renegade CIA plot mounted against the president, the other by place, which traces the nomadic life of Lee Harvey Oswald, that converge in Dallas at the novel's conclusion. As such, DeLillo's counternarrative subverts all semblance of totalizing structure in the composition of history.[2] Punctuated as well by the account of CIA analyst Nicholas Branch's frustrated attempts to write the secret history of the assassination of John F. Kennedy years later, the book also subverts all notions of complete originality, for the cumulative text that Branch is supposed to be writing only calls attention to the text of the Warren Commission—and its lone gunman master narrative—that DeLillo's work both inscribes and repudiates.[3]

According to Hayden White, who sees narrative as a dialogic "process of decodation and recodation" in which assumptions canonized by time and convention are continually reviewed and reinterpreted with respect to the new contexts within which they are cast (*Tropics* 96), it is only through such dialogic interchange that past events are given meaning. This view becomes particularly relevant when examining *Libra,* since the Warren Commission *Report* that functions as the prototext for DeLillo's novel has as its own foundational texts the fifteen volumes of testimony and eleven volumes of 3,154 exhibits that comprise the Warren Commission *Hearings* (1964). Within those twenty-six antecedent volumes, moreover, Lee Harvey Oswald, the central figure of the work DeLillo once considered calling *Texas School Book* ("Outsider" 55), only acquires presence through the reconstructions in other people's testimony and the autobiographical documents reprinted as part of the exhibits, texts within texts, one more representational step removed from those witnesses who got to testify in person. Represented in the first as an inveterate watcher of movies, television, and commercials, Oswald as American consumer defines his role in history with respect to the formulae proffered by visual media. Represented by the latter as artistic producer, Oswald grows up believing that posterity is to be found in print. Because so many others in the historical drama—such as Oswald's brother, wife, and, most of all, mother—shared similar authorial yearnings, DeLillo's Oswald in many ways functions as a traditional American type. Once he shifts from producer to object of consumption in order to achieve stardom through visual media, however, the kind of figure he typifies belongs exclusively to the postmodern period. From the social misfit we all avoid, he becomes the celebrity manqué we Americans all are.

A Short Story Writer on Contemporary American Life

Our first presidential assassin, it is worth recalling, already *was* a star at the time he shot Abraham Lincoln. More than "a star of real magnitude" (*New York World* 17 Mar. 1862), in fact, whose meteoric rise had made him "the pride of the American people, the youngest tragedian in the world!" as the playbill advertising his first headliner turn in the nation's capital declared (Samples 76, 106), John Wilkes Booth was a matinée idol. Sought by crowds who waited after performances to catch a glimpse of him, pursued by well-bred women who sent him morally compromising letters, paid an average of $650 a week, he was fully justified in admiring how much "[m]y goose does indeed hang high" ("*Right*" 83). Yet he was not, it would appear, someone who esteemed himself much of a writer—"at the best of times, the worst letter writer in the world" by his own account (72), who would "avail myself of any excuse to get rid of writing" (74)—as the few surviving manuscripts not destroyed by his family attest. Therefore, while the act for which he is most remembered was, as eyewitnesses at the time noted, choreographed by Booth with theatrical precision and panache—a sudden gunshot presumed to be part of the evening's entertainment, a daring tenand-a-half-foot leap from presidential box to stage, a gleaming dagger brandished in front of an audience, a melodramatic *"Sic Semper Tyrannis!"* delivered prior to final exit stage right—it was not an act over which he had much spin control after his performance had ended. The 14 April 1865 letter that Booth wrote to the editors of Washington's *National Intelligencer* in which he justified his anticipated action at Ford's Theatre as saving the South from the total annihilation to be visited upon it by a Caesarean oppressor was never received, much less printed: the actor whom Booth asked to deliver it burned the document for fear of its implicating himself.[4] The pocket diary in which Booth wrote while on the run as a fugitive was never introduced as evidence in the trial of the conspirators and was not even referred to in print until two years later, and then only sporadically, when Lafayette C. Baker's (ghostwritten) *History of the United States Secret Service* was published in 1867 (Hanchett 39–40, 43–44).[5]

As a result, when witnesses years later recalled Booth's actions on that fateful Good Friday night, they remembered not his politics but his performance, one for which the actor had been preparing all his life, and a rather hammy performance at that.[6] "He was acting a premeditated part from the beginning to end, it is true," stated Roeliff Brinkerhoff in an account reprinted in 1900,

> but it was entirely for stage effect, and for the glorification of the actor. His "sic semper tyrannis" was stagey. His whole attitude and walk before the audience at the theater were stagey. His double-edged gladiatorial dagger had been prepared purposely for stage effect. In fact, it was all a part of a play which was to make John Wilkes Booth immortal in history. (Good 112)

Because those same eyewitnesses did not have access to the written words with which Booth attempted to explain himself to posterity, Booth became immortal in ways he never wanted. "The little, the very little I left behind to clear my name, the Govmt will not allow to be printed," he wrote in his last remaining diary entry (*"Right"* 154). Having done, in his view, just "what Brutus was honored for, what made [William] Tell a Hero," and having done so in a manner "purer" than those predecessors since "[o]ne, hoped to be great himself" and "[t]he other had not only his countrys but his own wrongs to avenge," Booth was left "in despair" at being so misunderstood (154), "abandoned, with the curse of Cain upon me," reviled even in parts of that South whose cause he had sought to represent: "When if the world knew my heart, *that one* blow would have made me great, though I did desire no greatness" (155), "greatness" defined not as notoriety—that he already had as an actor—but in terms of the heroic stature he felt was his due.

The self that DeLillo portrays as Lee Oswald, by contrast, does not exhibit enough of a unified form to cast in any role, "great" or otherwise, illustrating as he does the end of the bourgeois ego or monad, as critics have noted.[7] As devised by Win Everett in the alternating chapters that portray the CIA's plan to stage a "spectacular miss" on the life of the president (51), the lone gunman that Lee Oswald is to incarnate is a fictional construct, a "character" Everett creates with the most banal items of consumer culture, "household things, small and cheap" (50, 145)—Q-tips, razor blades, his daughter's school eraser—held together by nothing stronger than Elmer's Glue-All, for which Oswald later will supply a vehicle of transmission: "a name, a face, a bodily frame they might use to extend their fiction into the world" (50). Comprised by "the contents of a wallet"—driver's license, credit card, address book, passport, Social Security card, in short, "[p]ocket litter," "ordinary dog-eared paper" (50)—Everett's Oswald exists purely as documentation, a function of letters on a requisite number of pages. As even the model intended to wear Everett's paper wardrobe realizes when musing upon one of his aliases, "Take the double-*e* from Lee. Hide the double-*l* in Hidell. Hidell means hide the *L*. Don't tell. White ideograms" (90).

But as the fact of Oswald's aliases also suggests, Lee Oswald is in the process of constructing himself, with the same kinds of cheap implements that Everett employs, in his case, a ninety-eight-cent stamping kit, and with respect to the same kinds of paper artifacts: draft cards, passports, vaccination certificates, committee membership cards. To the extent that this evidence of Oswald's efforts testifies to a reality of the man Everett cannot deny, forcing him to acknowledge Oswald as a "fiction living prematurely in the world" (179), Everett the conspirator feels panic. To the extent that the sloppiness of Oswald's work contrasts with the precision of Everett's own efforts, Everett the craftsman experiences the more jarring feeling of having been "displaced" (179), for the ease with which Oswald creates his multiple selves testifies to the ease with which identity defined by paper can be constituted. Oswald thus understands full well why he does not need the approval of the Fair Play for Cuba Committee to open a branch office: "He had his rubber stamping kit. All he had to do was stamp the committee's initials on a handbill or piece of literature. Stamp some numbers and letters. This makes it true" (313). The corollary of such easy paper construction, of course, is an equally easy destruction. "She knew exactly what Ruby was thinking," conspirator Larry Parmenter's wife, Beryl, thinks when watching Oswald's death replayed on television. "He wanted to erase that little man" (446). To put it another way, in a world that can " 'make Stalin disappear' " by blowing up his statue (207), how hard can it be to get rid of someone represented in far less durable matter? " 'How many letters do you have to lose before you disappear?' " Parmenter's wife wonders after her husband is issued a new badge with a diminished number of letters around its edges (118).

Viewed from one perspective, this portrayal of literary characters as alphabetical characters might suggest a literature of aesthetic detachment, as typified, for example, by a novel like Gilbert Sorrentino's *Mulligan Stew* (1979), composed entirely of documents and populated by characters whose names derive from earlier works of fiction *(The Great Gatsby, The Glass Key, Lolita, At Swim-Two-Birds)*, none of which is ascribed any more consistency from work to work than any letters grouped upon a page demand. As indicated by the one character whose name, Martin Halpin, derives from a mere footnote in Joyce's *Finnegans Wake,* "In a way, I *was* the letters, no more" (25). And DeLillo's earlier fiction is replete with passages that anticipate *Libra*'s reduction of character to linguistic configuration.[8] " 'I like literally to segment a name until nothing remains,' " says a crystal scientist who doubles as a musician in *Ratner's Star* (1976). " 'I remove one letter at a time, retaining meaning, it is hoped, to the very end' " (152). " 'Owen says 'character' comes from a Greek word' " that means " 'to brand or to sharpen,' " James Axton's son, Tap, informs his father in *The Names* (1982). " 'This is probably because 'character' in English not only means someone in a story but a mark or symbol,' " Axton replies, the similarity of which his son immediately grasps: " 'Like a letter of the alphabet' " (10).

Such a conception of characterization obviously corroborates Victor Burgin's denotation of "the 'post-modernist' subject" as an " 'effect of language' " (49). As a character in both historical fiction and the actual past, however, Oswald occupies a dual position, as both "object of history," or "referent of the proper name," as well as "object of perception," or "empirical, once alive" person, to quote Linda Hutcheon's paraphrasing of Lyotard (*Poetics* 145). Thus, *The Names* also asserts that those letters of the alphabet that now may appear as formal codings proposed by humans to make sense of the world around them through pattern and repetition in fact originated in ancient times as "pictographs" intended to represent that world in all its chaotic imperfections. " 'From nature, you see,' " explains archaeologist Owen Brademas to Axton. " 'The ox, the house, the camel, the palm of hand, the water, the fish. [. . . T]hese marks, these signs that appear so pure and abstract to us, began as objects in the world, living things in many cases' " (116). Those in the book who would forget these origins and use linguistic codings to assuage " 'the terror in our souls' " with systematization (308), as the cultists do who match the initials of their victims to the place names in which they are killed, embark upon a mission DeLillo views as both unnatural and unsuccessful: by the end of the book, the number of fractured cells indicates that "the cult was nearly dead" (290). As Andahl, the renegade cultist with whom Axton meets, admits, " 'Numbers behave, words do not' " (208).[9]

The contrast that Andahl draws is not altogether accurate, though, for in DeLillo's work numbers often prove as unstable as letters. In *Libra*, Nicholas Branch may begin thinking of the date of the Kennedy assassination as 11/22, but using "strictly numerical terms" to understand the events he is investigating affords him little help in mastering the data the CIA curator keeps sending him (377).[10] Yet just how much words misbehave in *Libra* is illustrated by the fact that neither Everett's nor Oswald's written script is directly responsible for the death of the president in DeLillo's novel. If plot in narrative, as Hayden White has argued, endows the individual events that comprise it with "a meaning by being identified as parts of an integrated whole" (*Content* 9), the components of the conspiracy to kill the president are drained of meaning as the plot that encloses them disintegrates into process. So many permutations does Everett's original plan undergo after it leaves the confines of his enclosed basement (and passes from Everett to Parmenter to T-Jay Mackey to shooters Raymo and Vásquez), and so many personae does Oswald sketch for himself (A. J. Hidell, O. H. Lee, H. O. Lee, D. F. Drictal, to name but a few), that it finally is only a large degree of coincidence that brings together the two men's scenarios.[11]

Everett, whose distinctly postmodern collages of information only hint at "secret symmetries in a nondescript life" (78), in fact admits the workings of chance into his plan by recognizing the necessity of withholding causal connections from his audience: "You have to leave them with coincidence, lingering mystery. This is what makes it real" (147). Oswald, in contrast, accepts no such dictum. Portrayed as a would-be author, quoted as having listed *"To be a short story writer on contemporary American life"* as his vocational interest when applying to Albert Schweitzer College in Switzerland (134), Oswald structures the script of his life according to much more traditional narrative principles—as the "word-blindness" from which he suffers dictates that he must (166). Because the inability to "clearly see the picture that is called a word" also leaves him unable to "get a grip on the runaway world" (211), he suffers a form of disorientation that proves particularly debilitating, living as he does in a world DeLillo anachronistically defines in terms of "curved space," devoid of all "plane surfaces" (164), a "postmodern hyperspace," to recall Jameson's term, that frustrates the attempts of individuals to locate themselves, both perceptually and cognitively, in a mappable external world (*Postmodernism* 44). Oswald therefore commits words to paper "to explain himself to posterity" (211), presuming that committing his story to paper will authenticate, organize, and—by extension—ascribe agency to his life: "It validated the experience," he thinks of his "Historic Diary," "as the writing of any history brings a persuasion and form to events" (211).

True, he takes his cues for action from events that are staged in visual media, as befits someone who also is presented as an inveterate watcher of movies and television. " 'I believe I shot myself,' " he says after shooting himself in the arm while in the marines. "Bushnell studied the perfect little scene. He thought Ozzie's remark sounded historical and charming, right out of a movie or TV play" (91). And he shapes those events with respect to plots that derive from the formulae of American visual media, *I Led Three Lives, Red River, Suddenly, We Were Strangers* being just four of the artifacts DeLillo cites. But when Oswald acts as the performing self that DeLillo depicts him as being, conscious of the representation of his acts at the time of their perpetration, he does so as artistic producer, assuming that the road to posterity is to be found in print.[12] He attempts suicide in Russia and imagines what he will and will not say for publication (152). He writes a "Historic Diary" in which he sees himself relating his story for *Life* or *Look,* in whose waiting rooms he sees himself sitting with a leather manuscript folder—"What is it called, morocco?" (206)—in his lap. He writes "The Kollective," and appends to it a foreword and a sketch titled "About the Author" (212–13).

Unlike the script devised for Oswald by the CIA Bay of Pigs veterans, which reflects a real political agenda, namely, making the attempt on Kennedy's life appear to come from Cubans in retaliation for plots against Castro, and thereby squelch any reconciliation between the United States and Cuba, none of the scripts that Oswald imagines for himself is motivated by any belief in organized politics one way or another. This, as it turns out, is quite consistent with the apolitical roles in which the actual Oswald tended to cast himself in those writings he composed while in Russia. It also is consistent with the schizophrenic self that permeates those autobiographical pieces included as exhibits in the Warren Commission *Hearings,* for if subjectivity requires a teleological sense of history for its support, Oswald's refusal to commit himself to any ideological belief left him as decentered in his own (self-)representation as he would later be in DeLillo's. The "Historic Diary" portrays him more as licentious (or, depending upon the woman, languishing) Lothario than lumpen proletariat: "Rosa about 23 blond attractive unmarried Excellant English, we attract each other at once" (XVI: 99); "A growing lonliness overtakes me in spite of my conquest of Ennatachina a girl from Riga," "I am having a light affair with Nell Korobka" (XVI: 101); "I am introduced to a girl with a French hair-do and red-dress with white slipper [. . .] Her name is Marina. We like each other right away" (XVI: 102).[13] Two self-questionnaires alternate between the expatriate living the good life ("I had plenty of money, an apartment rent-free lots of girls etc. why should

I leave all that?" [XVI: 436]) and the tourist frustrated at having to deal with bureaucratic red tape ("almost 1 year was spent in trying to leave the country. thats why I was there so long not out of desire!" [XVI: 439]) in explaining the reasons for his two-and-a-half-year stay abroad. Even the "New Era," political in nature in that it proposes no choice to exist between Russian Communism and American capitalism, as "[b]oth offer imperilistic injustice, tinted with two brands of slavery" (XVI: 429), concludes with an advocacy of "stoical readiness" as the vaguely defining trait of the equally vague pose of "radical futurist" that Oswald adopts (XVI: 430, 425).

In DeLillo's novel, this lack of political motivation is, in part, a function of Oswald's being a Libran, " 'sitting on the scales, ready to be tilted either way' " (319). And, as Jack Ruby will later recognize, it also is a function of Oswald's not having enough of a personality, his being "a complete nothing, a zero person in a T-shirt" (421), to maintain deeply held convictions of any sort. It is primarily the need to assuage the dreadful loneliness from which he suffers, almost a throwback to modernist alienation, that causes Oswald to affiliate himself with organized politics, an affiliation that begins with Oswald's early reading of Marxist books that "made him part of something" (41), since political movements offer him the prospects of ending his isolation by "merging with history." "History means to merge," he thinks. "The purpose of history is to climb out of your own skin" (101), the particular movement with which he opts to effect this merger varying with whatever movement seems to promise the greatest hope of community at any one time. Yet not only do all the movements Oswald samples frustrate his desire for community, they expose how ineffectual his attempts to define identity in terms of printed materials are. Feeling himself a " 'zero in the system' " of American capitalism (106), Oswald emigrates to the Soviet Union, thinking he will be "a man in history now" (149), only to discover he is a "zero in the system" there, too (151), Stateless Person Number 311479 according to his Identity Document (167). Presuming that "[d]ocuments are supposed to provide substance for a claim or a wish" because "[a] man with papers is substantial," he takes his papers to the Cuban embassy in Mexico City, and once again "the system floats right through him, through everything, even the revolution. He is a zero in the system" (357).

While Oswald's felt absence of self recalls that of another "true life novel" killer, Gary Gilmore, who described his personality as "[s]lightly less than bland" (Mailer, *Executioner's* 674), the violence through which he ultimately tries to fill that void springs from an altogether different motive. The suggestiveness of his remarks prior to shooting two bullets into Max Jensen's head notwithstanding (" 'This one is for me,' " " 'This one is for Nicole' " [227]), Gilmore's killing of two young men resonates as more than simple rage directed away from himself and his girlfriend. " 'I'll bet a nickel he knew those boys were Mormon before he killed them,' " a friend of his family wagers (456), so framing Gilmore's actions as reactions to a history of imprisoning American theocracies, the most recent of which is incarnated in Utah. Oswald's real motivating desire, by contrast, is not to merge with history, but to stand apart from history. As David Ferrie accurately points out, " 'I think you've had it backwards all this time. You wanted to enter history. Wrong approach, Leon. What you really want is out. Get out. Jump out. Find your place and your name on another level' " (384). In Marxism, after all, the individual is subservient to economic/historical processes; likewise, the CIA system that Oswald later seeks to penetrate "perpetuate[s] itself" (22).

For someone like Oswald, who feels himself a zero in system after system, the only "other level," to recall Ferrie's words, on which he will find a "place and name" of sufficient compensation is a marquee. Suspicions that the U.S. Marine Corps manual "had been written just for him" (42), that the military brig "was invented just for him" (100), that the Office of Naval Intelligence's false defector program "was written with him in mind" (162), that the television networks showing movies about assassination plots "were running this thing just for him" (370), in short, that "[t]hey had plans for him, whoever they were" (329) reflect far less Oswald's paranoid fears than they do his yearnings for centrality. Not surprisingly, the easiest way for anyone to enlist Oswald's support is to tell him how important he is. " 'You're an interesting individual,' " says George de Mohrenschildt, when approaching Oswald about talking to the CIA. " 'I'm sure they would very much like to learn about your contacts in the Soviet Union' " (238). " 'You're an interesting fellow,' " repeats CIA agent Marion Collings, with whom de Mohrenschildt sets up a meeting (247), only to have his flattery topped by Agent Bateman of the FBI, who attempts to secure Oswald's services for his own organization: " 'You're an interesting fellow. Every agency from here to the Himalayas has something in the files on Oswald, Lee' " (311).

Such insinuating remarks only reinforce the message continually sent by the one medium that encourages the zero person to believe that he truly has exceptional value: television. Yes, television frustrates the poverty-stricken Oswald in that the life of consumer fulfillment it promises is repudiated by the life in small rooms that he and his mother have been forced to live. Marguerite gets fired from a salesperson's job at Lerner's "because they said she did not use deodorant," DeLillo writes. "This was not true because she used a roll-on every day and if it didn't work the way it said on TV, why should she be singled out as a social misfit?" (38). Nevertheless, television's presence in DeLillo's work is treated ambivalently. On the one hand, television remains the only medium that dissolves those differences in social class that separate people. In *White Noise* (1985), it is a weather report on television that enables Howard Dunlap to recover from the state of malaise into which his mother's death has plunged him, since, as he points out, " 'Everyone notices the weather' " (55). As popular culture lecturer Murray Jay Siskind states, television " 'welcomes us into the grid' " (51). On the other hand, the grid into which television welcomes everyone also imprisons everyone, symptomatic as it is of the dominant mass media that no person can escape, as Oswald and his Russian wife experience one evening when they stop to look at a television set in a department store window and see "the most remarkable thing": "It was the world gone inside out. There they were gaping back at themselves from the TV screen. She was on television. Lee was on television, standing next to her, holding Junie in his arms. [. . .] She didn't know anything like this could ever happen" (227). Having thus discovered the "world inside the world" he has sought for years in the very medium he has watched since childhood (13), Oswald shifts from words to pictures, and concomitantly from artistic producer to object of consumption, as a means of ensuring his place in posterity. He poses in his backyard with rifle, revolver, and radical literature and imagines himself on the cover of *Time* magazine, entering "the frame of official memory" as "[t]he Castro partisan with his guns and subversive journals. [. . .] The man who shot the fascist general. A friend of the revolution" (279, 281), or, more simply, as DeLillo has stated in interviews, "almost the poor man's James Dean" ("Outsider" 56).

The Megaton Novel James Joyce Would Have Written
If He'd Moved to Iowa City

In this desire to be a media celebrity, DeLillo's Oswald is not the disaffected American, as the role of lone gunman would suggest, or even the lunatic American, as his prolonged habitations in small rooms would imply, but, as critics have argued, every American.[14] Such typicality, in fact, was exactly the point that Oswald's mother stressed in those interviews with Jean Stafford (1966) in which she tried to vindicate her place as " 'a mother in history' " (25). Portraying her son's childhood as defined by " 'regular trend[s]' " like chess, stamp collecting, comic books, and Monopoly (98, 19), she refused to see " 'anything abnormal about any part of his life' " and defended the Oswald family as " 'an average American family' " (19, 25) despite the fact that one "regular trend" in which her son engaged was prolonged truancy and the fact that the history of her own matrimonial misfortunes, as Stafford noted, "shoots off at a forty-five degree angle from the norm" (26). Yet even those Warren Commission counselors with less at stake personally contributed, however inadvertently, to the impression of Oswald's representative status through questions (often leading) posed to witnesses about how "typical" or "normal" Oswald was. "Your family was always a typical, loyal American family?" his brother Robert was asked (I: 375), "And Lee had what you would describe as a normal interest in firearms?" (I: 296), "And it is your opinion [. . .] that they [Lee and Marina] led a reasonably normal married life [. . .]?" (I: 414), all of which elicited answers in the affirmative. "Would you say that the course of conduct of Lee Oswald was normal, having in mind the problems he was facing?" (VIII: 7), childhood acquaintance Edward Voebel was made to recall. "And you don't think Lee was an outstanding student [. . .]? You think he was more or less average; is that right?" (VIII: 13), "Did he have any sex deviation of any kind? From your experience, he seemed to be perfectly normal in that respect?" (VIII: 15). Affirmative on all counts once again.[15] The difference—and it is crucial—is that DeLillo ironizes the protagonist as type from which the traditional historical novel generalized, his portrayal of the outsider Oswald as typical suggesting that what binds us as a nation is the sense that all of us are marginalized figures now.

DeLillo reinforces that representative status of Oswald with respect to the myriad characters who parade through his book, taking their cues for action from the various films that have left upon them the greatest impressions. Wayne Elko hires himself out as a mercenary in order to act as masterless *Seven Samurai* warrior (145). Parmenter stages Caribbean CIA invasions with "[c]ryptic messages from spy movies of the forties" (127). And so similar to Oswald is the figure of Jack Ruby introduced in the second half of the novel that he functions as Oswald's mirror image. A "nothing person," by his own admission, whose present domicile resembles "a lost-and-found" and whose past dwelling in hotel rooms recalls the isolated lives in small rooms that Oswald and his mother have led (342), Ruby also is a Jew in Texas, who inhabits a decentered space "off to the side" despite his club ownership making him "a known face, with ads in the paper, as only America can turn out" (350, 344), and a fragmented self, as suggested by the Mafia emissary who shows how " 'not outfit' " he is with a reference to Ruby's not being " *'connected'* " (256). As a result, Ruby the avenger must be "pieced together," as the epigraph to part two of the novel indicates (215), much like the figure of the lone gunman and from the same kind of movie scenarios. " 'You killed my President, you rat,' " the actual Ruby recalled himself exclaiming, à la James Cagney, at the moment he pumped lead into Oswald's body (V: 200). It is no wonder, then, that DeLillo describes the scene of Oswald being shot in the Dallas police station as a stage lit with spotlights and TV cameras, with Ruby "seeing everything happen in advance" (437), for Ruby, no less than Oswald, is acting as performing self seeking celebrity status at the point of a gun. " 'I am Jack Ruby,' " he said after the deed was done. " 'You all know me' " (V: 200).

Which is not to say, of course, that Oswald's end brings to an end the impulse toward celebrity that he typifies. All that changes is the means by which notoriety is achieved as the celebrity performer is replaced by the celebrity author. "I will write books about the life of Lee Harvey Oswald," his mother states to the Warren Commission in the final pages of DeLillo's novel (449), so echoing the aspirations that permeate the remarks entered into the actual transcribed document. "It is my story that some day I hope to write," Marguerite Oswald announces to the Warren Commission (I: 222), having already whetted its appetite with the "stories galore" she plans to narrate prior to beginning the "speaking tours" for which she is—pun intended—"booked" (I: 163, 236). Aware from the start that "[t]his is my life and my son's life going down in history" (I: 182), and having already obtained the commission's word that "you will let me have my life story from early childhood and Lee's life story from early childhood" (I: 196), she proceeds to relate the most minute details of her life since childhood—such as the fact that she wore a pink dress to her grammar school graduation and sang "Little Pink Roses" at the ceremony (I: 252)—and transform those relating to Oswald's to the degree that they affect her own. Hence her dismissal of any objections her son has had to an earlier book she has planned to write of his defection: " 'It has nothing to do with you and Marina. It is my life, because of your defection' " (I: 132). Not to be outdone, wife Marina writes "the story of my life from the time I met him [Oswald] in Minsk up to the very last days" (I: 3). Brother Robert begins a diary with the statement: " 'Dated December 6, 1963, for the history of the past 2 weeks as seen through my eyes, and heard with my ears, and felt with my body; I write for future reference for myself and for the future members of the family' " (I: 341).

If DeLillo then characterizes the Warren Commission *Report* and its accompanying twenty-six volumes as "the megaton novel James Joyce would have written if he'd moved to Iowa City and lived to be a hundred," containing as they do "a poetry of lives muddied and dripping in language" (181), it is because the witnesses in them jump at the chance to testify and elevate to public prominence the otherwise trivial details of their ordinary lives.[16] Presuming that "[e]ventually somebody would have to be coming after me," the man who shares Ruby's apartment comes before the commission of his own volition and shares insider information about the meals he cooks for Ruby: "After all, I was his roommate," George Senator states (XIV: 246). The woman with whom Marina lives from September 1963 until the assassination insists on introducing into the public record a letter she wrote her mother because, as Ruth Paine asserts, it shows how ordinary Oswald was from her privileged perspective as "one of the few people who can give it" (II: 509).

And with the passage of time enabling them to supplement the discovery of their prominence as witnesses with the discovery of their prominence as participants, the tragedy of the dead king itself is replaced by differently emplotted productions in which each has played a major role, much like Stoppard's Rosencrantz and Guildenstern. Robert concludes that the assassination is the product of sibling rivalry, of Lee's "realization that I had been lucky enough to achieve what he wanted and would never achieve," because he notices that his brother's "most reckless acts" occurred on "dates which had particular significance in my life" (his birthday, the birthday of his son, and his wedding anniversary) (*Lee* 240, 232). Marguerite, who earlier has reminded Lyndon Johnson in *Time* magazine " 'that he is only President of the United States by the grace of my son's action' " (I: 242), starts publicizing the history of her own contributions to the history of the Oval Office. " 'After all, I *am* responsible for two Presidents,' " she tells Stafford when explaining her refusal to discuss her " 'personal politics' " (62)—a contagious sense of obligation, as it turns out, for by the time these turns at center stage have been completed, each person has found himself or herself to be the one person who could have prevented the assassination of the president from occurring. "[I]f I had led my life differently President Kennedy might be alive," Ruth Paine declares in the opening statement to the litany of "if onlys" that comprise the piece titled "Oswald" that she submits to *Look* magazine at the time of the Warren Commission: "*If only* I had known that Lee Oswald had hidden a rifle in my garage. *If only* I had appraised this man as someone able to do such terrible violence. *If only* the job that I helped him find hadn't put him in a building along the President's route" (XVII: 179). This litany she repeats almost verbatim when speaking as "The Woman Who Sheltered Lee Oswald's family" to Jessamyn West for *Redbook*'s July 1964 cover story—" '*If only* I had known that Lee Oswald had hidden a rifle in my garage. *If only* I had realized that this man was capable of such an act. If only quite by accident I had or had not done a dozen things' " (92)—seconded this time by her husband, Michael, who speculates " 'if I gave up too soon with Lee' " (85).

This, of course, is hardly the first time that Americans have jumped on a celebrity bandwagon with participatory anecdotes in tow. Witnesses to the events surrounding the Lincoln assassination a century earlier were equally eager to trumpet their individually privileged perspectives with claims (often dubious) to fame that stemmed from a variety of services performed—boosting a surgeon up into the presidential theater box to tend to the wounded leader in the case of one businessman, escorting a neglected first lady across the street to see her dying husband in the case of a War Department clerk—and that culminated later in the simple (but oft disputed) claims to being not just the "only" person able to supply a missing detail, but the "last" living witness able to supply any information at all. Convinced that he was "[t]he only living man who can tell the story," as the title page of his book asserts, the man who provided Booth with a boat to escape from Maryland offered his *J. Wilkes Booth* (1893) to the public as *An Account of His Sojourn in Southern Maryland after the Assassination of Abraham Lincoln, His Passage across the Potomac, and His Death in Virginia.* This was despite the fact that the chapters in the account focus mainly on the trials and tribulations of its author, Thomas A. Jones ("My Connection with the Confederate Mail," "I am Offered $100,000.00 to Betray Booth by Captain Williams," "I Conduct Booth to the Potomac," "My Arrest and Imprisonment"), and the fact that Booth himself does not enter into the text until one-third of the way through it. Convinced, likewise, that she was " 'the only person that knows how Booth made his escape,' " ninety-four-year-old Mrs. Nelson Todd broadcast the tale of her experiences in Ford's Theatre, first over a 1934 national hookup and, afterward, in a cinematic talkie—so successfully, it seemed, that she returned to a New York studio the next day in order to lengthen the newsreel in which she had appeared (Good 176, 174).

Yet witnesses a century earlier also let time elapse before disclosing their own contributions to the public.[17] Asia Booth Clarke, for instance, specifically instructed that the 1874 memoir she wrote of her brother John Wilkes Booth not be read until after her death and stipulated that all monies that might accrue from any future publication go to the British writer to whom she entrusted the manuscript in 1888 (*Unlocked* 135, 204). That writer, B. L. Farjeon, in turn, made no attempt to get the text published until the last family members of Clarke's generation had died. As a result, the manuscript did not get issued until 1938, after Farjeon's daughter Eleanor decided to resume work on the project. Ably assisted by the disbursements that the media a hundred years later award them for whatever details of their lives they wish to proffer, the people on the fringes of the Kennedy assassination, in contrast, brook no delay: movie and television rights to Texitalia Films and World-Wide, photo rights to *Life* and the *London Daily Mirror*, serial and article rights to *Stern* and *This Week* magazines, and world book rights to Meredith Press net Marina $132,350 in contract fees (I: 496), in addition to $7,500 plus expenses for each filmed appearance and $1,500 plus expenses for each personal appearance (II: 23). So thoroughly implicated are these later participants that any complaints that arise concern less the fact of the media's scrutiny and more the division of the media's spoils. "This whole thing seems to me like I have been kind of made a patsy," whines James Martin, who has quit managing motels to manage Marina's business affairs, after Marina cancels their ten-year contract and his 15 percent cut (I: 491). Similarly humiliated by the paltry $900 she has received from charitable donors in contrast to the $35,000 mailed to Marina (I: 210), Marguerite instructs the

Secret Service men opening envelopes, " 'I definitely want my share' " (I: 176), and takes even sterner measures with respect to the media: " 'if we are going to have the life story with Life magazine [. . .] I would like to get paid' " (I: 145).[18]

The more immediate problem they face, however, stems from the distance between ambition and composition, for while quite willing to pose as celebrity authors, few are willing to do what Oswald himself did and proceed with the actual task of putting words on paper. Nowhere is that disparity between whim and work more trenchantly displayed than in Marguerite Oswald's attempts to get Jean Stafford to write the numerous stories she has available to tell. That Mrs. Oswald is a veritable well of authorial potential she quickly establishes for Stafford at the start of their first interview: the book she intends to write, alternately titled *One and One Make Two* or *This and That,* is to be the first of three or five projected books Marguerite could write " 'on what I know and what I have researched' " (12). But it is not until Stafford returns to Mrs. Oswald's home for their final interview and discovers Marguerite calmly eating her lunch while listening to her one-hundred-eighty-word-a-minute voice blare out the "Mother's Day Epistle" (Stafford's term) she has earlier that day fed into a tape recorder—a wonderful image of communications looping—that the full extent of the older woman's authorial yearnings becomes completely clear (85). Certain by this time that she has enough material for a series of books (94), enough, at the very least, to run " 'for two or three years every month in a big national magazine, and after that as a sort of a soap opera on radio or even on TV' " (101), Marguerite makes her a cappella pitch after the tape runs out: " 'Couldn't you take the summer off and come on down and rent the other side of the house so we could write it all up?' " (102). As her next remarks indicate, though, the "we" that she envisions is no authorial sorority, for underlying the added inducements of " 'a discount house where you could get a hot plate cheap' " and a back porch on which the two can work in housecoats is a division of labor that hardly qualifies as joint composition: " 'I mean, I would give of my time and voice and let you see the work I've done and we could split the proceeds' " (102).

DeLillo attributes Marguerite's rhetorical inability to move from orality to literacy to a narrative fixation with chronology and causation: "I cannot enumerate cold," she tells the Warren Commission in his novel. "I have to tell a story" (455). Yet as the picture of Nicholas Branch struggling to formulate any finished prose illustrates, it is virtually impossible to tell a story about the assassination of John F. Kennedy in the traditionally realist manner that Marguerite requires. All one *can* do, in fact, is enumerate or list the pieces of data that surround the event, as Branch does with the data the curator continues to send him, and *not* draw any connections among them, however provocatively they call out for assemblage, as Branch observes when listing the various deaths of those connected, however loosely, to the events of 22 November, and as DeLillo substantiates by the scattered presentation of those details throughout his text (58, 378–79, 442–43). If, as Hayden White contends, the demand for closure is a demand for moral meaning (*Content* 21), the relinquishing of the former implies the futility of uncovering the latter.

In the pre-Oprah 1960s, moreover, no appropriate visual forum exists for the assassination's authorial wannabes to hawk the instant literary wares they project, and so, like most performances by actors and actresses in supporting roles, they get consigned to virtual oblivion.[19] None is awarded by the Academy that middle name, which—even if not Oscar literally—serves to confer upon its recipient equivalent celebrity status. "Once you did something notorious, they tagged you with an extra name, a middle name that was ordinarily never used," DeLillo's Oswald realizes in Russia when confronted with the imprisoned Francis Gary Powers. "You were officially marked, a chapter in the imagination of the state" (198). Oswald himself is so catapulted in *Libra* after the assassination of the president who, having run for office as a box-office star, according to Norman Mailer, had been reconstituted as a media simulacrum of three names as early as 1960.[20] "After the crime comes the reconstruction," Oswald thinks in prison (434). "People will come to see him, the lawyers first, then psychologists, historians, biographers" (435). Ruby, who never gains that third name, continues to feel himself "a nothing person" (443), without ever understanding why. "All he knows for sure is that there is a missing element here, a word that they have canceled completely" (445). There is: Leon, his own middle name.

As Frank Lentricchia has noted, "The question, who or what is responsible for the production of *Lee Harvey Oswald* (or *John Fitzgerald Kennedy*), is inseparable from the question of where DeLillo imagines power to lie in contemporary America" (203–4). In the words of Marguerite Oswald's personification, "TV gave directions and down he went" (452). The irony is that the celebrity crossover that grants Oswald the singular self for which he strives, that "single clear subject now, called Lee Harvey Oswald" (435), gives him a self that he is incapable of recognizing. "It sounded extremely strange," he thinks when hearing his official name on radios and televisions. "He didn't recognize himself in the full intonation of the name. [. . .] It sounded odd and dumb and made up. They were talking about somebody else" (416). Whereas Oswald previously has imagined his sense of destiny in terms of "a network of connections" in which "the private world" of miniature rooms in which he has been locked would expand "out to three dimensions" (277), being encased in the black box that is network TV ends up reducing him to two dimensions, thereby imprisoning him in what, in effect, serves as the smallest of the small rooms in which he has been trapped throughout his life. Only now he is both literally and figuratively flattened and devoid of all depth, a postmodern subject defined by what Jameson views as "the supreme formal feature" of all postmodern art (*Postmodernism* 9).[21] "It was a process that drained life from the men in the picture, sealed them in the frame," Beryl Parmenter realizes when watching the footage of Oswald's death replayed on television (447). As such, Oswald ends up the "victim of a total frame" in more than the one way he means when the police first apprehend him (418), for the frame that victimizes him comes as much from a photograph as it does from the CIA, just as the shot that kills him comes as much from a camera as it does from Jack Ruby's gun, as DeLillo's description of the replayed footage of his death indicates: "He is commenting on the documentary footage even as it is being shot. Then he himself is shot, and shot, and shot, and the look becomes another kind of knowledge" (447).[22]

Reviewing the Kennedy assassination in an essay written for *Rolling Stone* two decades after it occurred, DeLillo saw Oswald as presaging all those media-receptive young men who took guns into their hands and committed acts of political violence for reasons other than politics: Arthur Bremer, John Hinckley, James Earl Ray ("American" [1983] 24, 27–28).[23] Bremer, we also might wish to remember, was another diarist, one who so strongly believed his 1972 journal would become "one of the most closely read pages since the Scrolls in those caves" (93) that he prohibited any unauthorized use of its material by copyrighting it (albeit with his own notarization) (124).[24] Yet, in a measure of the difference between the media-infused 1960s and the media-saturated 1970s, Bremer's diary repeatedly depicts its author as being completely impatient with the entire process of composition: "thruorly pissed off" when he cannot find a pen to write with (93), equally irate when he does find an implement, Bremer gets bored so quickly when making his entries that adding to his journal becomes equivalent to "writting, writting, a War & Peace" (102).[25] And once that diary turns into a testament to all his fumbled attempts to assassinate a public figure, the document whose sole purpose has been to immortalize further Bremer's deeds *after* the fact becomes a mockery of his total inability to act at all ("Two-hundred-forty-one pages—wow! I should of been dead about 60 or 70 pages ago" [117]), and writing itself becomes a feminized endeavor, evidence of all Bremer's accumulated failures, sexual and otherwise, to perform as a man ("Nothing has happened for so long, 3 months, the 1st person I held a conversation with in 3 months was a near naked girl rubbing my erect penis & she wouldn't let me put it thru her" [98]). Bremer thus repudiates in advance any conceit that his decision to shoot George Wallace instead of Richard Nixon will be viewed as "exciting & fasinating to readers 100 years from now—as the Booth conspricy seems to us today" or that his shift in strategy will be considered a surprise ending to a book in which "my inner character shall steal the climax and destroy the author and save the anti-hero from assasination" (105, 104). Convinced that the mediocrity of his proposed victim confirms the mediocrity of his own self, Bremer knows in advance he "won't get more than 3 minutes on network T.V. news" (105).

After Jean Harris killed Scarsdale Diet Doctor Herman Tarnower eight years later, she got considerably more time than that, not to mention two Barbara Walters interviews and two *People* magazine spreads. Unlike Tommy Roy Foster, the imprisoned killer with whom Jack Gladney's son plays chess in *White Noise*, who cares for his weapons obsessively, has an arsenal stashed in a " 'shabby little room off a six-story car park,' " makes tapes of his voice asking forgiveness of loved ones, hears voices on TV telling him " 'to go down in history,' " and goes out to kill six people in Iron City from a rooftop sniper's position (44), the respectable Harris acted out of a much simpler desire: not to be treated as disposable by a lover of fourteen years any longer. DeLillo's imprisoned killer, a cultural cliché by 1985, unfortunately forgets that Iron City is the one place in the country that has no media, and so, as Gladney's son ruefully notes, " 'He now knows he won't go down in history' " (45). Proof that representation trumps any previous lack of fame in the making of media spectacles that bypass class, race, and gender, Harris, as we shall see in the next chapter, was given a place in history that she never initially sought.

"I was just a screw or a cog in the great machine I called life, and when I dropped out of it I found I was of no use anywhere else. What can one do when one finds that one only fits into one hole? One must get back to it or be thrown out into the rubbish heap—and you don't know what it's like in the rubbish heap!"
—Lily Bart to Lawrence Selden, *The House of Mirth* (1905)

"To be jeered at, and called 'old and pathetic' made me seriously consider borrowing $5,000 just before I left New York and telling a doctor to make me young again—to do anything but make me not feel like discarded trash. I lost my nerve because there was always the chance I'd end up uglier than before."
—Jean Harris, letter to Herman Tarnower, 8–9 March 1980

"Two People Who Didn't Argue, Even, Except over the Use of the Subjunctive"
Jean Harris, the Scarsdale Diet Doctor Murder, and Diana Trilling

Living in an age in which actors gain sixty pounds in preparation to play washed-up boxers, I decided to reverse the process and go on the Scarsdale Diet in preparation for my work on Jean Harris and the murder of Scarsdale Diet Doctor Herman Tarnower. I puckered my lips for morning grapefruit, munched dry protein toast with wild abandon, and, casting caution to the wind, gorged myself on spinach leaves soaked in lemon juice, all the while chew-chew-chewing in conformance with the doctor's command.

I now knew why Herman Tarnower had to die.

So, apparently, did everybody else. For women's groups, Harris's taking a gun to Tarnower (with intent or not) was simply a final assumption of control after having endured fourteen years of psychological abuse and flagrant infidelity. For Shana Alexander, who found the chronology of Harris's life to parallel her own quite strikingly, the rage of romance novels and the repression of an entire lifetime combined to cause Tarnower's death, taking specific shape in jealousy over an office assistant that Harris was too proud to admit (300). Indeed, it seems that the only one who did not know why Herman Tarnower died was Jean Harris herself, who continued to remain mystified about "how something that ugly and sad could have happened between two people who didn't argue, even, except over the use of the subjunctive" (*Stranger* 139).

We smirk knowingly at such a comment, of course, particularly when it comes as testimony that claims to describe what killer and victim were feeling as one lay dying at the feet of the other. And yet the remark actually reveals a great deal about the factors that contributed to the events of 10 March 1980. Rhetorical ability means a great deal to Jean Harris. This, after all, is a woman whose main objection to prison's lack of privacy is the denotation of underpants as "panties," who sings "The Rain in Spain" ("a real show stopper") to fellow inmates as part of her war on double negatives and four-letter words, and who mourns a two-year-old's use of profanity as damning her "to live the way she speaks" (*Marking* 72; *Stranger* 331, 358). Why? Because, as her quotation of Alfred North Whitehead makes clear, "Style in its finest sense, is the last acquirement of the educated mind, it is also the most useful. [. . .] Style is the ultimate morality of mind" (*Marking* 128).

Diana Trilling, who long subscribed to Dewey's definition of "manners as small morals" (*We* 149), would have concurred completely. "We like to persuade ourselves that in any sense worth our notice, style is only of the arts," she writes near the beginning of *Mrs. Harris* (1981), her book on the diet doctor murder, only to end with a statement of how delusory such an assumption is: "In the style of life that any of us chooses there's contained a psychological, social, and moral message. [. . .] The bad esthetics of a society *matter* and so do the bad esthetics of the individual within the society; [. . .] style is a moral mode, a mode in morality" (40–41).[1] And morality, what Émile Durkheim termed the "human ideal," was part and parcel of the "national ideal" that the state, in his view, was meant to cultivate.[2] If Trilling then saw Tarnower's rise from card games with eastern European Jews in Flatbush to golfing with Alfred A. Knopf in Purchase as a story out of F. Scott Fitzgerald, and Harris's search for respectability at exclusive girls' schools as worthy of a George Eliot novel, she also recognized the changing roles that money, taste, and intellectualism had come to play in the postwar version of national definition: money might now buy class, but it did not confer moral stature; taste could be acquired by acts of intellectual will, but aesthetic sensibility did not guarantee social acceptance. In the conflict between these two very different approaches to social prestige, she found the motive that so escaped the drama's surviving protagonist.

Or did she? In contrast to those celebrated murder trials—the O. J. Simpson trial being an obvious example—devoted to uncovering the identity of the perpetrator, the Jean Harris case was never a whodunit. Police who arrived on the scene in response to a call from Tarnower's housekeeper found Harris in blood-stained clothing leaving the doctor's Purchase estate, allegedly on her way to a nearby community center to phone in the shooting herself. Harris, a fifty-six-year-old headmistress at the exclusive Madeira School outside of Washington, D.C., immediately confessed to having shot her companion of fourteen years after having driven five hours from Virginia to see him one last time. The only question that seemed to remain was whether the death of the doctor that ended that last visit was the result of Harris's desire to kill him for having replaced her in his affections with a woman twenty years her junior, as the prosecution claimed, or the result of Harris's botched attempt to kill herself, as the defense contended, in which Tarnower's efforts to stop her ended in his own accidental death during a struggle for the gun. During the actual trial, however, this narrative so easily framed in terms of love triangles, sexual jealousy, and a woman scorned, and lapped up by a public hungry for more on the lifestyles of the rich and famous, unraveled as more and more details of the case emerged. The discovery, for instance, that Harris was addicted to Desoxyn, which the doctor had been overprescribing for her for a decade, led to questions about whether her violent actions after a weekend without amphetamines reflected self-righteous feminist injustice or simple drug withdrawal. Therefore, in contrast, again, to the Simpson case, in which focusing on the determining issue of race—rightly or wrongly—became an even more central index of foundational American inequities as the trial (not to mention the testimony of Mark Fuhrman) progressed, focusing exclusively on the comparably central issues of gender and class in the Harris case became exercises in diminishing returns.

But if notorious legal cases become spectacular cases precisely because they serve as cultural litmus tests, just what kind of cultural issues were most at stake in the Jean Harris murder trial? According to the defense, which predicated its entire strategy upon Harris's being too much a "lady" to commit murder, it was a case of the inextricability of manners and morality, of "classiness" and class, linkages that, as Trilling acknowledges, do possess an inherent gender bias: "The idea of the gentleman has to all purposes disappeared from our culture, but not the idea of the lady; the title has been largely discarded but the concept remains. It seems to withstand all our rebellions against these presumably outmoded categories" (*Mrs.* 263). In his own examination of "Manners, Morals, and the Novel" (1948) years earlier, her husband, Lionel, ascribed such resilience to living in a bourgeois democratic society in which, money having produced a constant shifting of social classes, there remained a need for other criteria to define status in the United States. As a result, "[t]o appear to be established is one of the ways of becoming established" (204). By the time of the Harris case, such an emphasis on personal style would be revealed as a fetishizing of style, with bad taste synonymous with bad character and good taste with moral probity, a belief maintained not only by participants in the trial, like Harris, blocked from social distinction by lack of money, but also by commentators on the trial, like Diana Trilling, frustrated by the perceived constraints of marriage. What no one anticipated until the trial was under way was how much the well-educated and immaculately groomed defendant would vex that unstated social credo with behavior that was, from Trilling's perspective as observer, "often neither fine nor ladylike" (*Mrs.* 17). And, in the end, it was this crime in the courtroom, more than any prosecutorial evidence about bullet trajectories or blood splatters, that led to Harris's being convicted for the crime of which she was accused.

Stranger in Two Worlds

No such complications were provided by the victim in the case, Herman Tarnower, whose life provided incontrovertible proof of the connection between morality and manners. A man who played off one woman against another, to the extent of informing his assistant Lynne Tryforos of his itinerary when traveling with Jean Harris so that the older woman would be aware of letters sent by the younger rival, and of making certain that each woman knew of his sexual involvement with the other by keeping negligees of both in the same bathroom, he was, as Trilling points out, nothing but "a small-time emotional imperialist" (*Mrs.* 311). Certainly, such preying on the emotional vulnerabilities of others was at the heart of the Complete Scarsdale Medical Diet itself, a fourteen-day weight-loss plan whose advertised "simplicity" derived from the fact that *"the decisions have been made for you"* (Tarnower and Baker 10), specifically, the decisions of exactly what to eat for breakfast, lunch, and dinner, which Trilling analyzes in great detail to reveal both the diet's unnecessarily restrictive nature and its elitist social pretensions. Why, she asks, was it not until Tarnower went public with the two-page diet he had privately been supplying patients for close to two decades that he allowed a variety of vegetables in place of Thursday's meager cabbage? (*Mrs.* 38). Why are the gourmets on the "Diet for Epicurean Tastes" variation allowed three ounces of wine a day, not to mention the options of papaya, mango, and "Spinach Delight à la Lynne," when the proles on the "Money-Saver Diet" must make do with grapefruit and "[p]lenty of spinach"? (39, 40). For Trilling, in fact, the doctor's gastronomic tastes provide an index to the doctor's aesthetic tastes, as illustrated most vividly by his home, a former pool house turned into "a small monument to cultural inflatedness" (23), its dining room an homage to the art of taxidermy, its master bedroom a tribute to tourist-trade *tchotchkas*—all in all, a two-story "Japanese—Japanoid— manifestation, a sort of domestic pagoda," complete with pond and private Buddha (25). "I couldn't make out the little island in the pond or see whether the Buddha to which the doctor was said to have liked to row was bronze or stone, sat on its island or stood, whether it was a fat Silenus of a deity or flat-bellied as befitted the object of a diet doctor's reverence," Trilling admits after being denied access to the grounds upon her first visit (27). But of one thing the seventy-five-year-old matron skulking around during an April downpour is convinced: "Imagine one's private pond in Westchester with a private Buddha to row to—it was absurd!" (27).

Given that Tarnower's assimilationist social aspirations required speaking in front of a mirror for four years during college in order to lose his Brooklyn accent, it is not surprising that his cardiology expertise became obsolescent as his diet authority in particular grew. As Pierre Bourdieu notes, "Taste, a class culture turned into nature, that is, *embodied*, helps to shape the class body. [. . .] It follows that the body is the most indisputable materialization of class taste" (190). Nor should it be surprising that the Complete Scarsdale Medical Diet concerns itself as much with *how* to eat as it does with *what* to eat—"*Chew! Chew! Chew!*" "*Build a mountain* when you make a salad," "*Cup up your food*" (Tarnower and Baker 132–33)—for while the working-class person characterizes a meal by abundance, the bourgeois is concerned to eat with all due form (Bourdieu 194, 196).

For if Herman Tarnower was anything, he was bourgeois. True, his professional skills gave him entrée into the upper-class world of German Jewry, success this son of eastern European immigrants was able to achieve due to the democratization that the fact of Nazism had produced among American Jews.[3] And insofar as money was concerned, sales of *The Complete Scarsdale Medical Diet* made sure that he remained financially well established. Published in January 1979, the book's hardcover edition lasted forty-nine weeks on the *New York Times* best-seller list, thirty-one as number one, and sold 711,100 copies; the Bantam paperback, published a year later, lasted eighty weeks, forty as number one, and at the time of the doctor's death had sold 2.25 million copies (Alexander 152; Altman B4). (These two-year figures may be compared with the 5.25 million copies total of Robert Atkins's *Dr. Atkins' Diet Revolution* sold in the seven years since its 1973 publication [Altman B4].) Culturally, however, he provided living justification for those jeremiads against "the spreading ooze of Mass Culture" that people like Dwight Macdonald and Clement Greenberg were delivering in the middle decades of the century (Macdonald 73).[4] According to Harris,

Tarnower "grew up in a cultural Sahara. [. . .] He never mentioned a home that had books or music in it, but he tried to teach himself to understand and appreciate culture in all its forms," adding, "[h]e had an extensive record collection of symphonies, some with the seals still unbroken" (*Stranger* 50). A marvelous detail, which corroborates Trilling's invocation of Fitzgerald, the records specifically bring to mind Nick Carraway's encounter with an owl-eyed guest in Gatsby's library, whose delight in its holdings' "real"-ness is capped off by the fact that their pages are not cut (*Great* 45–46). Yet Harris misses the point of the unbroken seals completely. To her Tarnower is "a man who read Herodotus for fun," not a man whose favorite contemporary music was the soundtrack to the movie *Cleopatra* (qtd. in Alexander 262).

As her confusion here suggests, the midwestern Harris very much conformed to the role of young woman from the provinces; Trilling compares her to Emma Bovary and Anna Karenina, "people who were born to stay home rather than follow the beckonings of their imaginations" (*Mrs.* 244). And there is something horribly plaintive about the story Trilling recounts of Harris driving to Purchase from her home in Virginia to stand outside a window looking in at the doctor entertaining friends with Lynne Tryforos (156), much like that other provincial, Jude Fawley, looking in at Christminster in Thomas Hardy's novel. That horror is only exacerbated by the fact that Harris's position of "stranger in two worlds," as she titled her memoir (1986), was one that she straddled all her life, as indicated by the differences in social standing between her and the schools with which she was affiliated: from the Shaker Heights girls' school and Smith College she attended as a student, to the Grosse Pointe elementary school at which she worked as a teacher, to the Chestnut Hill middle school at which she served as director, to the Madeira School at which she became headmistress.

Unlike Tarnower, however, Harris could not use money to erase those differences. No Mildred Pierce pie conglomerate for her. Harris's 1945 Phi Beta Kappa graduation from Smith as an economics major *magna cum laude* coincided with the circumscribed job prospects available to women after their post–World War II demobilization. Her teaching career commenced at the time that the concept of gracious living was introduced into American popular culture, in which, as Trilling describes, "[i]t was the function of women to be nourishers and sustainers, not doers or achievers" (*Mrs.* 316).[5] Indeed, for all her obvious enjoyment of the things that money could buy, such as the ubiquitous mink accessories that so damned her in the jury's eyes during her trial, and her resentment of how little money her own employment granted her, as evidenced by her prison remark that "call girls" are "much richer than school teachers" (*Stranger* 219), Harris maintained an attitude toward money that was decidedly ambivalent. She had no objections to the Scarsdale Diet, for instance, just the fact that Tarnower started selling it (Alexander 151). She took a fifteen-thousand-dollar pay cut when moving to Madeira from a job at Allied Maintenance Corporation.[6] Reflecting more than mere desire for prestige that a job writing bids for industrial cleaning contracts could not provide, Harris's act betrays a discomfort about working for pay. She thus traced "the place and time when I began to be a non-person" to the time that she exchanged the role of school teacher for school administrator in order to make more money to support her family (*Stranger* 81). Far more comfortable with being a female than a feminist, she defined the kind of role model she would be at Madeira accordingly: "I wanted the role to be that of a woman first—a woman who happened to be a headmistress" (92).

This conflict between "feminism and 'female-ism'" is one that long concerned Trilling (*Claremont* 50). Her 1950 *Partisan Review* piece on Margaret Mead's *Male and Female* (1949) equates the "shuttle" that the anthropologist runs between being a popularizer and a professional to the "shuttle every sensitive professional woman in our culture runs between the need to protect and the wish to transcend her femininity" (*Claremont* 52); in Trilling's view, however, Mead's recognition that women were not sufficiently valued for their activities as wives and mothers does not lead to its logical conclusion, namely, "that because we do not value women for their femaleness, we force them to seek social prestige by emulating the activities of men" (61). Turning from the professional to the popular herself in 1959, Trilling, in her *Look* magazine piece, makes "The Case for the American Woman" dependent upon a similar sense of confusion: "her sex has lost its way" because the demands now placed on the American woman for a competence that was never before required—as chauffeur, economist, psychologist, mechanic, carpenter—have made her doubt her "womanly grace and charm" (51, 54); what is required, according to Trilling, is "simple recognition that the modern woman is begging for reassurance that she has not lost her femininity by her forced advance along new lines of masculine competence" (54).

Significantly, Trilling's article for *Look* locates this crisis most visibly in middle-class life, where the disappearance of servants and other household services demands more from women in compensation. Yet, as a 1971 trip to her college alma mater forces her to realize, it is the American middle class that ill equips its daughters to feel comfortable with, much less aspire to meet, the challenges of professional competence. On the contrary, Trilling's nine-week return to Radcliffe in "We Must March My Darlings" (1971–72) presents her with women not so much choosing their majors as having "fallen into" them (*We* 275), the particular major less important than "the degree of slackness it accommodates," "slackness" being defined as "the lack of pledge to continuing serious work in the field in which one is being trained" (276) and a quality Trilling finds to have characterized her own generation of women at the school. Thus she concludes:

> When the deepest assumptions of one's culture suggest that female independence is a condition of direst emergency, either a social holocaust or the death, bankruptcy, or incapacitating illness of one's father or husband, perhaps a daughter of the middle class is to be forgiven if she fails to bring to her education the bright purposive energies we generally associate with professional goals. (278–79)

Perhaps she also is to be forgiven for honing her aesthetic sensibility while practicing what Trilling calls this "art of self-deluding temporization" (279), as exemplified by one of the students Trilling interviews who has just purchased a silver coffeepot for display because "I'm used to crystal and Spode and so forth and I don't like Pyrex" (235). As the student notes, "It's probably my standard" (234).

As an educator, Jean Harris had to profess that such standards could be acquired by acts of intellectual will. "I still believe good teaching will cure almost anything short of the common cold," she writes in the epilogue to her memoir (*Stranger* 357), when explaining the reasons for her continued instruction of inmates and their children at the Bedford Hills Correctional Facility. Yet as the testimony she gave at her trial suggests, the standards of taste for Harris were more inborn than imbibed. "You felt she did not have the education you had?" the prosecutor asks when questioning the Phi Beta Kappa Harris about the Endicott Junior College dropout Lynne Tryforos.

> *Harris*: It wasn't a matter of education, Mr. Bolen.
> *Bolen*: Breeding?
> *Harris*: Perhaps just common sense and taste. (*Mrs.* 248)

Even worse, Tryforos's lack of taste is perceived as having produced a coarsening impact on those whom Harris sees as defined by taste, as the letter she mailed Tarnower right before she left Madeira with a gun makes clear.[7] "It isn't your style—but then Lynne has changed your style," she writes when chastising Tarnower for not responding to an earlier note she has sent him (Letter 257). "Tasteless behavior is the only kind Lynne knows," she asserts when reprimanding him for the "tasteless diatribes" he starts delivering about men needing wives half-their-ages-plus-seven-years, adding, "[u]nfortunately it seems to be catching" (259). Perhaps, worst of all, such infectious behavior may even be affecting Harris herself, who starts denoting her rival as a "thieving slut" and "psychotic whore" (257). "And are these words you customarily used?" the prosecutor asks her while on the witness stand later, to which the indignant

Harris—who has just pronounced "[a] whore is a whore is a whore"—responds with a vigorous defense of her own "integrity": "It's not like me to rub up against people like that" (*Mrs.* 251). Devoid of that integrity, tarred by the style of a rival deemed " '[d]ishonest, ignorant and tasteless' " (Letter 260), Harris is reduced to feeling "like discarded trash," "like a piece of old discarded garbage" (260, 258), to be "cremated as cheaply as possible and IMMEDIATELY THROWN AWAY," as the note she put in her handbag prior to driving to Purchase instructed (qtd. in Alexander 6).

Trilling, whose enthusiasm for Freud lasted through seven therapists and one botched analysis after another (*Beginning* 228), places great emphasis on another self-description that Harris provided in another letter she wrote just before leaving Virginia that night, a letter of resignation to the Madeira board, in which she portrayed herself as "a person and no one ever knew," a phrase that, upon questioning by her lawyer, she later elucidated to mean "I was a person sitting in an empty chair" (*Mrs.* 225). The empty chair signifying to Trilling the female body, the metaphor becomes for her one of female castration (225–26), and Harris's acquisition of a gun becomes a way of supplying herself "with what she'd been deprived of by biology" (320), an act of empowerment, in other words, however misguided.

Harris's memoir, however, presents a much more claustrophobic aftermath in chronicling her desperate attempts to regain her lost status through the only means she knows—the display of her own intellect and taste. If tests taken during ten days spent in a mental ward after Tarnower's death scare her because of "the very real threat that they would discover I wasn't intelligent and then everyone would know" (*Stranger* 144), years in prison provide an opportunity to assert aesthetic superiority over those around her, to the extent that Harris's intellectual pretensions increase in direct proportion to the decrease in social standing that she envisions. If headmistress Harris's letter to Tarnower mourns Somerset Maugham's dying before he could portray the two of them in fiction ("He could have come up with something to top a *Magnificent Obsession*" [Letter 258]), the incarcerated Harris starts comparing their affair to "a Noel Coward play" in which "my part hadn't quite jelled in the author's mind" (*Stranger* 34). If her pretrial literary touchstone is Edna St. Vincent Millay ("every woman must find herself somewhere in those poems" [*Stranger* 25]), her confinement confessors range from Simone Weil to Milan Kundera to Viktor Frankl to Umberto Eco to Francis Bacon to Thomas More, to name but a few of the intellectual luminaries whose names Harris repeatedly drops.[8] Harris ends, then, exactly where she begins. As the Madeira School motto would have it, "Function in disaster, finish in style."

Everyone's Story

Such assertions of intellectual and aesthetic supremacy, of course, destroy any belief in the representative status that Harris took pains to accord a life she introduces in her autobiography as so "totally steeped in all the comfortable mythology about America and Americans" that she bequeathed her fan mail to the Smith College archives so that graduate students could find in it "a piece of Americana" (*Stranger* xxiv, ix). For without such representative status, of what importance *is* the story of Jean Harris and Herman Tarnower? Nobody at the White Plains police station recognized Tarnower's name on the night the murder was phoned in (*Mrs.* 88). The shooting made the front page of the *New York Times* for two days (12–13 Mar. 1980), after which it was relegated to the metropolitan section, having been displaced on 15 March by the killing of former U.S. Representative Allard K. Lowenstein by Dennis Sweeney. The *Los Angeles Times* followed a front-page piece the day the story broke with three small columns on its twenty-eighth page the next day (13 Mar. 1980), and then nothing on the day after that. And in the *Chicago Tribune,* in which John Wayne Gacy dominated the front page for three days running (12–14 Mar. 1980) and in which the Tarnower shooting never got past page two, coverage of Harris's story increasingly shrank from three small columns (12 Mar. 1980), to nine small paragraphs (five of them just one sentence long) (13 Mar. 1980), to a minuscule one-fifteenth-of-a-page blurb (15 Mar. 1980).[9] No wonder the judge presiding over the trial declared at its start that nobody would be interested in the case after it was over (*Mrs.* 162).

By that time, though, the judge's words had become irrelevant. Tarnower's cook already had dyed her hair blond, lost weight, and begun referring to herself as Tarnower's "house-manager" and her husband as Tarnower's "estate-manager and gardener" (*Mrs.* 95). The court artist had a show of her drawings scheduled (71). *People* magazine had cited Jean Harris—along with Ronald Reagan, Goldie Hawn, Pat Benatar, Larry Hagman, Beverly Sills, and Robert Redford—as one of "The 25 Most Intriguing People of 1980" (29 Dec. 1980–5 Jan. 1981: cover).[10] NBC had produced a two-part miniseries, *The People vs. Jean Harris,* to be aired on 7–8 May 1981.[11] And—according to *People,* at least—Norton Simon had agreed to pay Diana Trilling one million dollars to adapt her book into a movie for his wife, Jennifer Jones (Diliberto 50). This later media hoopla notwithstanding, it still is important to keep in mind the point Joan Didion makes when comparing the media coverage of the 1989 Central Park Jogger case to the lack of such coverage of the 3,254 other rapes reported that same year in New York City: "crimes are universally understood to be news to the extent that they offer, however erroneously, a story, a lesson, a high concept" (*After* 255–56).[12]

The lesson that Harris tries to teach her readers is plain and simple: "This could happen to you" (*Stranger* 189). Trilling, in contrast, alternates between an awareness of Didion's point and a desire to transcend it. She hates the anointing of Harris as a champion of women, both for what choosing someone so emotionally fragile says about women as a group and for the careless generalizing from the particular that confuses "an irremediable and fatal collision between one man and one woman with a remediable attitude toward women in our society" (*Mrs.* 207). She recognizes that "there was something lowering in being cooped up in a White Plains courthouse, concentrating our attention on Mrs. Harris as if she were a world-historical event, when historical events were taking place in the world," notably the release of the hostages held in Iran (199). Yet she keeps returning to the wider relevance that Harris's story must have, quoting nineteenth-century legal historian Frederic Maitland's selection of a murder trial as providing "many hints as to a multitude of matters of the first importance" to any culture (162), and citing her own earlier work on the Hiss and Oppenheimer trials, cases that have "direct bearing on our contemporary society," and on subjects, like LSD and the death of Marilyn Monroe, "which bring into conjunction our private and our public dilemmas" (66).

Trilling justifies her search for wider relevance with reference to the lack of any such greater social significance provided by the current literary scene.

> It had once been the high function of literature to deal with just such material, to acquaint us with our social variousness and our human complexity, provide us with the surrogates of our known and unknown strengths, terrors, perils. Through the imaginative experience of the exaltation and pain, the triumph or downfall of the characters in books, we'd discovered our own capacity for exaltation and pain, learned the range of our humanity and the size of our world. But literature no longer gave us this instruction. It had become abstract, remote from the objects of our immediate personal and social curiosity. [. . .] Love and sexual passion, honor, money, envy, jealousy, greed, death, greatness and meanness of spirit, the anguishing anatomy of class differences: all these which were once the major themes of the novel were disappearing from literature to find their home in television, whose falsifications steadily weakened our understanding of life even while we boasted our superiority to its influence. (*Mrs.* 66–67)

Not a wholly original complaint, Trilling's remarks echo the tirade delivered by Norman Mailer in "Some Children of the Goddess" (1963) eighteen years earlier.[13] More to the point, they also depend upon a reading of competing writing that is, at best, less than accurate and, at worst, completely self-serving.

Thus, Trilling's acknowledgment of Truman Capote's self-proclaimed "nonfiction novel" *In Cold Blood* (1965) and Mailer's self-proclaimed "true life novel" *The Executioner's Song* (1979) as "gifted books" is followed by the caveat that their portrayals of crime "safely sealed it off from the middle class in some dark corner of life where the best dream was to see the blood splash" (*Mrs.* 68). Yet she is forgetful of the fact that Capote's careful balancing of his killers' aspirations for white-picket-fence marriages with their victims' realization of television-family success shows how *much* a middle-class story the shooting of the Clutters is, and that Mailer's filling his social tapestry with migrants both respectable (like Assistant Attorney General Earl Dorius) and unrespectable (like Gilmore girlfriend Nicole Baker) turns Gary Gilmore's life of transiency into an exemplary tale and his killing of two Mormons into one *more* example of the kind of violence to which so many of the gun-toting figures in the book are prone. In Trilling's view, it is the shooting of Herman Tarnower alone that "couldn't be sealed off from the middle class, it had erupted in our respectable midst" (68), a stance suggested by the title that her book originally was to bear, *A Respectable Murder* (19).

The irony, however, is that the more she seeks to obtain wider social relevance for her subject in the real world, the more Trilling is forced to portray the figures she discusses as literary characters instead of actual people—and not just primary protagonists like Tarnower, who morphs from a Semitic Jay Gatsby (*Mrs.* 28–29) to a socially successful Simon Rosedale (34). The introduction of defense witness Herbert MacDonnell, for example, relies less on his criminologist's credentials than on his character's conformity. "He's a character out of Chekhov," writes Trilling in what could pass for a Great Books in World Literature précis:

> He has the vaguely dilapidated look of one of the better-situated persons in a Chekhov story, a surveyor perhaps or a retired teacher, someone who brings the secret knowledge of defeat to his small successes. [. . .] His obsessiveness isn't exemplary in the modern American or German literary fashion and it hasn't the dimensions it would have in Balzac—for all his tensions, MacDonnell is too toneless for a French novel. Without question, he belongs in the classic literature of Russia. (195–96).

The introduction of John Chandler Jr., former headmaster of the Grosse Pointe school at which Harris taught, while more succinct, is similarly resonant: "He's not Santayana's last puritan, there'll never be a last" (155). When Trilling then admits, near the end of her book, that "[n]o character in art or in life is wholly of a piece" (298), her remark is completely appropriate since by that point the literary patchwork of which Jean Harris has been constructed has taken a piece of Emma Bovary (244, 335–36), a piece of Anna Karenina (244, 335–36), a piece of Lily Bart (34), and stitched them together with the thread of George Eliot

(180). Indeed, by the time that Trilling concludes her book, Harris's significance is found mainly to stem from the degree to which she is "just such a person as makes a significant figure in fiction," from the degree to which she presents to her audience "the raw state of life where we have only the making of art, without its seamlessness" (336). And Trilling's greatness, by implication, lies in the degree to which that raw material has been shaped by her into a work of art: "Mrs. Harris is gifted and bright. She writes well; she has a kind of native literacy. But she isn't an artist; she couldn't have created herself as a character in fiction. She never had the capacity for externalization that would have made it possible for her to use herself as a subject. She was material asking to be written but with no one to write her" (336). Not anymore.

It's a brilliant move, of course, and not only because it extricates Trilling from the strain of manufacturing a modern-day Middletown out of decidedly non-middle-class materials (how many in that "present-day American middle-class establishment" of which she finds Tarnower representative [*Mrs.* 23] have an estate next door to Alfred A. Knopf?) and the clumsiness of social commentary more snobbish than smart (the trial judge's courtroom demeanor qualifying him as "surely the best of middle America" [162]).[14] It's also a brilliant evasive tactic, for turning Harris's case into "everyone's story" (339) enables Trilling to deflect the particular relevance that the case had to have had to her own very personal history—specifically, the relevance that Harris's long-term relation-ship with a man she deemed, in Trilling's characterization, "a fitting partner of the superior intellectual life she led as a member of the academic profes-sion" (22) must have had to the unaffiliated Trilling, whose definition of her-self as an intellectual was inextricably linked to an even more fitting partner with whom she had an even lengthier involvement. This Diana Trilling is not the public essayist finding types wherever she turns, who viewed Profumo pan-derer Stephen Ward as "a representative figure, someone in whom we can read, if we will, a record of our times and of ourselves in our times" (*Claremont* 5); who saw in the political past of J. Robert Oppenheimer "the almost archetypi-cal political history of the idealistic temperament of his generation" (124); and who claimed that the moral contradictions in Norman Mailer bore "a striking resemblance to present-day America" (177). This Diana Trilling is the agora-phobic faculty wife who deemed the very private journal of Alice James "her last desperate stand for her earned place in the family hierarchy of distinction" (97–98) and diagnosed the sibling's physical and psychological infirmities as "an escape from the torturing, the impermissible, wish to rival brothers of unrivaled brilliance" (98). In short, this is the Diana Trilling who found membership in the middle class to be a matter of self-definition, but, in likening the idiosyn-crasies of that inclusion to "being an intellectual: an intellectual is someone who calls himself an intellectual" (*Mrs.* 181), revealed her own insecurities with both claims.

Nowhere are those insecurities more openly portrayed than in "A Visit to Camelot" (1997), Trilling's account of her visit to the Kennedy White House with her husband to honor the Nobel Prize laureates in 1962. From penny-by-penny accounts of what she spends ($250 for a black dress that turns out to be unsuited to the demands of a white-tie affair, $395 bargained down to $250 for a model's sample she then takes with alterations, $22 for white kid gloves) to listings of where she saves (coach seats instead of club car, take-out sandwiches instead of dining-car service, the house of a sister-of-a-friend instead of a hotel), Trilling's narrative traces a course of one narrowly missed faux pas after another, only to stop dead in its tracks with a blunt admission that proves that what she wears, in the end, hardly matters: "I had nothing to do with this occasion except as Lionel's wife" (63). Aware, moreover, that Lionel's name is familiar to most of the educated guests, she also knows how much cachet her own name has for that same audience ("But did they read the serious intellectual journals and know that I was a writer, too? I didn't have to ponder the answer. It was no" [63]), a fact that is made abundantly clear to her later in the evening when Jackie Kennedy, certain that Diana has found someone with whom to talk, turns her attention to Lionel alone "and never once gave a sign of having any interest in anyone else" (63).

As Trilling astutely recognizes, Jackie is the White House's "billion-dollar asset" ("Visit" 64), careful to refer to her husband "no fewer than a dozen times," while maintaining "a deliberately blank expression" when observing him in conversation with others (65). Trilling's own stock, by contrast, has far less market value. To hear her speak of it in *The Beginning of the Journey* (1993), Trilling's account of the early years of her marriage, life with Lionel was a history of insufferable slights delivered by one famous woman after another who thought he had chosen a woman who was beneath him—from Hannah Arendt, who just snubbed her, to Mary McCarthy, who told her she should inform readers at the start of an essay that she was the wife of Lionel Trilling (305)—which only culminated in her treatment by the president's wife. To hear her tell it, life with Lionel was a history of sacrificing her own authorial ambitions on the altar of his own inhibiting professional angst; she reshaped "draft after draft of his *Matthew Arnold*" (326), editing "every word he wrote" so relentlessly that she rewrote a quotation from its subject (19), and received in return either ambivalent appreciation or annihilating verbal attacks that reduced her to tears with regularity. Given that Trilling had never published a word of her own until the age of thirty-six and had never started on a book until the age of seventy-five (after her husband, significantly, had died[15]), are we then surprised at the outrage

Trilling recounts herself experiencing when F. W. Dupee, who loves to talk about decor and fabrics, takes her aside to discuss her living-room upholstery (306)?

And, viewed in retrospect, is it any wonder that the heroines Trilling continually would invoke in her writing are those "heroine[s] of spirit" who have "led women to be deceived that their possibilities in life are larger than they usually turn out to be" ("Liberated" 506)—no Margot Macombers here, or even Bathsheba Everdenes—fashioned by women novelists through whose work a "second voice" nevertheless speaks, rebuking their cultures "where culture, reinforced by biology, takes too easy an advantage of women of mind and spirit" (509)? Trilling's reading of *Middlemarch,* therefore, depends upon male-female relationships defined by inverse proportion: "Dorothea Brooke grotesquely underestimates her own intellectual capacities and overestimates those of Casaubon whom she has decided to marry in order to help him with his literary career instead of making a career of her own" (509). Eliot's most revealing comment on that union she locates, likewise, in analogical rhetoric: " 'She was always trying to be what her husband wanted, and never able to repose on his delight in what she was' " (509)—a comment that Trilling, in 1978, would extend beyond the covers of the novel to refer to Eliot's own relationship with George Henry Lewes and return to, years later, when describing her own dynamic with her husband: "Lionel wanted as much for me in self-realization [. . .] as he wanted for himself. I wanted as much for him as he wanted for himself and more than I wanted for myself" (*Beginning* 21).

"Reality-bound"—the exact same phrase she later would invoke to describe herself (*Beginning* 2)—is the phrase Trilling uses to denote her literary analogues ("Liberated" 504). A particularly apt phrase in that it connotes not just a state of sensibility but a state of imprisonment, it expresses well the self-portrait that emerges from the essay of hers that Trilling recalls her husband admiring most (*Beginning* 364), "The Other Night at Columbia" (1958). The piece opens with her deciding to go as one of "three wives from the English department" to hear a reading of beat poets at McMillin Theater and closes with her reabsorption into the spousal cell of her Claremont Avenue apartment, depicted metaphorically with respect to the group of faculty men who, dressed in "proper suit[s]," are meeting there when she returns home (*Claremont* 153, 173). All Trilling can do is try, in vain, "to bridge the unfathomable gap that was all so quickly and meaningfully opening up between the evening that had been and the evening that was now so surely reclaiming me" (173).

Writing in the quite literal cell meant to house her for a much longer fifteen-years-to-life incarceration, Jean Harris vigorously protested the lapses in etiquette that the conditions of confinement seemed to mandate. " 'As long as I am breathing I will be more than a disembodied hand,' " swears this Scarlett

O'Hara when referring to the way that head counts are taken each morning, a lowered hand her substitute for an upraised fist. " 'Christ as my witness, there is absolutely nothing they can threaten me with that will raise my hand to that window' " (*Stranger* 199). Nearly two years into her term, however, she still was lamenting the man whose first (and, blessedly, only) book she had taken great pride in editing and finding comfort in the idea of confinement itself. "I think about him constantly," she told Barbara Walters through a torrent of sobs into which she burst on national television. "It's one of the reasons I don't care if I get out, actually, I can't imagine what it would be like out there without him" (Interview [1982]).[16] Dressed in decorous cable-knit sweater and tortoise-shell headband, she still was distressed that nobody had understood what her case was really about:

> It did not become a feminist case. That to me is one of the sad things about it. There were lots of women covering that trial. Women, young women, attractive young women who probably considered themselves liberated because they wore blue jeans instead of skirts and hadn't washed their hair very recently, but not one of them really had a feminist point of view. There wasn't one article that said this woman has worked harder than most men work in their lifetimes and she's done it her entire adult life and she finally, for a lot of very sound reasons was burned out. (Interview [1982])

If, in the end, Trilling—the "sloppy little woman" Harris saw "stretched out, full length and shoeless, on one of the court benches quietly snoring" during her trial (*Stranger* 313)—understood more than most others, it was because she was as much a stranger in two worlds as Harris. "The histrionism of modern American women is a great unexamined scourge in our society," Trilling wrote a decade before her Jean Harris book, "but how should a woman frustrated in the belief that she is special among her sex, at once more talented, more energetic, and destined for more accomplishment than the general run of women, *not* be impelled to act out in gesture and facial expression the fantasies of personal power which were engendered in her at school but find no sustenance in her actual experience of life?" (*We* 287). It is this question—really a scream masquerading as a question—that serves as the "high concept," to recall Joan Didion's phrase, that Trilling's portrait of Harris seeks to inculcate. Harris answered it by stashing a .32-caliber gun in her purse and five rounds of ammunition in the pocket of a mink jacket, Trilling by inverting the image of writing as male violation of a feminine blank and excoriating her husband of forty-six years in print. Mrs. Harris left a corpse behind her. Mrs. Trilling, in contrast, did not have to. For her husband was already dead.

For the first time in his life, it occurred to him that if he wanted to get on he ought to insinuate himself into the good graces of people—do or say something that would make them like him. So now he contrived an eager, ingratiating smile, which he bestowed on Mr. Squires, and added: "If you'd like to give me a chance, I'd try very hard and I'd be very willing."

—Theodore Dreiser, *An American Tragedy* (1925)

Playboy: You headed to Utah. But so did swarms of media. Why were you able to get to Gilmore and his family when no one else could?

Schiller: Because I was the Fuller Brush man. I was the Avon salesman. I was able to knock on the door, get my foot in. Once again, I walked in and ingratiated myself.

—Lawrence Schiller, "*Playboy* Interview" (February 1997)

9 Your Trash Ain't Nothin' but Cash
Lawrence Schiller, O. J. Simpson, and the Trial (which one?) of the Century (again?)

Early in *American Tragedy* (1996), Lawrence Schiller and James Willwerth's "Uncensored Story of the Simpson Defense," the authors recount a set of previously undisclosed events more bizarre in many ways than the famous low-speed Bronco chase that they preceded. It is Friday, 17 June 1994, the day that an arrest warrant for the murders of Nicole Brown Simpson and Ronald Goldman has been issued for O. J. Simpson, and the suicidal Simpson is recording his thoughts for posterity in the home of his friend Robert Kardashian. He dictates a microcassette tape, urging people to " 'remember me as the Juice' " and " 'a good guy' " (51). He addresses letters to his children, his mother, and " 'To Whom It May Concern, press or public,' " asking his audience to " 'think of the real O.J. and not this lost person' " (53, 64). And then he takes a pistol wrapped in a towel and prepares to commit the act for which he has been planning. The only problem is that he cannot find an appropriate spot in Kardashian's nine-thousand-square-foot house in which to shoot himself. He can't do it in the room in which he has been staying because it is the bedroom of Kardashian's daughter. He can't do it in the shrubbery near the laundry room door because the bushes are too close to the house. He can't do it in the distant backyard because he doesn't want his body to bake in the sun. He can't do it in the area beside the driveway because he doesn't want cars to park over the place where he would lie. Finally, he can't do it by a side entrance where some empty cartons are stacked. "He rejects it. He doesn't want to be found in a pile of trash" (58).

Depending on whose view of the Simpson case one subscribes to, of course, that is exactly where O. J. Simpson ended up. "The Simpson case is like a great trash novel come to life," wrote Dominick Dunne in "L.A. in the Age of O.J.," one of his "Letter from Los Angeles" *Vanity Fair* columns, "a mammoth fireworks display of interracial marriage, love, lust, lies, hate, fame, wealth, beauty, obsession, spousal abuse, stalking, brokenhearted children, the bloodiest of bloody knife-slashing homicides, and all the justice that money can buy" (48). And by now we know just how many people were willing to write it.[1] Indeed, with lawyers and jurors, policemen and parasites all writing books about their roles in the Simpson saga, no one today needs to be persuaded of the point made by George Lipsitz in 1997: that if the Simpson trial was less than the trial of the century in terms of legal significance, it certainly was the sale of the century in terms of marketing opportunities (10).

As we have seen in chapter 7, such marketing is hardly a twentieth-century phenomenon. But if the fringe players surrounding the Kennedy assassination distinguished themselves from those of the Lincoln assassination by the speed with which they began hawking their wares, those involved in the Simpson case distinguished themselves by hawking their wares even before the trial had gotten very much under way. Witness Jill Shively, eight days after the murders, held up her grand-jury subpoena to *Hard Copy* cameras while telling of having seen Simpson erratically driving around Brentwood the night of 12 June 1994 at an hour he claimed to be at home. Confidante Faye Resnick, after a miraculous three-week gestation, produced *Nicole Brown Simpson: The Private Diary of a Life Interrupted* in time to appear in the middle of jury selection. Simpson himself, strapped for funds to pay for his defense, shared his *I Want to Tell You* response so as to coincide with opening statements.

The importance of this cash-for-trash phenomenon cannot be underestimated in any assessment of the impact that the O. J. Simpson spectacle had on the national consciousness. As Henry Louis Gates Jr. points out, "It's a cliché to speak of the Simpson trial as a soap opera—as entertainment, as theatre—but it's also true" in that "the trial provides a fitting rejoinder to those who claim that we live in an utterly fragmented culture, bereft of the common narratives that bind a people together" (60), a point that is confirmed by the frequency with which commentators compared the impact of its verdict, and in some instances the Bronco chase, to that of the Kennedy assassination.[2] Yet as Gates adds in an important caveat, "it's a fallacy of 'cultural literacy' to equate shared narratives with shared meanings" (62). Hence the variety of meanings ascribed to the case, meanings that, significantly, reflected no shared racialized interpretation on the part of their authors. What was "*Birth of a Nation* writ large" for Toni Morrison (xxviii) and "American Kabuki" for Patricia J. Williams (273) was "a novel by Zola" for Walter Mosley and "the 'Ring' cycle of Wagner" for Jessye Norman (qtd. in Gates 62). For someone like Diana Trilling, in fact, whose view derived from a comparison of the Simpson trial with that of Jean Harris, its meaning bypassed race entirely, having to do instead with "a general deterioration of manners" that the behavior in Judge Ito's courtroom evinced and, for her, the frightening consequences that can ensue in a democracy when that "root connection between civility and the sustaining processes of law" is abrogated ("Notes" 22). And it is precisely because of the trial's inability to lend itself to any monolithic interpretation that the role of the media in framing it—especially the tabloid media, whose breaking and usually accurate coverage gained them new credibility (Furno-Lamude 29–30; Thaler 122–28)—increased dramatically in importance. For if, as Morrison contends, spectacle has now become "the best means by which an official story is formed" and "a superior mechanism for guaranteeing its longevity," it is because "democratic discourses are suborned by sudden, accelerated, sustained blasts of media messages—visual and in print— that rapidly enforce the narrative and truncate alternative opinion" (xvi).

Enter Lawrence Schiller, whose initial role as a "material witness" for the Simpson defense was intended to truncate those opinions on Simpson's behalf. The man in whom *The New Yorker*'s Jeffrey Toobin saw reincarnated the Zero Mostel character who sells the public a show called *Springtime for Hitler* in *The Producers* (*Run* 252), Schiller already had sold the public the stories of Jack Ruby and Manson family member Susan Atkins in print, and those of Lee Harvey Oswald and Gary Gilmore on film prior to collaborating on *I Want to Tell You* with Simpson. As such, he personifies well the intertextual engagement with other media upon which commercial television in America is based. A photographer–movie producer–movie director who enhanced the sound quality of the Fuhrman tapes for the Simpson defense, Schiller personifies equally well the penetration of Hollywood into civil institutions even prior to the trial, as evidenced by an LAPD that boasts *Star Trek* creator Gene Roddenberry among its former officers and *Cagney and Lacey* model Margaret York (also wife of Lance Ito) among its women captains. Yet in works that transgress fiction/nonfiction generic conventions, Schiller also is distinguished by being a character in his own right and under his own name: an authorial surrogate in Norman Mailer's *The Executioner's Song* ("A True Life Novel" [1979]), a "triple agent" in the Simpson novel that Dominick Dunne's autobiographical journalist plans in *Another City, Not My Own* ("A Novel in the Form of a Memoir" [1997]),[3] finally, a figure introduced by Robert Kardashian to the Simpson defense team as someone who is " 'going to make some money for us' " in the "factual account" that would become Schiller's own *American Tragedy* (251, ix).

A particularly apt coinage, the title of this last book tropes both the caption that accompanied *Time*'s 27 June 1994 cover of Simpson's darkened mug shot and a Theodore Dreiser novel, emblems of both the sensationalist past and respectable future that Schiller seeks, respectively, to avoid and anticipate. For Schiller—fanatically concerned with "build[ing] integrity" and "do[ing] something respectable," compulsive in his belief that becoming "a man of substance" means "record[ing] history right"[4]—is as much obsessed with not ending up in the trash as O. J. Simpson. To the extent that the case portrayed in Dreiser's book prefigures Simpson's in being cast by the media as "a crime sensation of the first magnitude, with all of those intriguingly colorful, and yet morally and spiritually atrocious, elements—love, romance, wealth, poverty, death" (*American* 577), Schiller's choice of literary antecedent is astute. Unfortunately, in trying to enhance the importance of his own trial narrative by invoking a 1925 fictionalized murder trial based on an actual 1906 trial, juxtaposing the *fin de siècle* Simpson spectacle against the earlier one(s) that inaugurated the American Century, Schiller only interrogates any one trial's claim to singular status. In so doing, he also exposes what Guy Debord has recognized as the paradox of "spectacular time," in which a media event's shelf life—and, by extension, that of any text devoted to it—is reduced to that of "pseudo-event," "quickly forgotten, thanks to the precipitation with which the spectacle's pulsing machinery replaces one by the next" (114).

Real American Tragedies and Visible Men

Ten years after the publication of his gargantuan masterpiece, Theodore Dreiser was convinced that he had found "the real American tragedy" in Wilkes-Barre, Pennsylvania, where, in an uncanny reprise of the fictional Clyde Griffiths's experiences, Robert Allen Edwards was tried and convicted in 1934 for the murder of Freda McKechnie, a telephone operator struck on the head while swimming, whom he had impregnated. As Dreiser was quick to point out in the series of articles he originally wrote for the *New York Post*, and then expanded for *Mystery Magazine* in 1935, Edwards's was not the *only* such American tragedy.[5] Citing the cases of Carlyle Harris (1893), Roland Molineux (1899), Chester Gillette (1906), and Clarence Richesen (1911), and alluding to the seventeen such cases he personally had studied ("I Find" 40), Dreiser deduced that "between 1895 and this present year [1935] there has scarcely been a year in which some part of the country has not been presented with a crime of this type" (7), the crime in question defined by a young man "possessed of an ingrowing ambition to be somebody financially and socially" who had sought marriage to a rich woman as the quickest way of achieving those ends (5). Because such aspirations were both inculcated and encouraged by the dominant culture, and because the decedent was typically a young woman whose pregnancy prevented the man's desired union with another, Dreiser saw no *"anti-social"* element behind the criminal actions of the perpetrator (10). On the contrary, because the young man's preference for an improved social status showed an adherence to American mores, his act was profoundly *"pro-social"* in nature: "He merely wished to divest himself of the poorer relationship in order to achieve the richer one" (10, 11).

That this could only be effected by way of murder was, for the Freudian and mechanistic enthusiast, due to a combination of factors: insufficient finances (the lack of which, in preventing Edwards from visiting his upstate New York inamorata, caused him to resume relations with McKechnie), punitive religious dogma (sexual intimacy punishable by communal shunning, according to the Wilkes-Barre pastor), and, perhaps most important, the "deranging hypnotism of love" (a "chemical or quiescent content of the human body") ("I Find" 71, 73). The combined pressures of these "poisoned, tortured and betrayed and made emotionally insane his reasoning faculties" and resulted in an act that Edwards never would have ordinarily committed (72). Far from being a conniving and calculating killer—indeed, not even a very polished killer as the idiotic elements of his plan revealed (calling on McKechnie's relation-by-marriage before the murder, parking beside a lighted casino, bathing in the most conspicuous spot of the lake)—Edwards was, in Dreiser's view, "morally and spiritually guiltless" (64). As much *"the victim of a frenzy"* as the woman he killed and the woman he desired, he was, in fact, *"the key victim"* of the three in being both *"the one who is most violently involved"* and the one who had to suffer the added injustice of being *"judged to be a sane, coldly reasoning person who deliberately proceeded to murder"* by a state that refused to consider psychiatric evidence as a mitigating factor (73).

More "key" than the bludgeoned woman?

More "victim" than the corpse left floating in the water?

I don't think so.

That Dreiser evidently did reflected a habitual prioritizing of the abstract over the actual, a predilection that would result in his claim that the only "individuality" belonged to a transhistorical "eternal individual" ("Myth" 341), and that earlier infused the portrayals in the novel that the Edwards case so eerily mirrored. Therefore, for all Dreiser's reminders of those "chemisms" that afflict Clyde like "some sweet, disarranging poison," leaving "only panic and temporary unreason in [their] wake" (*American* 425, 463), Clyde's conflict is less physiological than representational, torn as he is between the "imaginative pull of such a girl as Sondra and all that she represented" and the "specter of Roberta and all that she represented" (308, 429). It is, moreover, a contest that bears little scrutiny. While Sondra's Finchley fortune satisfies the financial "desire for more—more" that propels Clyde throughout the book (804), the manufacture of electric sweepers from which it is derived does little to satisfy the craving for refinement that is awakened by his first sight of the Green-Davidson hotel, which "represented, as he saw it, the quintessence of luxury and ease" (31)— another impression that bears little scrutiny. But, then again, displacing the real for the representational is the *modus operandi* of every character in the book. Clyde's appeal to Sondra stems from his "represent[ing] physical as well as moral attributes which were agreeable to her" (329). The revulsion he inspires in the district attorney who prosecutes him is a function of a lifelong distaste for "[t]he wastrel and evil rich—a scion or representative of whom" he mistakenly assumes Clyde to be (519).

As the example of Jean Harris and Diana Trilling illustrates, however, representative cases are not born but made; lacking a famous victim (Kennedy for Oswald, Wallace for Bremer), and devoid of any personal celebrity themselves, both killer and chronicler opted for representative status to distinguish the case, and the books they wrote about it, from tales of tawdry love triangles. Such authorial transformation is presented as equally important in the *American Tragedy* society that Dreiser depicts, poised between class and mass, as evidenced by a Green-Davidson hotel that supplies " 'exclusiveness to the masses' " and a Griffiths collar factory that provides " 'polish and manner to people who wouldn't otherwise have them' " (32, 321). No such representative distinction was granted Chester Gillette in the *New York World* accounts from which Dreiser fashioned the novel,[6] despite an acknowledged mass appeal to which women clamoring to get into the courthouse (not just teenage girls, but "matrons who should know better") and a town setting "World's Fair prices" on every item testified (14 Nov. 1906: 3), and the placement given those accounts suffered accordingly. Pushed back to page two on the day the trial began by the trial of a more famous killer, Harry K. Thaw, who was said to "[RISK] HIS LIFE ON WIFE'S STORY AT HIS TRIAL," as the page-one banner headline read (13 Nov. 1906), Gillette's case was repeatedly eclipsed in subsequent days by the arrest of Enrico Caruso for having "rubbed, nudged and annoyed two young women" in the Central Park monkey house the previous December (17 Nov. 1906: 2). It was not until his victim's love letters were read in open court (20 Nov. 1906) and Gillette himself took the stand (28 Nov. 1906) that the case began edging onto the front page—still vying for attention with zookeeper testimony and an absent accuser in the tenor's trial, and coinciding, significantly, with a report of a possible postponement of the Thaw proceedings until the summer (3 Dec. 1906).[7]

Viewed within the framework of such a spectacular society, as Joseph Karaganis has superbly argued, Dreiser's protagonist experiences an American apotheosis rather than tragedy, beginning with his arrest and culminating in the trial that, by way of the press, provides individual subjectivity to its defendant and a communal locus to the nation (155–59). Far from repudiating Clyde's American Dream of social mobility, according to Karaganis, Dreiser's *American Tragedy* thematizes it with respect to new standards of measurement: not rags to riches, but invisibility to visibility. As Karaganis goes on to say:

> Visibility in the novel doesn't necessarily correspond to the class difference measured by one's relation to production or the nature and quantity of one's consumption. Clyde's infamy demonstrates that being a spectacle is not the same as being rich, and that moving toward spectacularity is not the same as moving up the social ladder. Status, in this context, is not the power to control others or buy leisure but an indicator of one's place in the *spectacular* economy—in the public circulation of fascinated gazes. (171–72)

But what of the defendant for whom all questions of visibility and invisibility are additionally charged by race? And what of the defendant, like O. J. Simpson, whose visibility is on the wane—so not newsworthy before his trial that the one *Los Angeles Times* piece on him the previous year, a brief ode to his 1968 Heisman Trophy win, had to dredge up a new telephone commercial of his mother racing to answer a call from him in order to justify its "Still Going Strong" title (L. White C10)?[8] (" '[I]t's only O.J. fame,' " writes Dominick Dunne of the perks that a courtroom seat affords his authorial surrogate. " 'It's not real fame' " [*Another* 238].) How to re-present someone as representative who already has been packaged as exceptional? Look to the subject's self-representations, I would say. More to the point, look to those texts that best show Simpson negotiating these very issues at pivotal points in his career: *O.J.: The Education of a Rich Rookie* (1970), which tries to restore Heisman Trophy stature to a disappointing first-round draft choice; *I Want to Tell You* (1995), which casts a murder defendant as yet another victim of LAPD conspiring; the *Playboy* interview (December 1976), which seeks to parlay athletics into acting; and the *Saturday Night Live* appearance (25 February 1978), broadcast the year before he retired from football, which seeks to fashion what Simpson later would describe as a "personality" through the art of parodic performance.

According to Simpson, who once informed sportswriter Robert Lipsyte, " 'I'm not black, I'm O.J.' " (qtd. in Toobin, *Run* 49), his career had little to do with a desire for racial visibility. Indeed, the oft-cited tale of his life-changing encounter with Willie Mays at age fifteen bespeaks just those kind of rags-to-riches values that Dreiser is generally viewed as depicting. At the end of a day spent with Mays, who has been asked to intervene in the young delinquent's affairs, the adolescent O. J. has the epiphanic vision that makes him abandon his truant's ways: "He had this $80,000 house. [. . .] It was the first time I saw the pot of gold at the end of the rainbow" (*I Want* 157). Shades of Clyde Griffiths alighting upon his rich uncle's Lycurgus domicile ("The beauty! The ease!" [*American* 188]), or the unemployed Dreiser himself "envying the rich and wishing that I was famous or a member of a wealthy family" while staring at Cleveland's Euclid Avenue mansions (qtd. in Orlov 62).

As Leola Johnson and David Roediger have documented, however, the cross-over success that later financed the purchase of a comparable residence for Simpson at Rockingham was based on the creation of an image that rested squarely on racial identity, namely, the promotion of Simpson as a nonmilitant black man at the precise time that, ironically, the Black Power movement had awakened advertising executives to the value of the African American market (200–209). Viewed within this context, the lesson Simpson learns from Mays in the version found in *I Want to Tell You*—"if this guy could make it, I could make it" (157)—involves as much the route *to* as it does the rewards *of* success. Specifically, it involves, first, a particular model of black masculinity in that it is Mays, the surrogate father, who appears at the Simpson household after Simpson's mother has retrieved him from police custody, and not the homosexual father who deserted them that he has expected to see called over to administer a whipping. And, as Simpson's opening reference to his initial awareness of the center fielder suggests, it involves, second, a model of black masculinity that is as acceptable to whites as it is to blacks. "I didn't know who Willie Mays was," Simpson recalls of his preteen self. "All the white teachers in school seemed to get just as excited about Mays and the Giants as my mother or my uncle Hollis did. And all of a sudden, I realized he was a black man" (*I Want* 156).[9] Having thus prefaced his story with this earlier recollection, Simpson ends his account with an identification that is tantamount to corporeal ingestion: "I remember that I didn't get his autograph; I didn't need to. I had him inside of me" (157).

Narrating his book in November 1994 while on trial for murder, facing a predominantly African American jury, and defended by lawyers who, as early as July, were planning to discredit Mark Fuhrman as a racist,[10] Simpson no doubt saw the advantage of putting a racialized rather than an economic spin on the Mays story in *I Want to Tell You*.[11] Yet even the earlier autobiographical work written under no such extenuating circumstances reveals Simpson defining himself largely with respect to race. *The Education of a Rich Rookie* thus traces his drive back to "a hunger that probably was born in the ghetto" (59–60), reiterates the hope that his success will "shatter a lot of white myths about black athletes" (12, 23), and asserts his intention "to take on the challenge of helping black kids" after he finishes with "the challenges of football" (12), based on the belief "that I can do as much for my people in my own way as a Tommie Smith, a Jim Brown, or a Jackie Robinson may choose to do in another way" (12). Nothing astonishing here, until one gets to Simpson's forthright acknowledgment that these assumed goals are a function of his own image consciousness ("That's part of the image I want, too," he states after distinguishing himself from the more activist athletes [12]), a trait to which he "plead[s] guilty" on the book's first page: "I have always wanted to be liked and respected; recognition has been far more important to me than money" (9). Unaware that his image of racial commitment is no more authentic than those "false images" of ghetto truculence he admits to having adopted while growing up, the kind that keep blacks "faceless and invisible" in American society (10), he is nonetheless acutely aware—in an almost textbook case of Lacanian mirroring—that it is only in the adulation of his audiences that he finds a discernible identity: "I loved it when kids stopped me for autographs, I loved it when people recognized me on the street. I loved it, I think, because I could at last recognize myself" (11–12).

It is not until much later in the book, however, that the "Question of Image" suggested by its opening chapter title—exceptional rookie or just typical rookie?—is answered. To be precise, it is not until Simpson realizes that his profitable business investments have made it possible for him to retire—at the age of twenty-two—from football entirely.

> That jolted me, because I'd always needed football—not from a financial point of view, just from a basic need. I needed the thrill and contact and challenge of the game, and I also needed to be respected for doing something special. Football had gained me that respect, and I wasn't ready to conclude that I no longer needed it. (135)

Once this realization is arrived at, the book metamorphoses into a cautionary tale, its education the lesson of what can happen when the pursuit of evil lucre (nine hundred thousand dollars in contracts) and the temptations of instant celebrity (commercial endorsements, public appearances, *Medical Center* guest shots) sidetrack a young naïf from tending to his remarkable God-given talent: no Rookie of the Year awards (à la Jim Brown), no NFL records (à la Gale Sayers's twenty-two-touchdown, 132-point first season), just lackluster stats (697 yards gained rushing) on an even more lackluster (4-10-0) team.[12]

Nothing, of course, could be more different than the moral of that later cautionary tale, *I Want to Tell You,* which depends for its success on portraying Simpson as a representative African American man. Hence the transformation of the Potrero Hill projects into a utopian socialist community: "If you had a 'roach' problem, [. . .] you couldn't solve it just in your home alone. The whole eight families or however many were in the building had to work together to solve that problem" (155). Hence the return of Simpson to the fold of religious fraternity: "I know that I will raise my children differently in relationship to God. [. . .] I won't play golf. Sunday we will go to church" (141)—not just any church, but Johnnie Cochran's downtown Second Baptist Church (142). Hence the surrounding of him with cohorts of similar devotional bent: not just the unsurprisingly "spiritual" mother and sister (178, 182), or the obviously "spiritual" Rosey Grier (191), but the "very spiritual" Robert Kardashian (188), and the remarkably (four times cited) "spiritual" Paula Barbieri (27, 40, 121, 191). (These are contrasted with the "false witness" Faye Resnick [140] and the former wife, Nicole, whose marriage to him failed because they "never took God and put Him in [their] relationship" [26]). Having discovered that the audience he now has, as opposed to those earlier drawn by "my football career, my acting, and some just out of curiosity," is a "much more spiritual audience" (137), Simpson is able to "preach" the new lesson (à la Jean Harris) that he has learned: "If this injustice could happen to me, it could happen to anybody" (168).

Obviously, this later portrait is no less an image, not to mention product of joint authorship, than the *Education of a Rich Rookie* earlier one—Simpson just doesn't identify it as a rhetorical construction. We even can reconcile the two as evidence of the kind of multiple role-playing at which Simpson, by the 1990s, had become quite adept: less negotiating the kind of contradictions that living in a state of "in-betweenness" mandates (Fanon 112; Bhabha, *Location* 44–45), as assuming the variety of roles that pursuit of an acting career necessitates. As that pursuit illustrates, moreover, the shift from visible exemplar to visible representative had begun long before legal affairs made it an advantageous role to perform.

Still claiming recognition as a bigger motivating force for him than money ("it's really hard to sit home and dream about *dollars*" [102]) in the 1976 *Playboy* interview given two years after his *Towering Inferno* (1974) film debut and the year before his numbers as a running back would plummet (from 1,503 yards gained rushing in 1976 to 557 in 1977),[13] Simpson talked at length to Lawrence Linderman about the seriousness of his commitment to acting. Not that playing roles was new to him, as the *Education* anecdote of giving "Burt Lancaster" as his name to a policeman when a teenager indicates (10). But pushing thirty in a field in which men of twenty-seven, twenty-eight, and thirty constitute an "old" offensive line (*Education* 106–7), Simpson has no interest in playing the trickster when he now cites Dustin Hoffman, Robert Redford, Clint Eastwood, and even Martin Balsam as his thespian role models. Yet at the same time that he bluntly states he is "not lookin' for parts that necessarily call for a black cat" (90), he also reveals the one film part for which he is ready to quit football immediately: Coalhouse Walker in *Ragtime* (85). An odd choice for someone whose expressed desire to cross casting color lines and exclusive mention of white actors would seem to imply complete white identification. For if Doctorow's book of multiple passings—class (the silhouette peddler Tateh returning as the Baron Ashkenazy), ethnic (Evelyn Nesbit posing as a Lower East Side Jewish seamstress), racial (Younger Brother masquerading as a black revolutionary)—illustrates anything, it is the very ineradicableness of that color line for a black man in America. Even more odd for a man whose entire public persona as "the best-liked athlete in American sport," as the *Playboy* introduction notes (77), was built around a position of nonmilitancy. What was he going to do if cast? Throw autographs instead of bombs?[14]

As the *Saturday Night Live* performance of fourteen months later suggests, the only way Simpson could have acted such a role and preserved his public image was by way of parody, for every sketch is built around black athleticism, black hostility, or black virility, the assumed traits that make the black man, in Frantz Fanon's term, a "phobogenic object" (151).[15] Thus we see Simpson, in *Masterpiece Theatre* armchair, relating the Babe Ruth–visits-dying-boy tale but this time failing to hit a home run for the child played by Garrett Morris, which leads him to the conclusion that "[i]t was yet another case of a white man breaking a promise to a poor little colored boy" and the moral: "Never underestimate the revenge of a black man. Because little Hank Aaron came through and went on to break all of Babe Ruth's records anyway." And we see Simpson—who turned down a lead in the film *Mandingo*—playing a bare-chested buck in "Mandingo II" and informing Laraine Newman, decked out in southern belle regalia, "Massa gon' give it to me, but fust I'm gon' give it to you." And Simpson, again bare chested, watching Newman, as a locker-room reporter, swear she's "never seen anything like this before" as she, in turn, looks in the direction of Simpson's crotch. And Simpson, now preening, inviting moderator Jane Curtin to retire with him and his white female "Celebrity Battle of the Sexes and Races" combatants, secure in the knowledge that "my mouth don't write no checks my body can't cash."

We don't laugh much at these sketches today—given subsequent events they're just too unsettling. Nevertheless, it is tempting to view their performative elements as destabilizing all notions of naturalized identity, the show's return to the subject of black eroticism evidence of that quality of repetition that Judith Butler finds so crucial in the exposure of identity as politically—and tenuously—determined (140–41). Yet, as Butler reminds us,

> Parody by itself is not subversive, and there must be a way to understand what makes certain kinds of parodic repetitions effectively disruptive, truly troubling, and which repetitions become domesticated and recirculated as instruments of cultural hegemony. [. . . P]arodic displacement, indeed, parodic laughter, depends on a context and reception in which subversive confusions can be fostered. (139)

No such context existed for the *Saturday Night Live* parodies because the receptive terms for later sketches already had been set by an initial "Samurai Night Fever" sketch in which Simpson, playing a priest, confesses to a desire that would seem to involve more than vacating his vocation: "I just don't wanna be black no more." Within the context of a sketch in which the obviously-not-Italian Bill Murray and Jane Curtin are playing Bay Ridge parents, and the obviously-not-Asian John Belushi is playing a Japanese samurai, such a wish seems eminently reasonable, color as easily removable as collar—and even achievable. When the brothers adjourn to a disco, and the Canadian Dan Ackroyd says in his best Brooklynese accent, "You look different tonight," Simpson replies with the affirmation: "I'm not black anymore." He still is, of course, and the laughter his declaration evokes from the audience, which far surpasses any it shows the other impersonations, springs from the fact that everyone else knows this as well. But he is in a completely unthreatening way, since engaging in a fantasy of minstrelsy in reverse has deprived him of those traits of excess and abandon that, as Eric Lott has shown, characterize the desires behind blackface mimicry (479).[16]

As was established by the monologue that opened the show, moreover, it was not as an actor that Simpson appeared on *Saturday Night Live* but as a host—a "personality," to use the word with which Simpson later characterized himself during his civil trial (Schuetz 13). As such, the two sketches that invoke Walter Payton parody not stereotypes of black men in general but the aging running back Simpson in particular. One even parodies Simpson's Hertz commercial parody of himself in showing the speedster arriving at the airport only to be told at the car rental desk that his vehicle has been given to Payton since Hertz, as well as its customers, "also ha[s] to go with the winner." In this emphasis, the sketches anticipate the *Naked Gun* pratfalls that parody his earlier athletic agility and films that cast him as one of the "People Who Acted in the Movie"—not an actor, but a person who acts—as the closing credits to all three state (1988, 1991, 1994). A phenomenon more suited to television than film, and one that continues what Richard Dyer has called the "embourgeoisement of the cinematic imagination" that the biographies of public figures in popular magazines began (22), the personality system refutes all notions of identity as a performative construct. Inherently conservative in that attributing to individuals "coherent identit[ies]" imparts coherence "to what is potentially a diverse and seemingly chaotic universe of events," as John Langer claims (357), it requires individuals that can be made, first, consumable and, second, typical in a medium in which, as Langer puts it, " 'the exceptional' is the exception rather than the rule" (354).

Simpson's *Playboy* interview indicates that he had no objections to either. When asked about what goals he had set for himself as an aspiring actor, he stated that he would settle for becoming "bankable," which he defined as "having enough of a following to know that people will go to see movies I'm in," and illustrated with reference to character actors rather than stars (90). In fact, as someone who relished being known by the name of a commodity ("But, hey, I know who *I* am: I'm the Juice" [90]), he'd been an object of consumption for quite some time (if ultimately less popular than the 1977 record-breaking Payton, who would go on to appear nine times on the Wheaties cereal box). Consumable and typical before Lawrence Schiller ever came on the scene for *I Want to Tell You,* Simpson didn't need anyone to make him over. It would be left for Schiller to produce a work that, inadvertently, would make him erasable.

A Writer without Hands

It should have been a perfect match: object of consumption and profligate consumer—or, given the junk food gastronomic preferences that media accounts of Schiller invariably note, trash compactor.[17] A man ahead of his time in this latter regard, Schiller anticipated the cash-for-trash explosion that is generally credited to two events of the 1990s: one, the 1991 Supreme Court ruling that the "Son of Sam" law passed by New York State in 1977, which would have prevented criminals from earning money from the sale of their stories, violated the First Amendment; and, two, the 1992 Amy Fisher–Joey Buttafuoco case, which garnered precedent-setting prices for its participants and made fees for selling scandal skyrocket (Toobin, "Cash" 36). Schiller's earlier contracts can't compete with the half-million-dollar sum handed over to Buttafuoco by *A Current Affair,* but they do testify to the amounts that were being paid and made decades earlier. Having snuck a tape recorder concealed in a Neiman Marcus briefcase into Parkland Memorial Hospital in 1966, Schiller bought Jack Ruby's deathbed interview by agreeing to pay Ruby's $4,500 debt to the Internal Revenue Service.

In 1969, he sold Susan Atkins's story of the Manson murders to the *London News of the World* for $40,000. In 1976, he paid $52,000 to Gary Gilmore and another $25,000 to Gilmore's girlfriend for exclusive rights to his life and their romance. And in 1994, he paid nothing for Simpson's *I Want to Tell You* response, and earned $170,000 for himself, $1.4 million for the defendant, plus an additional $100,000 and $640,000 for the two, respectively, from the victory party photographs taken at Simpson's home after the criminal trial verdict.[18]

Norman Mailer's *The Executioner's Song* offers perhaps the most trenchant comment on such hucksterism when it shows Schiller arriving in prison to witness Gilmore's execution and discovering that the pad on which he has planned to take notes is missing: "all he had with him was his checkbook. He would have to take notes on the backs of checks" (930). A most conclusive image in a work in which Schiller has been portrayed going *mano-à-mano* with David Susskind for ABC backing, dribbling out select morsels of Gilmore's story to the *National Enquirer,* optioning Gilmore's love letters to finance his own Utah operating costs, and shipping off his mother and girlfriend to broker foreign sales deals in Europe. Schiller tries to justify his acts by way of presence and perseverance: when told that Susskind has described their difference as producers as that between a high-school football team and the Dallas Cowboys, Schiller retorts that his team is suited up and in the stadium while Susskind is calling plays from a New York control room (633–34). Mainly, though, Schiller tries to rehabilitate himself, to shed the skin that has occasioned remarks involving a cross section of the animal kingdom: scavenger, snake, lizard, eel, carrion bird.[19] It is these efforts, in fact, that form the subplot of Mailer's work, the attempts of the Academy Award–winning film producer, made-for-TV movie director, and "best one-eyed photographer in the world" (581) to become the one thing he is not: a writer.

Set against the media circus that surrounds Gilmore in the second half of Mailer's work, it is not a surprising aspiration. As conceived by Schiller, however, it is an astonishingly anachronistic one. For in shifting from visual to print media (the exact opposite path Oswald takes in *Libra*) and presupposing a depth-model of human subjectivity ("he got weary of walking into people's lives, shaking their hands, photographing them, walking out. [. . .] Wanted to do people in depth" [581]), Schiller adopts standards that Mailer questions again and again in the rest of the book. The twenty-seven poses that Gilmore assumes in the interviews taped for *Playboy* testify to fluctuation, not fixity (806). The autopsy during which he is taken apart and put back together depicts any unified self as, quite literally, a matter of construction (981–83), of no more worth than the fifty-nine-cent loaf of bread once held by the plastic bag from which his ashes are finally scattered (993). Most of all, in assuming that "record[ing] history right" means "remain[ing] accurate to the facts" (585), not "get[ting] involved with it" (694), and, above all else, never "try[ing] to influence history, never forc[ing] the results" (801), Schiller subscribes to a model of historiography based on the transparency of the written product. When he finally has that revelatory moment in which, weeping and despondent, he questions the ethics of what he is doing, the diarrhetic answer he gets in response confirms the fact that his "desire to record history, true history, not journalistic crap" is nothing but, well, crap as far as distinguishing him from the other media vultures is concerned (832). Yet the inspiration this gastrointestinal moment affords him, "that all the people who were respected in all the worlds he had gone through, respected for their integrity, had maybe not all been born with it, not every last one, but built it, job by job and night by separate night" (833), still ends with a conception of historiography—" 'you can't fictionalize, you can't make it up, you can't *embroider*' " (833)—that is unaltered from his earlier conceit. This conception, in turn, is finally repudiated by a text that, for all Mailer's later describing it as a work of photographic realism,[20] is still cast as a *"true life story"* presented "as if it were a novel" (1022), or, as its subtitle states, "A True Life Novel." Last shown conducting interviews, the very grunt work that has made possible the successful works of others (Mailer, Barry Farrell, Albert Goldman[21]), Schiller remains until the end "a writer without hands" (1013).

We would do well to treat Mailer's portrait-of-an-artist-manqué with some skepticism, of course. The Johnny-on-the-spot interviewer Schiller is the same Schiller who, if Manson prosecutor Vincent Bugliosi is correct (259), never met Susan Atkins, much less wrote a word of the combined interview-text he later sold under his name as *The Killing of Sharon Tate* (1970) to New American Library. Likewise, the detached doctrinaire Schiller is also the Schiller who, according to Pat Wechsler and Roger D. Friedman (12), helped Gilmore divert his funds so as to prevent the widows of the men he killed from making wrongful-death claims against his estate. And the transparent transcriber Schiller is the same Schiller who, by his own admission, encoded the Fuhrman tapes with subtitles and low-frequency sounds, a twenty-eight-thousand-dollar state-of-the-art job—later dubbed "[a]n incidental event in which I participated in the case"—that he performed gratis for the Simpson defense (*American* 579, 687).

Commenting on said event in his own *Playboy* interview (February 1997), Schiller described his refusal to turn the tapes to his own profit as "another example of me thinking about the future of the project, not just the moment" (146). Ditto the restraint earlier shown the tapes Simpson recorded for *I Want to Tell You:* "I could have made millions of dollars with those tapes. [. . .] But here is an example of Larry Schiller keeping his eye on the prize" (51). Yet having thus defined his desire (much like Simpson in his *Playboy* interview) not by way of dollars, and discounting notoriety as something he's "already had" (52), of what then does the "prize" consist? Not just the opportunity to write *American Tragedy* or claim its $1.25 million advance. "It's the sense of accomplishment," he went on to say, "the sense of leaving something to my family that they might be proud of, something that juxtaposes the criticism and the controversies of my life" (52): *I Want To Tell You Deux,* in which the misunderstood Schiller, by way of Simpson's all-American saga, will prove once and for all "the story of Schiller is not only those things" (151).

When Mailer undertook a similar task in *The Armies of the Night* (1968), he was able to make his life signify beyond himself because he could situate his own figure of "monumental disproportions" within the chaos of an antiwar march that justified "egotism" as "the last tool left to History" and against a Washington, D.C., setting that allowed that protest to assume the contours of a "quintessentially American event" (68, 241). He later could portray Gilmore in *The Executioner's Song* as a "quintessentially American" example of what he had been talking about all his life and Utah as a modern-day theocracy because his opening invocation of a literal fall from a forbidden apple tree (17), with all its intimations of lapsed grace and lost Eden, had already established what Lauren Berlant has called a " 'nationalization' of utopia" (32).[22] Schiller's signs, in contrast, signify nothing beyond themselves. He opens *American Tragedy* with reference to the 1970 introduction of Simpson and Al Cowlings to the Kardashian brothers, all four men "living Everyman's—well, every twentieth-century American man's—fantasies" (xv), in an equally fantastical place the next chapter translates as "City of Angels—the name might have come from a fairy tale" (3). He then goes on to explain that for the Armenian Kardashians the city has been a very real source of salvation because emigrating to Los Angeles at the turn of the twentieth century saved their ancestors from genocidal extermination. No wonder Robert begins each day with a prayer: having already made one fortune in the music business, he is in the process of working on his second when the events of 12 June 1994 intervene to test his faith "that God's plan will be evident" (56). The resonance of his setting thus established, however, Schiller is left with the more pressing questions: Whose American Tragedy is it? And of what does it consist?

It's not about the victims, who emerge as abstractions as empty as the Bundy condo crime scene, stripped of all its furnishings (370). And it's certainly not about Schiller, whose appearances in the text constitute little more than a Hitchcock cameo. Is the tragedy then Kardashian's? The Jamesian loss of innocence of the one attorney who negotiates no fee for his labors and who steadily awakens to the fact that he is not in Kansas (celebrity version) anymore ("Was he really O.J.'s friend, or just the admirer of a mask the athlete always wore for him?"

[92]), as he is forced to recognize that the man he claims to know as well as any-one else is a longtime batterer, maybe even a murderer, and silently conclude that "if Simpson has withheld and hidden and disguised so much of himself for so many years, he must be hiding still more now" (682). *The Wings of the Dupe,* in other words. Or, finally, is it Simpson's? Not just " 'the All-American Hero, the clean-cut image of the American Man' " noted by Marcia Clark in her address to the jury pool (256), but "[a] superstar who had reinvented himself," as one of the DNA experts realizes, and, as such, "a contemporary American hero" (176), whose story could be titled *Gatsby II, the Sequel.*

Finally, it is neither. This is not due to Schiller's inability to crib a frame when necessary. His willingness to pitch Gilmore's story as "a woman's story" if he can only secure the rights to Gilmore's girlfriend or cast their romance as a con-temporary *Romeo and Juliet* should Gilmore be executed before he has been interviewed testifies to his ability to crib from all manner of sources.[23] And the foreword he appended to *I Want to Tell You* portrays the imprisoned Simpson as so manacled—handcuffs linked to belly restraint, belly restraint fastened to floor—and so surrounded by "sound[s] of force telling you more powerfully than words that you're entering a world where you are not in control" as to ap-proximate a remake of *Roots* (ix). But manacled himself in *American Tragedy* by a decision to portray Simpson, who tried to block the book's publication, "only through the eyes and ears of third parties" (687), Schiller ends up fragmenting Simpson when he is not completely disembodying Simpson. On the one hand, the Simpson that comes into focus through Schiller's third-party sources consis-tently complicates the expectations of those who meet him. To the pathologist who expects "another jock who'd sailed through college untouched by higher learning," Simpson turns out to be someone who asks "sharp, thoughtful ques-tions" (100). To the Cochran law associate who expects "a Bryant Gumble, a white man with dark skin" (299), Simpson turns out to be decidedly *"ethnic"* and unequivocally *"down"* (157, 299). On the other hand, the Simpson reduced to a voice on a conference-room speakerphone loses all presence entirely—despite Schiller's efforts to grant him agency by virtue of a voice barking "orders from the high command" to his lawyers about running- versus passing-game strategies, particular plays, and trial pacing (375, 305, 495, 592). Alone among a courtroom of performers—Fuhrman, who, even in disgrace, has "star qual-ity" (616); Barry Scheck, who puts on "a good show" (662); Marcia Clark, who delivers "[g]ood solid theater" (649)—Simpson is the only actor, his leading role notwithstanding, whose most impressive performances nobody gets to see. Never called to the stand by attorneys who know full well how disastrous his tes-timony would be, his cross-examination is conducted as a dialogue with himself (636). His closing arguments are delivered to an empty holding cell (662).

With his subject neither type nor typical, the only way that Schiller can assert the significance of his endeavor is by way of the trial itself. And this he does—ad infinitum. DNA lawyer Bob Blasier offers to work on the case for free because he thinks that "[w]orking on the trial of the century, win or lose, was an excellent career move" (285). Screenwriter Laura Hart McKinny's lawyers eagerly meet with Simpson's about the Fuhrman tapes because it gets them "involved in the trial of the century" (521). Barry Scheck is "a remarkable man" because, in refusing to take over in court for the increasingly erratic F. Lee Bailey, he declines—at least initially—"a starring role in the trial of the century" (317). Yet to have any real historical validity as a "trial of the century," as Claudia Brodsky Lacour astutely argues, a "crime of the century" is required, a "crime without equal in kind whose commission also ha[s] the unique subjective requirement *that it be done disinterestedly, for its own sake,* while with a modern enthusiasm for inventing and implementing technology" (384), the model of which she finds in the 1961 trial of Adolf Eichmann. Curiously, Schiller alluded to that trial in an early made-for-television movie he produced, *The Trial of Lee Harvey Oswald* (1976), in which Oswald, who has not been killed during the transfer to the Dallas county jail, sits through his own "trial of the century" as a man inside a glass booth. [24] In *American Tragedy,* by contrast, the repeated mention of Simpson's trial as "the trial of the century" only recalls how hackneyed the literary device is—not just because it was so frequently invoked by others discussing the Simpson case, as occurred when Diana Trilling compared it to the Dreyfus affair, which for France "was its trial of the century" ("Notes" 18, 20), but because it has such a long history of being invoked to accommodate almost any spectacle. As early as 1895, Hearst's *San Francisco Examiner* publicized the murder of two girls in church by Sunday school superintendent Theodore Durrant as "THE CRIME OF A CENTURY" (Swanberg 75). Three years later, Henry Hunt found *The Crime of the Century: Or the Assassination of Dr. Patrick Henry Cronin* in the hacking to death of a Chicago physician by members of an Irish secret society (Geis and Bienen 4).

Aware, after the subsequent trials-of-the-century of Leopold and Loeb (1924) and of Bruno Hauptmann (1935), that the only parlance the term can now have is ironic, E. L. Doctorow has his *Ragtime* narrator situate the trial of Harry K. Thaw for the murder of Stanford White in a relativistic context: "And though the newspapers called the shooting the Crime of the Century, [Emma] Goldman knew it was only 1906 and there were ninety-four years to go" (5). Unaware of—or refusing to concede—such irony, Schiller keeps invoking the Simpson case in his next attempt to write the great American exposé. Part of the "more complete context" he wishes to provide the JonBenét Ramsey case in *Perfect Murder, Perfect Town* (1999), as his "Author's Note" asserts (xi), the Simpson case becomes the touchstone that people keep returning to—after the obligatory reference to the Kennedy assassination ("It was like the day John F. Kennedy was killed: nothing seemed normal" [30])—in order to establish the death of the six-year-old as a "global story" that tells us " 'what world we live in, where we are' " (30, 125). The Ramseys' press representative thus tells them that their daughter's murder is "sure to become the next media circus after the oj business" (89). The Boulder chief of police, by contrast, announces, " 'It's not oj and it's not LA here in Boulder' " (111).

Only the effort completely backfires. For while invoking *the Ramsey thing* as succeeding *the Simpson thing, [and] the Susan Smith thing* may provide an effective rebuke to that complacency the insular residents of Boulder feel their setting affords them (214)—as does Schiller's opening "Part One: A Death in Paradise" with JonBenét's learning that the roses in her garden do, in fact, have thorns (3)—casting each "thing" as the latest in a succession of nationally destabilizing "things" only interrogates any one "thing's" singular status. Reduced to an empty signifier, the Simpson trial ends up a reference to be used at will. When the *Globe* stringer then tries to insinuate himself into the Ramseys' confidence by comparing the Boulder PD's treatment of them with the LAPD's of Simpson (220), ingratiate himself with their minister by citing biblical verses quoted by Christopher Darden to the Simpson jury (313–14), and gain access to the district attorney by showing him a copy of a paper he wrote on the Simpson case (251), his actions are less evidence of tabloid manipulations as they are legitimate appropriations of a trial that commentators like Schiller have voided of all meaning.

In the two-part miniseries broadcast on 12 and 15 November of the following year, the trial would be voided even more. Gone are the "trial of the century" references. Gone, for the most part, is O.J., whose presence in the script Schiller instructed teleplay writer Norman Mailer to reduce.[25] Visible only as a set of separate body parts—a hand playing blackjack in jail, a back rehearsing closing arguments in a holding cell, a left profile in the courtroom—the O. J. Simpson of the *American Tragedy* (2000) Schiller directed for CBS emerges as an act of ventriloquism: one actor assumes his body while another provides his voice. A drama now about a couple-a-middle-aged-guys with bald spots, bellies, and big convertibles, this *American Tragedy* deals as much with conspiracies that paranoid Dream Team members think are being mounted against them by their own colleagues as it does any massive LAPD conspiracy those attorneys are trying to prove was mounted against their client. If viewers get any sense of the context of what is supposed to be at stake, it is, ironically, by way of commercial interruptions, which, among ads for Lysol, Orajel, and Chloraseptic, include clips from a *48 Hours* episode on "America's Rage," a *60 Minutes II* feature on "what's it like to go through an execution," a late-news segment on "Celebrity Mug Shots," and promos for law-and-order dramas like *The Fugitive, Family Law,* and *The District* (the last featuring an episode in which a black child witnesses his mother's murder).

In Stephen Heath's view, it is in these interstices that the entire question of media representation discussed in all my chapters on W.A.S.T.E. is resolved, as television replaces a model defined by citizenship (the individual as embodiment of nation or social group) with a model defined by markets (the social group as serialized conglomerate). "The full alignment of representation with commodification and the solicitation of consumer desire is finally the loss of the sense of representation (its sense as in any way representative *of*)"; because "there is no representation for and of the American as subject and citizen, no stability from which representation could operate politically (no nationhood) or socially (only the dissolution of 'the American mainstream')," what television finally represents is television itself: "it 'represents' the reality it produces and imitates" (Heath 281–82). And, fittingly, it is among the commercial interstices of television that we finally locate Schiller—heretofore absent from Mailer's script as in any way involved with the defense—hiding in plain sight, much like the figure of the animal waiting to be found amidst the camouflage of a surrounding drawing. For, as viewers discover, it is not only Afrin and Alka-Seltzer, Sprint and Slim-Fast that they have the opportunity to consume while watching *American Tragedy.* With the steady stream of 1–800 numbers that flash upon their screens, they also learn that they can have their choice of "Now That's What I Call Music, Volume 5," "The Beatles 1," Yanni's "If I Could Tell You," and "Universal Smash Hits," to name but a few of the items available for instant order. None, however, can compete with the "exclusive one-time offer" that concludes the broadcast of the two-part television drama: a videotape of "the miniseries O.J. never wanted you to see," which, if purchased immediately, entitles them to a free copy of "the *New York Times* #1, best-selling book, *American Tragedy,* personally autographed by author Lawrence Schiller." In the end, it is this addendum that best suggests the literary model that has eluded the writer without hands all along: *Advertisements for Myself,* the frame within which he should have cast his work from the very beginning.

The Fresh Kills Landfill, which closed on Thursday, received New York City's garbage for 53 years. That was 48 years longer than originally planned.

At the height of the landfill's operations in 1987, the city shipped 29,000 tons of garbage a day to its 3,000 putrid acres, which 650 workers built into mountains of trash; six crane operators endlessly scooped fresh trash from barges; and 44 enormous dump trucks plied the steep roads that vein the landfill's surface.

Today, Fresh Kills is quieter. About 300 workers remain; a single crane still operates, and just six trucks rumble across surfaces that resemble the grasslands of Montana.

—"Requiem for a Garbage Dump," *New York Times* 25 March 2001

Hesh: Very smart. It could be major.

Tony: It could be as good as garbage.

Christopher: Hey, garbage is our bread and butter.

Tony: Was.

—*The Sopranos*, Episode 1

Conclusion

The number of people who *get* wasted on his series notwithstanding, Tony Soprano has a point: waste is no longer alive and well in New Jersey. Plans to build a major trash transfer station in Linden were rejected in September 2001 by the state's Department of Environmental Protection. Investigations by the attorney general's office revealed financial collusion between the mayor of Linden and the son-in-law who is part owner of the proposed transfer site. Even the Trash Museum located on Route 519 in Harmony—the only museum in the country devoted entirely to trash—faces an uncertain future after county freeholders voted in April to terminate its curator's job as "environmental education specialist."[1] Not that the situation in New Jersey's primary trash supplier is any better. The March 2001 closing of the " 'King Kong of American garbage mounds' " that the waste analyst in Don DeLillo's *Underworld* presumed would expand forever (163), before adequate alternatives to Fresh Kills could be put in place, has made trash, as I write in March 2002, the focus of heated debate—not to mention Republican mayoral politics—in New York City. " 'Dig[ging]' " trash might be fine for the dwarfs of Barthelme's *Snow White*, who assume that "there can no longer be any question of 'disposing' of it, because it's all there is" (97), but in a city that generates twenty-two million pounds of trash a day, disposal is precisely the question, what with a Giuliani legacy of borough self-sufficiency too sacred a cow to touch, legislation pending in Congress and the Pennsylvania General Assembly that could greatly restrict interstate transfers, and a new mayor announcing 50 percent cuts in recycling. Therefore, unlike Donald Barthelme's dwarfs, who calculate increases in the per-capita production of trash per day, Michael Bloomberg's city planners are calculating increases in the costs of trash removal per year—which between 1998 and 2000 already had more than tripled to a sum that is projected to more than double by 2004.[2]

Given my book's consideration of popular culture as trash whose recycling has been pivotal to the fashioning of nation-states during the twentieth century, the trash crisis that the closing of Fresh Kills has produced inevitably raises questions about the future of what I have termed, in my appropriation of Barthelme, a trash phenomenon. What does a *New York Times* requiem for a landfill suggest about the continued role that American popular culture can be expected to play in an era of globalization? If, as Michael Hardt and Antonio Negri argue, the media paradigm that underlies today's Empire is the deterritorialized network, democratically incarnated in the Internet, oligopolistically in the broadcast systems (294–300), what impact, symbolic or actual, can the territorially specific Hollywood continue to have in a world defined by imperial rather than imperialist sovereignty? And, by extension, what relevance can the Hollywood novel continue to have as a literary genre when independent film production has made Hollywood, as David Fine quips, "wherever movies are made" (156)?

Contemporary writers, of course, are not the first to employ a landfill metaphor when assessing the social residue of popular culture. Perhaps the most memorable use of it earlier can be found in the scene in *The Day of the Locust* (1939) in which Todd Hackett, Nathanael West's artistic surrogate, observes a ten-ton truck unloading sets and props onto the gigantic pile of sets and props that already comprises a Hollywood back lot:

> This was the final dumping ground. He thought of Janvier's "Sargasso Sea." Just as that imaginary body of water was a history of civilization in the form of a marine junkyard, the studio lot was one in the form of a dream dump. A Sargasso of the imagination! And the dump grew continually, for there wasn't a dream afloat somewhere which wouldn't sooner or later turn up on it, having first been made photographic by plaster,

canvas, lath and paint. Many boats sink and never reach the Sargasso, but no dream ever entirely disappears. (132)

Looking over the remarks of the authors surveyed in this book, however, one would have to say that West, like DeLillo's waste analyst, was premature in his judgment, for the disappearance of culturally induced dreams is one of the themes that permeates their works. American writers typically trace that disappearance to television's supplanting film as a dominant medium. The "*blessed* celluloid upon which have been imprinted in our century all the dreams and shadows that have haunted the human race since man's harsh and turbulent origins" that Gore Vidal glorifies in the opening of *Myra Breckinridge* is portrayed as no more returning than verse drama (5, 95), now that the MGM commissary is occupied by television technicians slurping what used to be called Louis B. Mayer Chicken Soup (31). Non-American authors, by contrast, typically blame the encounter with America itself. The trip to America that Dennis Potter claimed "open[ed] my very reclusive, narrow, insular head to what had been as a dream to me—the films I had seen as a child, the songs I still listened to" also left that dream "stripped of its fantasy, naked in front of me, because I could see the source of it" while working on the MGM version of *Pennies from Heaven* in Hollywood (*Potter* 116). Likewise, the "fantasy world" of American popular culture that obsessed Murakami Haruki while growing up in a suburb outside of Kobe (Murakami and McInerny 28) became completely demystified during the period in which he lived in the United States as an adult: " 'Listening to Jim Morrison in the United States is not the same as listening to him in Japan' " (Buruma, "Becoming" 70).

It is important to remember that the elegiac note sounded in these eulogies to American popular culture, especially the classic American film, has long been a central component of what can be called the classic Hollywood novel. F. Scott Fitzgerald's unfinished *The Last Tycoon* (1941) concludes its first chapter with images of descent and death, as the eponymous Monroe Stahr is described as returning to earth after a celestial flight in which "he saw which way we were going," bringing with him "a new way of measuring our jerky hopes and graceful rogueries and awkward sorrows" when "he came here from choice to be with us to the end" (20). Only in his case the end in question is not only the result of poor health but of the fact that the paternalistic form of management that his personalized approach to filmmaking yields is already anachronistic in a studio system succumbing to the pressure of labor unions. Budd Schulberg's *What Makes Sammy Run?* (1941) opens with a similar reference to its hustling protagonist's "running against time" (5), which later is elaborated in the portrayal of Sammy Glick "turning life into a race in which the only rules are fight for the rail and elbow on the turns and the only finish line is death" (191). Norman Mailer's *The Deer Park* (1955) traces the slide into mediocrity of one of the "few kind and honest men in the world" as Charles Eitel learns he is not an artist but a "commercial man" (20, 260), and not even a very good commercial man at that, ending up directing films that are "nothing remarkable" and that gross "middling returns" (314).

This is not to say that all Hollywood novels adopt this elegiac tone. If West recognized that "[i]t is hard to laugh at the need for beauty and romance, no matter how tasteless, even horrible, the results of that are" (61), John O'Hara had no difficulty characterizing Hollywood as " 'the big laugh' " in his 1962 novel of that name (257). Not surprisingly, it is the latter approach that tends to inform most recent works of the genre, such as Michael Tolkin's *The Player* (1988) and Bruce Wagner's *Force Majeure* (1991) and *I'm Losing You* (1996). But those novels that present the state of Hollywood as an emblem of the state of the union invariably depict the American nation-state as a fragile—if not feeble—construction. West, whose novella opens with an invocation of "quitting time" (59), portrays the people who "had come to California to die" as "the pick of America's madmen" whose violence will—and in the end does—erupt in "civil war" (60, 118). Fitzgerald's comparison of Stahr to Lincoln as another "leader carrying on a long war on many fronts" is undermined by an earlier portrait of an actor dressed as Lincoln eating a forty-cent special in the studio commissary, the sight of which causes a visiting Danish prince to stare "as a tourist at the mummy of Lenin in the Kremlin" (106, 49). Schulberg's depiction of Sammy Glick's tale as "a blueprint of a way of life that was paying dividends in America in the first half of the twentieth century" (276) offers the Rivington Street ghetto from which it has sprung as evidence not only of the "withering away in America" of the Judaism that is "thrown overboard as excess baggage" by those in a hurry to succeed, but of "all [the] Rivington Streets of all nationalities allowed to pile up in cities like gigantic dung heaps smelling up the world" (206, 226).

The nostalgia that often infuses these works conforms to Susan Stewart's definition of the term in being an inchoate longing for a past that "has never existed except as narrative" (23). In this sense, the "lavish, romantic past that perhaps will not come again into our time" that Fitzgerald cited in an explanatory note about *The Last Tycoon* (141) is the past of *The Great Gatsby* (1925), which itself, in infinite regress, is informed by an amorphous longing for that "fresh, green breast of the new world" with which it concludes (182). By contrast, the longing that infuses John Updike's *In the Beauty of the Lilies* (1996), the Hollywood novel with which I want to end my study, is the quite specific narrative of messianic historicism, the master narrative that has supported modern nationalism from its eighteenth-century inception. Spanning the American Century from 1910 to

1990, from the fall of Mary Pickford off a horse to the fall of a false prophet on television, and tracking the fortunes through four generations of a single family that dates back "to near the beginning" of the country (110), Updike's book resurrects all those binaries of elect and preterite and assumptions about chosen people that have supported the invention of America from its Calvinist origins. Indeed, each of the successive Wilmots that he portrays deliberately opts for a career that fosters spiritual and/or national unification: Clarence through the church, Teddy through the delivery of mail, Essie through the cinema, and Clark through the Temple of True and Actual Faith. More than simply nostalgic in an age in which, as Montserrat Guibernau contends, there are "no common memories to invoke" to summon up a consciousness of global identity (131), the novel would seem to announce its own obsolescence by establishing national memory as its very foundation.

Significantly, the strongest proof of the Wilmots' election does not come until the section of the novel that deals with the Wilmot who becomes a movie star. Raised by a crippled mother who worships her physically intact child as "perfection" (226), repeatedly reminded by relatives and admirers of the indescribable " 'it' " that makes her " 'special' " (273, 274, 298, 317), Essie grows up confident that God always answers her prayers and traces that phenomenon back to the Calvinist grandfather who has died before her birth. No such belief animates that paternal grandfather, whose loss of faith in God in the novel's first pages eventually leads to his leaving his New Jersey ministry and taking a job as a door-to-door salesman in Paterson. Yet having once preached that God " 'speak[s] to men in metaphors drawn from their daily lives' " (51), Clarence finds that he can satisfy his need for belief in cinematic "church[es]" in which he becomes one with another congregation of "worshippers" (105, 103). Within these catacombs in which "[t]he world was being created anew" (106), events that previously have confirmed his view of God as an "absurd bully, barbarically thundering through a cosmos entirely misconceived" (5), are recycled in such a way as to mitigate their sense of finality: "last year's sinking of the *Titanic,* sounding the absence of God to its very bottom, was recast as a flaming disaster in a Danish film, and Queen Elizabeth was reborn as an aging Sarah Bernhardt" (106). And even those facts that cannot be so re-created—such as the starving Jews of the Warsaw Ghetto and the frozen bodies on the Russian tundra during World War II—are given meaning by "the voice of God behind the movie newsreels" that "boomed and scolded," yet "enclos[ed] the audience in the ultimate security of an unfaltering American baritone" (255). Projection booth or burning bush, each emits a radiant source of light.

Because the novel also characterizes movies as "above all American" (104), however, the auratic processes by which they provide spiritual consolation are processes that create national consolidation. Essie's stardom is achieved while working at Columbia, the name given by Harry Cohn to Cohn-Brandt-Cohn in 1924 as a patriotic sign of this immigrants' son's assimilation. More important, in their displacement of the high culture, and especially the print culture, that has been so fundamental to the emergence of nationalism, movies also signal a paradigm shift in the way in which any such consolidation is achieved. The Benjamin West portraits of the "velvet-clad founders of our freedom" that Clarence's son Teddy sees in the Pennsylvania Academy of the Fine Arts only oppress him with their "oily clutter" (212, 211). The *Popular Encyclopedia* that Clarence pitches as " 'a down-to-earth encyclopedia, written and edited to patriotic native tastes,' " makes no impression at all on the immigrant *populus* to whom he tries to sell it because the "ladder of information" it is alleged to afford any person "regardless of how early circumstances had compelled him to quit formal schooling" is restricted to those who are literate (92, 86). Last seen sitting on the lowest shelf of a bookcase, its volumes of "crumbling yellow-brown leather" smell "so of the dead past" that nobody ever opens them (295). The national consolidation that movies successfully promote, by contrast, is presented as a transhistorical phenomenon. The inculcation of "unified emotions" from channeling "surging indignation, distress, suspense, and a relief that verged upon the comic in the violence of its discharge" that joins the "addict" Clarence to other scattered viewers (105, 108) is the same effect that the not quite "betranced" Teddy experiences when watching films that try "to get you to look over the edge, at something you would rather not see—poverty, war, murder" (146, 147), which, in turn, is what the youthful Essie experiences when looking at movies that "took you to an edge but left you safe, all shadows sealed shut inside a happy ending," and, in "wound[ing] only to heal," dismiss their consumers "back into reality as even better Americans and firmer Christians" (247, 311).

Such techniques of consolation/consolidation confirm Fredric Jameson's nomination of anxiety and hope as the two sides of mass culture's collective consciousness whereby legitimization of the existing order depends on giving expression to actual social concerns that then are resolved by the projection of illusory social harmony ("Reification" 141, 144). The same *noir* melodramas in which Essie gives voice to "the desolate America of earning and spending and eating and breeding" in a way that the refined Audrey Hepburn and Grace Kelly do not mainly serve as moral mechanisms "toward the elimination of all defective parts" and thus require that the characters she plays "be cast out—murdered, exiled, imprisoned—for failing to conform" (333). So effective are they in manufacturing this illusion of false consensus that, by the time Essie's son, Clark, is born, movies exported abroad have begun to direct their energies "from easing a nation's pain with entertainment to easing the pain of the entire free and third worlds, not excluding parts of Eastern Europe" (414). No wonder, on the last pages of the book, the success of video is described as having produced a whole new market, the creation of overseas audiences desperate to see "American old-timers" like Essie on film testifying to "an imperial nostalgia at work" (487).

Not coincidentally, the paradigm shift that Hardt and Negri see in the switch from *imperialist* to *imperial* sovereignty is one they trace back to the U.S. Constitution, whose model of checks and balances entrusted power into the hands of the multitude and left no room for the kind of transcendence of power that had characterized modern European conceptions of sovereignty (160–64). That being said, the contemporary Empire they see as distinguished by the global extension of American constitutional processes still does not grant the United States any more than a prominent—as opposed to a preeminent—position.

> The fundamental principle of Empire [. . .] is that its power has no actual and localizable terrain or center. Imperial power is distributed in networks, through mobile and articulated mechanisms of control. This is not to say that the U.S. government and the U.S. territory are no different from any other: the United States certainly occupies a privileged position in the global segmentations and hierarchies of Empire. As the powers and boundaries of nation-states decline, however, differences between national territories become increasingly relative. They are now not differences of nature (as were, for example, the differences between the territory of the metropole and that of the colony) but differences of degree. (384)

First evidenced by the Persian Gulf War, which presented the United States as the only power capable of managing international justice, *"not as a function of its own national motives but in the name of global right"* (180), that privileged position did indeed confirm the birth of a new world order, if not in quite the way that George Bush had intended.

Essie's brother, Danny, comes to this conclusion near the end of Updike's novel. A State Department political officer who admits to " 'lov[ing] this crazy, wasteful, self-hating country in spite of itself' " while the Vietnam War still rages (394), he confesses to " 'wondering lately if losing and winning are as different as we like to think' " upon being recalled from Southeast Asia to Washington, D.C., after the end of the Cold War and assigned to work on Middle Eastern affairs (488). Far more prescient than his character, though, Updike questions the binary premises that underlie American nationhood throughout the entire text. Like DeLillo in *Underworld*, his *inscription* of nationalist precepts does not imply his *subscription* to them. Thus, the election that distinguishes the Wilmots as "special" turns out to be a function of their own self-image. To those who marry them, they are alternately " '*self*ish' " or overly cautious (350, 270); to those who medicate them, they are simply " 'a little too fine-spun' " (204). Similarly, the interwoven presence of God that Essie has found "as dependable as her reflection in the mirror" turns out to be no more durable than her most recent cosmetic surgery (354). Having once imagined the camera endowing her with "immortal safety, beyond change and harm" (335), especially after the 1950 switch from film based on cellulose nitrate, which disintegrates into "chemical mush" in storage, to film based on cellulose acetate, which grants her "eternal return perennially called back to life" in archives and reruns (336), she discovers her "absolute immortality" turned into "a slow dissolution within a confused mass of perishing images like a colorful mountain of compressed and rotting garbage" as she is indiscriminately "mulched in" along with other actors and actresses in the memories of the moviegoing public (465). Even the celebrity that has made people consider her "a goddess [that] had descended to be among them" (467) turns out to be the deification, as Walter Benjamin long ago recognized, "not [of] the unique aura of the person but the 'spell of the personality,' the phony spell of a commodity" ("Work" 231).

The metaphor that Updike employs for the commodification that makes the cinematic elect no different from the working-class preterite is "stretching." Defined as the management principle behind the running of the Paterson silk mills, which entails increasing the number of machines operated by each worker, stretching is introduced by Updike as a product of advanced industrialization: with improvements in the looms no longer requiring hand-power to keep the machines working properly, more machines can be operated by fewer workers (28–29). Those who own the mills trumpet this advance as evidence of an inevitable progress by which all benefit " 'in a land God has favored with such a wealth of opportunity' " (31). Those who work in the mills, by contrast, recognize it full well as a means of keeping them jockeying for position in order to keep their menial places. Clarence's son Teddy thus recoils at the prospect of working in a bottle-cap factory after the impoverished family is forced to move from Paterson to Delaware upon Clarence's death: "He didn't want to have to compete, and yet this seemed the only way to be an American. Be stretched or strike" (139). Unfortunately, when Teddy's daughter, Essie, arrives in Hollywood, she discovers that "the Wilmot fineness" that was to have been her ticket out of Delaware has landed her in a dream factory that operates by the same principles, since the studios bring " 'a star along, and once you were up there they experimented a little, to see how far you could stretch and keep your audience' " (309, 357).

The great mistake made by those who join the Temple of True and Actual Faith that Updike portrays in the final section of the novel is the assumption that terms like election and preterition, player and nonplayer, insider and outsider apply in a nation whose citizenry is united in, if not equivalent, then synonymous forms of industrial exploitation. More than just giving voice to familiar countersubversive rants against the " 'Government of the Godless' " (401), then, Temple leader Jesse Smith also reprises those rants against reproduced popular culture familiar to us from the critics cited in my own introduction. Television makes viewers " 'worship images on a screen until nothing else means squat' " (421). Movies shown to soldiers in Vietnam served as weapons " 'to distract us poor boy-sinners from the dreadful deeds we were being asked to perpetrate' " (379). Clark, whose main memory of Vietnam is *Apocalypse, Now,* has " 'gorged' " himself on so much " 'ephemeral trash' " as to " 'remember every empty can, every orange peel' " (380). The product of such views, the City on the Hill that Jesse founds in Lower Branch, Colorado, is not just a utopian commune meant to return its followers to "God's country," to what was once called the " 'Territory of Jefferson' " (365, 369). It is a specifically preindustrial commune without even a telephone to commend it.

It doesn't stay that way, of course. In a perfect illustration of the national impinging upon the local, and the global impinging upon the national, the battle over the schooling of the Temple's children that leads to a confrontation with the FBI and the ATF results in the transformation of the surrounding area into "Satellite City," complete with hookups throughout the world: the ultimate Polo Lounge lunch for public relations director Clark, who doesn't "believe all of what he was saying" but "love[s] the sensation of saying it" into his airlifted Panasonic radiophone and "feeling the words being drunk up by a thirsty world" (451); the final Fall into technology for Jesse, who gets so addicted to his image on parachuted Zeniths as to make the compound's electric bills skyrocket (466). But finally just another standoff—like Ruby Ridge, like Waco—in which "[m]illions were fascinated, for a time" (453), just like all the successive spectacles considered in the last section of this book, after which "nothing, in any cosmic sense, had happened" and the world "rolled on, untransformed" (472).

Or maybe not. In a work in which characters desperately search for signs of God, and in which even the one character who abandons God for not having given his father the " 'little sign' " that would have helped him during his crisis of faith still views Nixon's resignation as a sign that " 'nothing's sacred' " (410), the expected conflagration of the Temple of True and Actual Faith that ends the novel provides an unexpected sign that " '[w]hat evaporates can recondense' " (81). Clark, in fact, receives one such sign when the Revelation-spouting Jesse is about to have his followers start sending women and children to Heaven at the point of a snub-nosed Colt .38 pistol. He imagines the women drifting around Heaven in "silken gowns falling in parallel folds like Elizabeth Taylor in a movie whose name he had forgotten," and he remembers his stepfather's admonition while playing Wiffle Ball: *"Start stretching, Superguy"* (482, 481).

Within the context of a novel in which stretching has been portrayed as joining all people in a postindustrial nation, it is an oxymoronic injunction. No one person can be a superhero when all are similarly chained to processes of mechanical enslavement. Yet within the context of a novel that also redefines doctrine as " 'the living, changing expression of a living God' " and " 'the subject of ongoing, at time radical, reconsideration' " (81), it is an injunction that enables Clark to reappropriate the artifacts of industrialization for his own salvific purposes. Much like the parody of Superman he once has tried to get made into a movie, featuring a character who "wouldn't be called Superman or after any superhero in copyright, and all of his superhuman effects like bending a crowbar or lifting a steam engine wouldn't come off" (411), the person who pumps two bullets into the body of the false savior Jesse Smith becomes a real savior by recovering all those memories of "ephemeral trash" that constitute his own history. Only this time, it is the alter ego Clark—Kent, not Gable—who, with his deed and subsequent death, prevents the slaughter of the innocents from occurring. Much like the congregants who, with his great-grandfather Clarence, are forced to leave "their scintillating bath into the bleak facts of life" upon exiting the cinematic churches in which they effortlessly join together (107), the women and children who exit the Temple's burning storm hutch after Clark's act of self-sacrifice step out "into the open, squinting, blinking" upon emerging from darkness into light (491). Only this time they step into a world that is no longer "gutted by God's withdrawal" (107). The Christ whom Julia Ward Howe celebrated in the "Battle-Hymn of the Republic" from which Updike's novel takes its title is a figure of inspiration who "was born across the sea." The movies that grant Clark the "inspired certainty" (485) to effect a salvation that is of this world, not the next, are a homegrown product, pure and simple.

Significantly, the intimations of futurity that such recycling affords are not limited to those of religious dispositions. Aware of the "strange beauty" that many kinds of trash can have, photographer Michael Falco visited the Fresh Kills landfill two or three times a week during the eight months before it shut its gates, documenting various operations at the site even as it was being prepared for its final closing. "Soon, All That Will Be Left of Fresh Kills Are the Pictures," wrote Jim O'Grady in the "Requiem for a Garbage Dump" that was printed as a "City Lore" fluff piece in a *New York Times* Sunday edition. As he also noted, the Department of Sanitation planned to place those pictures in an archive so that its "relic of a lost world" could encourage the public to "dream about the possibilities" of building a new park on the old grounds (3).

Writing in March 2001, he couldn't have known what kind of "relic" Fresh Kills would turn into when it was reopened six months later to receive the remnants of the World Trade Center, or, given what is included in that debris, how prescient his use of the word "requiem" would be. And it's still too early in time to know whether the "world" to which the landfill now testifies—of which the twin towers had seemed such a powerful emblem—is as irretrievably "lost" as O'Grady's piece suggests, since things "lost" have the possibility of becoming things "found." To someone like Ariel Dorfman, who reminded readers that it was on 11 September that Chile "lost its democracy" in a U.S.-supported military coup twenty-eight years earlier ("Unique" par. 1), and who found the sight of people wandering the streets of New York with photos of loved ones an eerie incarnation of men and women desperately seeking information about *desaparecidos* in South America (par. 5), what was lost on 11 September 2001 was nothing less than "(North) America's famous exceptionalism, that attitude which allowed the citizens of this country to imagine themselves as beyond the sorrows and calamities that have plagued less fortunate peoples around the world" (par. 7). To someone like Thomas L. Friedman, in contrast, who for years had been writing about "super-empowered angry m[e]n" that "hate America because it is the most powerful country in the world" ("Motives" A15) and warning against "layers of local operatives, who can't be traced to any country" as posing a greater threat than intercontinental ballistic missiles ("Memo" A19), what was found was renewed faith in American unilateralism. As his op-ed piece that compared allies' conditional support of the U.S. war in Afghanistan with their unqualified support during the Gulf War bluntly stated, "We Are All Alone"— indeed, "All Alone, Again," according to a later piece, should there be any talk of a return to Iraq, because of Saddam Hussein's ability to buy off adversaries with real money.[3]

It's not just fictional characters, then, who, like Updike's Rabbit Angstrom at the end of *Rabbit Is Rich*, are declaiming, "Who needs Afghanistan? Fuck the Russkis. Fuck the Japs, for that matter. We'll go it alone, from sea to shining sea" (436). For every person who sees in 9/11 proof that America is "Unique No More," as the title of Dorfman's essay asserts, there is a person who points to the nation's response as (re)affirming the "unique role in human events" that America has been called to play, as George W. Bush did in the conclusion to his 29 January State of the Union address.[4] For every person who, like Friedman, tempers pride that "America can fight everywhere in the dark" with provisos that "I wouldn't want it to have to fight everywhere alone" ("End" 15), there is a person who, like Bush, conflates Axis powers and Evil Empires—and, rhetorically, Roosevelt and Reagan—to produce an "axis of evil"; invokes Cold War melodrama ("the midnight knock of the secret police") and *Road Warrior* postapocalypse ("weapons of mass destruction") with similar disregard; and, with reminders of American troops stationed in the Philippines, Bosnia, and Africa, recalls if not the American Century's greatest hits (Somalia *is*, after all, mentioned), at least the American Century's latest blitzes. The European Union's foreign affairs minister Christopher Patten accuses Bush of taking an "absolutist" approach to the world. German foreign minister Joschka Fischer claims that coalition partners are being treated like "satellites."[5] And Walt Disney Company chairman Michael D. Eisner announces plans to "capture the post-Sept. 11 surge in patriotism" and make a new version of *The Alamo*.[6]

I can't claim to be immune to that surge. But in assessing how much shared grief has once again produced that "one country, mourning together and facing danger together," that Bush acclaimed at the end of his State of the Union address, or that bipartisan consensus, the "we" who "want to work together," that House minority leader Richard A. Gephardt repeatedly cited in his response,[7] I want to forgo the discourse of politics and return to the discourse of detritus. For in that it is the twenty-two-hundred-acre landfill that currently is receiving the remains of the World Trade Center that is said—the denials of NASA notwithstanding—to be one of two human-made structures visible to the naked eye from space, it is the landfill that might provide a more distanced perspective as to what the response to 9/11 might have yielded. To what other surges, or impulses, then, does this site of rubble and remains—now known, simply, as "The Hill"—give evidence?

Addressing the question of the "Meanings and Legacies of Garbage" in a discussion held the weekend of 12–13 January at the Snug Harbor Cultural Center on Staten Island, performance artist Michael Bramwell described an art piece in which he swept the halls of a decrepit tenement in Harlem and learned from it that garbage removal could serve as a "cultural model for care and concern."[8] At the time that I write, approximately 1.4 million tons of rubble have been carted to Fresh Kills.[9] At the time that I write, it also is becoming clear to the men and women who are working at both the site of collapse and the site of collection that their task is coming to an end, and with the number of bodies yet to be recovered still high and the amount of rubble yet to be examined growing smaller, the gap between the two will forever remain, since, as one firefighter put it, "we can't make more dirt."[10] Still they look to find more.

If this is the view from space that the landfill now offers for contemplation, its meaning may not be altogether different from that of the photographs that Michael Falco took to commemorate what was meant to be the Fresh Kills final closing. "At the moment, only sanitation workers really know that the site can be stunningly beautiful," wrote Jim O'Grady in March 2001 ("Requiem" 3). At this moment—one year later—maybe it's not the sanitation site, but the people who form the site's unflagging army of workers—and all that their efforts represent—that truly deserve the accolade.

NOTES

Introduction

1. I am aware that usage of the term "popular culture" is problematic, and for reasons that Stuart Hall has already delineated quite persuasively ("Notes" 231–34). Like him, I "settle" for it as a description of "those forms and activities which have their roots in the social and material conditions of particular classes; which have been embodied in popular traditions and practices" because its treatment of cultural forms and activities as "a constantly changing field" (234–35) offers a more dialectical approach to my subject than does the fixity implied by the term "mass culture."

2. See Barth, "Literature of Exhaustion" 29–34.

3. For representative examples of the qualifications and refutations that have been made over the years, see Lynes, *Tastemakers;* Katz and Lazarsfeld, *Personal;* Klapper, *Effects;* Fiedler, *Cross;* Huyssen, *After;* L. Levine, *Highbrow/Lowbrow;* Hawkins, *Classics;* Jameson, *Signatures;* P. Simmons, *Deep;* Johnston, *Information;* and Simon, *Trash.* A helpful historical overview of many of these arguments is provided by the essays collected in Gurevitch et al., *Culture.* An invaluable exploration and critique of the various conceptions of cultural imperialism may be found in Tomlinson, *Cultural.*

4. As Eric Hobsbawm has pointed out, the invocation of this kind of binary was particularly important in creating Americans out of the influx of immigrants who arrived during the late nineteenth and early twentieth century for whom "[t]he concept of Americanism as an act of *choice*—the decision to learn English, to apply for citizenship— and a choice of specific beliefs, acts and modes of behaviour implied the corresponding concept of 'un-Americanism' " ("Mass-Producing" 280).

5. Douglas Kellner, for instance, follows his assertion that "[p]opular culture per se is not manipulative, an instrument of class domination, nor a monolithic reproduction of capitalist ideology" with the qualification that "in the historically specific form of popular culture produced by the culture industries controlled by corporate capital, popular culture has tended to reproduce hegemonic ideology" ("TV" 484). Stuart Hall makes a similar point when talking about the limited range of decodings that is available to cultural receivers due to the tendency of the media, "a systematic tendency, not an incidental feature," to "reproduce the ideological field of a society in such a way as to reproduce, also, its structure of domination" ("Culture" 346). He thus follows his contrast between the fixed denotative level and polysemous connotative level of television signs with this reminder: "Polysemy must not, however, be confused with pluralism" ("Encoding" 134). Even John Fiske, who views the possibilities for textual polysemy much more optimistically than most cultural critics and who finds oppositional readings activated quite frequently by television watchers, still concedes that "[g]enres are popular when their conventions bear a close relationship to the dominant ideology of the time" (112). Many views like the ones just quoted derive from Gramsci's earlier recognition that the

"compromise equilibrium" formed by the groups over which hegemony is exercised and the "leading group" to which consent is accorded "cannot touch the essential; for though hegemony is ethical-political, it must also be economic, must necessarily be based on the decisive function exercised by the leading group in the decisive nucleus of economic activity" (161).

6. For a comparison of Pynchon and DeLillo that, in finding the former to be "the real lyricist of rubbish" (63), comes to conclusions that are very different from my own, see Tanner 59–65.

7. I discuss the role of the American musical in promoting viewer uniformity at greater length in chapters 5 and 6.

8. Descriptions of aesthetic shock therapy like the ones just quoted lead critics such as Philip Nel to see DeLillo as reviving the role played by the historical avant-garde (724–44). While agreeing with the view of the avant-garde as politically engaged in a way that modernists were not that underlies such evaluations, as evidenced by those manifestoes of André Breton that defined Surrealism as "a tenet of total revolt, complete insubordination, of sabotage according to rule," whose simplest act would consist of "dashing down into the street, pistol in hand, and firing blindly, as fast as you can pull the trigger, into the crowd" ("Second Manifesto of Surrealism" [1930] 125), I depart from it in seeing the priority ascribed to art as far exceeding that ascribed to politics. With Freud rather than Marx the inspiration for the techniques of automatic writing, juxtaposed images, and dream narratives that he advocated, and his goal "the total recovery of our psychic force by a means which is nothing other than the dizzying descent into ourselves," Breton specified "conditions of moral asepsis," free of any and all constraints emanating from the social world, as the environment in which the creative act had to take place (136–37, 187). Only after the "psychological conscience" that Breton deemed primary was awakened could a secondary "moral conscience" emerge ("Political Position of Today's Art" [1935] 212).

9. For additional discussion of the art of salvage as it is portrayed in *Underworld*, see Osteen, *American* 253–59. For discussions of the way DeLillo employs *Underworld* to fashion an authorial persona that approach this subject from a different perspective, with respect to poststructuralist reductions of the concept of authorship, see Kavadlo 384–400; and R. Simmons 675–93.

10. In substituting recycling for repetition and proposing recycling as culturally enabling, my analysis obviously differs from those of Jeffrey Karnicky, who endorses repetition as an authorial model (352–53), and Molly Wallace, who substitutes representation for recycling when discussing DeLillo's novel (379–80).

11. Ohmae Kenichi, qtd. in Giddens, *Runaway* 26; Hobsbawm, *Age* 565; Baudrillard, *America* 115, 29.

12. Obviously, any such survey of contemporary women writers is necessarily schematic. The career of Sontag provides a case in point. Her early espousal of popular culture as a disengaged phenomenon changes dramatically by the time she turns her attention to the films of Leni Riefenstahl in "Fascinating Fascism" (1974). Once the celebrator of time's liberating art from "moral relevance" and "delivering it over to the

Camp sensibility" (*Against* 285), she becomes the excoriator when time seems to invite people to look at recycled Nazi art with only "knowing and sniggering detachment, as a form of Pop Art" (*Under* 94). Thus she concludes: "The hard truth is that what may be acceptable in elite culture may not be acceptable in mass culture, that tastes which pose only innocuous ethical issues as the property of a minority become corrupting when they become more established. Taste is context, and the context has changed" (98). Her later portrayal of Emma Hamilton's transformation into a Camp artifact in *The Volcano Lover: A Romance* (1992), during the precise time that England, which needs an untarnished Lord Nelson, is "about to become the greatest imperial power the world has ever known" (348), links popular culture and nation building in exactly the manner that my own book examines.

13. Qtd. in Colás 193.

14. In treating foreign authors whose foundational experiences of America are more imaginative than actual, I am adopting an approach that is closer to that of Robert Weisbuch's *Atlantic Double-Cross* than Peter Conrad's *Imagining America*. In its consideration of the impact that the physical encounter with the United States has had on British writers, Conrad's excellent book functions as a study of travel writing. In its focus on Anglo-American literary influences, Weisbuch's equally excellent book anticipates the assumptions governing my own investigation of aesthetic cross-fertilization.

15. See Baudrillard, *Illusion* 10–13, 25–27, for a particularly vitriolic condemnation of aesthetic recycling as evidence of "the last stage of the history of art" and waste as a collection of "the defunct ideologies, bygone utopias, dead concepts and fossilized ideas which continue to pollute our mental space" (26).

16. See, for instance, Hall, "Culture" 342.

1. Vidal's *Empire* Strikes Back

1. See, for instance, Nasaw 125–33; and Mugridge 15–18, 144–52.

2. James Tatum provides an especially detailed examination of the connection between the United States and Rome that Vidal habitually portrays (199–220). See, especially, his distinction between the Republican image that constitutes the Rome of Brutus, Cincinnatus, and the early books of Livy's history and the later imperial Rome of Vergil, Ovid, Tacitus, Petronius, and Suetonius (208–9).

3. To give but one example, Vidal's portrayal of Jefferson distancing himself from his own plan to take New Orleans from Spain in *Burr* deliberately recalls the Bay of Pigs fiasco (180–82). For additional examples of the correlation between the past and the present in Vidal's historical novels, see Parini 22–23; Hines 94; and Pease 268.

4. Vidal varies the dates of these beginnings and endings by a year or so in different essays but remains consistent in characterizing the three American republics in terms of increasing consolidation over time. See, for instance, his "Last Note on Lincoln" (1991; *United* 707).

5. The one notable exception to such discomfort is Clay Overbury, the John F. Kennedy–like rising star of *Washington, D.C.* (1967), who, while celebrating the dying

Franklin Delano Roosevelt's assemblage of "the fragments of broken empires into a new pattern with himself at center, proud creator of the new imperium," also retains no illusions that "the United States [was] anything more than just another power whose turn at empire had come" (242, 243).

6. See Vidal's "The Day the American Empire Ran Out of Gas" (1986; *United* 1009–14).

7. The final pages of *The New Empire* offer an especially vivid example of a United States primed for centralization at the beginning of the twentieth century: "The West Indies drift toward us, the Republic of Mexico hardly longer has an independent life, and the city of Mexico is an American town. With the completion of the Panama Canal all Central America will become a part of our system. We have expanded into Asia, we have attracted the fragments of the Spanish dominions, and reaching out into China we have checked the advance of Russia and Germany, in territory which, until yesterday, had been supposed to be beyond our sphere. We are penetrating into Europe, and Great Britain especially is gradually assuming the position of a dependency, which must rely on us as the base from which she draws her food in peace, and without which she could not stand in war" (208–9). If, according to Adams's prognostications, the next fifty years continued the process evidenced by the previous half century, the nation's future was assured: "the United States will outweigh any single empire, if not all empires combined. The whole world will pay her tribute" (209).

8. Early attempts at cartel formation, as Kerry Segrave chronicles (1–20), can be seen in the 1908 establishment of the Film Service Association (fsa), led by the Edison Company, which merged with the Biograph Association of Licensees, led by American Biograph, to form the Motion Picture Patents Company (mppc) later that same year. Yet, as Segrave argues (11), it was not until 1914–22 that the U.S. film industry developed into a formidable cartel, dominated by eight companies: Metro-Goldwyn-Mayer, Paramount Pictures, Twentieth Century–Fox Film Corporation, rko Radio Pictures, Inc., and Warner Bros., Inc., all of which were vertically integrated in a system of production, distribution, and exhibition; and Universal Pictures, United Artists, and Columbia Pictures, which at the beginning were uninvolved in exhibition.

9. Amy Kaplan approaches this issue through a fascinating examination of those first "imperial films" that framed the Spanish-American War through domestic narratives, which, with time, became foundational imagistic texts for later films that predicated the birth of the American nation on the restoration of an imperiled home by white male saviors (1068–79).

10. All parenthetical citations to the *Creel Report* refer to the text officially attributed to the United States Committee on Public Information. Complete bibliographic information for this text appears under the latter heading in the list of works cited.

11. As Larry Wayne Ward makes clear, the Committee on Public Information film effort did not begin as quickly as Creel suggests in his *Report:* the Film Division was not established until 25 September 1917, more than five months after the committee's formation on 14 April 1917, and it took another six months before it began operating effectively (45). For a discussion of the reasons for this delay, see L. Ward 45–90.

12. It was, in fact, the desire for greater distribution of war film footage to larger au-

diences that inspired the Film Division, reorganized under Charles S. Hart, to undertake production on its own behalf in 1918. Prior to that time, the Film Division, under the direction of Louis B. Mack, had been limited to using the war footage made by the Signal Corps, some of which was distributed to the weekly film services, the remainder of which was compiled into features and distributed to patriotic societies and state Councils of Defense "in such manner as to avoid competition with the commercial motion picture industry" (*Creel* 47). The first features made under Hart's reorganization, in contrast, received gala openings at New York theaters (the Lyric Theater, the George M. Cohan Theater, the Rivoli and Rialto Theaters on Broadway), which were preceded by two-week publicity campaigns that included department store and hotel lobby displays, streetcar cards, newspaper ads, and banners, aimed at stimulating attendance at subsequent showings at local movie houses (Creel, *How* 121–23).

13. Such opportunistic substitution of title cards is exactly what was done to D. W. Griffith's World War I epic, *Hearts of the World* (1918). See Slide 110; and Brownlow 152.

14. Will H. Hays, who came to his presidency of the Motion Picture Producers and Distributors of America (MPPDA) after stints as chairman of the Republican National Committee and Postmaster General, saw it as "wholly natural" that his organization "should appreciate the help that government departments could render" (510). Much like Creel, he denied having been engaged in censorship at home or propagandizing abroad (327, 524) and, like Creel, described the policies he did promote with a set of euphemisms, such as "self-regulation" (327), "harmonization" (329), "policyship" (377). Even these euphemisms do not disguise the increasing degree of enforced compliance that permeates Hays's descriptions once he begins discussing the policies leading up to the Production Code: a "system of rules" consisting of "Don'ts and Be Carefuls" (433), establishment of a Hollywood Jury to "give a semblance of compulsion" to those "Don'ts and Be Carefuls" (435), a production ethic "capable of uniform interpretation and based not on arbitrary do's and don'ts, but on principles" and rooted in "immutable laws" (438), a Legion of Decency to promote "Code enforcement" (450), a "thorough house cleaning" of distributors and exhibitors akin to "police power" (452), and, finally, a Production Code Administration with the power to impose twenty-five-thousand-dollar fines (454).

15. See also Vidal's remarks in *Palimpsest* (1995), in which he describes the marriage between movies and politics as inevitable due to Hollywood's and Washington's each being "completely obsessed with itself" in comparable ways (289). See, as well, Vidal's 1983 essay "Ronnie and Nancy: A Life in Pictures" (*United* 980–94), in which he talks about the inevitability of the "carefully packaged persona of the old-time movie star" and the "carefully packaged persona of today's politician" coinciding in one person, Ronald Reagan (982).

16. Hearst's first successes in politics, his election to Congress in 1902 and reelection in 1904, proved to be his only successes.

17. As Lawrence W. Levine has persuasively argued, the increase in immigration around the turn of the twentieth century was pivotal to the emergence of cultural hierarchy in the United States. Unable to restrict access to those public places in which art

was on display, those who saw themselves as the arbiters of culture devoted themselves to controlling what Levine calls the "terms of access" (231), regulating the manner in which an already sacralized art had to be experienced. For a more detailed discussion of this point, see Levine's superb chapter on "Order, Hierarchy, and Culture" 169–242.

18. In making this claim, I am deliberately discounting the Hearst-Selig News Pictorial, whose first newsreel was introduced on 28 February 1914, one month before *The Perils of Pauline*'s first episode premiered. In referring to the serials as I do here, my concern is with those films conceived as pure fiction.

19. Proverbial cash cows, the serials also anticipated the promotional tie-ins of today. The *Patria* waltz, for example, was sold as sheet music, played and sung in ballrooms, and advertised in window displays in the McCrory and Woolworth chains (*New York American* 28 Jan. 1917: 8-M).

20. *New York American* 21 Jan. 1917: L-5; 22 Apr. 1917: 2-LH.

21. For a more extended discussion of the preparedness serial, see Stedman 39–43; and Lahue 38–65.

22. Whenever possible, quoted passages from silent films derive from the films themselves. When failure to preserve film makes citation from serial novelizations the only available option, newspaper dates and pages are supplied in endnotes.

23. Hints of Yellow Peril hysteria do occur in the two Hearst serials that preceded *The Romance of Elaine,* as seen in the introductions of the villainous Long Sin near the end of *The Exploits of Elaine* and Wu Fang in its first sequel, *The New Exploits of Elaine* (Stedman 39; Lahue 28). For additional evidence of Hearst's stance toward Asians, see his *Selections* 256–58, 566–72, 576–86. For evidence of his policy toward Mexico, see *Selections* 426–30; for additional discussion of the commercial interests guiding that policy, see Mugridge 133–36; and Swanberg 296–98, 394–403.

24. For a detailed history of the controversy surrounding *Patria* after the United States formally entered the First World War, see Nasaw 261–63.

25. I am grateful to the staff of the Museum of Modern Art for screening an archival copy of *Patria* for me.

26. See, especially, Banta 499–552.

27. For examples of film scholars who have argued these particular points, see Simmon 8; Rogin, "Sword" 262–63, 267–68, 273–80; and Lang 8–20.

28. *New York American* 21 Jan. 1917: CE-3; 28 Jan. 1917: 2-CE; 25 Mar. 1917: 3-CE.

29. *New York American* 21 Jan. 1917: L-5; 28 Jan 1917: 3-CE.

30. *New York American* 21 Jan. 1917: CE-3.

31. See the Castles' *Modern Dancing* 134–36, 177 for examples of proper dancing etiquette; see 139–49 for a discussion of dancing's reformation of the fashions decreed by "old Dame Style" (144).

32. *New York American* 4 Feb. 1917: 3-BE.

33. *New York American* 18 Feb. 1917: 3-BE.

34. Susan Ware's chapter on "Iconography and Representation" (144–74) provides a particularly informative discussion of the role that Earhart's clothing played in the public

perception of her. See, especially, the reproduced photographs of Earhart that depict her juxtaposition of mixed gender symbols both in and out of the cockpit (154, 162).

35. *New York American* 14 Jan. 1917: CE-3.

36. See *New York American* 8 Apr. 1917: CE-2; 22 Apr. 1917: CE-3.

37. The particular quotations cited in this sentence appear in Nasaw 25, 47, 136. Yet examples of Hearst's feminine traits abound in biographies. See, especially, Swanberg, who opens his biography with a reference to Hearst's sleeping with his mother until he was three and a half (8), and then goes on to provide one illustration after another of his "womanly" nature (101, 145, 155, 191, 234, 526). See also the minibiography that appears in Dos Passos's *The Big Money* (466–77), in which Hearst is depicted as forever tied to his mother's "gilded apronstrings" (468).

38. *New York American* 18 July 1915: CE-7; 25 July 1915: CE-7.

39. In an important discussion of *The City and the Pillar* (1948), Robert J. Corber sees Vidal's rejection of the phallic binarisms that link sexuality to gender as resulting in a reconceptualization of a subject position that can be both masculine and homosexual (30–32, 39–50). This reconceived subject position he compares to gay macho style, which, in Corber's view, originated as an oppositional response to the domestication of masculinity that the rise of the American "organization man" in the 1940s and 1950s produced (34–39). For a contrasting discussion of *The City and the Pillar* that sees the novel as completely refuting Vidal's claims about the natural bisexuality of all humans, see Summers 56–75.

40. In these claims, I obviously am in full agreement with Richard Poirier's reading of *Myra Breckinridge, Myron,* and *Duluth* as "comic-nightmare versions of Vidal's more realistic historical novels" (237). See also Catharine R. Stimpson's discussion of Myra's pursuit of sexual power, political power, and movie industry power (183–98), which also posits a connection between Myra's mission and Caroline Sanford's less stridently articulated endeavors (301).

41. *United* 957. For examples of Vidal's essays that trace the demise of the nation-state, see "Conglomerates" (1973), "The Second American Revolution" (1981), and "Patriotism" (1991), all republished in *United* 787–91, 956–79, 1045–47, and "Notes on Our Patriarchal State" (1990) 185, 202–4. For those conversations from which the final installment of the American Chronicle series gains its title, see *Golden* 295, 450, 462–63. The initial conversation in which the phrase appears is worth citing, as it suggests quite clearly on what basis, according to Vidal, America's preeminence during its brief period of global hegemony rested. " 'How can you have a golden age after Roosevelt took us off the gold standard?' " Gore Vidal as character asks, to which a character named after the founder of Rome gives the following reply: " 'Uranium,' said Aeneas, 'will do just as well' " (295).

2. Rabbit Rerun

1. Critics who have noted this decline of America that Updike portrays in the Rabbit novels conceive of it in different terms. For representative examples, see Larry E. Taylor's

discussion of antipastoral elements (74–75), Donald J. Greiner's account of 1960s social collapse (65), and Gordon E. Slethaug's overview of American history since the nation's inception (249–51). The most extended discussion of Harry Angstrom as American representative may be found in Dilvo I. Ristoff's *Updike's America,* predicated as it is on the first three Rabbit novels constituting "a story of middle America as much as it is Harry Angstrom's" (8). With the publication of *John Updike's* Rabbit at Rest: *Appropriating History,* Ristoff's "scene-centered approach" (4) is extended to the last work in the tetralogy.

2. See Lefebvre 12–26; and de Certeau xi–xxiv. For a helpful overview of such theories of the everyday, see Miller and McHoul 1–27.

3. As anyone familiar with Updike's work knows, the old milk carton is far more likely to appear than the rose or the tree, and thus his locating the connection between the tangible and the transcendental in Whitman rather than Emerson is understandable. For an excellent discussion of Emersonian elements in Updike's work, however, particularly Updike's "angular bias" of "eye" for the "subjective geography" of "I," see Regan 81–88.

4. In evaluating Updike's reliance on tangible things in his fiction, critics have tended to base their judgments on the degree to which the incorporated things signify beyond themselves. Critics who condemn Updike's practice tend to see the things as nothing but mere objects and Updike's prose dwelling too much on "the visible exterior texture of the object" and suggesting too little "the complex engagements of the social and psychic selves reflected within the human being," as James Gindin asserts (44). Raymond A. Mazurek thus finds *Rabbit Is Rich* the "most formless" of the first three Rabbit novels because the myriad details that evoke middle-class life in the 1970s "do not come together to promote any deep understanding of the period" (153), a failure he traces to Updike's inability, in all the Rabbit books, to provide any sustained alternative to Rabbit's perspective that would allow for social analysis and critique (147, 155–59). And Joseph Waldmeir simply alleges that Updike relies on things perceived "with no revelation beyond the perception" because "he honestly has no revelation to make" (16). Critics who praise Updike's prose, in contrast, often extend the significance of things somewhat further than I would argue. Defining "reification" as "the proposition that human nature is best thought of as a state of matter," Terrence A. Doody sees Updike's work justifying the view "that people are really things" (207). Robert Detweiler's assertion that *Rabbit Redux* "is not grounded in history and reinforced by fictive imagery; it is based on the imagery and is reinforced by history" (130–31) contradicts Updike's own remarks about the actual historical events that served as catalysts for the Rabbit novels ("Why" 24–25). For an interesting defense of Updike's technique that correlates the novelist's finding the extraordinary in the ordinary with Vermeer's conception of portraiture, see Plath 207–30.

5. *Rabbit Redux* 176; *Rabbit Is Rich* 211; *Rabbit, Run* 24–25. Harry's nostalgia, then, is not primarily for the Eisenhower era in which his own adolescent athletic career soared, as some critics claim (Detweiler [37], Waldmeir [19], Greiner [69]). Nor is it mainly for an early Cold War period in which clearly identifiable global antagonists helped to promote a stable sense of self, as D. Quentin Miller contends (38–40, 56–71). Directed more toward

the years of childhood, as both Kathleen Verduin (255) and J. A. Ward (38) recognize, the period enshrined is one of at least a decade earlier. For Updike's memories of what it was like to listen to Jack Benny on "those little late-30's radios," see "Evening" 55. For Updike's account of the effects that watching old films of Bing Crosby and listening to "a honeyed bit" of Doris Day have on him today, see *Self-Consciousness* 245.

6. For an account of the Lone Ranger's origins at the hands of George Trendle, a Detroit businessman, see Horton 570.

7. As Gaizka S. de Usabel has shown, Disney's *Three Little Pigs* also contributed not a little to assumptions about the kind of success that American films could hope to achieve in the Latin American film market (106–7). This, in turn, contributed to the pivotal role that Disney's films would play in the Pan-American efforts of the Office of the Coordinator for Inter-American Affairs (CIAA) in the early 1940s (163–64). The exportation of American films to Latin American countries is explored more fully in chapter 5.

8. See also Updike's introduction to *The Art of Mickey Mouse* (1991), in which he describes the cartoon character's initial appeal as that of "the overlookable democratic man," whose image, in the 1930s, bypassed national borders, as evidenced by those African tribesmen who had tiny mosaic Mickey Mouses inset into their front teeth and those world leaders, like King George V and Theodore Roosevelt, who insisted that all film showings they attended include Mickey Mouse on the program. As that appeal began assuming iconic status after 1940, Mickey Mouse grew in importance to the extent that, in Updike's view, "[t]he America that is not symbolized by that imperial Yankee Uncle Sam is symbolized by Mickey Mouse. He is America as it feels to itself—plucky, put-on, inventive, resilient, good-natured, game" (n.pag.).

9. Disney himself realized he no longer could buck the trend to television: the man who, in 1950, turned down one million dollars to televise his cartoon shorts out of a belief in their " 'timeless' " theatrical quality decided, four years later, to produce a *Disneyland* series of his own (Maltin 20).

10. Such divergence between the circulation of cultural and economic capital thus qualifies the dominance model of early communications theorists, such as Herbert I. Schiller and Cees J. Hamelink, who subscribe to a view of the American mass media as "the ganglia of national power and expansionism" (H. Schiller 192). For a refutation of this argument, see Tracey 17–54.

11. For additional examples, see J. Schwartz 64.

12. See also Updike's repeated remarks about his original cinematic conception for *Rabbit, Run* and his deliberate choice of present tense to approximate the temporal manner in which viewers experience film ("Art" 109–10; *Hugging* 850; "Why" 1). For a comprehensive listing of films and film personalities cited in Updike's works, see appendix I and II in De Bellis 184–87.

13. For the most complete discussions of Updike's portrayal of the televised moon shot, see Berryman 120–24; G. Held 333–41; and D. Miller 56–62.

14. In 1968 Updike noted the difference that television had made in its audience's capacity for engagement: "Where we once used to spin yarns, now we sit in front of the T.V. and receive pictures. I'm not sure the younger generation even knows how to gossip"

("Art" 115). In 1989 he reiterated his diagnosis with the greater force that twenty-one more years of media overload warranted: "Our brains are no longer conditioned for reverence and awe. We cannot imagine a Second Coming that would not be cut down to size by the televised evening news, or a Last Judgment not subject to pages of holier-than-Thou second-guessing in *The New York Review of Books*" (*Self-Consciousness* 216).

15. For examples of the diametrically opposed critical positions that debate over Updike's own degree of detachment has generated, see Doody 204–20; and Regan 77–96. Whereas Doody's notion of reification ascribes to Updike the objectivity of a camera lens (209), Regan's neo-Kantian analysis applauds the subjective eye that perceives the picture (81–84).

16. Much like the question of the degree to which the tangible signifies the transcendental in Updike's work, the issue of the degree to which Rabbit should be considered typical has generated a great deal of criticism, most of which condemns Updike's portrayal of American normativity as white male masculinity. For an especially strong presentation of this argument, see Robinson 342–60.

17. Updike anticipates this picture of Harry in his early essay "The American Man: What of *Him*?" (1957) in which the American Man is depicted as "*big*—a big man," who "does things in a big way," so much so that "[t]he popcorn alone that he devours every year would outweigh Mont Blanc" (*Assorted* 5).

18. This ambivalence in viewing Rabbit as superior to or symptomatic of his environment reflects an ambivalence that Updike suggests about his own position vis-à-vis American society. He cites, among his novelist's assets, "the taste for American life acquired in Shillington" but compares continued residence there to the entrapment felt by victims in a mining disaster (*Self-Consciousness* 109, 110). He notes complete disinterest in Ipswich's North Shore upper-class society but admits that penetrating "average, public-school, supermarket America" is achievable only in the guise of "literary spy" (53).

19. In the 1996 novel that takes its title from the "Battle-Hymn," Updike focuses on four generations of an American family to consider explicitly whether election is a matter of individual choice or of being chosen by God. See, especially, the initial presentation of this question in *In the Beauty of the Lilies* 43–54. I discuss this novel at greater length in my conclusion.

3. Cut and Print!

1. Unless otherwise noted, page numbers cited refer to the Pantheon edition of *American Hero*.

2. In portraying the Gulf War in this manner, Beinhart both reiterates and anticipates Hollywood's actual incursions into Middle Eastern affairs. In 2000 a declassified CIA paper titled "C.I.A. Goes Hollywood: A Classic Case of Deception" described a 1980 operation staged to free six Americans who had taken refuge with Canadian diplomats after Iranian militants had seized the American embassy in Tehran in November 1979. The operation involved working with Hollywood professionals to create a fake production company, "Studio Six Productions," that was publicized as scouting Iranian locations

for a fabricated film, "Argo" ("A cosmic conflagration. . . . story by Teresa Harris"), and getting the Americans out of the country by disguising them as Hollywood dandies. Prior to the "official" dissolution of the production company, it received twenty-six scripts, including one from Steven Spielberg (Sciolino 7). At the time that I write, March 2002, *Variety* has recently reported that the Pentagon is teaming up with Jerry Bruckheimer, producer of *Pearl Harbor* and *Black Hawk Down,* and Bertram van Munster, of television's *Cops,* to make a thirteen-part docudrama, to be broadcast by ABC, about the war on terrorism. According to the *Los Angeles Times,* the Pentagon also will be cooperating with a VH1 show, titled the *Military Diaries Project,* which will spotlight sixty soldiers pointing digital cameras at themselves so as to star in their own home movies (Dowd 13).

3. See, for examples, Kellner, *Persian* 62–71, 113, 255–60; Prince 243–44, 248–49; and Gerbner 252.

4. Leslie H. Gelb, qtd. in P. Taylor 46. See also Applebome 3.

5. As Lynda Boose's comparison of the two waves of Vietnam War films makes clear, gone also is the destructible body of the male hero, as the smallness of actors like Michael J. Fox, Willem Dafoe, and Tom Cruise is replaced by the " 'techno-muscularity' " of Sylvester Stallone, Chuck Norris, and Arnold Schwarzenegger (588–91). In Boose's view, such replacement conveys the message that an invincible America did not so much "lose" the war as it was prevented from winning it (591).

6. Another example of film displacing fact, the image of John Wayne winning World War II single-handedly that movies like *Sands of Iwo Jima* (1949) promoted is blatantly contradicted by the actor's notable absenteeism from the war. For a more extended discussion of the actor's efforts to avoid being drafted, see Wills 102–13.

7. The *New Republic* adhered to this particular framing to the letter during the months of Desert Shield, as evidenced by Rob Wood's retouching of the Susan May Tell photograph of Saddam Hussein that appeared on the 13 August 1990 cover of *Time* ("Iraq on the March"). In the resulting version that graced the 3 September 1990 cover of the *New Republic,* which included the heading "Furor in the Gulf," the word "Furor" was stamped in block Germanic letters across the forehead of a Hussein airbrushed to look like the Nazi chancellor.

8. Equally fabricated is the role invented by Beinhart for Baker, who, as long as it was possible to do so, favored diplomatic rather than military solutions to the Gulf crisis (Woodward 300, 316, 338, 353). This is not to suggest the novel's complete lack of conformity to those occurrences that led to the war. On the contrary, the idea of the Gulf War as an attempt at replaying World War II is fully in keeping with a president whose anti-appeasement stance derived, in large part, from his reading of Martin Gilbert's *The Second World War: A Complete History.* Likewise, the idea of a fictional Atwater gaining the inspiration for his deathbed memo from Margaret Thatcher's 1982 success in the Falklands dovetails with Bush's relinquishing his noninterventionist position on Kuwait after meeting with the British prime minister at the Aspen Institute in Colorado. Perhaps most provocative, Beinhart's thesis that the financing of the war with *"Other People's Money"* is finally "[t]he thing that really stands out and screams Hollywood" (117, 430),

in that such is the way that movies get bankrolled, is corroborated by the fact that the war in actuality was underwritten by Germany ($11 billion), Japan ($14 billion), and the oil-rich Gulf states (Smith 143–44, 149, 155–56).

9. See, for instance, Combs 262–65.

10. An adaptation of *Defenseless America,* written by munitions manufacturer Hudson Maxim, *The Battle Cry of Peace* was produced by the same man, J. Stuart Blackton, who had also filmed *Tearing Down the Spanish Flag* the day after war against Spain was declared in 1898. For a discussion of Blackton's role as a preparedness impresario, and a history of *The Battle Cry of Peace* as the preparedness film *par excellence,* see Isenberg 100–104; and L. Ward 36–39.

11. For a listing of the main loopholes by which the 1974 amendments to the federal election laws still can be circumvented, see DeParle 34.

12. One index of this point can be found in the fact that just two feature films that deal with the Gulf War have been released to date: *Courage under Fire* (1996) and *Three Kings* (1999). *Wag the Dog* (1997), the film described in its opening credits as "based on" Beinhart's *American Hero,* removes the entire scenario to the realm of the hyperreal, as the opening images of characters introduced by way of White House surveillance cameras suggest, and the filmmakers involved in the production of the war in question (against Albania) complete all their work in a Hollywood studio.

13. See Denton 33; Kellner, *Persian* 234; and Prince 236–37.

14. The Ballantine paperback edition of *American Hero* includes three additional chapters that separate the hardcover's final two. These added sections (369–86) recount the experiences of an author named Larry Beinhart who is interrupted while working in his upstate New York studio by the knock of Joe Broz on the door. Broz completes the story of what occurs in his narrative between 2 August 1990, the day that Iraq invades Kuwait, and 12 August, the day that he appears on Beinhart's doorstep. Beinhart then describes his subsequent transformation of those events into a novel.

4. Dennis Potter, *Pennies from Heaven,* and the Dream of a Common Culture

1. I am indebted to Joseph Angier for making the televised version of *Cold Lazarus* available for my viewing. I am also indebted to the staff of the Museum of Television and Radio in New York City for providing me access to those television dramas written by Potter that were not broadcast in the United States. Where published scripts for Potter's dramas exist, page numbers are included for quotations cited.

2. A third version of *Pennies from Heaven* was published in 1981 (London: Quartet) as Potter's novelization of his film screenplay.

3. Both Williams and Hoggart are cited with admiration by Potter in his first published book, *The Glittering Coffin* (1960). See 8, 40, 118.

4. The opening shot of Philip as a child appears only in the television version of *The Singing Detective,* not in the published script of the scene (78–79).

5. This elegiac note of Potter's writing is in marked contrast to the claustrophobic

quality sounded in his 1961 BBC documentary *Between Two Rivers*, in which the Forest of Dean is presented as a prison fortress and the Berry Hill community of his youth is made to emblematize "this miserable pile of dull villages [that] could not possibly be reconciled with great art, great thought, vital emotions, and classical music" (*Potter* 2).

6. When recalling *The Glittering Coffin* and *The Changing Forest* (1962) in his preface to *Waiting for the Boat* (1984), Potter discredited these first two published works as "weighed down with political and sociological cant" (22). Their somewhat hyperbolic rhetoric, however, should not obscure the validity of much of what they describe. Potter's portrait of a Forest of Dean overrun by "television aerials, now as universal and as unremarkable as chimney pots or curtains at the window" (*Changing* 20), for example, is corroborated by the statistics that Harry Hopkins provides of the growing prevalence of television in Great Britain after the Second World War: in 1949, two-thirds of the population had never even seen a television working; by the winter of 1957–58, almost one-half of the adult population spent Sunday evenings in front of the set, with 45 percent of working-class viewers spending an average of four hours every night of the week in front of it (403–4). See also the statistics quoted by Sinfield: 4.3 percent of homes had television sets in 1950, which increased to 49.4 percent by 1954 and to over 90 percent by 1964 (268).

7. This inversion of Houseman's sentimentalism characterizes every scene in Potter's work in which the betrayals of cosmopolitan adulthood are traced back to the cruelties of working-class youth. In *Vote, Vote, Vote for Nigel Barton* (1965), for instance, Nigel Barton's political manipulation of citizens to get elected is no different from his earlier manipulation of his schoolmates to escape the punishment due him for destroying a class flower. *The Singing Detective* later would recycle this childhood scene to show the young Philip Marlow getting his classmates to denounce another boy for his own having defecated on their teacher's desk after school.

8. A complete view of Potter's *New Statesman* columns can be ascertained by looking at the issues that appeared between the following dates: 14 July–1 Sept. 1967; 11 Jan.–31 May 1974; 6 Sept. 1974–27 June 1975; 10 Oct.–7 Nov. 1975; 6 Feb.–28 May 1976. For an overview of Potter's career as a television reviewer, see Purser, "Dennis's" 179–91.

9. For the period's pivotal manifesto of nonnaturalism in television, see Troy Kennedy Martin, " 'Nats Go Home' " 21–33, which was followed by Potter's "Reaction" 40.

10. Critics typically compare the estranging impact of Potter's use of music to Brecht's *Verfremdung* effect (Marinov 200–203; Bondebjerg 171–73), after which they then argue for Potter's subscription to a view of popular culture consistent with that of recent cultural theorists (e.g., Stuart Hall, Tony Bennett, Jim Collins) who conceive of popular culture as a site of contestation between producers and more actively involved consumers. Against this view, one should note the more empirical reception analysis work begun by Steve Brie that suggests that the musical devices in Potter's work induce audience pleasures that are extradiegetic in that they enable viewers to experience the songs as decontextualized pieces of nostalgic entertainment (205–13); in thus divorcing viewers from the narratives themselves, the musical sequences may operate as powerful

distancing devices, "but perhaps not always in the pedagogical way Potter appears to have imagined they would" (210). These conclusions are consistent with the argument earlier expounded by Iain Colley and Gill Davies, who also see the songs' separation from the diegetic space of the surrounding narrative as enabling them to be experienced as acts of nostalgic recuperation (68–75).

11. For a more extended discussion of the exact impact of these postwar events on the British economy, see Calvocoressi 9–22, 208.

12. For a detailed discussion of the contributions of the various people involved in the BBC production, see J. Cook 167–72. For an argument against viewing any of Potter's works in terms of auteur theory, see Coward 79–87.

13. See, for instance, Adorno's chapter on "Popular Music" 21–38, especially 27–28, 37–38.

14. Isaac Goldberg provides a list of these "how to" manuals and their authors: Charles K. Harris, *How to Write a Popular Song* (1906); F. B. Haviland, *How to Write a Popular Song* (1910); E. M. Wickes, *Writing the Popular Song* (1916); Harry J. Lincoln, *How to Write and Make a Success Publishing Music* (1919); Jack Gordon, *How to Publish Your Own Music Successfully* (1925); Abel Green, *Inside Stuff on How to Write Popular Songs* (1927); anonymous, *Hints on Popular Song Writing* (1928). See Goldberg 225.

15. Sheet music sales were the means by which the success of a song was measured prior to the advent of gramophone records. The availability of gramophone records, however, produced a sharp decline in sheet music sales, both in the United States and in Great Britain, beginning in the 1920s. By 1930, sales of sheet music in the United States were down 75 percent below normal (Goldberg 316; Ewen 321). Ronald Pearsall provides corresponding figures for revenue from sheet music sales in Britain: from a total of £566,459 in 1925, sheet music sales decreased to £453,564 in 1929 and £284,691 in 1933 (83). Arthur is thus correct in assuming "[t]he days of sheet music is numbered" in Potter's drama (96), but his decision to open up a shop that would sell gramophone records is not particularly well conceived given the impact that radio had on record sales once people started realizing that they now could hear the music they desired for free.

16. Such restriction of BBC programming under Reith was fully consistent with the regulated quality of the transmission and reception of broadcasting in Great Britain from the start, regulation that, as Asa Briggs has shown, arose, in large part, in reaction to what was perceived as the " 'chaos of the ether' " in the United States (19–20). See also 89–90.

17. Some critics see these renditions of American songs by British bands and vocalists as leading to a recontextualization of American mass culture, whereby the music is able to transcend the circumstances of its manufacture and become an authentically English product. According to Glen Creeber, for instance, who posits a cultural Fall in the 1950s and 1960s, lip-synching to these British recordings offers a mode of ideological resistance in conjuring up memories of an organic, and Edenic, working-class folk culture that existed before the invasion of the mass media into people's homes and minds (127–28, 142–46).

18. See, for instance, Reith's 1926 memorandum to Stanley Baldwin, the Conservative prime minister, concerning the General Strike: "Assuming the BBC is for the people and

that the Government is for the people, it follows that the BBC must be for the Government in this crisis too" (qtd. in Burns 16–17).

19. Examples of such purchases would include Fox's acquisition of the Red Star Publishing Company; Warner Brothers's reassembling of M. Witmark and Sons, T. B. Harms, and Jerome W. Remick and Company as the Music Publishers Holding Corporation; and Metro-Goldwyn-Mayer's takeover of the Robbins Music Corporation.

20. The Cinematograph Films Act of 1927, which was to run for ten years, required renters (distributors) to offer a set quota ($7\frac{1}{2}$ percent) and exhibitors to show a set quota (5 percent) of British film footage each year, footage that was to rise by annual $2\frac{1}{2}$ percent increments to reach a 20 percent figure by the time the act expired. In addition, all film had to be registered with the Board of Trade, thereby limiting the practice of blind booking, in which exhibitors had to accept a number of low-quality films in order to obtain the few high-quality films that they desired. American studios were able to circumvent the act, however, by having subsidiaries in Britain produce what became known as "quota quickies." The act of 1938 retained the renters' quota but reduced it from 20 percent to 15 percent and, in an attempt to eliminate "quota quickies," instituted a seventy-five-hundred-pound minimum cost for any long film submitted as fulfilling the quota. The quota was suspended in October 1942. For detailed tables indicating quota registrations during the years 1928–29 through 1940, see Low 276–81.

21. See, for instance, J. Cook 173–74; Colley and Davies 65–66; and Purser, "Dennis" 187. As John Baxendale and Chris Pawling conclude, "there is the implication that the 'reality' of any historical period is constituted both at the level of objective structures and subjective consciousness" (173).

22. *Sufficient Carbohydrate* (1983), which juxtaposes an Englishman and an American in much the same way as *The Bonegrinder,* complicates the earlier drama's portrayal of American economic superiority by introducing an element of American artistic superiority: in this drama of two multinational food processing executives vacationing with their wives on an unspoiled, which is to say, Coca-Cola deprived, Greek island, adulterated foodstuffs are synonymous with marital adultery, and gastronomic taste with aesthetic taste. Deficient in energy-producing carbohydrates, the Englishman, Jack, is, as he himself admits, as "limp as a piece of airline celery" (37). His priapic American boss, Eddie, who recommends Sidney Sheldon and Arthur Hailey to his son with the advice, "You can do worse than open a good meaty book now and then" (30), would seem to revel in literature as fecal as the food his company manufactures. Yet it is he who outmatches his English opponent in completing the lines to Keats's "Ode to a Nightingale," a blindsiding of Jack he is able to achieve because Jack continues to subscribe to a view of Americans as "unreformed colonials just one step away from the spittoon," as his wife puts it, "[a]nd England as the Greece to your Roman Empire—*civilizing* you" (20).

23. This unconcern with class hierarchy is made quite clear when the speech that the British Arthur makes to his fellow salesmen about the ability of songs to overcome the barriers of education and birth is compared to the speech made by the American Arthur, a paean to "what a fantastic world it is we live in" and to the transcendence it is possible to

achieve when "the whole place is shining." Instead of the salesmen puncturing Arthur's remarks with comments about the way songs are manufactured by the music industry, they simply respond to Arthur's vague beatitudes with equally vague statements of disbelief: "Sounds like a crate of eggs to me," "A slice of bologna, more like it."

24. For a more extended discussion of the Hopper and Evans allusions, see Kael 122.

25. For a more extended discussion of space and discourse in Berkeley musicals, see Rubin 37–40.

26. See Barrios for all information concerning which musicals of the 1930s include which particular songs. The songs noted here are cited on 348, 399, and 239 respectively.

27. Rogers's remark to the Italian clothing designer who wants to separate her from Astaire in *Top Hat* (1935) provides an example of the minimal degree to which the Depression intrudes into the Astaire-Rogers films: "Alberto, up to the present our relationship has been purely a business one, but if you start interfering in my personal affairs, I'll go back to America and live on the dole."

28. For a frame-by-frame discussion of the Astaire-Rogers dance by itself, see J. Harvey 183–92.

29. Fittingly, Potter's last piece of writing, a short story titled "Last Pearls," published in the *Daily Telegraph* (4 June 1994), addresses this very predilection for recycling in portraying a writer, dying of cancer, who attempts to write one last work that will correct the wrongs he feels he has inflicted on his own talent with his most recent piece of fiction, *Black Pearls*. At the end of the story, the writer turns out to have rewritten *Black Pearls* word for word. See Carpenter 575–78 for a reprinting of the story in its entirety. For additional information on Potter's last days, see Carpenter 545–81; and Gilbert 292–96.

30. See Jameson, *Postmodernism* 16–25; and Barth, "Literature of Exhaustion" 29–34 and "Literature of Replenishment" 65–71.

5. Flotsam and Peronism in the Novels of Manuel Puig

1. According to Puig, the word "parody" carried a degree of scorn that did not reflect accurately the characterizations he intended as recorded imitations of people whose mimicking of cinematic or musical models already was parodic. See his remarks in Puig and Levine 35; "Interview" (1977) 58; "Interview" (1979) 27; and "Brief" 168. See also Puig's comments about film exciting him with the desire "to copy, not to create" ("Growing Up" 50). This is not to suggest, however, that Puig's scorn for the word "parody" implies an absence of the parodic impulse in his work. As Lucille Kerr has persuasively argued, "The parodic inversions created by Puig's writing could be said to reevaluate historically devalued (i.e., potentially repressed) forms by generating inversions of those already inverted models" (*Suspended* 14). For additional examples of the cultural subversion inherent in these carnivalesque reversals and the various terms with which critics have designated it, see Ross Chambers's discussion of "appropriative opposition" in *Kiss of the Spider Woman* (201–21); Gustavo Pellón's consideration of "contradictory strategy"

in *Kiss of the Spider Woman* and *Pubis Angelical* (186–99); and David Román and Alberto Sandoval's depiction of a "citational politics of resistance" in both the novel and musical version of *Kiss of the Spider Woman* (553–79).

2. I am altering slightly Elena Brunet's translation of this term as "Factory of Dreams" in the English version of the novel, since "Dream Factory" is the actual term that was used to describe Hollywood.

3. The description is from Martínez, "Eva Perón" 43. See also Emir Rodríguez Monegal's review of *The Buenos Aires Affair,* "Sueños" 34–36, for a discussion of the kind of "sueños enlatados" (canned dreams) that join together Evita and the characters in Puig's first three novels. I am grateful to Suzanne Jill Levine's biography for bringing this review to my attention (236, 410), as I am grateful for her generosity in assisting me in the preparation of this chapter.

4. The irony of such legislation of film content, as Tim Barnard points out (43–49), is that the Argentine films produced during Perón's first presidency became more Europeanized than ever, reflecting the sensibilities of a second-generation middle class more interested in adaptations of European literature and what would become known as "white telephone" salon dramas.

5. For a comprehensive history of the invasion of Argentina by the United States film industry, with a particular emphasis on the role of United Artists, see de Usabel 43–48, 68–71, 174–82, 229–40.

6. Additional confirmation of this replacement would be provided by the $125 million "credit" Perón was forced to seek from the United States in 1949 (Williamson 469). For a brief discussion of Argentina's triangular trading relationship with Great Britain and the United States during this period, in which manufactured products needed from the United States for industrial expansion were not offset by agricultural goods exported to the United States, and agricultural goods exported to Great Britain were not balanced by machinery purchased by Argentina, see Page, *Perón* 171–73.

7. Gaizka S. de Usabel provides especially revealing statistics of this decline in a table that compares the number of films produced by Argentina and Mexico between 1940 and 1948. In 1940, Argentina produced forty-nine films to Mexico's twenty-seven; in 1945, Argentina produced twenty-two to Mexico's seventy-nine (181).

8. In fact, no character even remotely like this duke appears in the actual film, in which politics disappears after the Revolution of 1848 has provided a pretext for Strauss to be stranded in the Vienna Woods with a manipulative diva. The film also fails to mention the fact that the Revolution of 1848 was brutally suppressed in Austria, that it was followed by a restoration of Metternich's old order, and that the emperor who came to power as a result of it was Franz Josef, whose difficult reign would end with his declaration of the war that spawned World War I.

9. Critical discussion of movies in *Kiss of the Spider Woman* is by now quite extensive. For representative examples, see Masiello 15–23; Merrim, "Through" 300–310; Weber 163–81; Moses 247–56; and Pinet 19–32. For examples of discussions that compare the various adaptations of the novel that have subsequently appeared—play (1981), movie

(1985), musical (1992)—see Boccia 417–25; M. Dunne 14–23; Cheever 13–24; Santoro 120–38; and, especially, Román and Sandoval 553–79, who view the musical as an AIDS allegory.

10. As is the case with the movies included in *Kiss of the Spider Woman,* the incorporated footnotes that trace the origins of homosexuality have generated much critical discussion. In his *Christopher Street* interview with Ronald Christ (1979), Puig described his motivation as having been primarily informative—the dissemination of information on homosexuality to which people previously had not had access, especially people in Latin America and Spain—and presented his own voice as transparently transmissive: "I simply repeat in a condensed form the judgments of specialists" (28). Such a renunciatory pose dovetails with the abnegation of authorial omniscience to which Puig also alluded in that same interview, based on the assumption that any such privileging would reproduce the very kind of repression his novels condemn (27, 30–31). In that "[a]ll quotations are *transportations,*" however, as Lisa Block de Behar correctly notes (612), every transmission entails a transmutation. And, as Lucille Kerr has shrewdly argued, "The subject who lurks behind or outside the theories of other authoritative subjects unveils another authorial impulse at the end," in the case of *Kiss of the Spider Woman,* an authorial impulse presented in the guise of an invented female doctor, Anneli Taube, to whom Puig attributes his own point of view (*Suspended* 225). For additional discussion of this important point as it relates to Puig's entire *oeuvre,* see Kerr, *Suspended* 236–53; "Dis-Appearance" 89–110; and "Reading" 617–23.

11. The statistics from Gerd Albrecht's *Nationalsozialistische Politik* compendium that are quoted by Eric Rentschler are particularly revealing of this focus on formulaic plot and escapist diversion in Nazi cinema: of the 1,904 feature films made, 523 were comedies and musicals (*heitere* or "cheerful" films), 295 were melodramas and biopics, and 123 were detective films and adventure epics (7). For additional discussion of the inspiration that classical Hollywood cinema provided filmmakers during the Third Reich, see Rentschler 99–145. For discussion of the management of audience desire rather than ideas that these films were intended to facilitate, see Schulte-Sasse 1–43. For a history of the collaborative/competitive relationship between the American and the German film industries during the Weimar period, see Saunders 51–83.

12. For further discussion of this point, see La Place 34–43; and Dyer 54–59. See also Rodríguez Monegal, "Sueños" 35, for discussion of Puig's identification of women in films by the stars' professional names, instead of the names of the characters played, and reduction of everyone else to a subordinate role (e.g., "handsome young man," "faithful companion," "husband").

13. See, for instance, Chambers 203–4; Rice-Sayre 248, 256; Pinet 24, 28–29; Santoro 128, 138; and Tuss 330–31.

14. For a particularly trenchant portrait of the rooms devoted to storing these items of feminine adornment, see Freund 190–94. See also Copi's play *Eva Perón,* which imagines Evita planning for the display of her own corpse, surrounded by her designer dresses in display cases, and wondering where the American television cameras are (45).

15. For an extremely helpful summation of the shifts that the concept of Peronism underwent, from an ideology of *justicialismo,* or social justice, formulated by Perón to counter any attraction communism might have for the working class, to the mobilization of the Peronist masses by a Left that came to recognize the inapplicability of Cuba's rural *foco* as a blueprint for revolution in Argentina, see Colás 100–117.

16. The version of Evita's autobiography drafted by Penella de Silva was later rewritten by Raúl Mendé, one of Perón's speechwriters, at the president's request. In attributing to Evita the belief that "the world today suffer[s] from a great absence: that of woman" (*My Mission* 195), the manuscript finally published combines elements of its original author and echoes of the public Perón, who acclaimed the participation of women in Argentina's June Revolution based on the assumption that "if man is a rationalist, woman possesses what is above masculine rationalism: an intuition which is always superior to the success we men may be able to attain" (J. Perón 40).

17. The titles cited appear in Rodríguez Monegal, "Sueños" 34. The others included bear quoting as exemplifying so well the kind of discourse they perpetuated: *Snow on My Dreams* (Alexandra Fedorovna, the Last Czarina), *An Angel Comes on Stage* (Sarah Bernhardt), *The Maid from Martinique* (Josephine of France), *A Tear in the Wind* (Catherine of Russia), *Queen of Kings* (Lola Montes), *The Dancer of Paradise* (Isadora Duncan), *The Blood of Queens Smells of Carnations* (Eugenia of Montijo), *Fire in the Dead City* (Eleonora Duse), *The Eagle's Dove* (Lady Hamilton), and *The Chess Game of Glory* (Anna of Austria). For these, and all other translations from the Spanish cited in this chapter, I am most grateful to Joaquín Martínez Pizarro.

18. As biographers agree, the extent to which Evita's experiences as an actress, in particular a soap opera actress, informed her later role in a regime defined by spectacle and stages cannot be overestimated (see, in this regard, Fraser and Navarro 25–26, 112–13). For discussion of her career as an actress (which included twenty plays, five movies, and over twenty-six soap operas), see Barnes 17–24; Ortiz 29–47; and, especially, Fraser and Navarro 20–33, 41–48. For a useful chronology of that career, which also documents the magazine covers on which Evita appeared *(Antena, Cine Argentino, Radiolandia, Sintonía),* see Page, "Chronology" 115–16. Information about Evita's emulation of Hollywood actresses, and particular interest in Norma Shearer, whose early years in Montreal poverty seemed to correspond so closely to her own background, can be found in Ortiz 21–23; Fraser and Navarro 9–10; and Martínez, *Santa* 70–72, 75 (the last based on interviews with the hairdresser, Julio Alcaraz, who claimed to have " 'made her' ").

19. The list of feminist film theorists whose work is informed by such claims is by now a lengthy one. For representative examples, see Mulvey 14–26; Bergstrom 47–59; Kuhn 57–65; and Doane 1–37. For an example of the psychoanalytic approach that informs most of these critical works, see Metz 3–80. For examples of the ongoing discussion of female spectatorship, see the special issue of *Camera Obscura* (1989: 20–21) devoted to "The Spectatrix."

20. The Lamarr autobiography achieves a similar effect. Having opened with the actress's declaration that "in my life, as in the lives of most women, sex has been an impor-

tant factor" (*Ecstasy* 11), the memoir goes on to defuse that potential threat in a variety of ways. The "MGM family" of Hollywood, headed by "Old Man" Mayer and "Father De Mille," returns her to the fold of patriarchal authority (142–43, 174). Psychiatry reminds her of women's delight in "keep[ing] the house in order and themselves in order" (224). Thus, the woman who has admitted to lesbian encounters and confessed to Harry Cohn to having slept with one hundred men (214) comes to lament the fact that the word "cozy" has lost its meaning, acclaim the pleasures of "picnics, babies, sitting on the floor, and playing Santa Claus," and curse the face that has "attracted all the wrong people into my boudoir and brought me tragedy and heartache for five decades" (231, 273). No mention, it should be added, is made of her co-invention with George Antheil of a "Secret Communications System" (U.S. Patent Number 2,292,387, granted 11 August 1942), originally designed to protect radio-guided torpedoes from Nazi interception, which later became the basis of spread spectrum technology.

21. For more extended considerations of Puig's appropriation of Lacanian psychoanalytic theory in *Pubis Angelical,* see Davies 400–410; Zimmerman 65–77; and Merrim, "For a New" 148–57. For an excellent discussion of the correlation between the kind of Freudian psychoanalytic theory that seeks to explain everything in terms of sexual difference and a state premised on surveillance and control, see Labanyi's analysis of *The Buenos Aires Affair* 105–15.

22. I am grateful to Pamela Bacarisse, *Necessary* 140, for bringing this source to my attention.

23. The original screenplay assigned LUH 3417 a worse ending, as in it she is raped and then beaten to death on television (Baxter 100).

24. V. S. Naipaul makes much the same point when describing torture as an old and accepted Argentine institution, in which the difference between "good torture" and "bad torture" (162) simply depends on whether the victim is portrayed as a destroyer or a savior of the nation (111–12, 157–67).

25. For additional discussion of more recent science fiction that delineates feminist utopias, see Lefanu, especially 52–70; Le Guin, "Is Gender Necessary?" 130–39, and the revised "Is Gender Necessary? Redux" 7–16; and the essays included in Barr, *Future,* especially Sanders 42–58; Pearson 63–70; and Russ, "Some Recent" 71–84.

26. For contrasting views of what the sexless angel at the novel's end signifies, see Davies 409–10, who interprets the figure as neutralizing those sexual binaries that underlie a national psychology defined by male mastery and order; and Hughes 151–54, who draws upon the work of Luce Irigaray in order to view it as testifying to a kind of female solidarity that stretches beyond woman's already dual (if not plural) physical morphology.

27. According to biographers, the symptoms of Evita's illness, even before it was actually diagnosed, prevented her from having conjugal relations from 1949 until her death in 1952. See J. Taylor 57, 77; Page, *Perón* 237; and Martínez, *Santa* 122.

28. Qtd. in S. Levine 245; "Interview" (1979) 28, 30.

6. Murakami Haruki's Garbage-Collecting/Snow-Shoveling Consortium

1. In conformance with established practice among Japanologists, Japanese names are indicated by surnames followed by given names. Exceptions are names of Japanese-Americans and names quoted from English translations of novels in which the order is reversed in conformance with the habits of English readers.

2. See Buruma, "Becoming" 60; and Strecher, "Beyond" 375.

3. Boku refers not to the character's name, but to Murakami's use of first-person singular familiar to denote his narrator. In making the differences between Murakami's use of the familiar "Boku" and the formal "Watashi" clear to me, I am grateful to Matthew C. Strecher ("Beyond 'Pure' Literature" 361), as I am grateful for his generosity in sharing his own work on Murakami with me and in supplying me with recommendations for additional critical resources.

4. Barthes's 1970 treatment of Japan as a land of empty signs is typical of much recent criticism that depicts Japan's postmodernity as irrespective of any particular chronological period. For a listing of other critics who adopt a similar approach, see Tobin 6–7. John Whittier Treat adopts a somewhat different approach in tracing the evolution of the *shōjo* (young girl) from domestic laborer prior to the Meiji period to symbol of postmodern consumption in Japan's period of late-model capitalism (362–63).

5. For a discussion of the origin of this metaphor and a history of its application, see Dower 146–97.

6. Critics have made this point about cultural recoding with respect to a variety of disciplines and artifacts. See Mary Yoko Brannen's discussion of Tokyo Disneyland (617–30), Miriam Silverberg's discussion of 1920s Japanese mass culture (61–89), and Isozaki Arata's discussion of Tsukuba Science City architecture (47–62) for representative examples.

7. Murakami and McInerny 28. *Junbungaku,* commonly translated as "pure," as opposed to *taishūbungaku* or "pop," literature, is distinguished by its sense of social responsibility. Ōe Kenzaburō, whose work is often given as an example of *junbungaku,* chronicles the origin of the genre as well as its demise, the latter of which he locates in 1970 (359–69). For a discussion of the *shōsetsu,* see Miyoshi 17–36. For a complete transcription of Murakami's remarks about his place vis-à-vis Japanese literature, as well as a discussion of his American literary influences, see his 22 Oct. 1994 interview with Strecher that forms the appendix to Strecher's doctoral dissertation ("Hidden").

8. Both statements about Japan's demographics have been subject to debate, in part because the information upon which they are based derives from official statistics—the designation of Japan as a 90 percent middle-class society, for instance, derives from annual public opinion surveys conducted by the Prime Minister's Office since 1967. Yet even those scholars who interrogate the erasure of ethnic and social differences by considering the position of the Chinese and Koreans in Japan or the constitution of what has been termed Japan's New Middle Class often end by acknowledging what William W. Kelly has called "typifications of areas of life that have gained enormous ordering power in the last three decades" ("Rationalization" 605). See also Kelly, "Finding" 189–216; Katō 312–16; and Upham 325–27.

9. The terms quoted derive from the following sources: Hassan 81; Tobin 4 and Miyoshi 9; Kelly, "Rationalization" 613 and Ivy, *Discourses* 3; and Alexandre Kojève, qtd. in Miyoshi and Harootunian xiii.

10. See Strom A1, A8.

11. Because of Columbia's outstanding debt of $1.6 billion, the actual cost of acquisition was closer to $5 billion (Fabrikant D8).

12. Typifying that history was the experience of C. Itoh and Co. Ltd., Suntory Ltd., and the Tokyo Broadcasting System paying MGM/UA fifteen million dollars for a stake in three films that subsequently flopped (Hammer 48).

13. The year 1989 also marked the peak of Japanese investment in American real estate, mid- to late-1980s purchases that generated controversy similar to that of the Columbia Pictures acquisition because of the symbolic value that was attached to the purchases of "trophy" buildings like the Exxon building and Rockefeller Center in New York, the Arco Tower and Pebble Beach golf course in California, and the *U.S. News and World Report* complex in Washington, D.C. Since Japanese investment in U.S. property at its height constituted no more than 1 or 2 percent of Japanese holdings of U.S. assets (Edgington 155), such controversy was another example of symbolic values being given priority over actual, or monetary, values. See Edgington 153–73 for an extended analysis of this point. See, especially, 169–73 for discussion of the factors that forced Japanese companies to sell many of those properties acquired in the 1980s at a loss in the early 1990s. For further discussion of the difference between economic growth and economic success, see Hein 99–102.

14. For financial information on *Hudson Hawk,* see Perry 160. For reproduced internal Columbia financial statements on both production costs and profit-and-loss for *Last Action Hero,* see J. Stewart 44, 45.

15. See Weinraub, "Turmoil" D12; and Weinraub, "Sony" D1.

16. Complete publication information for these quoted headlines is as follows: Seiichi Kanise and Elaine Lafferty, *Time* 9 Oct. 1989: 70; Brent Schlender, *Fortune* 12 June 1995: 70; Ronald Grover, *Business Week* 9 Oct. 1989: 44; Mark Landler and Ronald Grover, *Business Week* 5 Dec. 1994: 44; *Newsweek* 9 Oct. 1989: cover; James B. Stewart, *New Yorker* 28 Feb. 1994: 43.

17. This was not the first time that the release of a bootlegged translation evoked American fears of Japanese ascendancy. Anticipating the plot of *Patria,* William Randolph Hearst's *New York American* featured in 1915 a translation of a book titled *The War between Japan and America,* alleged to have been sponsored by high Japanese officials and to have sold over a million copies, which told of Japan's plans to invade the United States in alliance with Mexico and to destroy the Panama Canal. The actual book was written by a Japanese newspaperman, had no official support, sold only a few thousand copies, and made no mention at all of the Panama Canal. See Swanberg 296.

18. I quote here from the authorized translation published in 1991 under Ishihara's name alone.

19. I allude here, of course, to Fredric Jameson's discussion of the Bonaventure Hotel as a paradigmatic example of postmodern hyperspace in which the individual no

longer can cognitively locate its position in a mappable external world (*Postmodernism* 39–44).

20. Contemporary scholars are not the only ones to comment upon the similarities between Western and Japanese aggression. Writing in 1933, K. K. Kawakami described Pan-Asianism in the following manner: "a nonwhite race has undertaken to carry the white man's burden" (qtd. in A. Cook 1: 63). Major General Frank R. McCoy, an American who was part of the 1932 League of Nations commission sent to investigate Japan's actions in Manchuria, was more blunt: "I took the same measures of self-defense in Cuba" (qtd. in A. Cook 1: 50).

21. I quote here from Ivy's English translation of Kurihara's *Kanri shakai to minshū risei: Nichijō ishiki no seiji shakaigaku* (1982) ("Formations" 252).

22. See, for instance, Ivy, "Critical" 38.

23. As Painter goes on to argue (320–21), these characteristics of television viewing, which also might seem applicable to television viewing in the United States, for instance, are in fact unique to Japan. Reflecting the American cultural bias in favor of individualism, American talk shows delineate conflicts as social in origin while presenting solutions as personal in nature and arrived at by individual introspection. Reflecting the Japanese cultural bias in favor of harmony, Japanese *waidoshō* portray problems as arising when individuals do not fulfill their social roles and obligations.

24. These figures would seem to confirm the "peanuts theory of TV" proposed by Ohya Souchi in response to the introduction of television into Japan, in which he compared a person's indiscriminate viewing of television to a person's unconscious eating from a bowl of peanuts (Katō 311).

25. For an extended discussion of the "curtain" that Murakami portrays "creaking down on the shambles of the sixties" (*Wild* 5), see Strecher, "Hidden" 15–53.

26. *Dance, Dance, Dance* provides a similar example of films bleeding into each other as Boku imagines a historical spectacle about ancient Egypt that begins with *The Bathing Beauty* and *The King and I* but keeps lapsing into Twentieth Century–Fox's *Cleopatra,* this time starring Jodie Foster and Michael Jackson instead of Elizabeth Taylor and Richard Burton, as Boku's "dream scenario" takes on "a life of its own" (72).

27. Such historical precision dovetails with Murakami's more recent forays into nonfiction: *Shinzō wo tsuranukarete* (1996), a translation of *Shot in the Heart* (1994), Mikal Gilmore's narrative of his brother Gary; *Underground* (*Andaguraundo,* 1997), a compilation of interviews with people who survived the 20 March 1995 Aum Shinrikyō poison gas attack in the Tokyo subway system; and *Post-Underground* (*Yakusoku sareta basho de,* 1998), a compilation of interviews with former and current Aum members, originally published in monthly installments in *Bungei Shunju* from April to October 1997.

28. Significantly, this pre–World War II period also saw Japanese government officials placing restrictions on the importation of foreign movies—a 1937 licensing system for all imports, a 1938 dollar ceiling on American imports in particular—which, after the bombing of Pearl Harbor in 1941, culminated in the banning of all exhibition of "enemy films" and the confiscation of any such films already in Japan as "enemy property" (Kasza 233–34, 247).

29. Hirohito became emperor on 25 December 1926, the day his father, the Taishō emperor, died. The official enthronement ceremony, or *Gotaiten*, did not take place until two years later (Irokawa 74). For statistics detailing the increase in receivers' contracts in response to the imperial spectacles cited, see Ito 21, 13. See also Stronach 131 for discussion of the 1939–40 experimental television broadcasts undertaken in preparation for Japan's scheduled hosting of the 1940 Olympics (prior to the event's cancellation due to the international political situation).

30. Ian Buruma comes to a similar conclusion in his depiction of Japanese popular culture's violent excesses as projected fantasies that enable the preservation of order to be maintained in Japanese society. See Buruma, *Behind* 219–25.

31. See Buruma, "Becoming" 71.

32. Harootunian's discussion, in fact, closes by portraying the "new age of culture" underlying the Ōhira government's announced program for the 1980s as another form of cultural exceptionalism in which, this time, it is the model of the Japanese business firm that is naturalized (84–86). Critics as different from Harootunian as Chalmers Johnson (86–87) and Karel van Wolferen (245–72) reach similar conclusions in assessing the appeals to cultural exceptionalism that accompanied Japan's period of high-speed growth as ideological constructions.

33. Murakami and McInerny 29. Critics who have discussed Murakami in terms of subjectivity and individual identity portray the nature of those qualities emerging through a variety of means: a Sartrean dialectic between self and other (Iwamoto 297–99), a Zen Buddhist bifurcation of subject-object ego consciousness (Loughman 90–93), a recovery of human sexuality (Strecher, "Hidden" 222–29, 246–61). Stephen Snyder thus makes an important point with respect to this issue when he claims that in *Hard-Boiled Wonderland and the End of the World*, "Murakami is both deconstructing and reinventing the I-novel by dramatizing the fragility and friability of its central preoccupation, the modern 'subject,' while at the same time he labors, through his elaborate and formally structured scheme, to maintain the integrity of that subject, if only by elaboration itself" (76).

34. For examples of *The Wind-Up Bird Chronicle*'s depiction of identity in terms of "'[h]ouse physiognomy'" (290), see 44, 263, 372, 397, 413. For examples of its depiction of identity in terms of boxes and containers, see 44, 172, 306, 425.

35. This image of an underground obviously is at the heart of Murakami's analysis of the 1995 Tokyo subway poison gas attack in *Underground*. In the "Blind Nightmare: Where Are We Japanese Going?" essay (224–41) that follows his interviews with the survivors, Murakami discusses Aum Shinrikyō as a mirror of the Japanese collective unconscious (229) and notes that the two events that constituted "the gravest tragedies in Japan's postwar history," the gas attack and 1995 Kobe earthquake, were both "nightmarish eruptions beneath our feet—from underground—that threw all the latent contradictions and weak points of our society into frighteningly high relief" (237).

7. A Mother (and a son, and a brother, and a wife, et al.) in History

1. DeLillo alternately gives the amount of time for this rupture as 5.6 seconds ("American" 21) and 7 seconds (*Libra* 181). My sentence joins the time cited in DeLillo's essay with the characterization included in the novel.

2. Critical approaches to DeLillo's portrayal of history have employed a variety of theoretical paradigms in their presentations: John Johnston invokes Gilles Deleuze's concepts of "intensive system" and "internal resonance" ("Superlinear" 336–38); Joseph Kronick investigates the "grammaticality" of historical events with respect to Paul de Man's theories of reading (120, 127–29); and Christopher M. Mott joins Hayden White's notions of narratological duplicity to Michel Foucault's notions of epistemological skepticism (132–33, 135–36, 144–45).

3. That recovering the past is a matter of examining the texts in which traces of that past reside is by now a critical commonplace. Just how much inscription involves critical interrogation, however, remains a matter of some debate. Locating in postmodern intertextuality "the history of aesthetic styles displac[ing] 'real' history," Fredric Jameson laments "a new and original historical situation in which we are condemned to seek History by way of our own pop images and simulacra of that history, which itself remains forever out of reach" (*Postmodernism* 20, 25). As Linda Hutcheon points out, though, saying that the past is known to us through textual traces does not imply, as some forms of poststructuralism contend, that the past itself is only textual: "This ontological reduction is not the point of postmodernism: past events existed empirically, but in epistemological terms we can only know them today through texts. Past events are given *meaning*, not *existence*, by their representation in history" (*Politics* 81–82).

4. For information about what happened to the three other versions Booth wrote of this letter, see Samples 165–66.

5. As William Hanchett documents, Baker also provided testimony about Booth's diary to the U.S. House of Representatives Judiciary Committee during the impeachment hearings for Andrew Johnson. For a discussion of how this testimony, which referred to pages that allegedly had been cut out of the diary between the time it was recovered from Booth and the time it was surrendered to the Judiciary Committee, fueled Lincoln assassination conspiracy theories, see Hanchett 42–50.

6. In her memoir, *The Unlocked Book*, Booth's sister Asia depicts that role as one to which Booth was driven by "the impetus of a desperate fate" (138). That "fate" she traces back to two events of his childhood: a "vision" that his mother had of his end when he was six months old (41–43) and a fortune told to him when a schoolboy, in which a Gypsy predicted for him " 'a fast life—short, but a grand one' " (57).

7. See, for instance, O'Donnell 6–11; and Thomas 111–19. To the extent that Oswald has any analogue among the Lincoln conspirators, it would be David E. Herold, an unemployed druggist's clerk deemed so "light," "trifling," and "boyish" by every witness called to testify in his defense (*Assassination* 96–97; in mind "about eleven years of age" according to one such witness [97]), that the attorney who argued against his death sentence used the very fact of Herold's inconsequentiality as the basis of his appeal (274). Interestingly, Gore Vidal attributes to the figure of Herold in *Lincoln* the same motivation

that DeLillo attributes to the figure of Oswald in *Libra,* as the ending to the penultimate chapter of Vidal's work makes clear: "Word was beginning to spread through the area, not to mention the world, that John Wilkes Booth had murdered the President. There was no news, David was sorry to hear, of Mr. Seward. Anyway, all that mattered was that Wilkes thought that he, David Herold, had done as he was told, and that they were now, the two of them, friends and true brothers, immortal" (651).

8. DeLillo's remarks in interviews contribute to the temptation to read his novels as examples of modernist aesthetic detachment, as illustrated by his description of writing as "trying to make interesting, clear, beautiful language" and his depiction of *Ratner's Star* in particular as "naked structure" ("Interview" 82, 86). Complicating the issue are other remarks of DeLillo that repudiate a pose of complete aesthetic disengagement: "I've always had a grounding in the real world, whatever esoteric flights I might indulge in from time to time" ("Outsider" 62). For a representative sampling of the variety of critical positions taken with respect to this issue of aesthetic detachment, see Kucich 334–41; Johnston, "Generic" 262–63; and Molesworth 147–51.

9. For a more detailed discussion of the way in which aesthetic formalism in *The Names* is depicted as leading to abuses of power with respect to sexism and colonialism in particular, see Morris 122–23. See also Bryant's consideration of the cultists as motivated by a desire that is fundamentally reactionary in that it is fueled by "nostalgia for a language system that never was and never will be, a language of stasis and order" (19).

10. Tom LeClair's consideration of Pythagorian mathematics in *Ratner's Star,* in fact, makes the point that Pythagoras specifically associated pure numbers with concrete objects or qualities (126), which links the history of the alphabet recounted in *The Names* and the history of mathematics delineated in the earlier novel.

11. For a discussion of the way in which coincidence is the means by which chance and necessity are reconciled in *Libra,* see Kronick 120, 116–17, 125–26. For a discussion of the contingent as anchoring the conspiratorial, and the way that astrology resolves the antimony between the two, see Willman, "Traversing" 405–31; and Willman, "Art" 630–37.

12. Almost every critic of *Libra* has recognized this element of Oswald's performing in considering DeLillo's fictional protagonist. See, for instance, Cain 279; and Civello 48–52. To the extent that the novel's Oswald initially seeks his place in history through the medium of print, however, he complicates these earlier critical readings of his intentions.

13. Parenthetical citations to volumes designated by Roman numerals refer to the twenty-six volumes of testimony and exhibits that comprise the *Hearings before the President's Commission on the Assassination of President Kennedy.* All grammatical infelicities and misspellings of words that appear in the quoted writings of the actual Lee Harvey Oswald duplicate those in the original documents.

14. For earlier critical commentary on this point, see, for instance, Goodheart 129; and Lentricchia 205.

15. These questions concerning Oswald's "normalcy" are in decided contrast to those questions about possible "abnormal" behavior patterns that the Warren Commission

counselors posed to witnesses who testified about their knowledge of Jack Ruby, especially their knowledge of Jack Ruby's sex life. Not only was Ruby's roommate George Senator questioned about his observation of traits that might suggest "the possibility of homosexuality" and asked if he himself was sleeping with Ruby (XIV: 203, 246), he even was examined on Ruby's attitude toward his dogs ("Was it a normal attitude that people have to dogs?"), particularly Ruby's attitude toward the one dog with which he allegedly had "a strange sort of relationship" (XIV: 195).

16. Norman Mailer comes to a similar conclusion about the *Report* in *Oswald's Tale: An American Mystery* (1995). Acknowledging that as an inquiry into the events surrounding the Kennedy assassination the Warren Commission's work "resembles a dead whale decomposing on a beach," he goes on to describe the twenty-six volumes of testimony and exhibits as "a Comstock Lode of novelistic material, not of much use in solving a mystery—so little is followed through to the end!—but certainly to be honored for its short stories, historical vignettes, and vast cast of characters [. . .]" (351).

17. For additional confirmation of this point, see the bibliographic entries of Good 205–12; and Samples 191–95.

18. One notable exception to this cavalcade of greed was Abraham Zapruder, who sold the original roll of film he shot on 22 November to *Time* and *Life* magazines, and then donated the twenty-five thousand dollars he received to the Firemen's and Policemen's Benevolence Fund "with a suggestion for Mrs. Tippit" (VII: 575–76).

19. DeLillo's two-act play *Valparaiso* (1999) provides a remedy for this pre-Oprah omission in its portrayal of the cultural role of the television talk show.

20. See Mailer, "Superman" 38.

21. *White Noise*'s portrait of Babette Gladney reduced to black and white, looking "flat, distanced, sealed off, [and] timeless" as her face is projected to her family through the magic of television (104), anticipates this later depiction of Oswald as postmodern prisoner.

22. For a discussion of the televised killing of Oswald as forging a national collectivity around the collapse of public and private spaces, see Green 585–93.

23. DeLillo's portrait of Oswald also presages his portrait of the fictional Texas Highway Killer in *Underworld*. For discussion of the Highway Killer's frustrated attempts to control his own image, see Walker 460–61; and Parrish 709–13.

24. According to Vidal, who ascribes the shooting of George Wallace to a Republican plot to defuse a political threat to Richard Nixon's reelection, it should have been E. Howard Hunt who had the pages in question copyrighted since, in Vidal's view, the diary exhibits all the characteristics of the popular paperback fiction at which Hunt excelled (*United* 879–83).

25. As in the case of passages quoted from texts written by Lee Harvey Oswald, all grammatical infelicities and misspellings of words in passages quoted from Arthur H. Bremer's diary appear in the original document.

8. "Two People Who Didn't Argue, Even, Except over the Use of the Subjunctive"

1. For additional examples of the variety of ways in which Trilling denotes style as moral form, see "The Oppenheimer Case: A Reading of the Testimony" (1954) (*Claremont* 112–13) and "The Liberated Heroine" (1978) 508.

2. Such cultivation of human morality, according to Durkheim in *Leçons de sociologie*, marked a decided shift in the state's main function over time. Earlier that function was simply "[t]o keep on expanding its power and to add lustre to its fame" (*Émile* 194), which meant that the private concerns of the individual were subordinated to collective aspirations and common beliefs. But as history advanced and "the circle of individual activity expands and becomes the primary object of moral respect," it was the individual who came to "serve as the axis of public as well as private conduct" and it became "the role of the state to help him to realise his nature" (195). For further discussion of this point, see Guibernau 28–31; and Giddens, *Giddens* 59–72.

3. For discussion of the separation between, and later democratization of, Jews of German and eastern European descent, see Glazer and Moynihan 138–41; and Birmingham 403–4.

4. See also Greenberg 103–4.

5. For a discussion of women, work, and domesticity after 1945, which includes statistics on what occupations working women entered, see Gatlin 24–48. For information on women who entered the teaching profession in particular, see Gatlin 27–28, 32, 34–35.

6. Depending upon what sources list Harris's salary at Allied Maintenance as having been, the pay cut that moving to Madeira entailed fluctuates between seven thousand and fifteen thousand dollars. For Shana Alexander, who gives Harris's Allied Maintenance salary as forty thousand dollars a year and the starting salary at Madeira as twenty-five thousand dollars a year, the cut is fifteen thousand dollars (118–19). For Anthony Haden-Guest, who cites the Allied Maintenance salary as thirty-two thousand dollars a year, the salary cut is reduced to seven thousand dollars (39, 40).

7. This letter, which became known as the "Scarsdale letter," was sent to Tarnower at his Scarsdale clinic by certified mail, returned to Harris as undelivered mail by the local postal authorities, and eventually introduced as evidence at the trial by the prosecution. More than any other piece of evidence, it refuted the defense strategy that had been predicated upon Jean Harris's being too much a "lady" to commit murder. The letter is reprinted in full in Trilling, *Mrs.* 256–61, and in Alexander 193–99. All subsequent page citations to the letter refer to its reprinting in Trilling's book.

8. A complete listing of the intellectuals cited in Harris's memoir would also include Learned Hand, Thomas Jefferson, Gustave Flaubert, Sigmund Freud, George Santayana, H. L. Mencken, Alfred North Whitehead, Jerome Bruner, Fyodor Dostoyevsky, W. H. Auden, Boris Pasternak, Saul Bellow, Franz Kafka, Adam Smith, Ayn Rand, Herman Melville, Lewis Thomas, James Boswell, Henrik Ibsen, Edward Banfield, David Reisman, Daniel Bell, Wassily Leontief, Michael Harrington, Loren Eiseley, Henry Smith, Albert Schweitzer, Alan Dershowitz, John Connery, and Gabriel García Márquez.

9. The one notable exception to such limited coverage at the time of the shooting was

the *Washington Post*, which followed its initial front-page report of Tarnower's death, complete with photographs of Harris on the way to her arraignment and Tarnower in a white lab coat (Lescaze and Harden 12 Mar. 1980: A1), with continued coverage in subsequent days: a second front-page story, "Romance Cited in Diet Author's Death," and follow-up headline, "Slain Diet Author Allegedly Jilted Madeira Headmistress," which emphasized the love triangle central to the event (Harden and Lescaze 13 Mar. 1980: A1, A15); an article in the Metro section on "Madeira Coping in Crisis" and "Madeira Officials, Faculty Coping in 'Disaster' " (Feinberg 14 Mar. 1980: B1, B5); a third front-page story titled "Headmistress Planned to Die, Officer Testifies" (Lescaze 15 Mar. 1980: A1); and more Metro section accounts of "Madeira Headmistress' Secret Life" and "Headmistress Kept Troubles Secret from Friends Here" (Harden and Mansfield 16 Mar. 1980: B1, B3). Such extended coverage, no doubt, reflected the fact that the Madeira School, as the *Post* noted in its initial article, "trains the daughters of some of Washington's most affluent and powerful residents" (Lescaze and Harden 12 Mar. 1980: A1).

10. For the article on Harris that appeared in that issue of *People*, see "Accident or Murder? Only the Quiet Headmistress Knows" 48–49.

11. Tellingly, the rapid eight-week production of the NBC miniseries was initiated four days before the jury even handed in its 24 February verdict in the Jean Harris case. See T. Schwartz 48. For information on the responses of the trial participants to the show, see Feron 48.

12. Didion's outrage at the conflation of victim and city in the Central Park Jogger case coverage, an abstraction made easier due to the jogger's remaining nameless in most press reports, is at variance with her own practice of according representative status to the kind of public figures on whom she regularly reports, such as Patricia Hearst ("Girl of the Golden West," *After* 95–109), James Pike ("James Pike, American," *White* 51–58), John Wayne ("John Wayne: A Love Song," *Slouching* 29–41), and Joan Baez ("Where the Kissing Never Stops," *Slouching* 42–60). The difference, to Didion, would appear to be the difference between skilled and unskilled rhetorical performances.

13. See, especially, Mailer's concluding remarks: "This difficulty has always existed for the novelist, but today it may demand more antithesis and more agony than before. The writer who would explore the world must encounter a society which is now conscious of itself, and so resistant (most secretly) to an objective eye. Detours exist everywhere. There was a time when a writer had to see just a little bit of a few different faces in the world and could know that the world was still essentially so simple and so phrased that he might use his imagination to fill in unknown colors in the landscape. Balzac could do that, and so could Zola. But the arts of the world suffered a curious inversion as man was turned by the twentieth century into mass man rather than democratic man. [. . .] The Tolstoyan novel begins to be impossible. Who can create a vast canvas when the imagination must submit itself to a plethora of detail in each joint of society?" ("Some" 129).

14. Mark Krupnick traces a direct connection between Trilling's abandonment of communism and what he considers her "nearly dogmatic insistence on middle-class values" (217). In his assessment, "Mrs. Trilling turned to middle-class ideas of order when she

left communism behind. But she was as rigid in her middle-class tastes and in her anti-communism as she had been as a communist fellow traveler" (218).

15. As Trilling added when commenting upon this fact to Lis Harris, "We don't know what the meaning of that is" (L. Harris 92).

16. Ten more years in prison seem to have changed Harris's stance. Interviewed again by Walters after she was granted clemency by Mario Cuomo on 29 December 1992, Harris announced, "I'm not that interested in men anymore, to tell you the truth. There are too many babies to worry about to worry about men, Barbara. There's a new list of priorities in my life today" (Interview [1993]). I am grateful to Joseph Angier for making the tapes and transcripts of Harris's two *20/20* interviews available to me.

9. Your Trash Ain't Nothin' but Cash

1. For a comprehensive list of books written by Simpson trial participants and hangers-on, see Geis and Bienen 200–204.

2. For examples of the wide variety of commentators who have invoked the Kennedy assassination for comparative purposes, see Bender xi; D. Dunne, *Another* 354; Gates 56; Toobin, *Run* 434; and A. White 341.

3. See D. Dunne, *Another* 165, 168, 283.

4. See Mailer, *Executioner's* 833, 585; and L. Schiller, "*Playboy*" 49, 48.

5. Dreiser's articles, which also were published in the *Philadelphia Record,* appeared in the *New York Post* in 1934 on the following dates and pages: 2 Oct.: 1, 6; 3 Oct.: 3; 4 Oct.: 23; 5 Oct.: 12; and 6 Oct.: 3. Subsequent to their newspaper publication, Dreiser expanded his articles into "I Find the Real American Tragedy," which was serialized in *Mystery Magazine* 11 in 1935: Feb. 9–11, 88–90; Mar. 22–23, 77–79; Apr. 24–26, 90–92; May 22–24, 83–86; and June 20–21, 68–73. See Salzman 3–4 for complete bibliographic information.

6. For an extended discussion of the use made by Dreiser of the *New York World* accounts of the Gillette case in the composition of *An American Tragedy,* see Pizer 215–27.

7. Completely unreported in the *World* in the days following the 5 December 1906 verdict, reduced to four paragraphs on page three the day after the 10 December sentence of death was pronounced, the Gillette case passed into reportorial oblivion after reappearing as a second-page story of Christian redemption the day after his 30 March 1908 execution.

8. Nothing illustrates this diminution of public visibility more clearly than Jeffrey Toobin's reference to Simpson, the former Hertz spokesperson, pitching a questionable arthritis-relief product called "Juice Plus" at a Dallas convention two months before the murders (*Run* 387). Even if one discounts this example as reflecting Toobin's expressed belief in Simpson's guilt, there is no questioning the fact that the mainstream press's interest in Simpson had become nominal by 1994: for instance, he appears not once in the *New York Times Index* for the previous year.

9. In the version of this story told to Pat Jordan in a recent issue of *The New Yorker* (9 July 2001), Simpson makes this point even more bluntly when describing Willie Mays

as " 'the single biggest influence' " he had while growing up: " 'I saw how he made white people happy. I wanted to be like Willie Mays' " (42).

10. See, for instance, Toobin's 25 July 1994 "An Incendiary Defense" (56–59), in which this defense strategy—leaked by an unnamed, but clearly suggested Robert Shapiro—was first publicized.

11. Nowhere does the sanitized *I Want to Tell You* account mention that it was for a liquor store robbery that Simpson was apprehended by the police, just that he "got in trouble" (156). The only time Simpson actually alludes to the robbery occurs earlier in the text, while making the point that assuming a docile pose around the police is essential for a black male (117–18). Likewise, the version narrated to Lawrence Linderman in Simpson's 1976 *Playboy* interview describes the incarceration as having to do "with a fight I had had" (94). When he later mentions a robbery that got him remanded to the Youth Guidance Center in San Francisco, Simpson describes himself as never going into the liquor store with his friends and, in fact, urging them not to do so themselves (100).

12. Simpson's concluding *mea culpa* is worth quoting in full: "A year ago I was overwhelmed by the sheer magnitude of the business opportunities ahead of me; in the excitement and confusion, I let myself drift through the off-season. The hardest thing in the world for a poor kid who suddenly becomes a rich and busy businessman is to keep things in perspective. I lost that perspective for a while, and it took some crushing tackles and bitter disappointments to jolt everything back into place for me. It was a rugged lesson that I don't want to go through twice; business won't get in the way of football anymore" (*O.J.* 253). The consensus among sportswriters today, however, is that Simpson's unimpressive first season—which was followed by two more unimpressive seasons—was more the result of a head coach, John Rauch, who refused to build his offense around any one back. With the return of Lou Saban and his passing game in 1972, Simpson's numbers increased dramatically, culminating in his 2,003-yard record-breaking 1973 season. For all statistics cited for Simpson, see the "Player Register" provided in Carroll et al. 1170; for individual NFL records, see Aiken and Rowe 68–69. For his help in clarifying the intricacies of football to me, I am grateful to Eric Haralson.

13. These figures should be compared to those of Walter Payton, whose numbers began skyrocketing during this same period, from 679 yards gained rushing in 1975 to 1,390 in 1976 to 1,852 in 1977. That last year was also the year Payton was selected the NFL's Most Valuable Player, Player of the Year, and Offensive Player of the Year. For all statistics and awards cited, see Carroll et al. 1170, 1068, 270.

14. The reason Simpson gave for pursuing so fervently a role that could have been a public relations disaster is revealing. It was, he stated, the kind of part "that can build a movie career very quickly," very much like Robert Redford's role in *Butch Cassidy and the Sundance Kid* did for him ("*Playboy*" 85, 88). The right movie role thus assumes the quick fix quality here that marriage to a wealthy woman does in Dreiser's work.

15. I actually saw this *Saturday Night Live* episode when it was first broadcast. Memory being what it is, I am grateful to the Museum of Television and Radio for giving me the opportunity to re-view it.

16. For examples of *Saturday Night Live*'s treatment of Simpson in the wake of his criminal trial, see the "NFL on NBC" sketch broadcast on 7 October 1995, four days after the verdict, and the ongoing "Weekend Update" segments broadcast on 9 December 1995, 23 March 1996, 14 December 1996, 15 February 1997, 10 January 1998, and 4 December 1999.

17. See, for instance, Sipchen E1; Margolick, "Back" 31, 41; Margolick, "O.J.'s" 108, 110; and Toobin, *Run* 252.

18. In addition to those sums paid Gilmore and his girlfriend that are cited in Mailer's *The Executioner's Song* (601, 687), information on the sums listed in this paragraph may be found in the following sources: Tobin, "Cash" 36; Margolick, "O.J.'s" 116, 110; Bugliosi 259; Wechsler and Friedman 12; Farrell, "Merchandising" 71; and L. Schiller, "*Playboy*" 47. In Simpson's case, the profits from *I Want to Tell You* were supplemented by the profits from a marketed video, photographs, interviews, and autographs during the time of his criminal and civil trials; the combined earnings netted him $2.8 million ("Squeezed" 30). For figures on the money that Brown family members earned from the sale of Nicole Brown Simpson's photographs, wedding video, and diary, see Reibstein and King 30.

19. For examples of these depictions, see Mailer, *Executioner's* 612, 622, 628, 629, 698, 801.

20. See Mailer, "Interview" 181.

21. In addition to *The Executioner's Song*, see Mailer's *Oswald's* (1995), Farrell's "Scientists" (1966), and Goldman's *Ladies* (1974).

22. See Mailer, "Interview" 182, 175.

23. See Farrell, "Merchandising" 69; and Mailer, *Executioner's* 689–90.

24. Schiller's made-for-television movie was based on Amram Ducovny and Leon Friedman's Broadway play of the same name. The movie opens with the statement: "Lee Harvey Oswald was killed before he could stand trial for the assassination of John F. Kennedy. In creating the following drama certain names and events have been changed. While inferences are made at the trial, the testimony and the historical scenes of November 21 through November 24, 1963, including the film of the assassination of John F. Kennedy, have a factual basis, and were recreated for this motion picture at the actual locations where the events took place." Cross-cutting between the invented trial of Oswald and flashbacks that re-create Oswald's history, the movie goes on to suggest a conspiracy theory very much like that portrayed in DeLillo's *Libra*. By having Oswald killed while being taken to court to hear the jury's verdict, however, the movie refuses to draw any definite conclusions, asserting only, as its final voice-over states, "In creating the trial of Lee Harvey Oswald we have relied on documented fact. We have assumed the roles of prosecutor and defense attorney. We do not assume the role of the jury. The final judgment is yours."

25. See Margolick, "Back" 31.

Conclusion

1. Information cited on the state of garbage in New Jersey may be found in the following sources: Lipton A20; K. Johnson, "To City's" B4; and J. Miller 8.

2. For information on New York City's trash disposal policy, past and present, see Purnick B1; K. Johnson, "To City's" A1, B4; K. Johnson, "Commissioner" B4; and K. Johnson, "As Options" A1, B2. Figures for daily trash amounts and trash removal costs may be found in K. Johnson, "To City's" B4; and K. Johnson, "As Options" A1.

3. For further discussion of this point, especially as it concerns the distinction between alliances and coalitions, see Marquis 5.

4. The complete text of George W. Bush's 29 January 2002 State of the Union address appears in the *New York Times* 30 Jan. 2002: A22. Subsequent quotations from it that are included in my conclusion derive from that transcription.

5. Qtd. in Sanger 18.

6. Qtd. in Barra 5.

7. The complete text of Richard A. Gephardt's 29 January 2002 response to George W. Bush's State of the Union address appears in the *New York Times* 30 Jan. 2002: A23.

8. Qtd. in O'Grady, "To an Artist's Eyes" 4.

9. See Lipton and Glanz 42.

10. Qtd. in Lipton and Glanz 1.

WORKS CITED

"Accident or Murder? Only the Quiet Headmistress Knows: Jean Harris." *People* 29 Dec. 1980–5 Jan. 1981: 48–49.

Acker, Kathy. *Blood and Guts in High School.* 1978. New York: Evergreen–Grove Weidenfeld, 1989.

———. *Great Expectations.* 1982. New York: Evergreen-Grove, 1989.

Adams, Brooks. *America's Economic Supremacy.* New York: Macmillan, 1900.

———. *The Law of Civilization and Decay: An Essay on History.* London, 1895; New York: Macmillan, 1896. New York: Knopf, 1943.

———. *The New Empire.* 1902. New York: Bergman, 1969.

Adorno, Theodor W. *Introduction to the Sociology of Music.* Trans. E. B. Ashton. New York: Seabury, 1976. Trans. of *Einleitung in die Musiksoziologie.* 1962.

Aiken, Miles, and Peter Rowe. *American Football: The Records.* 1985. Rev. ed. Enfield, Middlesex, Eng.: Guinness, 1986.

Alexander, Shana. *Very Much a Lady: The Untold Story of Jean Harris and Dr. Herman Tarnower.* Boston: Little, 1983.

Altman, Lawrence K. "Tarnower Was a Busy Physician, Too." *New York Times* 12 Mar. 1980, late city ed.: B4.

America. Dir. D. W. Griffith. Prod. D. W. Griffith, Inc. Scenario by Robert W. Chambers. United Artists, 1924.

"An American Tragedy." *Time* 27 June 1994: cover.

Anderson, Benedict. *Imagined Communities: Reflections on the Origin and Spread of Nationalism.* London: Verso, 1983.

Anderson, Perry. "The Prussia of the East?" *Boundary 2* 18.3 (1991): 11–19.

Applebome, Peter. "Mood of the Nation: Sense of Pride Outweighs Fears of War." *New York Times* 24 Feb. 1991, late ed., sec. 4: 1+.

Arnold, Matthew. *Culture and Anarchy: An Essay in Political and Social Criticism.* 1869. Ed. Ian Gregor. Indianapolis: Bobbs, 1971.

The Assassination of President Lincoln and the Trial of the Conspirators. Comp. Benn Pitman. 1865. New York: Funk, 1954.

Auerbach, Erich. *Mimesis: The Representation of Reality in Western Literature.* Trans. Willard R. Trask. Princeton: Princeton University Press, 1953. Trans. of *Mimesis: dargestellte Wirklichkeit in der abendändischen Literatur.* 1946.

Babington, Bruce, and Peter William Evans. *Blue Skies and Silver Linings: Aspects of the Hollywood Musical.* Manchester: Manchester University Press, 1985.

Bacarisse, Pamela. *The Necessary Dream: A Study of the Novels of Manuel Puig.* Cardiff: University of Wales Press, 1988.

———. "The Projection of Peronism in the Novels of Manuel Puig." *The Historical Novel in Latin America: A Symposium.* Ed. Daniel Balderston. Gaithersburg, Md.: Hispamérica, 1986. 185–99.

Bakhtin, M[ikhail] M[ikhailovich]. *The Dialogic Imagination.* Ed. Michael Holquist. Trans. Caryl Emerson and Michael Holquist. University of Texas Press Slavic Ser. 1. Austin: University of Texas Press, 1981. Trans. of *Voprosy literatury i estetiki.* 1975.

Balibar, Étienne. "The Nation Form: History and Ideology." *Race, Nation, Class: Ambiguous Identities.* By Étienne Balibar and Immanuel Wallerstein. Trans. Chris Turner. London: Verso, 1991. Trans. of *Race, nation, classe: Les identités ambiguës.* 1988. Rpt. in *Becoming National: A Reader.* Ed. Geoff Eley and Ronald Grigor Suny. New York: Oxford University Press, 1996. 132–50.

Banta, Martha. *Imaging American Women: Idea and Ideals in Cultural History.* New York: Columbia University Press, 1987.

Barnard, Tim. "Popular Cinema and Populist Politics." *Argentine Cinema.* Ed. Tim Barnard. Toronto: Nightwood, 1986. 5–63.

Barnes, John. *Evita, First Lady: A Biography of Eva Perón.* New York: Grove, 1978.

Barr, Marleen S. *Alien to Femininity: Speculative Fiction and Feminist Theory.* Westport, Conn.: Greenwood, 1987.

————, ed. *Future Females: A Critical Anthology.* Bowling Green: Bowling Green State University Popular Press, 1981.

Barra, Allen. "Alamo Redux: A Mission Impossible." *New York Times* 10 Mar. 2002, late ed., sec. 4: 5.

Barrios, Richard. *A Song in the Dark: The Birth of the Musical Film.* New York: Oxford University Press, 1995.

Barth, John. "The Literature of Exhaustion." *Atlantic Monthly* Aug. 1967: 29–34.

————. "The Literature of Replenishment." *Atlantic Monthly* Jan. 1980: 65–71.

Barthelme, Donald. *The Dead Father.* 1975. New York: Penguin, 1986.

————. *Snow White.* 1967. New York: Atheneum, 1980.

Barthes, Roland. *Empire of Signs.* Trans. Richard Howard. New York: Hill and Wang–Farrar, 1982. Trans. of *L'empire des signes.* 1970.

Basinger, Jeanine. *The World War II Combat Film: Anatomy of a Genre.* New York: Columbia University Press, 1986.

Baudrillard, Jean. *America.* Trans. Chris Turner. 1988. London: Verso, 1989. Trans. of *Amérique.* 1986.

————. *The Gulf War Did Not Take Place.* Trans. Paul Patton. Bloomington: Indiana University Press, 1995. Trans. of *La Guerre du Golfe n'a pas eu lieu.* 1991.

————. *The Illusion of the End.* Trans. Chris Turner. Cambridge, Eng.: Polity, 1994. Trans. of *L'illusion de la fin: Ou la grève des événements.* 1992.

Baxendale, John, and Chris Pawling. "*Pennies from Heaven:* Revisiting the Thirties as Popular Culture." *Narrating the Thirties—A Decade in the Making: 1930 to the Present.* Houndmills, Eng.: Macmillan, 1996. 168–87, 230–31.

Baxter, John. *Mythmaker: The Life and Work of George Lucas.* New York: Spike-Avon, 1999.

Beattie, Ann. *Chilly Scenes of Winter.* 1976. New York: Fawcett, 1978.

Bederman, Gail. *Manliness and Civilization: A Cultural History of Gender and Race in the United States, 1880–1917.* Chicago: University of Chicago Press, 1995.

Beinhart, Larry. *American Hero.* New York: Pantheon, 1993.

————. *American Hero.* 1993. Rev. ed. New York: Ballantine, 1994.

————. *Foreign Exchange.* New York: Harmony-Crown, 1991.

————. *No One Rides for Free.* New York: William Morrow, 1986.

————. *You Get What You Pay For.* New York: William Morrow, 1988.

Bender, David. *The Confession of O. J. Simpson: A Work of Fiction.* New York: Berkley, 1997.

Benjamin, Walter. "The Work of Art in the Age of Mechanical Reproduction." 1936. Rpt. in *Illuminations.* Ed. Hannah Arendt. Trans. Harry Zohn. 1968. New York: Schocken, 1969. 217–51.

Bergstrom, Janet. "Enunciation and Sexual Difference (Part I)." *Camera Obscura* 3–4 (1979): 32–69.

Bergstrom, Janet, and Mary Ann Doane, eds. *The Spectatrix.* Spec. issue of *Camera Obscura* 20–21 (1989): 1–378.

Berlant, Lauren. *The Anatomy of National Fantasy: Hawthorne, Utopia, and Everyday Life.* Chicago: University of Chicago Press, 1991.

Berryman, Charles. "The Education of Harry Angstrom: Rabbit and the Moon." *Literary Review* 27 (1983): 117–26.

Beveridge, Albert J. "The Taste of Empire." 16 Sept. 1898. *William McKinley 1843–1901.* Ed. Harry J. Sievers. Dobbs Ferry, N.Y.: Oceana, 1970. 57–63.

Bhabha, Homi K. "Interrogating Identity: The Postcolonial Prerogative." *Anatomy of Racism.* Ed. David Theo Goldberg. Minneapolis: University of Minnesota Press, 1990. 183–209.

————. *The Location of Culture.* London: Routledge, 1994.

Birmingham, Stephen. *"Our Crowd": The Great Jewish Families of New York.* 1967. New York: Wallaby-Pocket, 1977.

The Birth of a Nation. Dir. D. W. Griffith. Prod. Epoch Producing Corporation. Scenario by D. W. Griffith and Frank E. Woods. Epoch Producing Corporation, 1915.

Block de Behar, Lisa. "Narration under Discussion: A Question of Men, Angels, Proper Names, and Pronouns." *World Literature Today* 65 (1991): 607–16.

Boccia, Michael. "Versions (Con-, In-, and Per-) in Manuel Puig's and Hector Babenco's *Kiss of the Spider Woman,* Novel and Film." *Modern Fiction Studies* 32 (1986): 417–26.

Bondebjerg, Ib. "Intertextuality and Metafiction: Genre and Narration in the Television Fiction of Dennis Potter." *Media Cultures: Reappraising Transnational Media.* Ed. Michael Skovmand and Kim Christian Schrøder. London: Routledge, 1992. 161–80.

Boose, Lynda. "Techno-Muscularity and the 'Boy Eternal': From the Quagmire to the Gulf." *Cultures of United States Imperialism.* Ed. Amy Kaplan and Donald E. Pease. New Americanists. Durham: Duke University Press, 1993. 581–616.

Booth, John Wilkes. *"Right or Wrong, God Judge Me": The Writings of John Wilkes Booth.* Ed. John Rhodehamel and Louise Taper. Urbana: University of Illinois Press, 1997.

Bourdieu, Pierre. *Distinction: A Social Critique of the Judgement of Taste.* Trans. Richard Nice. Cambridge: Harvard University Press, 1984. Trans. of *La distinction: Critique sociale du jugement.* 1979.

Brannen, Mary Yoko. " 'Bwana Mickey': Constructing Cultural Consumption at Tokyo Disneyland." *Cultures of United States Imperialism.* Ed. Amy Kaplan and Donald E. Pease. New Americanists. Durham: Duke University Press, 1993. 617–34.

Branson, Noreen, and Margot Heinemann. *Britain in the 1930's.* New York: Praeger, 1971.

Braudy, Leo. *The Frenzy of Renown: Fame and Its History.* New York: Oxford University Press, 1986.

Bremer, Arthur H. *An Assassin's Diary.* New York: Harper's Magazine–Harper, 1973.

Breton, André. *Manifestoes of Surrealism.* Trans. Richard Seaver and Helen R. Lane. Ann Arbor: University of Michigan Press, 1969.

Breuilly, John. *Nationalism and the State.* New York: St. Martin's, 1982.

Brie, Steve. " 'Yesterday Once More': Thoughts on the Relationship between Popular Music, Audience and Authorial Intention in Dennis Potter's *Pennies from Heaven, The Singing Detective* and *Lipstick on Your Collar.*" *The Passion of Dennis Potter: International Collected Essays.* Ed. Vernon W. Gras and John R. Cook. New York: St. Martin's, 2000. 205–17.

Briggs, Asa. *The* BBC: *The First Fifty Years.* Oxford: Oxford University Press, 1985.

The Broadway Melody. Dir. Harry Beaumont. Prod. Lawrence Weingarten. Story by Edmund Goulding. Dialogue by Norman Houston and James Gleason. MGM, 1929.

Brownlow, Kevin. *The War, the West, and the Wilderness.* New York: Knopf, 1978.

Brownstein, Ronald. *The Power and the Glitter: The Hollywood-Washington Connection.* New York: Pantheon, 1990.

Bryant, Paula. "Discussing the Untellable: Don DeLillo's *The Names.*" *Critique* 29 (1987): 16–29.

Bugliosi, Vincent. *Helter Skelter: The True Story of the Manson Murders.* With Curt Gentry. 1974. New York: Bantam, 1995.

Burgin, Victor. *The End of Art Theory: Criticism and Postmodernity.* Atlantic Highlands, N.J.: Humanities Press International, 1986.

Burns, Tom. *The* BBC: *Public Institution and Private World.* London: Macmillan, 1977.

Buruma, Ian. "Becoming Japanese." *New Yorker* 23–30 Dec. 1996: 60–62, 64–71.

——. *Behind the Mask: On Sexual Demons, Sacred Mothers, Transvestites, Gangsters, and Other Japanese Cultural Heroes.* 1984. New York: Meridian–New American Library, 1985.

Bush, George W. State of the Union Address. United States Congress. Washington, D.C. 29 Jan. 2002. Transcribed as "President Bush's State of the Union Address to Congress and the Nation." *New York Times* 30 Jan. 2002, late ed.: A22.

Butler, Judith. *Gender Trouble: Feminism and the Subversion of Identity.* New York: Routledge, 1990.

Cain, William E. "Making Meaningful Worlds: Self and History in *Libra.*" *Michigan Quarterly Review* 29 (1990): 275–87.

Calvocoressi, Peter. *The British Experience, 1945–75.* New York: Pantheon, 1978.

Camille. Dir. George Cukor. Prod. Irving Thalberg and Bernard Hyman. Screenplay by Zoe Akins, Frances Marion, and James Hilton. MGM, 1936.

Capote, Truman. *In Cold Blood: A True Account of a Multiple Murder and Its Consequences.* 1965. New York: Signet–New American Library, 1980.

Carpenter, Humphrey. *Dennis Potter: A Biography.* 1998. New York: St. Martin's, 1999.

Carroll, Bob, et al., eds. *Total Football: The Official Encyclopedia of the National Football League.* New York: HarperCollins, 1997.

Castle, Mr. and Mrs. Vernon [Vernon and Irene Castle]. *Modern Dancing.* New York: Harper, 1914.

Certeau, Michel de. *The Practice of Everyday Life.* Trans. Steven F. Rendall. Berkeley: University of California Press, 1984. Trans. of *Arts de faire.* 1980.

Chambers, Ross. "Opposition by Appropriation: Manuel Puig's *Kiss of the Spider Woman.*" AUMLA 74 (1990): 201–23.

Cheever, Leonard A. "Puig's *Kiss of the Spider Woman:* What the Movie Version *Couldn't* Show." *Publications of the Arkansas Philological Association* 13.2 (1987): 13–27.

Chicago Tribune 12–15 Mar. 1980.

Ching, Leo. "Imaginings in the Empires of the Sun: Japanese Mass Culture in Asia." *Boundary 2* 21.1 (1994): 198–219.

Civello, Paul. "Undoing the Naturalistic Novel: Don DeLillo's *Libra.*" *Arizona Quarterly* 48.2 (1992): 33–56.

Clarke, Asia Booth. *The Unlocked Book: A Memoir of John Wilkes Booth by His Sister Asia Booth Clarke.* 1938. New York: Benjamin Blom, 1971.

Cohen, Paula Marantz. *Silent Film and the Triumph of the American Myth.* New York: Oxford University Press, 2001.

Colás, Santiago. "Beyond Valentín's Dream: From the Crisis of Latin American Modernity." *Postmodernity in Latin America: The Argentine Paradigm.* Post-Contemporary Interventions. Durham: Duke University Press, 1994. 100–117, 192–94.

Colley, Iain, and Gill Davies. "*Pennies from Heaven:* Music, Image, Text." *Screen Education* 35 (summer 1980): 63–78.

Combs, James. "From the Great War to the Gulf War: Popular Entertainment and the Legitimation of Warfare." *The Media and the Persian Gulf War.* Ed. Robert E. Denton Jr. Praeger Ser. in Political Communication. Westport, Conn.: Praeger, 1993. 257–83.

Connery, Christopher. "Pacific Rim Discourse: The U.S. Global Imaginary in the Late Cold War Years." *Boundary 2* 21.1 (1994): 30–56.

Conrad, Peter. *Imagining America.* New York: Oxford University Press, 1980.

Cook, Alvin D. *Nomonhan: Japan against Russia, 1939.* 2 vols. Stanford: Stanford University Press, 1985.

Cook, John R. *Dennis Potter: A Life on Screen.* Manchester: Manchester University Press, 1995.

Coover, Robert. *A Night at the Movies, Or, You Must Remember This.* 1987. New York: Collier-Macmillan, 1988.

———. *The Public Burning.* 1977. New York: Bantam, 1978.

Copi. *Eva Perón.* Paris: Christian Bourgois, 1969.

Corber, Robert J. "Gore Vidal and the Erotics of Masculinity." *Western Humanities Review* 48 (1994): 30–52.

Courage under Fire. Dir. Edward Zwick. Prod. John Davis, Joseph M. Singer, and David T. Friendly. Screenplay by Patrick Sheane Duncan. Twentieth Century–Fox, 1996.

Coward, Rosalind. "Dennis Potter and the Question of the Television Author." *Critical Quarterly* 29.4 (1987): 79–87.

Cowart, David. *Literary Symbiosis: The Reconfigured Text in Twentieth-Century Writing.* Athens: University of Georgia Press, 1993.

Creeber, Glen. *Dennis Potter: Between Two Worlds.* London: Macmillan, 1998.

Creel, George. *How We Advertised America: The First Telling of the Amazing Story of the Committee on Public Information That Carried the Gospel of Americanism to Every Corner of the Globe.* New York: Harper, 1920. New York: Arno, 1972.

Creighton, Millie R. "The *Depāto:* Merchandising the West While Selling Japaneseness." *Re-Made in Japan: Everyday Life and Consumer Taste in a Changing Society.* Ed. Joseph J. Tobin. New Haven: Yale University Press, 1992. 42–57.

Croce, Arlene. *The Fred Astaire and Ginger Rogers Book.* New York: Outerbridge and Lazard-Dutton, 1972.

Crowther, Bosley. "'Love Is Better Than Ever,' With Elizabeth Taylor and Larry Parks, Has Premiere Here." *New York Times* 4 Mar. 1952, late city ed.: 23.

Cushman, John H., Jr. "The Electronic Battlefield: Crucial Tests for Tools of Command." *New York Times* 20 Jan. 1991, late ed., sec. 4: 1–2.

Davies, Lloyd. "Psychoanalysis, Gender, and Angelic Truth in Manuel Puig's *Pubis angelical.*" *Modern Language Review* 93 (1998): 400–410.

De Bellis, Jack. "'It Captivates . . . It Hypnotizes': Updike Goes to the Movies." *Literature/Film Quarterly* 23 (1995): 169–87.

Debord, Guy. *The Society of the Spectacle.* Trans. Donald Nicholson-Smith. 1994. New York: Zone, 1995. Trans. of *La société du spectacle.* 1967.

DeLillo, Don. "American Blood: A Journey through the Labyrinth of Dallas and JFK." *Rolling Stone* 8 Dec. 1983: 21–22, 24, 27–28, 74.

———. "An Interview with Don DeLillo." With Tom LeClair. *Anything Can Happen: Interviews with Contemporary American Novelists.* Ed. Tom LeClair and Larry McCaffery. Urbana: University of Illinois Press, 1983. 79–90.

———. *Libra.* 1988. New York: Penguin, 1989.

———. *The Names.* 1982. New York: Vintage-Random, 1983.

———. "'An Outsider in This Society': An Interview with Don DeLillo." With Anthony DeCurtis. *Introducing Don DeLillo.* Ed. Frank Lentricchia. Durham: Duke University Press, 1991. 43–66. Expansion of "Matters of Fact and Fiction." *Rolling Stone* 17 Nov. 1988: 114–15, 117, 119, 121, 164.

———. *Ratner's Star.* 1976. New York: Vintage-Random, 1980.

———. *Underworld.* New York: Scribner, 1997.

———. *Valparaiso: A Play in Two Acts.* New York: Scribner, 1999.

———. *White Noise.* 1985. New York: Penguin, 1986.

Denton, Robert E., Jr. "Television as an Instrument of War." *The Media and the Persian*

Gulf War. Ed. Robert E. Denton Jr. Praeger Ser. in Political Communication. Westport, Conn.: Praeger, 1993. 27–42.

DeParle, Jason. "The First Primary." *New York Times Magazine* 16 Apr. 1995: 28–35, 42, 48, 53–54.

Detweiler, Robert. *John Updike*. 1972. Rev. ed. Boston: Twayne-Simon, 1984.

Didion, Joan. *After Henry*. 1992. New York: Vintage-Random, 1993.

———. *Slouching towards Bethlehem*. 1968. New York: Touchstone-Simon, 1979.

———. *The White Album*. 1979. New York: Pocket-Simon, 1980.

Diliberto, Gioia. "Schoolmistress Jean Harris Gets an 'A' for Effort in Prison." *People* 11 May 1981: 49–50.

Doane, Mary Ann. *The Desire to Desire: The Woman's Film of the 1940s*. Theories of Representation and Difference. Bloomington: Indiana University Press, 1987.

Doctorow, E. L. *The Book of Daniel*. 1971. New York: Signet–New American Library, 1972.

———. *Ragtime*. New York: Random, 1975.

Doody, Terrence A. "Updike's Idea of Reification." *Contemporary Literature* 20 (1979): 204–20.

Dorfman, Ariel. *The Empire's Old Clothes: What the Lone Ranger, Barbar, and Other Innocent Heroes Do to Our Minds*. With trans. by Clark Hansen. New York: Pantheon, 1983.

———. "Unique No More." *CounterPunch* 3 Oct. 2001. <http://counterpunch.org/dorfman.html>.

Dos Passos, John. *The Big Money*. 1936. Vol. 3 of *U.S.A.* 3 vols. 1938. New York: Modern-Random, n.d.

Dowd, Maureen. "Coyote Rummy." *New York Times* 24 Feb. 2002, late ed., sec. 4: 13.

Dower, John W. "Occupied Japan and the American Lake, 1945–1950." *America's Asia: Dissenting Essays on Asian-American Relations*. Ed. Edward Friedman and Mark Selden. New York: Pantheon-Random, 1971. 146–206.

Dreiser, Theodore. *An American Tragedy*. 1925. New York: Signet–New American Library, 1981.

———. "I Find the Real American Tragedy." *Mystery Magazine* 11 (Feb. 1935): 9–11, 88–90; (Mar. 1935): 22–23, 77–79; (Apr. 1935): 24–26, 90–92; (May 1935): 22–24, 83–86; (June 1935): 20–21, 68–73. Rpt. in *Resources for American Literary Study* 2 (1972): 5–74.

———. "The Myth of Individuality." *American Mercury* 31 (Mar. 1934): 337–42.

Dunne, Dominick. *Another City, Not My Own: A Novel in the Form of a Memoir*. 1997. New York: Ballantine, 1999.

———. "L.A. in the Age of O.J." *Vanity Fair* Feb. 1995: 46, 48, 50–52, 54, 56.

Dunne, Michael. "Bakhtinian Dialogics in Hector Babenco's *Kiss of the Spider Woman*." *Post Script* 14.3 (1995): 14–24.

Durkheim, Émile. *Émile Durkheim: Selected Writings*. Ed. and trans. Anthony Giddens. Cambridge: Cambridge University Press, 1972.

Duvall, John N. "Baseball as Aesthetic Ideology: Cold War History, Race, and DeLillo's 'Pafko at the Wall.'" *Modern Fiction Studies* 41 (1995): 285–313.

Dyer, Richard. *Stars*. 1979. London: British Film Institute, 1998.

Edgington, David W. "The Search for Paradise: Japanese Property Investors in North America." *Japan and the West: The Perception Gap*. Ed. Keizo Nagatani and David W. Edgington. Aldershot, Eng.: Ashgate, 1998. 153–78.

Egan, Jack. "Sony's Big-Picture Strategy." With Jim Impoco and Mike Tharp. *U.S. News and World Report* 9 Oct. 1989: 35–36, 38.

Eliot, T. S. "Tradition and the Individual Talent." 1920. Rpt. in The Waste Land *and Other Writings*. New York: Modern-Random, 2001. 99–108.

Engelhardt, Tom. "The Gulf War as Total Television." *Seeing through the Media: The Persian Gulf War*. Ed. Susan Jeffords and Lauren Rabinovitz. Communications, Media, and Culture. New Brunswick: Rutgers University Press, 1994. 81–95.

Erenberg, Lewis A. *Steppin' Out: New York Nightlife and the Transformation of American Culture, 1890–1930*. Westport, Conn.: Greenwood, 1981.

"Eva Perón: Between Two Worlds, an Argentine Rainbow." *Time* 14 July 1947: cover, 32–34, 36.

Ewen, David. *The Life and Death of Tin Pan Alley: The Golden Age of American Popular Music*. New York: Funk, 1964.

Fabrikant, Geraldine. "Deal Is Expected for Sony to Buy Columbia Pictures." *New York Times* 26 Sept. 1989, late ed.: A1+.

Fallows, James. "Containing Japan." *Atlantic Monthly* May 1989: 40–48, 51–54.

Fanon, Frantz. *Black Skin, White Masks*. Trans. Charles Lam Markmann. New York: Grove, 1967. Trans. of *Peau noire, masques blancs*. 1952.

Farrell, Barry. "Merchandising Gary Gilmore's Dance of Death." *New West* 20 Dec. 1976: 64–71.

———. "Scientists, Theologians, Mystics Swept Up in a Psychic Revolution." *Life* 25 Mar. 1966: 31–33.

Feild, Robert D. *The Art of Walt Disney*. New York: Macmillan, 1942.

Feinberg, Lawrence. "Madeira Coping in Crisis." *Washington Post* 14 Mar. 1980, final ed.: B1+.

Feron, James. "Portrayal on TV Reportedly Displeases Jean Harris." *New York Times* 9 May 1981, late city ed.: 48.

Fiedler, Leslie A. *Cross the Border—Close the Gap*. New York: Stein, 1972.

———. *What Was Literature? Mass Culture and Mass Society*. New York: Simon, 1982.

Fine, David. "Sargasso of the Imagination: The Hollywood Novel." *Imagining Los Angeles: A City in Fiction*. Albuquerque: University of New Mexico Press, 2000. 153–77, 266–68.

First Blood. Dir. Ted. Kotcheff. Prod. Buzz Feitshans. Screenplay by Michael Kozoll, William Sackheim, and Sylvester Stallone. Orion, 1982.

Fischer, Lucy. *Shot/Countershot: Film Tradition and Women's Cinema*. Princeton: Princeton University Press, 1989.

Fiske, John. *Television Culture*. 1987. London: Routledge, 1989.

Fitzgerald, F. Scott. *The Great Gatsby*. New York: Scribner's, 1925.

———. *The Last Tycoon*. New York: Scribner's, 1941.

Follow the Fleet. Dir. Mark Sandrich. Prod. Pandro S. Berman. Screenplay by Dwight Taylor and Allan Scott. RKO Radio, 1936.

Footlight Parade. Dir. Lloyd Bacon. Prod. Robert Lord. Screenplay by Manuel Seff and James Seymour. Dance Dir. Busby Berkeley. Warner Bros., 1933.

Foucault, Michel. *Discipline and Punish: The Birth of the Prison.* Trans. Alan Sheridan. New York: Vintage-Random, 1979. Trans. of *Surveiller et punir: Naissance de la prison.* 1975.

Fraser, Nicholas, and Marysa Navarro. *Eva Perón.* 1980. New York: Norton, 1985.

Freund, Gisèle. "A Controversial Lady: Evita Perón." *The World in My Camera.* Trans. June Guicharnaud. New York: Dial, 1974. 183–94.

Friedman, Thomas L. "All Alone, Again." *New York Times* 19 Dec. 2001, late ed.: A35.

———. "Desert Fog: The Uncertain Time beyond High Noon." *New York Times* 24 Feb. 1991, late ed., sec. 4: 1+.

———. "The End of NATO?" *New York Times* 3 Feb. 2002, late ed., sec. 4: 15.

———. "A Memo from Osama." *New York Times* 26 June 2001, late ed.: A19.

———. "Motives for the Bombing." *New York Times* 8 Aug. 1998, late ed.: A15.

———. "We Are All Alone." *New York Times* 26 Oct. 2001, late ed.: A23.

Friedman, Thomas, and Patrick E. Tyler. "From the First, U.S. Resolve to Fight: The Path to War." *New York Times* 3 Mar. 1991, late ed., sec. 1: 1+.

Frith, Simon. *Performing Rites: On the Value of Popular Music.* Cambridge: Harvard University Press, 1996.

Furno-Lamude, Diane. "The Media Spectacle and the O. J. Simpson Case." *The O. J. Simpson Trials: Rhetoric, Media, and the Law.* Ed. Janice Schuetz and Lin S. Lilley. Carbondale: Southern Illinois University Press, 1999. 19–35.

"Furor in the Gulf." *New Republic* 3 Sept. 1990: cover.

Gates, Henry Louis, Jr. "Thirteen Ways of Looking at a Black Man." *New Yorker* 23 Oct. 1995: 56–60, 62–65.

Gatlin, Rochelle. *American Women Since 1945.* Jackson: University Press of Mississippi, 1987.

Geis, Gilbert, and Leigh B. Bienen. *Crimes of the Century: From Leopold and Loeb to O. J. Simpson.* Boston: Northeastern University Press, 1998.

Gellner, Ernest. *Nations and Nationalism.* New Perspectives on the Past. Ithaca: Cornell University Press, 1983.

Gephardt, Richard A. Response to the State of the Union Address. Washington, D.C. 29 Jan. 2002. Transcribed as "Democrats' Response: Trying to Put Aside Partisanship." *New York Times* 30 Jan. 2002, late ed.: A23.

Gerbner, George. "Persian Gulf War, the Movie." *Triumph of the Image: The Media's War in the Persian Gulf—A Global Perspective.* Ed. Hamid Mowlana, George Gerbner, and Herbert I. Schiller. Critical Studies in Communication and in the Cultural Industries. Boulder: Westview, 1992. 243–65.

Giddens, Anthony. *The Giddens Reader.* Ed. Philip Cassell. Stanford: Stanford University Press, 1993.

————. *Runaway World: How Globalization Is Reshaping Our Lives.* 1999. New York: Routledge, 2000.

Gilbert, W. Stephen. *Fight and Kick and Bite: The Life and Work of Dennis Potter.* 1995. London: Sceptre–Hodder and Stoughton, 1996.

Gilda. Dir. Charles Vidor. Prod. Virginia Van Upp. Story by E. A. Ellington. Screenplay by Marion Parsonnet. Columbia, 1946.

Gindin, James. "Megalotopia and the WASP Backlash: The Fiction of Mailer and Updike." *Centennial Review* 15 (1971): 38–52.

Glasgall, William. "Foreign Investors Are Keeping the Pot Boiling." *Business Week* 24 Nov. 1986: 84.

Glazer, Nathan, and Daniel P. Moynihan. *Beyond the Melting Pot: The Negroes, Puerto Ricans, Jews, Italians, and Irish of New York City.* 1963. Cambridge: MIT Press, 1970.

Glickman, Norman, and Douglas P. Woodward. *The New Competitors: How Foreign Investors Are Changing the U.S. Economy.* New York: Basic, 1989.

Goldberg, Isaac. *Tin Pan Alley: A Chronicle of American Popular Music.* 1930. New York: Frederick Ungar, 1961.

Gold Diggers of 1935. Dir. Busby Berkeley. Prod. Robert Lord. Story by Robert Lord and Peter Milne. Screenplay by Manuel Seff and Peter Milne. Dance Dir. Busby Berkeley. Warner Bros., 1935.

Gold Diggers of 1933. Dir. Mervyn LeRoy. Prod. Robert Lord. Story by Erwin Gelsey and James Seymour. Dialogue by David Boehm and Ben Markson. Dance Dir. Busby Berkeley. Warner Bros., 1933.

Goldman, Albert. *Ladies and Gentlemen—Lenny Bruce!!* From the journalism of Lawrence Schiller. 1974. New York: Penguin, 1991.

Good, Timothy S., ed. *We Saw Lincoln Shot: One Hundred Eyewitness Accounts.* Jackson: University Press of Mississippi, 1995.

Goodheart, Eugene. "Some Speculations on Don DeLillo and the Cinematic Real." *Introducing Don DeLillo.* Ed. Frank Lentricchia. Durham: Duke University Press, 1991. 117–30.

Gramsci, Antonio. *Selections from the Prison Notebooks of Antonio Gramsci.* Ed. and trans. Quintin Hoare and Geoffrey Nowell Smith. London: Lawrence and Wishart, 1971.

Grand Hotel. Dir. Edmund Goulding. Prod. Irving Thalberg. Screenplay by William A. Drake. MGM, 1932.

The Great Waltz. Dir. Julien Duvivier. Prod. Bernard Hyman. Story by Gottfried Reinhardt. Screenplay by Samuel Hoffenstein and Walter Reisch. MGM, 1938.

The Great Ziegfeld. Dir. Robert Z. Leonard. Prod. Hunt Stromberg. Screenplay by William Anthony McGuire. MGM, 1936.

Green, Jeremy. "Disaster Footage: Spectacles of Violence in DeLillo's Fiction." *Modern Fiction Studies* 45 (1999): 571–99.

Greenberg, Clement. "Avant-Garde and Kitsch." *Partisan Review* 6.5 (1939): 34–49. Rpt. in *Mass Culture: The Popular Arts in America.* Ed. Bernard Rosenberg and David Manning White. 1957. New York: Free-Macmillan, 1964. 98–107.

Greenblatt, Stephen. "Racial Memory and Literary History." PMLA 116 (2001): 48–63.

Greiner, Donald J. *John Updike's Novels*. Athens: Ohio University Press, 1984.

Grover, Ronald. "*When Columbia Met Sony* . . . A Love Story." *Business Week* 9 Oct. 1989: 44–45.

Guibernau, Montserrat. *Nationalisms: The Nation-State and Nationalism in the Twentieth Century*. Cambridge, Eng.: Polity, 1996.

Gunther, John. *Inside Asia*. New York: Harper, 1942.

Gurevitch, Michael, et al., eds. *Culture, Society and the Media*. London: Methuen, 1982.

Haden-Guest, Anthony. "The Headmistress and the Diet Doctor." *New York* 31 Mar. 1980: cover, 36–41.

Hall, Stuart. "Culture, Media and the 'Ideological Effect.'" *Mass Communication and Society*. Ed. James Curran, Michael Gurevitch, and Janet Woollacott. London: Edward Arnold, 1977. 315–48.

———. "Encoding/Decoding." *Culture, Media, Language: Working Papers in Cultural Studies, 1972–79*. Centre for Contemporary Cultural Studies, University of Birmingham. London: Hutchinson, 1980. 128–38.

———. "Notes on Deconstructing 'The Popular.'" *People's History and Socialist Theory*. Ed. Raphael Samuel. London: Routledge, 1981. 227–40.

———. "The Rediscovery of 'Ideology': Return of the Repressed in Media Studies." *Culture, Society and the Media*. Ed. Michael Gurevitch et al. London: Methuen, 1982. 56–90.

Hamelink, Cees J. *Cultural Autonomy in Global Communications: Planning National Information Policy*. New York: Longman, 1983.

Hammer, Joshua. "Next Stop, Tinseltown." With Bill Powell and Michael Reese. *Newsweek* 20 Mar. 1989: 48–49.

Hanchett, William. "Booth's Diary." *Journal of the Illinois State Historical Society* 72 (1979): 39–56.

Harden, Blaine, and Lee Lescaze. "Romance Cited in Diet Author's Death." *Washington Post* 13 Mar. 1980, final ed.: A1+.

Harden, Blaine, and Stephanie Mansfield. "Madeira Headmistress' Secret Life." *Washington Post* 16 Mar. 1980: B1+.

Hardt, Michael, and Antonio Negri. *Empire*. 2000. Cambridge: Harvard University Press, 2001.

Hardy, Thomas. *Jude the Obscure*. 1895. Boston: Riverside-Houghton, 1965.

Harootunian, H. D. "Visible Discourses/Invisible Ideologies." *Postmodernism and Japan*. Ed. Masao Miyoshi and H. D. Harootunian. Post-Contemporary Interventions. Durham: Duke University Press, 1989. 63–92.

Harris, Jean. Interview with Barbara Walters. *20/20*. ABC. WABC, New York. 18 Nov. 1982.

———. Interview with Barbara Walters. *20/20*. ABC. WABC, New York. 5 Mar. 1993.

———. Letter to Herman Tarnower. 8–9 Mar. 1980. *Mrs. Harris: The Death of the Scarsdale Diet Doctor*. By Diana Trilling. New York: Harcourt, 1981. 256–61.

———. *Marking Time*. 1991. New York: Zebra-Kensington, 1993.

———. *Stranger in Two Worlds*. New York: Macmillan, 1986.

Harris, Lis. "Di and Li." *New Yorker* 13 Sept. 1993: 91–99.

Harvey, James. *Romantic Comedy in Hollywood, from Lubitsch to Sturges.* New York: Knopf, 1987.

Harvey, Paul A. S. "*Nochan's Dream:* NHK Morning Serialized Television." *The Worlds of Japanese Popular Culture.* Ed. D. P. Martinez. Cambridge: Cambridge University Press, 1998. 133–51.

Hassan, Ihab. "The Burden of Mutual Perceptions: Japan and the United States." *Salmagundi* 85–86 (winter–spring 1990): 71–86.

Hawkins, Harriett. *Classics and Trash: Traditions and Taboos in High Literature and Popular Modern Genres.* Theory/Culture 1. Toronto: University of Toronto Press, 1990.

Hays, Will H. *The Memoirs of Will H. Hays.* Garden City, N.Y.: Doubleday, 1955.

Hearings before the President's Commission on the Assassination of President Kennedy. 26 vols. Washington, D.C.: United States Government Printing Office, 1964.

Hearst, William Randolph. *Selections from the Writings and Speeches of William Randolph Hearst.* Ed. E. F. Tompkins. San Francisco: n.p., 1948.

Hearts of the World. Dir. and prod. D. W. Griffith. Scenario by Gaston de Tolignac [D. W. Griffith]. Paramount-Artcraft, 1918.

Heath, Stephen. "Representing Television." *Logics of Television: Essays in Cultural Criticism.* Ed. Patricia Mellencamp. Theories of Contemporary Culture 11. Bloomington: Indiana University Press, 1990. 267–302.

Heide, Robert, and John Gilman. *Dime-Store Dream Parade: Popular Culture, 1925–1955.* New York: Dutton, 1979.

Hein, Laura E. "Growth versus Success: Japan's Economic Policy in Historical Perspective." *Postwar Japan as History.* Ed. Andrew Gordon. Berkeley: University of California Press, 1993. 99–122.

Held, David. "The Decline of the Nation State." *New Times: The Changing Face of Politics in the 1990s.* Ed. Stuart Hall and Martin Jacques. London: Lawrence and Wishart, 1990. 191–204. Rpt. in *Becoming National: A Reader.* Ed. Geoff Eley and Ronald Grigor Suny. New York: Oxford University Press, 1996. 407–16.

Held, George. "Men on the Moon: American Novelists Explore Lunar Space." *Michigan Quarterly Review* 18 (1979): 318–42.

Hines, Samuel M., Jr. "Political Change in America: Perspectives from the Popular Historical Novels of Michener and Vidal." *Political Mythology and Popular Fiction.* Ed. Ernest J. Yanarella and Lee Sigelman. Westport, Conn.: Greenwood, 1988. 81–99.

Hobsbawm, Eric. *The Age of Extremes: A History of the World, 1914–1991.* New York: Pantheon, 1994.

———. "Inventing Traditions." Introduction. *The Invention of Tradition.* Ed. Eric Hobsbawm and Terence Ranger. Cambridge: Cambridge University Press, 1983. 1–14.

———. "Mass-Producing Traditions: Europe, 1870–1914." *The Invention of Tradition.* Ed. Eric Hobsbawm and Terence Ranger. Cambridge: Cambridge University Press, 1983. 263–307.

Hoggart, Richard. *The Uses of Literacy: Changing Patterns in English Mass Culture.* Fair Lawn, N.J.: Essential, 1957.

Holquist, Michael. "How to Play Utopia: Some Brief Notes on the Distinctiveness of

Utopian Fiction." *Yale French Studies* 41 (1968): 106–23. Rpt. in *Science Fiction: A Collection of Critical Essays*. Ed. Mark Rose. Englewood Cliffs, N.J.: Prentice, 1976. 132–46.

Hopkins, Harry. *The New Look: A Social History of the Forties and Fifties in Britain*. Boston: Houghton, 1964.

Horkheimer, Max, and Theodor W. Adorno. *Dialectic of Enlightenment*. Trans. John Cumming. 1972. New York: Continuum, 1997. Trans. of *Dialektik der Aufklärung: Philosophische Fragmente*. 1944

Horton, Andrew S. "Ken Kesey, John Updike and the Lone Ranger." *Journal of Popular Culture* 8 (1974): 570–78.

Hughes, Psiche Bertini. "Traditional and New Readings of Puig's *Pubis angelical*." *Revista Interamericana de Bibliografía* 42 (1992): 148–55.

Huntington, John. "Science Fiction and the Future." *College English* 37 (1975): 345–52. Rpt. in *Science Fiction: A Collection of Critical Essays*. Ed. Mark Rose. Englewood Cliffs, N.J.: Prentice, 1976. 156–66.

Hutcheon, Linda. *A Poetics of Postmodernism: History, Theory, Fiction*. London: Routledge, 1988.

———. *The Politics of Postmodernism*. New Accents. London: Routledge, 1989.

Huyssen, Andreas. *After the Great Divide: Modernism, Mass Culture, Postmodernism*. Theories of Representation and Difference. 1986. Bloomington: Indiana University Press, 1987.

Inoue Osamu. "Advertising in Japan: Changing Times for an Economic Giant." *Advertising in Asia: Communication, Culture, and Consumption*. Ed. Katherine Toland Firth. Ames: Iowa State University Press, 1996. 11–38.

International Commission for the Study of Communication Problems. *Many Voices, One World: Towards a New More Just and More Efficient World Information and Communication Order*. London: Kogan Page, 1980.

"Iraq on the March." *Time* 13 Aug. 1990: cover.

Irokawa Daikichi. *The Age of Hirohito: In Search of Modern Japan*. New York: Free, 1995.

Isenberg, Michael T. *War on Film: The American Cinema and World War I, 1914–1941*. Rutherford, N.J.: Fairleigh Dickinson University Press, 1981.

Ishihara Shintaro. *The Japan That Can Say No*. Trans. Frank Baldwin. New York: Simon, 1991. Trans. of *Nō to ieru Nihon*. 1989.

Isozaki Arata. "Of City, Nation, and Style." *Postmodernism and Japan*. Ed. Masao Miyoshi and H. D. Harootunian. Post-Contemporary Interventions. Durham: Duke University Press, 1989. 47–62.

Ito Masami. *Broadcasting in Japan*. London: Routledge, 1978.

Ivy, Marilyn. "Critical Texts, Mass Artifacts: The Consumption of Knowledge in Postmodern Japan." *Postmodernism and Japan*. Ed. Masao Miyoshi and H. D. Harootunian. Post-Contemporary Interventions. Durham: Duke University Press, 1989. 21–46.

———. *Discourses of the Vanishing: Modernity, Phantasm, Japan*. Chicago: University of Chicago Press, 1995.

———. "Formations of Mass Culture." *Postwar Japan as History*. Ed. Andrew Gordon. Berkeley: University of California Press, 1993. 239–58.

Iwamoto, Yoshio. "A Voice from Postmodern Japan." *World Literature Today* 67 (1993): 295–300.

Jacobs, Naomi. "The Frozen Landscape in Women's Utopian and Science Fiction." *Utopian and Science Fiction by Women: Worlds of Difference*. Ed. Jane L. Donawerth and Carol A. Kolmerten. Syracuse: Syracuse University Press, 1994. 190–202, 228–29.

Jameson, Fredric. *Postmodernism, or, The Cultural Logic of Late Capitalism*. Post-Contemporary Interventions. Durham: Duke University Press, 1991.

———. "Reification and Utopia in Mass Culture." *Social Text* 1 (winter 1979): 130–48.

———. *Signatures of the Visible*. New York: Routledge, 1990.

"Japan Invades Hollywood." *Newsweek* 9 Oct. 1989: cover.

Jarvie, Ian. *Hollywood's Overseas Campaign: The North Atlantic Movie Trade, 1920–1950*. Cambridge Studies in the Hist. of Mass Communications. Cambridge: Cambridge University Press, 1992.

Johnson, Chalmers. "The People Who Invented the Mechanical Nightingale." *Daedalus* 119.3 (1990): 71–90.

Johnson, Kirk. "As Options Shrink, New York Revisits Idea of Incineration." *New York Times* 23 Mar. 2002, late ed.: A1+.

———. "Commissioner Defends Plan for Garbage and Recycling." *New York Times* 21 Mar. 2002, late ed.: B4.

———. "To City's Burden, Add 11,000 Tons of Daily Trash." *New York Times* 28 Feb. 2002, late ed.: A1+.

Johnson, Leola, and David Roediger. " 'Hertz, Don't It?' Becoming Colorless and Staying Black in the Crossover of O. J. Simpson." *Birth of a Nation'hood: Gaze, Script, and Spectacle in the O. J. Simpson Case*. Ed. Toni Morrison and Claudia Brodsky Lacour. New York: Pantheon, 1997. 197–239.

Johnston, John. "Generic Difficulties in the Novels of Don DeLillo." *Critique* 30 (1989): 261–75.

———. *Information Multiplicity: American Fiction in the Age of Media Saturation*. Baltimore: Johns Hopkins University Press, 1998.

———. "Superlinear Fiction or Historical Diagram? Don DeLillo's *Libra*." *Modern Fiction Studies* 40 (1994): 319–42.

Jones, Thomas A. *J. Wilkes Booth: An Account of His Sojourn in Southern Maryland after the Assassination of Abraham Lincoln, His Passage across the Potomac, and His Death in Virginia*. 1893. Bowie, Md.: Heritage, 1990.

Jordan, Pat. "The Outcast: Conversations with O. J. Simpson." *New Yorker* 9 July 2001: 42–47.

Kael, Pauline. "Dreamers." Rev. of *Pennies from Heaven*, dir. Herbert Ross. *New Yorker* 21 Dec. 1981: 122–26.

Kanise, Seiichi, and Elaine Lafferty. "From Walkman to Showman." *Time* 9 Oct. 1989: 70–71.

Kantor, Kenneth Aaron. *The Jews on Tin Pan Alley: The Jewish Contribution to American Popular Music, 1830–1940*. New York: Ktav, 1982.

Kaplan, Amy. "The Birth of an Empire." PMLA 114 (1999): 1068–79.

Karaganis, Joseph. "Naturalism's Nation: Toward *An American Tragedy*." *American Literature* 72 (2000): 153–80.

Karnicky, Jeffrey. "Wallpaper Mao: Don DeLillo, Andy Warhol, and Seriality." *Critique* 42 (2001): 339–56.

Kasza, Gregory J. *The State and the Mass Media in Japan, 1918–1945*. Berkeley: University of California Press, 1988.

Katō Hidetoshi. "Japanese Popular Culture Reconsidered." *Handbook of Japanese Popular Culture*. Ed. Richard Gid Powers and Hidetoshi Katō. Westport, Conn.: Greenwood, 1989. 301–18.

Katz, Elihu, and Paul F. Lazarsfeld. *Personal Influence: The Part Played by People in the Flow of Mass Communications*. Foundations of Communications Research 2. Glencoe, Ill.: Free, 1955.

Kavadlo, Jesse. "Recycling Authority: DeLillo's Waste Management." *Critique* 42 (2001): 384–401.

Kellner, Douglas. *The Persian Gulf TV War*. Critical Studies in Communication and in the Cultural Industries. Boulder: Westview, 1992.

————. "TV, Ideology, and Emancipatory Popular Culture." *Socialist Review* 9.3 (1979): 13–53. Rpt. in *Television: The Critical View*. Ed. Horace Newcomb. 1976. 4th ed. New York: Oxford University Press, 1987. 471–503.

Kelly, William W. "Finding a Place in Metropolitan Japan: Ideologies, Institutions, and Everyday Life." *Postwar Japan as History*. Ed. Andrew Gordon. Berkeley: University of California Press, 1993. 189–216.

————. "Rationalization and Nostalgia: Cultural Dynamics of New Middle-Class Japan." *American Ethnologist* 13 (1986): 603–18.

Kennedy, Paul. *The Rise and Fall of the Great Powers: Economic Change and Military Conflict from 1500 to 2000*. New York: Random, 1987.

Kerr, Lucille. "The Dis-Appearance of a Popular Author: Stealing around Style with Manuel Puig's *Pubis angelical*." *Reclaiming the Author: Figures and Fictions from Spanish America*. Durham: Duke University Press, 1992. 89–110, 193–99.

————. "Reading between the Lines, Reading between the Lies: Manuel Puig's *Maldición eterna a quien lea estas páginas*." *World Literature Today* 65 (1991): 617–24.

————. *Suspended Fictions: Reading Novels by Manuel Puig*. Urbana: University of Illinois Press, 1987.

Klapper, Joseph T. *The Effects of Mass Communication*. Foundations of Communications Research 3. Glencoe, Ill.: Free, 1960.

Kracauer, Siegfried. "The Mass Ornament." Trans. Barbara Correll and Jack Zipes. *New German Critique* 5 (spring 1975): 67–76. Trans. of "Das Ornament der Masse." *Frankfurter Zeitung* 9–10 July 1927.

Krauss, Ellis S. "Portraying the State: NHK Television News and Politics." *Media and Politics in Japan.* Ed. Susan J. Pharr and Ellis S. Krauss. Honolulu: University of Hawai'i Press, 1996. 89–129.

Kristof, Nicholas D. "A Would-Be Anthem in Search of a Meaning." *New York Times* 15 July 1999, late ed.: A8.

Kroker, Arthur, and David Cook. *The Postmodern Scene: Excremental Culture and Hyper-Aesthetics.* New World Perspectives, CultureTexts Ser. Houndmills, Eng.: Macmillan Education, 1988.

Kronick, Joseph. "*Libra* and the Assassination of JFK: A Textbook Operation." *Arizona Quarterly* 50.1 (1994): 113–32.

Krupnick, Mark. "The Trillings: A Marriage of True Minds?" Rev. of *The Beginning of the Journey: The Marriage of Diana and Lionel Trilling,* by Diana Trilling. *Salmagundi* 103 (1994): 213–24.

Kucich, John. "Postmodern Politics: Don DeLillo and the Plight of the White Male Writer." *Michigan Quarterly Review* 27 (1988): 328–41.

Kuhn, Annette. *Women's Pictures: Feminism and Cinema.* London: Routledge, 1982.

Labanyi, Jo. "Voyeurism and Narrative Pleasure in Manuel Puig's *The Buenos Aires Affair.*" *Romance Studies* 19 (1991): 105–16.

Lacour, Claudia Brodsky. "The 'Interest' of the Simpson Trial: Spectacle, National History, and the Notion of Disinterested Judgment." *Birth of a Nation'hood: Gaze, Script, and Spectacle in the O. J. Simpson Case.* Ed. Toni Morrison and Claudia Brodsky Lacour. New York: Pantheon, 1997. 367–413.

Lahue, Kalton C. *Continued Next Week: A History of the Moving Picture Serial.* Norman: University of Oklahoma Press, 1964.

Lamarr, Hedy. *Ecstasy and Me: My Life as a Woman.* New York: Bartholomew, 1966.

Landler, Mark, and Ronald Grover. "Sony's Heartaches in Hollywood." With David Greising. *Business Week* 5 Dec. 1994: 44.

Lang, Robert. "*The Birth of a Nation:* History, Ideology, Narrative Form." The Birth of a Nation: *D. W. Griffith, Director.* Ed. Robert Lang. Rutgers Films in Print 21. New Brunswick: Rutgers University Press, 1994. 3–24.

Langer, John. "Television's 'Personality System.'" *Media, Culture and Society* 3 (1981): 351–65.

La Place, Maria. "Bette Davis and the Ideal of Consumption." *Wide Angle* 6.4 (1985): 34–43.

LeClair, Tom. *In the Loop: Don DeLillo and the Systems Novel.* Urbana: University of Illinois Press, 1987.

Lefanu, Sarah. *Feminism and Science Fiction.* Bloomington: Indiana University Press, 1989.

Lefebvre, Henri. *Everyday Life in the Modern World.* Trans. Sacha Rabinovitch. Classics in Communication and Mass Culture. New Brunswick: Transaction, 1984. Trans. of *La vie quotidienne dans le monde moderne.* 1968.

Le Guin, Ursula K. "American SF and The Other." *Science-Fiction Studies* 2 (1975): 208–
10. Rpt. in *The Language of the Night: Essays on Fantasy and Science Fiction*. Ed. Susan
Wood. New York: Putnam's, 1979. 97–99.

———. "Is Gender Necessary?" *Aurora: Beyond Equality*. Ed. Vonda N. McIntyre and
Susan J. Anderson. Greenwich, Conn.: Fawcett, 1976. 130–39.

———. "Is Gender Necessary? Redux." 1987. *Dancing at the Edge of the World: Thoughts
on Words, Women, Places*. New York: Grove, 1989. 7–16.

Lentricchia, Frank. "*Libra* as Postmodern Critique." *Introducing Don DeLillo*. Ed. Frank
Lentricchia. Durham: Duke University Press, 1991. 193–215.

Lescaze, Lee. "Headmistress Planned to Die, Officer Testifies." *Washington Post* 15 Mar.
1980, final ed.: A1+.

Lescaze, Lee, and Blaine Harden. "Diet Author Slain; Madeira School Headmistress
Held." *Washington Post* 12 Mar. 1980, final ed.: A1+.

Levin, Meyer. *Compulsion*. 1956. New York: Cardinal-Pocket, 1958.

Levine, Lawrence W. *Highbrow/Lowbrow: The Emergence of Cultural Hierarchy in America*. 1988. Cambridge: Harvard University Press, 1990.

Levine, Suzanne Jill. *Manuel Puig and the Spider Woman: His Life and Fictions*. New York:
Farrar, 2000.

Lipsitz, George. "The Greatest Story Ever Sold: Marketing and the O. J. Simpson Trial."
Birth of a Nation'hood: Gaze, Script, and Spectacle in the O. J. Simpson Case. Ed. Toni
Morrison and Claudia Brodsky Lacour. New York: Pantheon, 1997. 3–29.

Lipton, Eric. "Trash Transfer to New Jersey Is Postponed." *New York Times* 19 Sept. 2001,
late ed.: A20.

Lipton, Eric, and James Glanz. "In Last Piles of Rubble, Fresh Pangs of Loss." *New York
Times* 17 Mar. 2002, late ed.: 1+.

Los Angeles Times 12–13 Mar. 1980.

Lott, Eric. "White Like Me: Racial Cross-Dressing and the Construction of American
Whiteness." *Cultures of United States Imperialism*. Ed. Amy Kaplan and Donald E.
Pease. New Americanists. Durham: Duke University Press, 1993. 474–95.

Loughman, Celeste. "No Place I Was Meant to Be: Contemporary Japan in the Short
Fiction of Haruki Murakami." *World Literature Today* 71 (1997): 87–94.

Low, Rachel. *Film Making in 1930s Britain*. London: George Allen and Unwin, 1985.

Lukács, Georg. *The Historical Novel*. Trans. Hannah and Stanley Mitchell. 1962. Boston:
Beacon, 1963. Trans. of *A történelmi regény*. 1937.

Lynes, Russell. *The Tastemakers*. New York: Harper, 1954.

Mac Adam, Alfred J. "Manuel Puig's Chronicles of Provincial Life." *Revista Hispánica
Moderna* 36 (1970–71): 50–65.

Macdonald, Dwight. "A Theory of Mass Culture." *Diogenes* 3 (summer 1953): 1–17. Rpt. in
Mass Culture: The Popular Arts in America. Ed. Bernard Rosenberg and David Manning White. 1957. New York: Free-Macmillan, 1964. 59–73.

Mailer, Norman. *The Armies of the Night: History as a Novel, the Novel as History*. New
York: Signet–New American Library, 1968.

———. *The Deer Park*. 1955. New York: Berkley Windhover, 1976.

————. *The Executioner's Song.* 1979. New York: Warner, 1980.

————. "An Interview with Norman Mailer." With John W. Aldridge. *Partisan Review* 47 (1980): 174–82.

————. *Oswald's Tale: An American Mystery.* New York: Random, 1995.

————. "Some Children of the Goddess." *Esquire* July 1963: 63–69, 105. Rpt. in *Cannibals and Christians.* 1966. New York: Dell, 1967. 104–30.

————. "Superman Comes to the Supermart." *Esquire* Nov. 1960: 119–27. Rpt. as "Superman Comes to the Supermarket." *The Presidential Papers.* 1963. New York: Berkley Medallion, 1970. 25–61.

Maltin, Leonard. *The Disney Films.* New York: Bonanza, 1973.

Margolick, David. "Back in the Courtroom for People v. Simpson." *New York Times* 12 Nov. 2000, late ed., sec. 2: 31+.

————. "O.J.'s Ghost." *Vanity Fair* Nov. 1996: 108, 110, 112, 114, 116, 118, 121–22, 124, 126.

Marie Antoinette. Dir. W. S. Van Dyke II. Prod. Hunt Stromberg. Screenplay by Claudine West, Donald Ogden Stewart, Ernest Vajda. MGM, 1938.

Marinov, Samuel G. "*Pennies from Heaven, The Singing Detective* and *Lipstick on Your Collar:* Redefining the Genre of Musical Film." *The Passion of Dennis Potter: International Collected Essays.* Ed. Vernon W. Gras and John R. Cook. New York: St. Martin's, 2000. 195–204.

Marquis, Christopher. "For Allies, 'I Do' Becomes 'Hey, Want to Dance?' " *New York Times* 14 Apr. 2002, late ed., sec. 4: 5.

Martin, Emily. "The End of the Body?" *American Ethnologist* 19 (1992): 121–40.

Martin, Troy Kennedy. " 'Nats Go Home': First Statement of a New Drama for Television." *Encore* 11.2 (Mar.–Apr. 1964): 21–33.

Martínez, Tomás Eloy. "Eva Perón, semidiosa de Hollywood." *Panorama* 24 Feb. 1970: 43–44.

————. *Santa Evita.* Trans. Helen Lane. New York: Knopf, 1996. Trans. of *Santa Evita.* 1995.

Masiello, Francine R. "Jail House Flicks: Projections by Manuel Puig." *Symposium* 32 (1978): 15–24.

Mason, Bobbie Ann. *In Country.* 1985. New York: Perennial-Harper, 1986.

Mazurek, Raymond A. " 'Bringing the Corners Forward': Ideology and Representation in Updike's Rabbit Trilogy." *Politics and the Muse: Studies in the Politics of Recent American Literature.* Ed. Adam J. Sorkin. Bowling Green: Bowling Green State University Popular Press, 1989. 142–60.

Mellencamp, Patricia. "TV Time and Catastrophe, or *Beyond the Pleasure Principle* of Television." *Logics of Television: Essays in Cultural Criticism.* Ed. Patricia Mellencamp. Theories of Contemporary Culture 11. Bloomington: Indiana University Press, 1990. 240–66.

Merrim, Stephanie. "For a New (Psychological) Novel in the Works of Manuel Puig." *Novel* 17 (1984): 141–57.

————. "Through the Film Darkly: Grade 'B' Movies and Dreamwork in *Tres tristes tigres* and *El beso de la mujer araña.*" *Modern Language Studies* 15.4 (1985): 300–312.

Metz, Christian. *The Imaginary Signifier: Psychoanalysis and the Cinema.* Trans. Celia Britton, Annwyl Williams, Ben Brewster, and Alfred Guzzetti. Bloomington: Indiana University Press, 1982. Trans. of *Le signifiant imaginaire: Psychanalyse et Cinéma.* 1977.

Miller, D. Quentin. *John Updike and the Cold War: Drawing the Iron Curtain.* Columbia: University of Missouri Press, 2001.

Miller, Jonathan. "Trash Museum Is, Um, Trashed." *New York Times* 27 May 2001, late ed., sec. 14NJ: 8.

Miller, Toby, and Alec McHoul. *Popular Culture and Everyday Life.* London: Sage, 1998.

Miyoshi, Masao. *Off Center: Power and Culture Relations between Japan and the United States.* Convergences: Inventories of the Present. Cambridge: Harvard University Press, 1991.

Miyoshi, Masao, and H. D. Harootunian. Introduction. *Postmodernism and Japan.* Ed. Masao Miyoshi and H. D. Harootunian. Post-Contemporary Interventions. Durham: Duke University Press, 1989. vii–xix.

Modleski, Tania. *Loving with a Vengeance: Mass-Produced Fantasies for Women.* New York: Routledge, 1996.

Molesworth, Charles. "Don DeLillo's Perfect Starry Night." *Introducing Don DeLillo.* Ed. Frank Lentricchia. Durham: Duke University Press, 1991. 143–56.

Morris, Matthew J. "Murdering Words: Language in Action in Don DeLillo's *The Names.*" *Contemporary Literature* 30 (1989): 113–27.

Morrison, Toni. "The Official Story: Dead Man Golfing." Introduction. *Birth of a Nation'hood: Gaze, Script, and Spectacle in the O. J. Simpson Case.* Ed. Toni Morrison and Claudia Brodsky Lacour. New York: Pantheon, 1997. vii–xxviii.

Moses, Gavriel. "You Can't Imagine." *The Nickel Was for the Movies: Film in the Novel from Pirandello to Puig.* Berkeley: University of California Press, 1995. 233–56, 297–300.

Mott, Christopher M. "*Libra* and the Subject of History." *Critique* 35 (1994): 131–45. ✔

Mugridge, Ian. *The View from Xanadu: William Randolph Hearst and United States Foreign Policy.* Montreal: McGill-Queens University Press, 1995.

Mulvey, Laura. *Visual and Other Pleasures.* Theories of Representation and Difference. Bloomington: Indiana University Press, 1989.

Murakami Haruki. *Dance, Dance, Dance.* Trans. Alfred Birnbaum. 1994. New York: Vintage-Random, 1995. Trans. of *Dansu dansu dansu.* 1988.

———. *The Elephant Vanishes.* Trans. Alfred Birnbaum and Jay Rubin. 1993. New York: Vintage-Random, 1994.

———. *Hard-Boiled Wonderland and the End of the World.* Trans. Alfred Birnbaum. 1991. New York: Vintage-Random, 1993. Trans. of *Sekai no owari to hādo-boirudo wandārando.* 1985.

———. *Underground.* Trans. Alfred Birnbaum and Philip Gabriel. 2000. New York: Vintage-Random, 2001. Trans. of *Andaguraundo* and *Yakusoku sareta basho de.* 1997, 1998.

———. *A Wild Sheep Chase.* Trans. Alfred Birnbaum. 1989. New York: Plume-Penguin, 1990. Trans. of *Hitsuji o meguru bōken.* 1982.

————. *The Wind-Up Bird Chronicle*. Trans. Jay Rubin. New York: Knopf, 1997. Trans. of *Nejimaki-dori kuronikuru*. 1994, 1995.

Murakami Haruki, and Jay McInerny. "Roll Over Basho: Who Japan Is Reading, and Why." *New York Times Book Review* 27 Sept. 1992: 1, 28–29.

Murphy, Robert. "Under the Shadow of Hollywood." *All Our Yesterdays: 90 Years of British Cinema*. Ed. Charles Barr. London: British Film Institute, 1986. 47–71.

The Museum of Television and Radio. *The Television of Dennis Potter*. New York: 23 Jan.–31 May 1992. 1991.

Musser, Charles. *The Emergence of Cinema: The American Screen to 1907*. Hist. of the Amer. Cinema 1. New York: Scribner's, 1990.

Naipaul, V. S. "The Return of Eva Perón." *The Return of Eva Perón, with the Killings in Trinidad*. London: André Deutsch, 1980. 93–170.

The Naked Gun. Dir. David Zucker. Prod. Robert K. Weiss. Screenplay by Jerry Zucker, Jim Abrahams, David Zucker, and Pat Proft. Paramount, 1988.

Naked Gun 33$^1/_3$: The Final Insult. Dir. Peter Segal. Prod. Robert K. Weiss and David Zucker. Screenplay by Pat Proft, David Zucker, and Robert LoCash. Paramount, 1994.

The Naked Gun 2$^1/_2$: The Smell of Fear. Dir. David Zucker. Prod. Robert K. Weiss. Screenplay by David Zucker and Pat Proft. Paramount, 1991.

Nasaw, David. *The Chief: The Life of William Randolph Hearst*. Boston: Houghton, 2000.

Nel, Philip. " 'A Small Incisive Shock': Modern Forms, Postmodern Politics, and the Role of the Avant-Garde in *Underworld*." *Modern Fiction Studies* 45 (1999): 724–52.

Newman, Judie. *John Updike*. New York: St. Martin's, 1988.

————. "*Rabbit at Rest*: The Return of the Work Ethic." *Rabbit Tales: Poetry and Politics in John Updike's Rabbit Novels*. Ed. Lawrence R. Broer. Tuscaloosa: University of Alabama Press, 1998. 189–206.

New York [Sunday] American 13 June–29 Aug. 1915; 14 Jan.–22 Apr. 1917.

New York Times 12–15 Mar. 1980.

New York World 13 Nov.–11 Dec. 1906; 31 Mar. 1908.

"The NFL on NBC." *Saturday Night Live*. 7 Oct. 1995. Transcript. <http://snltranscripts.jt.org/scripts/95bnflonnbc.phtml>.

Norris, Christopher. *Uncritical Theory: Postmodernism, Intellectuals and the Gulf War*. Amherst: University of Massachusetts Press, 1992.

Norris, Margot. "Only the Guns Have Eyes: Military Censorship and the Body Count." *Seeing through the Media: The Persian Gulf War*. Ed. Susan Jeffords and Lauren Rabinovitz. Communications, Media, and Culture. New Brunswick: Rutgers University Press, 1994. 285–300.

O'Donnell, Patrick. "National Trauma and the Cultural Imaginary: Narrating Paranoia in DeLillo's *Libra* and Stone's *JFK*." Narrative: An International Conference. Society for the Study of Narrative Literature. Desmond Hotel, Albany. 2 Apr. 1993.

Ōe Kenzaburō. "Japan's Dual Identity: A Writer's Dilemma." *World Literature Today* 62 (1988): 359–69.

O'Grady, Jim. "Requiem for a Garbage Dump." *New York Times* 25 Mar. 2001, late ed., sec. 14: 3.

———. "To an Artist's Eyes, Beauty Is Trash, and Trash Beauty." *New York Times* 20 Jan. 2002, late ed., sec. 14: 4.

O'Hara, John. *The Big Laugh.* 1962. Hopewell, N.J.: Ecco, 1997.

Older, Mrs. Fremont [Cora Baggerly Older]. *William Randolph Hearst: American.* New York: Appleton Century, 1936.

Orlov, Paul A. An American Tragedy: *Perils of the Self Seeking "Success."* Lewisburg, Pa.: Bucknell University Press, 1998.

Orphans of the Storm. Dir. D. W. Griffith. Prod. D. W. Griffith, Inc. Scenario by Marquis de Trolignac [D. W. Griffith]. United Artists, 1921.

Ortiz, Alicia Dujovne. *Eva Perón.* Trans. Shawn Fields. New York: St. Martin's, 1996. Trans. of *Eva Perón.* 1995.

Osteen, Mark. *American Magic and Dread: Don DeLillo's Dialogue with Culture.* Penn Studies in Contemporary American Fiction. Philadelphia: University of Pennsylvania Press, 2000.

———. "Children of Godard and Coca-Cola: Cinema and Consumerism in Don DeLillo's Early Fiction." *Contemporary Literature* 37 (1996): 439–70.

Oswald, Robert L. *Lee: A Portrait of Lee Harvey Oswald by His Brother.* With Myrick and Barbara Land. New York: Coward-McCann, 1967.

Page, Joseph A. "Chronology of Eva Perón's Life." *In My Own Words: Evita.* Ed. Joseph A. Page. New York: New Press, 1996. 115–19.

———. *Perón: A Biography.* New York: Random, 1983.

Painter, Andrew A. "Japanese Daytime Television, Popular Culture, and Ideology." *Journal of Japanese Studies* 19 (1993): 295–325.

Parini, Jay. "Gore Vidal: The Writer and His Critics." *Gore Vidal: Writer against the Grain.* Ed. Jay Parini. New York: Columbia University Press, 1992. 1–30, 291–93.

Parrish, Timothy L. "From Hoover's FBI to Eisenstein's *Unterwelt:* DeLillo Directs the Postmodern Novel." *Modern Fiction Studies* 45 (1999): 696–723.

Patria. Dir. Theodore Wharton, Leo Wharton, and Jacques Jaccard. Prod. International Film Service. Pathé, 1917. 15 episodes.

Pearsall, Ronald. *Popular Music of the Twenties.* Totowa, N.J.: Rowman and Littlefield, 1976.

Pearson, Carol. "Women's Fantasies and Feminist Utopias." *Frontiers* (fall 1977): 50–61. Rev. and rpt. as "Coming Home: Four Feminist Utopias and Patriarchal Experience." *Future Females: A Critical Anthology.* Ed. Marleen S. Barr. Bowling Green: Bowling Green State University Popular Press, 1981. 63–70.

Pease, Donald E. "Citizen Vidal and Mailer's America." *Raritan* 11.4 (1992): 72–98. Rev. and rpt. as "America and the Vidal Chronicles." *Gore Vidal: Writer against the Grain.* Ed. Jay Parini. New York: Columbia University Press, 1992. 247–77, 303–5.

Pellón, Gustavo. "Manuel Puig's Contradictory Strategy: Kitsch Paradigms *versus* Paradigmatic Structure in *El beso de la mujer araña* and *Pubis angelical.*" *Symposium* 37 (1983): 186–201.

"Pennies from Heaven." Music by Arthur Johnston. Lyrics by John Burke. 1936. *Songs of the 30's: The Decade Series.* Milwaukee: Hal Leonard, 1989. 144–46.

The Perils of Pauline. Dir. Louise Gaznier and Donald MacKenzie. Pathé, 1914. 20 episodes.

Perón, Eva. *History of Peronism.* Buenos Aires: Servicio Internacional Publicaciones Argentinas, 1951.

———. "My Message." Trans. Laura Dail. *In My Own Words: Evita.* Ed. Joseph A. Page. New York: New Press, 1996. 47–92. Trans. of *Mi mensaje.* 1987.

———. *My Mission in Life.* Trans. Ethel Cherry. New York: Vantage, 1952. Trans. of *La razón de mi vida.* 1951.

Perón, Juan Domingo. *Perón Expounds His Doctrine.* 1948. New York: AMS, 1973.

Perry, Nancy J. "Will Sony Make It in Hollywood?" *Fortune* 9 Sept. 1991: 158–60, 162, 164, 166.

Pinet, Carolyn. "Who Is the Spider Woman?" *Rocky Mountain Review of Language and Literature* 45 (1991): 19–34.

Pizer, Donald. *The Novels of Theodore Dreiser: A Critical Study.* Minneapolis: University of Minnesota Press, 1976.

Plath, James. "Verbal Vermeer: Updike's Middle-Class Portraiture." *Rabbit Tales: Poetry and Politics in John Updike's Rabbit Novels.* Ed. Lawrence R. Broer. Tuscaloosa: University of Alabama Press, 1998. 207–30.

Poirier, Richard. "American Emperors." *New York Review of Books* 24 Sept. 1987: 31–33. Rev. and rpt. as "Vidal's *Empire.*" *Gore Vidal: Writer against the Grain.* Ed. Jay Parini. New York: Columbia University Press, 1992. 230–38.

Potter, Dennis. *Between Two Rivers.* Prod. Anthony de Lotbinière. BBC. London. 3 June 1960.

———. *Blade on the Feather.* Dir. Richard Loncraine. Prod. Kenith Trodd. ITV. London. 19 Oct. 1980.

———. *Blue Remembered Hills.* Play for Today. Dir. Brian Gibson. Prod. Kenith Trodd. BBC-1. London. 30 Jan. 1979. *Waiting for the Boat: On Television.* London: Faber, 1984. 37–85.

———. *The Bonegrinder.* Playhouse. Dir. and prod. Joan Kemp-Welch. ITV. London. 13 Mar. 1968.

———. "Bunk Holiday." *New Statesman* 30 May 1975: 736–37.

———. *The Changing Forest: Life in the Forest of Dean.* London: Secker and Warburg, 1962.

———. *Cold Lazarus.* Dir. Renny Rye. Prod. Kenith Trodd and Rosemarie Whitman. Channel Four. London. 26 May–16 June 1996. *Karaoke and Cold Lazarus.* London: Faber, 1996. 193–392.

———. "Embalmed." *New Statesman* 27 Feb. 1976: 268–69.

———. "Flay It Again." *New Statesman* 28 Mar. 1975: 428.

———. *Follow the Yellow Brick Road.* The Sextet. Dir. Alan Bridges. Prod. Roderick Graham. BBC-2. London. 4 July 1972. *The Television Dramatist.* Ed. Robert Muller. London: Paul Elek, 1973. 301–82.

———. *The Glittering Coffin.* London: Gollancz, 1960.

———. *Karaoke.* Dir. Renny Rye. Prod. Kenith Trodd and Rosemarie Whitman. BBC-

1. London. 28 Apr.–19 May 1996. *Karaoke and* Cold Lazarus. London: Faber, 1996. 1–192.

––––––. "Last Pearls." *Daily Telegraph* 4 June 1994, arts sec.: 2. Rpt. in *Dennis Potter: A Biography.* By Humphrey Carpenter. 1998. New York: St. Martin's, 1999. 575–78.

––––––. *Lipstick on Your Collar.* Dir. Renny Rye. Prod. Dennis Potter. Channel Four. London. 21 Feb.–28 Mar. 1993. London: Faber, 1993.

––––––. "Mimic Men." *New Statesman* 13 Sept. 1974: 357.

––––––. *Moonlight on the Highway.* Saturday Night Theatre. Dir. James MacTaggart. Prod. Kenith Trodd. ITV. London. 12 Apr. 1969.

––––––. *The Nigel Barton Plays.* Harmondsworth, Eng.: Penguin, 1967.

––––––. *Pennies from Heaven.* Dir. Piers Haggard. Prod. Kenith Trodd. BBC-1. London. 7 Mar.–11 Apr. 1978. London: Faber, 1996.

––––––. *Pennies from Heaven.* Dir. Herbert Ross. Prod. Nora Kaye and Herbert Ross. MGM, 1981.

––––––. *Pennies from Heaven.* London: Quartet, 1981.

––––––. "Poisonous Gas." *New Statesman* 28 May 1976: 724–25.

––––––. *Potter on Potter.* Ed. Graham Fuller. London: Faber, 1993.

––––––. "Reaction: Replies to Troy Kennedy Martin's Attack on Naturalistic Television Drama." *Encore* 11.3 (May–June 1964): 40.

––––––. *Seeing the Blossom: Two Interviews and a Lecture.* London: Faber, 1994.

––––––. *The Singing Detective.* Dir. Jon Amiel. Prod. Kenith Trodd and John Harris. BBC-1. London. 16 Nov.–21 Dec. 1986. New York: Vintage-Random, 1988.

––––––. *Stand Up, Nigel Barton.* The Wednesday Play. Dir. Gareth Davies. Prod. James MacTaggart. BBC-1. London. 8 Dec. 1965. *The Nigel Barton Plays.* Harmondsworth, Eng.: Penguin, 1967. 23–75.

––––––. "Stay Out of Our Parlour." *New Statesman* 24 May 1974: 744.

––––––. *Sufficient Carbohydrate.* London: Faber, 1983.

––––––. "Take a Break." *New Statesman* 27 Dec. 1974: 940–41.

––––––. Television Reviews. *New Statesman* 14 July–1 Sept. 1967; 11 Jan.–31 May 1974; 6 Sept. 1974–27 June 1975; 10 Oct.–7 Nov. 1975; 6 Feb.–28 May 1976.

––––––. *Traitor.* Play for Today. Dir. Alan Bridges. Prod. Graeme McDonald. BBC-1. London. 14 Oct. 1971.

––––––. "Violence Out of a Box." *New Statesman* 29 Nov. 1974: 796.

––––––. *Vote, Vote, Vote for Nigel Barton.* The Wednesday Play. Dir. Gareth Davies. Prod. James MacTaggart. BBC-1. London. 15 Dec. 1965. *The Nigel Barton Plays.* Harmondsworth, Eng.: Penguin, 1967. 77–125.

––––––. *Waiting for the Boat: On Television.* London: Faber, 1984.

––––––. *Where the Buffalo Roam.* The Wednesday Play. Dir. Gareth Davies. Prod. Lionel Harris. BBC-1. London. 2 Nov. 1966.

––––––. "Why Import This Trash?" *Daily Herald* 6 Aug. 1964: 7.

"Power without Purpose." Prod. Joseph Angier. Writ. Joseph Angier and Carl Byker. *Power in the Pacific.* Prod. Bruce Belsham. Australian Broadcasting Corporation and Community Television of Southern California. PBS. KCET, Los Angeles. 11 Nov. 1990.

Prestowitz, Clyde V., Jr. *Trading Places: How We Allowed Japan to Take the Lead.* New York: Basic, 1988.

Prince, Stephen. "Celluloid Heroes and Smart Bombs: Hollywood at War in the Middle East." *The Media and the Persian Gulf War.* Ed. Robert E. Denton Jr. Praeger Ser. in Political Communication. Westport, Conn.: Praeger, 1993. 235–56.

Puig, Manuel. *Betrayed by Rita Hayworth.* Trans. Suzanne Jill Levine. 1971. New York: Vintage-Random, 1981. Trans. of *La traición de Rita Hayworth.* 1968.

———. "Brief Encounter: An Interview with Manuel Puig." With Jorgelina Corbatta. Trans. Ilan Stavans. *Review of Contemporary Fiction* 11.3 (1991): 165–76. Trans. of "Encuentros con Manuel Puig." *Revista Iberoamericana* 49 (1983): 591–620.

———. *The Buenos Aires Affair: A Detective Novel.* Trans. Suzanne Jill Levine. 1976. New York: Vintage-Random, 1980. Trans. of *The Buenos Aires Affair: Novela policial.* 1973.

———. "Cinema and the Novel." Trans. Nick Caistor. *On Modern Latin American Fiction.* Ed. John King. New York: Noonday-Farrar, 1989. 283–90.

———. *Eternal Curse on the Reader of These Pages.* Trans. Manuel Puig. New York: Random, 1982. Trans. of *Maldición eterna a quien lea estas páginas.* 1980.

———. "Growing Up at the Movies: A Chronology." *Review* 4–5 (1971–72): 49–51.

———. *Heartbreak Tango: A Serial.* Trans. Suzanne Jill Levine. 1973. New York: Vintage-Random, 1981. Trans. of *Boquitas pintadas: Folletín.* 1969.

———. "An Interview with Manuel Puig." With Ronald Christ. *Partisan Review* 44 (1977): 52–61.

———. "Interview with Manuel Puig." With Ronald Christ. *Christopher Street* Apr. 1979: 25–31.

———. *Kiss of the Spider Woman.* Trans. Thomas Colchie. 1979. New York: Vintage-Random, 1980. Trans. of *El beso de la mujer araña.* 1976.

———. "Losing Readers in Argentina." *Index on Censorship* Oct. 1985: 55–57.

———. *Pubis Angelical.* Trans. Elena Brunet. New York: Vintage-Random, 1986. Trans. of *Pubis angelical.* 1979.

———. *Tropical Night Falling.* Trans. Suzanne Jill Levine. New York: Simon, 1991. Trans. of *Cae la noche tropical.* 1988.

Puig, Manuel, and Suzanne Jill Levine. "Author and Translator: A Discussion of Manuel Puig's *Heartbreak Tango.*" *Translation* 2 (1974): 32–41.

Purnick, Joyce. "The Politics of Garbage, Forever Ripe." *New York Times* 14 Mar. 2002, late ed.: B1.

Purser, Philip. "Dennis Potter." *British Television Drama.* Ed. George W. Brandt. Cambridge: Cambridge University Press, 1981. 168–93.

———. "Dennis's Other Hat." *The Passion of Dennis Potter: International Collected Essays.* Ed. Vernon W. Gras and John R. Cook. New York: St. Martin's, 2000. 179–93.

Pynchon, Thomas. *The Crying of Lot 49.* 1966. New York: Bantam, 1967.

———. *Vineland.* Boston: Little, 1990.

Radway, Janice A. *Reading the Romance: Women, Patriarchy, and Popular Literature.* 1984. Chapel Hill: University of North Carolina Press, 1991.

Rambo: First Blood Part II. Dir. George P. Cosmatos. Prod. Buzz Feitshans. Story by Kevin Jarre. Screenplay by Sylvester Stallone and James Cameron. Tri-Star, 1985.

Rambo III. Dir. Peter MacDonald. Prod. Buzz Feitshans. Screenplay by Sylvester Stallone and Sheldon Lettich. Carolco, 1988.

Reeve, Arthur B. *The Romance of Elaine.* With Charles W. Goddard. *New York [Sunday] American* 13 June 1915–29 Aug. 1915.

Regan, Robert Alton. "Updike's Symbol of the Center." *Modern Fiction Studies* 20 (1974): 77–96.

Reibstein, Larry, and Patricia King. "O.J. Family Values." *Newsweek* 17 Feb. 1997: 28–31.

Renan, Ernest. "What Is a Nation?" Trans. Martin Thom. *Nation and Narration.* Ed. Homi K. Bhabha. London: Routledge, 1990. 8–22. Trans. of "Qu'est-ce qu'une nation?" Sorbonne, Paris. 11 Mar. 1882. *Oeuvres Complètes.* Vol. 1. 887–907.

Rentschler, Eric. *The Ministry of Illusion: Nazi Cinema and Its Afterlife.* Cambridge: Harvard University Press, 1996.

Reynolds, David S. *Beneath the American Renaissance: The Subversive Imagination in the Age of Emerson and Melville.* 1988. Cambridge: Harvard University Press, 1989.

Rice-Sayre, Laura. "Domination and Desire: A Feminist-Materialist Reading of Manuel Puig's *Kiss of the Spider Woman*." *Textual Analysis: Some Readers Reading.* Ed. Mary Ann Caws. New York: Modern Language Association, 1986. 245–56.

Ristoff, Dilvo I. *John Updike's* Rabbit at Rest: *Appropriating History.* New York: Peter Lang, 1998.

———. *Updike's America: The Presence of Contemporary American History in John Updike's Rabbit Trilogy.* New York: Peter Lang, 1988.

Robinson, Sally. " 'Unyoung, Unpoor, Unblack': John Updike and the Construction of Middle American Masculinity." *Modern Fiction Studies* 44 (1998): 331–63.

Rock, David. *Argentina, 1516–1982: From Spanish Colonization to the Falklands War.* Berkeley: University of California Press, 1985.

———. *Authoritarian Argentina: The Nationalist Movement, Its History and Its Impact.* Berkeley: University of California Press, 1993.

Rodríguez Monegal, Emir. "A Literary Myth Exploded." Trans. Mary A. Kilmer. *Review* 4–5 (1971–72): 56–64. Trans. of "*La traición de Rita Hayworth* una tarea de desmistificación." *Imagen* 34 (Oct. 1968).

———. "Los sueños de Evita (a propósito de la última novela de Manuel Puig)." *Plural* 22 (1972): 34–36.

Rogin, Michael. " 'Make My Day!': Spectacle as Amnesia in Imperial Politics." *Representations* 29 (1990): 99–123. Rpt. with "The Sequel" in *Cultures of United States Imperialism.* Ed. Amy Kaplan and Donald E. Pease. New Americanists. Durham: Duke University Press, 1993. 499–534.

———. *Ronald Reagan, the Movie and Other Episodes in Political Demonology.* Berkeley: University of California Press, 1987.

———. " 'The Sword Became a Flashing Vision': D. W. Griffith's *The Birth of a Nation*." *Representations* 9 (1985): 150–95. Rpt. in The Birth of a Nation: *D. W. Griffith, Director.*

Ed. Robert Lang. Rutgers Films in Print 21. New Brunswick: Rutgers University Press, 1994. 250–93.

Román, David, and Alberto Sandoval. "Caught in the Web: Latinidad, AIDS, and Allegory in *Kiss of the Spider Woman, the Musical.*" *American Literature* 67 (1995): 553–85.

The Romance of Elaine. Dir. George B. Seitz. Pathé, 1915. 12 episodes.

Roosevelt, Theodore. *American Ideals.* 1897. New York: Review of Reviews, 1910.

———. *The Strenuous Life.* 1900. New York: Review of Reviews, 1910.

Roth, Mark. "Some Warners Musicals and the Spirit of the New Deal." *Velvet Light Trap* 17 (winter 1977): 1–7. Rpt. in *Genre: The Musical.* Ed. Rick Altman. British Film Institute Readers in Film Studies. London: Routledge, 1981. 41–56.

Rubin, Martin. *Showstoppers: Busby Berkeley and the Tradition of Spectacle.* New York: Columbia University Press, 1993.

Russ, Joanna. "The Image of Women in Science Fiction." 1971. *Images of Women in Fiction: Feminist Perspectives.* Ed. Susan Koppelman Cornillon. Bowling Green: Bowling Green State University Popular Press, 1972. 79–94.

———. "Some Recent Feminist Utopias." *Future Females: A Critical Anthology.* Ed. Marleen S. Barr. Bowling Green: Bowling Green State University Popular Press, 1981. 71–85.

Sack, Kevin. "Democrats Raise Money; Republicans Make Hay." *New York Times* 15 Sept. 2000, late ed.: A30.

Sakai, Naoki. "Modernity and Its Critique: The Problem of Universalism and Particularism." *Postmodernism and Japan.* Ed. Masao Miyoshi and H. D. Harootunian. Post-Contemporary Interventions. Durham: Duke University Press, 1989. 93–122.

Salzman, Jack. Introduction. "I Find the Real American Tragedy." By Theodore Dreiser. *Resources for American Literary Study* 2 (1972): 3–4.

Samples, Gordon. *Lust for Fame: The Stage Career of John Wilkes Booth.* Jefferson, N.C.: McFarland, 1982.

Sanders, Scott. "Woman as Nature in Science Fiction." *Future Females: A Critical Anthology.* Ed. Marleen S. Barr. Bowling Green: Bowling Green State University Popular Press, 1981. 42–59.

Sanger, David E. "Allies Hear Sour Notes in 'Axis of Evil' Chorus." *New York Times* 17 Feb. 2002, late ed.: 18.

Santoro, Patricia. "*Kiss of the Spider Woman,* Novel, Play, and Film: Homosexuality and the Discourse of the Maternal in a Third World Prison." *Framing Latin American Cinema: Contemporary Critical Perspectives.* Ed. Ann Marie Stock. Minneapolis: University of Minnesota Press, 1997. 120–40.

Sargent, Pamela. "Women in Science Fiction." *Futures* 7 (1975): 433–41.

Saunders, Thomas J. *Hollywood in Berlin: American Cinema and Weimar Germany.* Berkeley: University of California Press, 1994.

Scarface. Dir. Howard Hawks. Prod. Howard Hughes. Story by Ben Hecht. Dialogue by Seton I. Miller, John Lee Mahin, and W. R. Burnett. United Artists, 1932.

Schiller, Herbert I. *Mass Communications and American Empire.* 1969. 2nd ed. Critical Studies in Communication and in the Cultural Industries. Boulder: Westview, 1992.

Schiller, Lawrence, dir. and prod. *American Tragedy*. By Lawrence Schiller and James Willwerth. Teleplay by Norman Mailer. 2 parts. CBS. WCBS, New York. 12 and 15 Nov. 2000.

———. Foreword. *I Want to Tell You: My Response to Your Letters, Your Messages, Your Questions*. By O. J. Simpson. Boston: Little, 1995. vii–xiv.

———. *The Killing of Sharon Tate*. With Susan Atkins. New York: Signet–New American Library, 1970.

———. *Perfect Murder, Perfect Town: JonBenét and the City of Boulder*. With Charles Brennan. New York: HarperCollins, 1999.

———. "*Playboy* Interview." With David Sheff. *Playboy* Feb. 1997: 47–52, 146–51.

———, supervising prod. *The Trial of Lee Harvey Oswald*. By Amram Ducovny and Leon Friedman. Dir. David Greene. Prod. Richard Freed. Teleplay by Robert E. Thompson. 2 parts. 1976. Worldvision, 1986.

Schiller, Lawrence, and James Willwerth. *American Tragedy: The Uncensored Story of the Simpson Defense*. New York: Random, 1996.

Schilling, Mark. *The Encyclopedia of Japanese Pop Culture*. New York: Weatherhill, 1997.

Schlender, Brent. "They Can Make a Walkman, But Can They Make a Batman?" *Fortune* 12 June 1995: 70.

Schuetz, Janice. "Telelitigation and Its Challenges to Trial Discourse." Introduction. *The O. J. Simpson Trials: Rhetoric, Media, and the Law*. Ed. Janice Schuetz and Lin S. Lilley. Carbondale: Southern Illinois University Press, 1999. 1–18.

Schulberg, Budd. *What Makes Sammy Run?* 1941. New York: Vintage-Random, 1993.

Schulte-Sasse, Linda. *Entertaining the Third Reich: Illusions of Wholeness in Nazi Cinema*. Post-Contemporary Interventions. Durham: Duke University Press, 1996.

Schwartz, John. "Japan Goes Hollywood." With Joshua Hammer, Michael Reese, and Bill Powell. *Newsweek* 9 Oct. 1989: 62–67.

Schwartz, Tony. "Drama Based on the Jean Harris Trial." *New York Times* 2 May 1981, late city ed.: 48.

Sciolino, Elaine. "When a Little Production in Hollywood Freed Six Americans Trapped in Iran." *New York Times* 15 Apr. 2001, late ed., sec. 4: 7.

Segrave, Kerry. *American Films Abroad: Hollywood's Domination of the World's Movie Screens from the 1890s to the Present*. Jefferson, N.C.: McFarland, 1997.

Sella, Marshall. "The Stiff Guy vs. the Dumb Guy." *New York Times Magazine* 24 Sept. 2000: 72–80, 102.

Shall We Dance. Dir. Mark Sandrich. Prod. Pandro S. Berman. Screenplay by Allan Scott and Ernest Pagano. RKO Radio, 1937.

Silverberg, Miriam. "Constructing a New Cultural History of Prewar Japan." *Boundary* 2 18.3 (1991): 61–89.

Simmon, Scott. *The Films of D. W. Griffith*. Cambridge Film Classics. Cambridge: Cambridge University Press, 1993.

Simmons, Philip E. *Deep Surfaces: Mass Culture and History in Postmodern American Fiction*. Athens: University of Georgia Press, 1997.

Simmons, Ryan. "What Is a Terrorist? Contemporary Authorship, the Unabomber, and *Mao II*." *Modern Fiction Studies* 45 (1999): 675–95.

Simon, Richard Keller. *Trash Culture: Popular Culture and the Great Tradition*. Berkeley: University of California Press, 1999.

Simpson, O. J. *I Want to Tell You: My Response to Your Letters, Your Messages, Your Questions*. Boston: Little, 1995.

———. *O.J.: The Education of a Rich Rookie*. With Pete Axthelm. New York: Macmillan, 1970.

———. "*Playboy* Interview." With Lawrence Linderman. *Playboy* Dec. 1976: 77–78, 82, 85, 88, 90–91, 94–96, 98, 100–102.

———, host. *Saturday Night Live*. Dir. David Wilson. Prod. Lorne Michaels. Writ. Dan Ackroyd et al. NBC. WNBC, New York. 25 Feb. 1978.

Sinfield, Alan. *Literature, Politics, and Culture in Postwar Britain*. The New Historicism: Studies in Cultural Poetics 12. Berkeley: University of California Press, 1989.

Sipchen, Bob. "Schiller's Twist." *Los Angeles Times* 3 Feb. 1995: E1+.

Slethaug, Gordon E. "*Rabbit Redux:* 'Freedom Is Made of Brambles.'" *Critical Essays on John Updike*. Ed. William R. Macnaughton. Critical Essays on Amer. Lit. Boston: Hall, 1982. 237–53.

Slide, Anthony. *Early American Cinema*. 1970. Rev. ed. Metuchen: Scarecrow, 1994.

Smith, Jean Edward. *George Bush's War*. New York: Henry Holt, 1992.

Snyder, Stephen. "Two Murakamis and Marcel Proust: Memory as Form in Contemporary Japanese Fiction." *In Pursuit of Contemporary East Asian Culture*. Ed. Xiaobing Tang and Stephen Snyder. Boulder: Westview-Harper, 1996. 69–83.

Sontag, Susan. *Against Interpretation*. 1966. New York: Anchor-Doubleday, 1990.

———. *Styles of Radical Will*. 1969. New York: Anchor, 1991.

———. *Under the Sign of Saturn*. 1980. New York: Anchor-Doubleday, 1991.

———. *The Volcano Lover: A Romance*. New York: Farrar, 1992.

"The Sopranos." Dir. David Chase. Prod. Ilene S. Landress. Writ. David Chase. Episode 1 of *The Sopranos*. HBO. 10 Jan. 1999.

Sorrentino, Gilbert. *Mulligan Stew*. New York: Evergreen-Grove, 1979.

"Squeezed: Where Did O.J.'s Money Go?" *Newsweek* 17 Feb. 1997: 30.

Stafford, Jean. *A Mother in History*. New York: Farrar, 1966.

Stedman, Raymond William. *The Serials: Suspense and Drama by Installment*. Norman: University of Oklahoma Press, 1971.

Stewart, James B. "Sony's Bad Dream." *New Yorker* 28 Feb. 1994: 43–51.

Stewart, Susan. *On Longing: Narratives of the Miniature, the Gigantic, the Souvenir, the Collection*. Baltimore: Johns Hopkins University Press, 1984.

Stimpson, Catharine R. "My O My O Myra." *Gore Vidal: Writer against the Grain*. Ed. Jay Parini. New York: Columbia University Press, 1992. 183–98, 300–303.

Strecher, Matthew C. "Beyond 'Pure' Literature: Mimesis, Formula, and the Postmodern in the Fiction of Murakami Haruki." *Journal of Asian Studies* 57 (1998): 354–78.

———. "Hidden Texts and Nostalgic Images: The Serious Social Critique of Murakami Haruki." Diss. University of Washington, 1996.

————. "Murakami Haruki: Japan's Coolest Writer Heats Up." *Japan Quarterly* 45.1 (1998): 61–69.

Strom, Stephanie. "In Japan, Mired in Recession, Suicides Soar." *New York Times* 15 July 1999, late ed.: A1+.

Stronach, Bruce. "Japanese Television." *Handbook of Japanese Popular Culture*. Ed. Richard Gid Powers and Hidetoshi Katō. Westport, Conn.: Greenwood, 1989. 127–65.

Strychacz, Thomas. *Modernism, Mass Culture, and Professionalism*. Cambridge Studies in Amer. Lit. and Culture. Cambridge: Cambridge University Press, 1993. 84–116, 212.

Summers, Claude J. " 'The Cabin and the River': Gore Vidal's *The City and the Pillar*." *Gay Fictions: Wilde to Stonewall: Studies in a Male Homosexual Literary Tradition*. New York: Continuum, 1990. 112–29, 230–32. Rev. and rpt. as "*The City and the Pillar* as Gay Fiction." *Gore Vidal: Writer against the Grain*. Ed. Jay Parini. New York: Columbia University Press, 1992. 56–75, 293–95.

Swanberg, W. A. *Citizen Hearst: A Biography of William Randolph Hearst*. New York: Scribner's, 1961.

Tanizaki Jun'ichirō. *Naomi*. Trans. Anthony H. Chambers. New York: Knopf, 1985. Trans. of *Chijin no ai*. 1924.

Tanner, Tony. "Afterthoughts on Don DeLillo's *Underworld*." *Raritan* 17.4 (1998): 48–71.

Tarnower, Herman, and Samm Sinclair Baker. *The Complete Scarsdale Medical Diet*. 1979. New York: Bantam, 1980.

Tatum, James. "The *Romanitas* of Gore Vidal." *Raritan* 11.4 (1992): 99–122. Rev. and rpt. in *Gore Vidal: Writer against the Grain*. Ed. Jay Parini. New York: Columbia University Press, 1992. 199–220.

Taylor, J. M. *Eva Perón: The Myths of a Woman*. Chicago: University of Chicago Press, 1979.

Taylor, Larry E. *Pastoral and Anti-Pastoral Patterns in John Updike's Fiction*. Carbondale: Southern Illinois University Press, 1971.

Taylor, Paul, and Richard Morin. "Poll Finds Americans Back U.S. Response, but Warily." *Washington Post* 10 Aug. 1990, final ed.: A1+.

Taylor, Philip M. *War and the Media: Propaganda and Persuasion in the Gulf War*. Manchester: Manchester University Press, 1992.

Thaler, Paul. *The Spectacle: Media and the Making of the O. J. Simpson Story*. Westport, Conn.: Praeger, 1997.

Thomas, Glen. "History, Biography, and Narrative in Don DeLillo's *Libra*." *Twentieth Century Literature* 43 (1997): 107–24.

Thompson, Kristin. *Exporting Entertainment: America in the World Film Market, 1907–34*. London: British Film Institute, 1985.

Three Kings. Dir. David O. Russell. Prod. Charles Roven, Paul Junger Witt, and Edward L. McDonnell. Story by John Ridley. Screenplay by David O. Russell. Warner Bros., 1999.

THX 1138. Dir. George Lucas. Prod. Lawrence Sturhahn. Story by George Lucas. Screenplay by George Lucas and Walter Murch. Warner Bros., 1970.

Tobin, Joseph J. "Domesticating the West." Introduction. *Re-Made in Japan: Everyday*

Life and Consumer Taste in a Changing Society. Ed. Joseph J. Tobin. New Haven: Yale University Press, 1992. 1–41.

Tolkin, Michael. *The Player.* 1988. New York: Vintage-Random, 1989.

Tomlinson, John. *Cultural Imperialism: A Critical Introduction.* Parallax Re-visions of Culture and Society. Baltimore: Johns Hopkins University Press, 1991.

Toner, Robin. "Bush in the Afterglow: Did Someone Say 'Domestic Policy'?" *New York Times* 3 Mar. 1991, late ed., sec. 4: 1–2.

Toobin, Jeffrey. "Cash for Trash." *New Yorker* 11 July 1994: 34–41.

———. "An Incendiary Defense." *New Yorker* 25 July 1994: 56–59.

———. *The Run of His Life: The People v. O. J. Simpson.* New York: Random, 1996.

Top Hat. Dir. Mark Sandrich. Prod. Pandro S. Berman. Story by Dwight Taylor. Screenplay by Dwight Taylor and Allan Scott. RKO Radio, 1935.

Tracey, Michael. "The Poisoned Chalice? International Television and the Idea of Dominance." *Daedalus* 114.4 (1985): 17–56.

Treat, John Whittier. "Yoshimoto Banana Writes Home: *Shōjo* Culture and the Nostalgic Subject." *Journal of Japanese Studies* 19 (1993): 353–87.

Trilling, Diana. *The Beginning of the Journey: The Marriage of Diana and Lionel Trilling.* 1993. New York: Harvest-Harcourt, 1994.

———. "The Case for the American Woman." *Look* 3 Mar. 1959: 50–54.

———. *Claremont Essays.* New York: Harcourt, 1964.

———. "The Liberated Heroine." *Partisan Review* 45 (1978): 501–22.

———. *Mrs. Harris: The Death of the Scarsdale Diet Doctor.* New York: Harcourt, 1981.

———. "Notes on the Trial of the Century." *New Republic* 30 Oct. 1995: 18, 20–22.

———. "A Visit to Camelot." *New Yorker* 2 June 1997: 54–60, 62–65.

———. *We Must March My Darlings: A Critical Decade.* 1977. New York: Harvest-Harcourt, 1978.

Trilling, Lionel. "Manners, Morals, and the Novel." *Kenyon Review* 10 (1948): 11–27. Rpt. in *The Liberal Imagination: Essays on Literature and Society.* New York: Anchor-Doubleday, 1950. 199–215.

Tuchman, Barbara W. *The First Salute: A View of the American Revolution.* New York: Knopf, 1988.

Tuss, Alex J. "Deconstructing and Reconstructing Masculinity in Manuel Puig's *Kiss of the Spider Woman.*" *Journal of Men's Studies* 8 (2000): 323–32.

"The Twenty-five Most Intriguing People of 1980." *People* 29 Dec. 1980–5 Jan. 1981: Cover.

Twitchell, James B. *Carnival Culture: The Trashing of Taste in America.* New York: Columbia University Press, 1992.

United States Committee on Public Information. *The Creel Report: Complete Report of the Chairman of the Committee on Public Information 1917: 1918: 1919.* Washington, D.C.: Government Printing Office, 1920. New York: Da Capo, 1972.

Updike, John. "The Art of Fiction XLIII: John Updike." With Charles Thomas Samuels. *Paris Review* 45 (1968): 84–117.

———. *Assorted Prose.* New York: Knopf, 1965.

———. "An Evening with John Updike." With Robert Boyers et al. *Salmagundi* 57 (1982): 42–56.

———. *Hugging the Shore: Essays and Criticism.* New York: Knopf, 1983.

———. *In the Beauty of the Lilies.* New York: Knopf, 1996.

———. Introduction. *The Art of Mickey Mouse.* Ed. Craig Yoe and Janet Morra-Yoe. New York: Hyperion, 1991. N. pag.

———. *Picked-Up Pieces.* New York: Knopf, 1975.

———. *Rabbit at Rest.* New York: Knopf, 1990.

———. *Rabbit Is Rich.* 1981. New York: Fawcett Crest–Ballantine, 1982.

———. *Rabbit Redux.* 1971. New York: Fawcett Crest–Ballantine, 1972.

———. *Rabbit, Run.* Greenwich, Conn.: Fawcett Crest, 1960.

———. *Self-Consciousness: Memoirs.* New York: Knopf, 1989.

———. "Why Rabbit Had to Go." *New York Times Book Review* 5 Aug. 1990: 1, 24–25.

Upham, Frank K. "Displaced Persons and Movements for Place." *Postwar Japan as History.* Ed. Andrew Gordon. Berkeley: University of California Press, 1993. 325–46.

Usabel, Gaizka S. de. *The High Noon of American Films in Latin America.* Studies in Cinema 17. Ann Arbor: UMI Research Press, 1982.

Vance, Louis Joseph. *Patria. New York [Sunday] American* 14 Jan. 1917–22 Apr. 1917.

Vargo, Edward. "Corn Chips, Catheters, Toyotas: The Making of History in *Rabbit at Rest.*" *Rabbit Tales: Poetry and Politics in John Updike's Rabbit Novels.* Ed. Lawrence R. Broer. Tuscaloosa: University of Alabama Press, 1988. 70–88.

Verduin, Kathleen. "Fatherly Presences: John Updike's Place in a Protestant Tradition." *Critical Essays on John Updike.* Ed. William R. Macnaughton. Critical Essays on Amer. Lit. Boston: Hall, 1982. 254–68.

Vidal, Gore. *Burr: A Novel.* New York: Random, 1973.

———. *Duluth.* 1983. New York: Penguin, 1998.

———. *1876: A Novel.* New York: Random, 1976.

———. *Empire: A Novel.* 1987. New York: Ballantine, 1988.

———. *The Golden Age: A Novel.* New York: Doubleday-Random, 2000.

———. *Hollywood: A Novel of America in the 1920s.* New York: Random, 1990.

———. *Lincoln: A Novel.* New York: Random, 1984.

———. *Myra Breckinridge.* 1968. *Myra Breckinridge/Myron.* 1986. New York: Penguin, 1997. 1–213.

———. *Myron.* 1974. *Myra Breckinridge/Myron.* 1986. New York: Penguin, 1997. 215–417.

———. "Notes on Our Patriarchal State." *Nation* 27 Aug.–3 Sept. 1990: 185, 202–4.

———. *Palimpsest: A Memoir.* New York: Random, 1995.

———. *Screening History.* Cambridge: Harvard University Press, 1992.

———. *United States: Essays, 1952–1992.* New York: Random, 1993.

———. *Washington, D.C.* Boston: Little, 1967.

Wagner, Bruce. *Force Majeure.* 1991. New York: St. Martin's, 1993.

———. *I'm Losing You.* New York: Villard-Random, 1996.

Wag the Dog. Dir. Barry Levinson. Prod. Jane Rosenthal, Robert De Niro, and Barry Levinson. Screenplay by Hilary Henkin and David Mamet. New Line, 1997.

Waldmeir, Joseph. "It's the Going That's Important, Not the Getting There: Rabbit's Questing Non-Quest." *Modern Fiction Studies* 20 (1974): 13–27.

Walker, Joseph S. "Criminality, the Real, and the Story of America: The Case of Don DeLillo." *Centennial Review* 43 (1999): 433–66.

Wallace, Molly. " 'Venerated Emblems': DeLillo's *Underworld* and the History-Commodity." *Critique* 42 (2001): 367–83.

Ward, J. A. "John Updike's Fiction." *Critique* 5.1 (1962): 27–40.

Ward, Larry Wayne. *The Motion Picture Goes to War: The U.S. Government Film Effort during World War I.* Studies in Cinema 37. Ann Arbor: UMI Research Press, 1985.

Ware, Susan. *Still Missing: Amelia Earhart and the Search for Modern Feminism.* New York: Norton, 1993.

Washington Post 12–16 Mar. 1980.

Weber, Frances Wyers. "Manuel Puig at the Movies." *Hispanic Review* 49 (1981): 163–81.

Wechsler, Pat, and Roger D. Friedman. "O. J. Simpson's Newest Sleazy Friend." *New York* 23 Jan. 1995: 12.

"Weekend Update." *Saturday Night Live.* 9 Dec. 1995; 23 Mar. 1996; 14 Dec. 1996; 15 Feb. 1997; 10 Jan. 1998; 4 Dec. 1999. Transcripts. <http://snltranscripts.jt.org/scripts/95hupdate.phtml>.

Weinraub, Bernard. "Sony Is Overhauling Its Film Studios." With Geraldine Fabrikant. *New York Times* 11 Jan. 1995, late ed.: D1+.

———. "Turmoil and Indecision at Sony's Film Studios." *New York Times* 24 Oct. 1994, late ed.: D1+.

Weisbuch, Robert. *Atlantic Double-Cross: American Literature and British Influence in the Age of Emerson.* 1986. Chicago: University of Chicago Press, 1989.

West, Jessamyn. "Prelude to Tragedy: The Woman Who Sheltered Lee Oswald's Family Tells Her Story." *Redbook* July 1964: 52–53, 84–88, 90, 92.

West, Nathanael. *The Day of the Locust.* 1939. Rpt. in Miss Lonelyhearts *and* The Day of the Locust. New York: New Directions, 1962. 59–185.

Wharton, Edith. *The House of Mirth.* 1905. New York: Signet–New American Library, 1964.

White, Armond. "Eye, the Jury." *Birth of a Nation'hood: Gaze, Script, and Spectacle in the O. J. Simpson Case.* Ed. Toni Morrison and Claudia Brodsky Lacour. New York: Pantheon, 1997. 339–66.

White, Hayden. *The Content of the Form: Narrative Discourse and Historical Representation.* Baltimore: Johns Hopkins University Press, 1987.

———. *Tropics of Discourse: Essays in Cultural Criticism.* Baltimore: Johns Hopkins University Press, 1978.

White, Lonnie. "Still Going Strong." *Los Angeles Times* 11 Dec. 1993: C10.

White, Theodore H. "The Danger from Japan." *New York Times Magazine* 28 July 1985: 19–22, 31, 37–38, 40, 42–43, 57, 59.

Wiegman, Robyn. *American Anatomies: Theorizing Race and Gender.* New Americanists. Durham: Duke University Press, 1995.

Williams, Patricia J. "American Kabuki." *Birth of a Nation'hood: Gaze, Script, and Spectacle in the O. J. Simpson Case.* Ed. Toni Morrison and Claudia Brodsky Lacour. New York: Pantheon, 1997. 273–92.

Williams, Raymond. *Culture and Society, 1780–1950.* 1958. New York: Columbia University Press, 1983.

————. *The Sociology of Culture.* 1981. New York: Schocken, 1982.

————. *Television: Technology and Cultural Form.* 1974. New York: Schocken, 1975.

Williamson, Edwin. *The Penguin History of Latin America.* London: Penguin, 1992.

Willman, Skip. "Art after Dealey Plaza: DeLillo's *Libra*." *Modern Fiction Studies* 45 (1999): 621–40.

————. "Traversing the Fantasies of the JFK Assassination: Conspiracy and Contingency in Don DeLillo's *Libra*." *Contemporary Literature* 39 (1998): 405–33.

Wills, Garry. *John Wayne's America.* 1997. New York: Touchstone-Simon, 1998.

Witte, Karsten. "Visual Pleasure Inhibited: Aspects of the German Revue Film." Trans. J. D. Steakley and Gabriele Hoover. *New German Critique* 24–25 (fall 1981–winter 1982): 238–63.

Wolferen, Karel van. *The Enigma of Japanese Power: People and Politics in a Stateless Nation.* New York: Knopf, 1989.

Woodward, Bob. *The Commanders.* New York: Simon, 1991.

"Your Cash Ain't Nothin' but Trash." Music and lyrics by Charles Calhoun. Progressive Music Publishing Co., Inc., 1954.

Zimmerman, Shari A. "*Pubis Angelical:* Where Puig Meets Lacan." *Critique* 39 (1997): 65–80.

INDEX

homosexuality, 23, 103, 110, 120, 221 (n. 39), 232 (n. 10)

Hoover, J. Edgar, 5, 9

Hopper, Edward, 97

Horkheimer, Max, 3

Hoskins, Bob, 98

How We Advertised America (Creel), 28, 29, 30, 219 (n. 12)

Hudson Hawk (film), 126

Hugging the Shore (Updike), 45, 52, 223 (n. 12)

Hunt, Henry, 199

Huntington, John, 116

Hussein, Saddam, 74, 212, 225 (n. 7)

Hutcheon, Linda, 152, 239 (n. 3)

Huyssen, Andreas, 3, 4

"I Find the Real American Tragedy" (Dreiser), 185–86, 244 (n. 5)

Imagining America (Conrad), 217 (n. 14)

I'm Losing You (Wagner), 205

imperialism: and Adams's, Brooks, economic theories, 26–27; American, 14, 15, 22–23, 24–27, 46, 70, 89, 208; British, 15, 58–59, 95–96; cultural, 5, 15, 59–61, 81–83, 88–90, 94–95, 123, 131, 208; Japanese, 15, 124, 129–30, 136, 139–41; land purchases, 25–26

In Cold Blood (Capote), 177

In Country (Mason), 13

International Commission for the Study of Communication Problems, 15

In the Beauty of the Lilies (Updike), 205–11

investments, foreign, in the United States, 50–51, 125–26, 236 (n. 13)

Ishihara Shintaro, 126

Ivy, Marilyn, 124, 125

I Want to Tell You (O. J. Simpson), 184, 188, 189–90, 191, 194, 195, 196, 198, 245 (n. 11), 246 (n. 18); Foreword to (L. Schiller), 198

Jackson, Andrew, 24

Jacobs, Naomi, 118

James, Alice, 178

James, Henry, 23

Jameson, Fredric, 10, 83, 101, 153, 164, 207, 236–37 (n. 19), 239 (n. 3)

Japan, 14–15; and China, 123, 128–29; common culture of, 123–24, 139, 235 (n. 8); economy of, 46, 50, 51, 61, 125–26; and Greater East Asia Co-Prosperity Sphere, 129–30; imperialism of, 15, 124, 129–30, 136, 139–41; and Manchukuo, 129–30, 136, 139; and the Manchurian Incident, 136, 137, 139; mass media in, 130–133, 136–37; Meiji Restoration in, 123; and *Nihonjinron*, 15, 124, 139; and *Patria*, 34; and television, 50, 131–33, 136–37; and the United States, 15, 44, 46, 50–51, 60–61, 123, 124–28, 130, 131, 140

Japan That Can Say No, The (Morita and Ishihara), 126

Jarvie, Ian, 95

Jefferson, Thomas, 24, 25–26, 27

Jennings, Peter, 63, 64

Johnson, Leola, 189

Jones, Thomas A., 161

journalism: and celebrity, 149, 156–57, 158, 161, 163–65; and communications technology, 14, 74–75; and the Gulf War, 61, 63, 64, 65, 67, 74–76, 225 (n. 7); and Hearst, 14, 23, 24, 31–33, 39–40, 236 (n. 17); and Japanese acquisitions, 125–26; new, 54, 175–76, 177, 195–96, 197, 237 (n. 27), 243 (n. 12); newspaper, 41, 61, 67, 74, 161, 175–76, 185–88, 242–43 (n. 9); newsreel, 31, 206, 220 (n. 18); and September 11, 2001, 212–13; sports, 72, 189; tabloid, 183–84, 194–95, 196; television, 137, 181, 200–201, 225 (n. 2), 238 (n. 29); —, and Kennedy assassination events, 158, 161, 163–65; —, in *Rabbit* [Angstrom] tetralogy, 49, 52, 54–55, 56; and the Vietnam War, 74–75; wire service, 30, 161; yellow, 14, 23, 24, 32, 236 (n. 17). *See also individual news organizations and publications*

Joyce, James, 157, 159; *Finnegans Wake*, 152

Judith of Bethulia (film), 35

J. Wilkes Booth (Jones), 161

Puig, Manuel: background of, 14–15, 123; and common culture, 15, 103; on gender and sexual roles, 102–4, 108–10, 111–12, 117–18; on homosexuality, 103, 110, 232 (n. 10); interviews with, 103, 110, 118, 120, 230 (n. 1), 232 (n. 10); machismo in the novels of, 107–10; Peronism in the novels of, 103, 104, 106–7, 108–9, 110, 112–13, 117, 119–20; on submission inculcated by American films, 103, 109–10, 114–15. Works: *Betrayed by Rita Hayworth*, 103, 106–7; *The Buenos Aires Affair*, 102–3; *Eternal Curse on the Reader of These Pages*, 120; *Heartbreak Tango*, 103; *Kiss of the Spider Woman*, 103, 108–10, 111, 232 (n. 10); *Pubis Angelical*, 103, 104, 111–20; *Tropical Night Falling*, 120, 121

Pynchon, Thomas: *The Crying of Lot 49*, 7, 58, 147; *Vineland*, 10

Rabbit [Angstrom] tetralogy (Updike): Harry as national symbol in, 56–58; nostalgia in, 46–47; *Rabbit at Rest*, 43–61 passim, 75; *Rabbit Is Rich*, 43–59 passim, 212; *Rabbit Redux*, 44, 47, 48, 49, 50, 52, 53, 55, 57, 63; *Rabbit, Run*, 48, 49, 52, 58; television in, 45–46, 49–50, 51–56

Ragtime (Doctorow), 10, 16, 192, 199

Rainer, Luise, 107, 108, 109, 110

Rambo (film series), 63

Ramsey, JonBenét, 199–200

Rank, Otto, 108

Ratner's Star (DeLillo), 152, 240 (nn. 8, 10)

Ray, James Earl, 164

Reagan, Ronald, 5, 14, 31, 47, 54, 61, 72, 212, 219 (n. 15)

recycling, 11; of American artifacts in Puig, 102–3, 104, 109, 113–14, 115; choice of artifacts for, 17–18; of musicals, 8–9, 83, 90–91, 97–101; of news events, 148–49, 177–78, 185, 192–93, 197, 198, 200–201; versus repetition, 10; and television, 53, 56; of war movies, 66–67, 69–70

Redbook (magazine), 160

Reid, Whitelaw, 123

Reith, John, 94, 228–29 (n. 18)

Renan, Ernest, 148

Rentschler, Eric, 232 (n. 11)

Report of the President's Commission on the Assassination of President John F. Kennedy, 147, 148, 149, 159, 241 (n. 16)

Resnick, Faye, 191; *Nicole Brown Simpson: The Private Diary of a Life Interrupted*, 183

Reynolds, David S., 4

Richesen, Clarence, 186

Riefenstahl, Leni, 70, 216 (n. 12)

Rise and Fall of the Great Powers, The (P. Kennedy), 60

Ristoff, Dilvo I., 50, 222 (n. 1)

Rock, David, 105

Roddenberry, Gene, 184

Rodia, Sabato, 9

Rodríguez Monegal, Emir, 107, 231 (n. 3), 233 (n. 17)

Roediger, David, 189

Rogers, Ginger, 99–100, 101, 230 (n. 27)

Rogin, Michael, 5, 72, 76

Rolling Stone (magazine), 73–74, 164

Romance of Elaine, The (serial), 23, 33–34, 39

Romeo and Juliet (film), 107

Roosevelt, Franklin Delano, 22, 23, 47, 48, 98, 212

Roosevelt, Theodore, 23–24, 26, 31; *American Ideals*, 38, 39; "National Duties," 108; *The Strenuous Life*, 39, 108

Root, Elihu, 25

Rosenberg, Ethel, 16

Rosenberg, Julius, 16

Ross, Harold, 45

Roszak, Theodore, 118

Roth, Mark, 98–99

Rubin, Martin, 91

Ruby, Jack, 155, 158, 159, 163, 164, 194, 241 (n. 15)

Sanders, Deion, 49

San Francisco Examiner (newspaper), 199

Santa Evita (Martínez), 120

Saturday Night Live (television program), 188–89, 192–93, 246 (n. 16)

Scarface (film), 100

Schary, Dore, 46

Scheck, Barry, 198, 199

Schiller, Herbert I., 3, 223 (n. 10)

Schiller, Lawrence: authorial yearnings of, 185, 195–97; financial dealings of, 184, 194–95, 196–97, 198, 201, 246 (n. 18); and involvement with Simpson, O. J., defense, 184, 196, 197; as literary character, 184–85, 195–96, 197; "*Playboy* Interview" with, 182, 196–97; portrayal of Simpson, O. J., trial, 185, 199–201. Works: *American Tragedy* (book), 182–83, 185, 196, 197–99, 201; *American Tragedy* (television miniseries), 200–201; Foreword to *I Want to Tell You*, 198; *The Killing of Sharon Tate*, 196; *Perfect Murder, Perfect Town*, 199–200; *The Trial of Lee Harvey Oswald*, 199, 246 (n. 24)

Schmoedipus (Potter), 100

Scholes, Percy, 93–94

Schulberg, Budd, 204–5

science fiction, 111, 115–19

Scott, Sir Walter, 11–12

Screening History (Vidal), 21

Secret of the Submarine, The (serial), 33

Selections (Hearst), 32, 38–39

Self-Consciousness (Updike), 45, 48, 56, 58, 223 (n. 5), 224 (nn. 14, 18)

Senator, George, 159, 241 (n. 15)

September 11, 2001, tragedy, 212–14

Sergeant York (film), 46, 70

Seven Samurai (film), 158

Seward, William, 24

Shall We Dance (film), 100, 101

Shearer, Norma, 107, 113, 119, 233 (n. 18)

Shively, Jill, 183

Silverberg, Miriam, 137

Simon, Norton, 175

Simpson, Nicole Brown, 182, 183, 191, 246 (n. 18)

Simpson, O. J.: and acting, 191–94, 245 (n. 14); collaboration of, with Schiller,

Lawrence, 184, 194, 195, 196, 198; and football, 190–92; "*Playboy* Interview" with, 188, 191–92, 194, 196, 245 (n. 11); portrayal of, in *American Tragedy* (book), 182–83, 198; portrayal of, in *American Tragedy* (television miniseries), 200–201; and race, 16, 168, 189–91, 192–93; *Saturday Night Live* appearance of, 188–89, 192–93; trial of, 15–16, 168, 183–85, 199–200. Works: *I Want to Tell You*, 184, 188, 189–90, 191, 194, 195, 196, 198, 245 (n. 11), 246 (n. 18); *O.J.: The Education of a Rich Rookie*, 188, 190–92, 245 (n. 12)

Sinfield, Alan, 85, 227 (n. 6)

Singing Detective, The (Potter), 83, 85–86, 88, 227 (n. 7)

Slouching towards Bethlehem (Didion), 54, 243 (n. 12)

"Slow Boat to China, A" (Murakami), 128

Snow Queen, The (Vinge), 118

Snow White (Barthelme), 1–2, 7, 10, 18, 203

Snyder, Stephen, 238 (n. 33)

Sociology of Culture, The (R. Williams), 53–54

"Some Children of the Goddess" (Mailer), 176, 243 (n. 13)

"Son of Sam" law, 194

Sontag, Susan: *Against Interpretation*, 13; "Fascinating Fascism," 216–17 (n. 12); *Styles of Radical Will*, 103; *The Volcano Lover*, 217 (n. 12)

Sony Corporation, 125–26

Sophie's Choice (film), 135

Sopranos, The (television series), 202

Sorrentino, Gilbert, 152

Spanish-American War, 14, 22, 24, 25, 27, 41, 69, 218 (n. 9)

spectacles, 15–17, 65, 75–76, 163, 165, 175–76, 183–85, 187–88

Springsteen, Bruce, 73

Stafford, Jean, 157, 162

Stand Up, Nigel Barton (Potter), 88

Star Mother (Van Scyoc), 118

Statue of Liberty, 35, 57, 60, 126

Stewart, Susan, 205
Stranger in Two Worlds (J. Harris), 167, 171, 172, 173, 174, 175, 176, 180–81, 242 (n. 8)
Strauss, Johann, 106, 110, 231 (n. 8)
Strecher, Matthew C., 141, 143, 235 (nn. 3, 7)
Strenuous Life, The (T. Roosevelt), 39, 108
Strychacz, Thomas, 9
Styles of Radical Will (Sontag), 103
Sufficient Carbohydrate (Potter), 100, 229 (n. 22)
"Sugar Shack" (song), 134
Sun Tzu, 67
"Superman Comes to the Supermart" (Mailer), 163
Surrealism, 216 (n. 8)
Susskind, David, 195
Sykes, John, 74

Tarnower, Herman: character of, 169–71, 173, 177, 178; *The Complete Scarsdale Medical Diet*, 169–70, 171–72; murder of, 165, 166–67, 168, 174, 175, 181. *See also* Harris, Jean
Taylor, Elizabeth, ix, 52, 210
Tearing Down the Spanish Flag (film), 69
television: advertisements on, 55–56, 88–89; and American commerce, 50; in *Cold Lazarus*, 81–82; disasters on, 54–55; effects on conduct of, 53–56, 86–88, 223–24 (n. 14); in Great Britain, 86–90; and the Gulf War, 64, 65, 68, 74–76; in *In the Beauty of the Lilies*, 210; in Japan, 131–33, 136–37; in *Libra*, 156–57, 163–64; in political campaigns, 73; in the Rabbit [Angstrom] tetralogy, 45–46, 49–50, 51–56; and the Vietnam War, 64, 74; in *The Wind-Up Bird Chronicle*, 136, 137–38
Television: Technology and Cultural Form (R. Williams), 88–89
Thatcher, Margaret, 69, 225 (n. 8)
Thaw, Harry K., 16, 187–88, 199
Thompson, Kristin, 27
Thomson, Bobby, 4, 5, 6, 8

Three Little Pigs, The (animated film), 48, 223 (n. 7)
THX 1138 (film), 104, 115–16, 234 (n. 23)
Time (magazine), 126, 157, 185
Todd, Mrs. Nelson, 161
Tolkin, Michael, 205
Toobin, Jeffrey, 184, 194, 244 (n. 8), 245 (n. 10)
Top Hat (film), 100, 230 (n. 27)
Towering Inferno, The (film), 191
Track 29 (Potter), 100
Traitor (Potter), 90
trash: landfill metaphor of, 2, 203–4; as metaphor for marginalization, 7–8, 147, 166, 174, 183, 185; as metaphor for popular culture, 1–4, 9, 13, 81, 102–3, 122–23, 183, 203, 210, 211; as metaphor for tabloids, 182, 183, 194, 196; recycling of, 9–11, 17–18, 102–3, 203, 209
Trash Museum, 202
Treat, John Whittier, 134
Tregaskis, Richard, 70
Trial of Lee Harvey Oswald, The (television film), 199, 246 (n. 24)
Trilling, Diana: on aesthetics, 167, 169–70; on Harris, Jean, trial significance, 176, 177–78, 187; on manners and morality, 167, 168–69; relationship of, with husband, 178–80; on Simpson, O. J., trial significance, 184; on women, 171, 172–73, 174, 176, 181. Works: *The Beginning of the Journey*, 174, 179–80; "The Case for the American Woman," 172; *Claremont Essays*, 172, 178, 180; "The Liberated Heroine," 180; *Mrs. Harris*, 167–79 passim; "Notes on the Trial of the Century," 184, 199; "The Other Night at Columbia," 180; "A Visit to Camelot," 179; "We Must March My Darlings," 172–73, 181
Trilling, Lionel, 180; "Manners, Morals, and the Novel," 168–69; *Matthew Arnold*, 179
Triumph of the Will (film), 66, 70
Tropical Night Falling (Puig), 120, 121
Tryforos, Lynne, 169, 171, 173

Tuchman, Barbara W., 60; *The First Salute,* 43, 44, 58–59
"TV People" (Murakami), 131–32, 134
Twitchell, James B., 3

Underground (Murakami), 237 (n. 27), 238 (n. 35)
Underworld (DeLillo), 2–18 passim, 148, 208, 241 (n. 23)
UNESCO, 15
United Artists, 104, 105
United States: and American Century, 11, 14, 15, 22, 69, 148, 185, 205, 213; and Argentina, 15, 103, 105–6, 231 (n. 6); and binarism, 5, 206, 208, 209–10; decline of, 42, 44, 45, 46, 50, 54, 57–61; economic expansionism of, 14, 15, 22–23, 25–27, 38–39, 218 (n. 7); and exceptionalism, 5, 14, 25, 56–61; foreign investments in, 50–51, 125–26, 236 (n. 13); and Great Britain, 15, 83, 88–90, 93, 94–95; imperialism of, 5, 14, 24–25, 35, 39, 70, 123, 203, 208; involvement of, in world affairs, 212–13; and Japan, 15, 44, 46, 50–51, 60–61, 123, 124–28, 130, 131, 140; and Monroe Doctrine, 23; as nation-state, 4–8, 11, 15–17, 22, 24–25, 148, 167, 183–84, 206–7, 213. *See also individual wars*
United States: Essays (Vidal), 24, 25, 31, 39, 217 (n. 4), 219 (n. 15), 221 (n. 41)
Unlocked Book, The (A. Clarke), 161, 239 (n. 6)
Updike, John: and consumerism, 45, 48–49, 50–51; and the decline of America, 14, 42, 44, 45, 50–51, 57–61; and Disney, 47–49, 223 (n. 8); and films, 44, 47, 52; interviews with, 45, 48, 223 (nn. 5, 12, 14); and realism, 45–46; and television, 45–46, 49–50, 51–56. Works: "The American Man: What of Him?" 224 (n. 17); *Assorted Prose,* 50; *Hugging the Shore,* 45, 52, 223 (n. 12); *In the Beauty of the Lilies,* 205–11; Introduction to *The Art of Mickey Mouse,* 223 (n. 8); *Picked-Up Pieces,* 45; *Rabbit at Rest,* 43–61 passim, 75; *Rabbit Is Rich,* 43–59 passim,

212; *Rabbit Redux,* 44, 47, 48, 49, 50, 52, 53, 55, 57, 63; *Rabbit, Run,* 48, 49, 52, 58; *Self-Consciousness,* 45, 48, 56, 58, 223 (n. 5), 224 (nn. 14, 18); "Why Rabbit Had to Go," 222 (n. 4), 223 (n. 12)
Usabel, Gaizka S. de, 104, 223 (nn. 5, 7), 231 (n. 7)
Uses of Literacy, The (Hoggart), 84–85
U.S. News and World Report (newspaper), 125
utopian fiction, 116–17, 119

Valparaiso (DeLillo), 241 (n. 19)
Vance, Louis Joseph, 34, 36
Vanity Fair (magazine), 183
Van Scyoc, Sydney J., 118
Victory in the West (film), 66
Victory through American Power (film), 48
Vidal, Gore: on American imperialism, 22–23, 24–26, 33, 39, 42; on gender and sexuality, 23, 39–41, 221 (n. 39); on the Hollywood–Washington, D.C., connection, 14, 27, 29, 30–31, 40–41, 72, 73; and silent films, 22–23, 28–29, 32–33, 34, 39–41; and yellow journalism, 28–29, 32–33, 39–40. Works: *Burr,* 22, 24, 25–26, 27, 39; *The City and the Pillar,* 221 (n. 39), "The Day the American Empire Ran Out of Gas," 42; *Duluth,* 5–6; *1876,* 26; *Empire,* 21, 22, 23–25, 27, 28–29, 31–32, 39–40, 41–42; *The Golden Age,* 41, 221 (n. 41); *Hollywood,* 22, 25, 27, 28–29, 31–33, 34, 39–41, 73; *Lincoln,* 22, 24, 27, 30–31, 239–40 (n. 7); *Myra Breckinridge,* 40, 43, 46, 204; *Myron,* 40, 46; "Notes on Our Patriarchal State," 41; *Palimpsest,* 39, 219 (n. 15); *Screening History,* 21; *United States: Essays,* 24, 25, 31, 39, 217 (n. 4), 219 (n. 15), 221 (n. 41); *Washington, D.C.,* 22, 31, 217–18 (n. 5)
Vietnam War, 5, 13, 61, 63; in *American Hero,* 64, 66, 67, 71, 74, 75–77; in *In the Beauty of the Lilies,* 208, 210; in the Rabbit [Angstrom] tetralogy, 44, 57

Villa, Francisco (Pancho), 69
Vineland (Pynchon), 10
Vinge, Joan D., 118
Visitors (Potter), 100
"Visit to Camelot, A" (D. Trilling), 179
Voebel, Edward, 158
Volcano Lover, The (Sontag), 217 (n. 12)
Vote, Vote, Vote for Nigel Barton (Potter), 88, 227 (n. 7)

Wagner, Bruce, 205
Wake Island (film), 66
Walcamp, Marie, 33
Walken, Christopher, 71
Wallace, George, 164, 187, 241 (n. 24)
Walters, Barbara, 165, 181, 244 (n. 16)
War Cooperation Committee (U.S.), 28
Ward, Larry Wayne, 29, 218 (n. 11)
Ward, Stephen, 178
Warren Commission *Hearings,* 147, 149, 154–55, 157–60, 161–62, 240 (n. 13), 241 (nn. 15, 18)
Warren Commission *Report,* 147, 148, 149, 159, 241 (n. 16)
wars. *See individual wars*
Washington, D.C. (Vidal), 22, 41, 217–18 (n. 5)
Washington, George, 22, 25, 39, 64, 72
Washington Post (newspaper), 67, 242–43 (n. 9)
Wasserman, Lew, 72
Wayne, John, 54, 66–67, 225 (n. 6)
Wechsler, Pat, 196
Weinstein, Harvey, 73
Weisbuch, Robert, 217 (n. 14)
Welles, Orson, 41
"We Must March My Darlings" (D. Trilling), 172–73, 181
Wenner, Jann, 74
West, Jessamyn, 160
West, Nathanael, 203–4, 205
What Makes Sammy Run? (Schulberg), 204–5
Where the Buffalo Roam (Potter), 87

White, Hayden, 149, 153, 163
White, Pearl, 33
White, Stanford, 199
White, Theodore H., 126
White Album, The (Didion), 243 (n. 12)
Whitehead, Alfred North, 167
White Noise (DeLillo), 156–57, 165, 241 (n. 21)
Whitman, Walt, 45
"Why Import This Trash?" (Potter), 81
"Why Rabbit Had to Go" (Updike), 222 (n. 4), 223 (n. 12)
Wiegman, Robyn, 142
Wild Sheep Chase, A (Murakami), 122, 123, 127–28, 129–30, 133, 140–41
William Randolph Hearst: American (Older), 35
Williams, Patricia J., 184
Williams, Raymond: *Culture and Society,* 84–85; *The Sociology of Culture,* 53–54; *Television: Technology and Cultural Form,* 88–89
Willwerth, James, 182; *American Tragedy: The Uncensored Story of the Simpson Defense,* 182–83, 185, 196, 197–99, 201
Wilson, Edith, 27
Wilson, Woodrow, 25, 27, 31, 33, 34
Wind-Up Bird Chronicle, The (Murakami): bodily imagery in, 136, 141–43; historical consciousness in, 136, 140–41, 142–44; individual identity in, 141–43, 238 (n. 34); Japanese imperialism in, 124, 130, 136, 139–40; and Manchukuo, 130, 136, 139; and the Manchurian Incident, 136, 139; and Nomonhan, 136, 140; television in, 136, 137–38
Witte, Karsten, 109
women: in American films, 107–8, 109–10, 114–15; and careers, 171–73; in *Empire* and *Hollywood,* 39–41; in *Kiss of the Spider Woman,* 108–10; and National Socialism, 108–9, 113; in *Patria,* 34–39; and Peronism, 108–9, 112–13, 119–20; in *Pubis Angelical,*